Books on the events of the early months of 1940 are dominated by the ~~~~~~ the British Expeditionary Force in Northern France and Belgium following the German invasion of May 10th and it is often overlooked that prior to this another British expeditionary force was involved in fierce fighting in Norway. Indeed, the invasion on April 9th saw the first use of airborne troops in the war and was also one of the very few amphibious operations undertaken by the Germans during the Second World War. It is hoped that Niall Cherry's new two-volume work covering the Allied intervention in Norway 1940 will fill this significant gap.

The author provides a detailed account of the German invasion and the Allied reaction, including the land, sea and air battles. This includes such actions as the sinking of HMS *Glowworm* and HMS *Glorious*, the Gladiators on the frozen lakes and Maurice Force, the sacrifice of the Territorial Battalions at Tretten and the Independent Companies, to name but a few. Volume 1 focuses on the prelude to and early phases of the German invasion and Allied response.

As in Niall's previous books, detailed research has been carried out using official reports, war diaries and veterans' accounts, supported by photographs and maps.

Niall Cherry was born in London in 1959 and recalls becoming interested in military history as a schoolboy from watching such classic war films as *'The Battle of Britain'* and *'A Bridge Too Far'*. He later found out that one of his Grandfathers fought in the Great War, serving as a chemical corporal at Loos in 1915 and ended up as a Captain. His father served in the REME in the 1950s and Niall continued in the family tradition by serving in the RAMC. During his time he qualified as a Combat Medical Technician Class 1 and an instructor in First Aid and Nuclear, Biological and Chemical Warfare, ending up as a Senior NCO.

Deeply interested in the major conflicts of the 20th Century, he has visited numerous battlefields including the Western Front, Arnhem, Gallipoli, Normandy and North Africa. He is a long standing member of the Western Front Association, the Military Heraldry Society and 23 Parachute Field Ambulance Old Comrades Association. He also has the honour to be the UK representative for the Society of Friends of the Airborne Museum Oosterbeek, secretary of the Arnhem 1944 Veterans' Club and secretary and a trustee of the Arnhem 1944 Fellowship.

He has now written ten books - *Red Berets and Red Crosses, I Shall Not Find His Equal, Most Unfavourable Ground, With Nothing Bigger than a Bren Gun, Striking Back, Arnhem Surgeon, Tunisian Tales, A Few Vital Hours, Four Days at Arnhem* and *Desert Rise Arnhem Descent*. Since 2000 he has led various groups around battlefields, contributed articles to After the Battle and Battlefields Review and has helped with around 30 books on the airborne forces and the Great War. Niall currently lives in Lancashire and works for BAE Systems in the aerospace industry.

could obtain this vital export. Even then, to stay in a relatively safe shipping channel, the ships had to sail down the narrow sea lane known as the Norwegian Leads, which lay close to the western coast of Norway.

In the 1930s, who was in either direct or indirect control of Norwegian territorial waters was of major importance to both Britain and Germany. As the decade progressed, it was believed that a war between Britain and Germany would happen sooner or later, and as it was felt that the German Navy was weaker than the Royal Navy, it would be better for the Germans that Norway remain neutral.

Adolf Hitler's rapid rise to power in Germany was made possible because of the terrible state the country was in during the years after its defeat in the Great War. Post-war German politics was one of extremes, often involving violence on the streets between supporters of opposing parties. One of those parties was the extreme right wing Nationalsozialistische Deutsche Arbeiterpartie, otherwise known as the NSDAP (National Socialist German Workers Party) led by Adolf Hitler. Under his leadership, the party rapidly rose to power.

In 1932, after a series of elections, Hitler's Nazi party - as the NSDAP was popularly known - became the single largest party in the parliament, or Reichstag. The following year, Hitler was appointed Reich Chancellor, effectively becoming the power behind the throne of Reich President Paul von Hindenburg, the ageing Great War leader.

Hitler quickly gained the Army's support by assuring them that he would tear up the Treaty of Versailles and make rearmament his top priority. Then, after either bullying or imprisoning his political rivals, he transferred the power to govern from the parliament into his own hands under an Enabling Act. The Nazis staged a Day of National Rising at Potsdam to celebrate the birth of the Third Reich and the union of Reichswehr (the German 'Army' from 1919 until 1935, when it was merged with the newly created *Wehrmacht* to form a modern army) and Party.

Various laws were then passed, which dismissed all Jews and political opponents from the Civil Service and dissolved all the trade unions. This was followed by the banning of the Social Democratic Party, and with the dissolving of all the other parties this left the Nazis in sole charge

With the internal position in Germany stitched up, Hitler was able in the autumn of 1933 to turn his attention to international policy. His first act was to remove Germany from the League of Nations and the disarmament talks going on at Geneva in Switzerland. The western superpowers failed to react to these moves and so Poland (with probably more to lose than most other countries) suggested an agreement for a 10-year non-aggression pact with Germany. This was formally signed on 26 January 1934.

By the middle of 1934 it was clear that the Reich President, von Hindenburg, was very ill and close to death. Hitler visited him on 1 August, but von Hindenburg failed to recognise him. That evening Hitler had the cabinet agree to a law combining the office of Reich President with that of Reich Chancellor. On the following day, von Hindenburg died and Hitler assumed the title of Führer and Reich Chancellor. To cement his grip, he got his Army Minister, General Blomberg, to arrange on this day for all members of the armed forces to swear an oath of unconditional loyalty to the office of Führer. With the army's support, Hitler could now start to concentrate more on "righting the wrongs of Versailles". The first step on this journey came in January 1935 when the Saarland (a disputed area on the French-German border), which had been placed under the control of the League of Nations after Versailles but was ruled by the French, held a referendum on whether to return to Germany. The inhabitants voted to return to German control by over 90 per cent after a clever Nazi propaganda campaign. The actual change took place on 1 March. Hitler had also, as promised to the army, increased expenditure on armaments and the Germans were doing all they could to circumvent the provisions of the Versailles and Locarno Treaties. This latter treaty sought to ratify territory settlements as a result of the break-up of the old European superpowers such as Austro-Hungary. It was against this backdrop that on 3 February 1935 a joint British-French communiqué was issued which condemned unilateral rearmament and suggested limits on arms and an international agreement against "terror from the air". On 10 March, the Reich Commissioner for Aviation, Hermann Göring, revealed the existence of an air force, formed in a flagrant breach of the Versailles Treaty. To further impress or scare diplomats, the Germans announced they had double the number of aircraft they actually had.

Around this time France renewed her military pact with Belgium and increased its length of national service to two years. In retaliation, and to appease the military leaders, the ruling Nazis made a further announcement on 16 March. This outlined the growth of the German army with the reintroduction of conscription, planning an army of 24 divisions with an expansion to a peacetime strength of 36 divisions containing around 500,000 men. It went further, stating that should there be a war by 1939 the army would be expanded to 63 divisions. To try to allay any fears amongst the western European superpowers Hitler claimed that Germany had no further designs on any French territory. The French and Italians were aghast at these developments and made threatening noises, but only the British formally protested. They pushed for talks, and on 25 March the British Foreign Secretary, Sir John Simon, and the Privy Seal, Anthony Eden, arrived in Berlin. They returned home with the message that Germany wanted parity in air force strength with Britain and 35 per cent of the Royal Navy's strength (roughly equivalent to the size of the French Navy). In June, Germany's newly appointed Ambassador Extraordinary, Joachim von Ribbentrop, went to London to negotiate with the Admiralty on the German naval build-up. To his surprise, Sir John Simon announced almost immediately that the British accepted Hitler's proposal, following the policy of appeasement then in vogue. This was formally agreed in an Anglo-German Naval Agreement, which was signed on 18 June, and von Ribbentrop returned in triumph with another major breach of the Versailles Treaty in favour of Germany.

Hitler shrewdly guessed that neither Britain nor France had much stomach for a fight and so decided at the beginning of March to send troops back into the Rhineland sector of Germany. This had been established as a demilitarised German zone at the end of the Great War to ensure that Germany could never again launch an attack on France from the region. Allied troops, which had occupied this zone, had been gradually withdrawn over the years. The last troops had left in June 1930. Hitler judged the time was right and on 7 March1936, in front of the world's press, German troops marched over the Hohenzollern Bridge in Cologne, which spanned the Rhine, and re-entered the "forbidden" zone, again in a clear breach of the Versailles Treaty. In a speech in the Reichstag just after announcing the re-occupation, Hitler declared: "Germany has no further claims to make from France nor will she make any." In the same speech, he said Germany would be prepared to rejoin the League of Nations and enter into non-aggression pacts with France and Belgium, promises he had no intention of keeping. The only real voice of opposition came from the Council of the League of Nations, which merely condemned Germany for breaking the terms of the Treaty of Versailles. To try and stop any further action, Hitler dissolved the Reichstag and called for the Germans to vote on 29 March to show whether they approved of his actions. The result was an astounding 98.8 per cent vote in favour. The road to a future conflict took another turn in July, when another Fascist leader, General Francisco Franco, asked for assistance in the bloody civil war then being fought against the communists in Spain. Germany agreed to send some elements of the *Luftwaffe* there, including transport aircraft, fighters, bombers and anti-aircraft guns.

Things went quiet for a year or so, although behind the scenes, Hitler was becoming convinced that Germany was unable to feed and re-arm itself from her own resources and might need to expand into other areas. This would mean that she would be ready to go to war in four years' time. Meanwhile, Italy, another Fascist state, was not happy with the apparently growing relationship between Britain and Germany. Benito Mussolini, who had been in power in Italy since 1922, sent Count Galeazzo Ciano, his son-in-law and Italian Foreign Minister, to Berlin for talks in October 1936. These resulted in an alliance known as the Axis Pact. Hitler also committed more assistance to Franco, and in November 1936 Germany signed an Anti-Comintern Pact with Japan in mutual support against the Soviet Union.

In September 1937, Mussolini paid a visit to Berlin for talks with Hitler. While no formal agreements were signed, the two leaders did agree that neither would get too close to Britain without the other party's say-so. It was also agreed that Italy would have a free hand in the Mediterranean and Germany could "have" Austria. With this agreement in the bag and the lack of any foreign objection to the actions taken so far, Hitler felt able to plan further territorial ambitions. The impression of a lack of serious opposition at that time was further strengthened on 19 November 1937, when the British Foreign Secretary, Lord Halifax, visited Hitler on behalf of the new government led by Neville Chamberlain to explain their appeasement policy. In exchange for a German commitment to a permanent European peace settlement, Britain would be prepared to allow Germany to settle territorial disputes in Austria, Czechoslovakia and Danzig in accordance with her wishes. However, Hitler primarily wanted a free hand in the east, and although he would have preferred a pact or alliance with Britain, he did not deem it essential to his plans.

The following year, on 12 February, Hitler invited Austrian Chancellor Kurt von Schuschnigg to the Berghof, his mountaintop retreat in Bavaria for so-called talks. There, von Schuschnigg was bullied into accepting an unfavourable agreement whereby the Austrian Nazi Party was allowed to be a part of the Austrian government, with control of the Ministry of the Interior and consequently the Austrian Police. Schuschnigg thought he could sidestep this by announcing on 9 March a plebiscite for three days later, but Hitler again managed to bully him into cancelling it. Hitler threatened to send in troops if von Schuschnigg did not resign in favour of the leader of the Austrian Nazis –

Arthur Seyss-Inquart. Schuschnigg appealed to the Western powers for help but got no response, and late on 11 March German troops entered Austria. Two days later, Austria was formally annexed to form the Greater German Reich. Hitler commented in defence of his actions:

> On Friday night I was asked to order German troops to march into Austria in order to prevent grave internal disorders in that country. Toward 10:00 p.m. troops were already crossing the frontier at numerous points. At 6:00 a.m. the main body began to march in. They were greeted with tremendous enthusiasm by the population, which was thus at last free. On Saturday, 13 March, at Linz, I decreed the incorporation of the Ostmark into the Reich and caused the members of the former Austrian Army to swear allegiance to me as the Commander-in-Chief of the German Forces.

Britain condemned the manner in which this Anschluss had been achieved, but went on to recognise the new state of affairs.

Buoyed up by this success, Hitler decided that Czechoslovakia was his next target, the main reason for this interest being given as protection of the Sudeten Germans. The area of Sudeten had been given to the newly formed Czechoslovakia just before the end of the Great War. This region comprised mainly ethnic Germans, who campaigned over the next 20 years either to be independent or become part of Germany. In February 1938, Hitler instructed Goebbels, his Propaganda Minister, to mount a campaign against the Czech Government, accusing it of ill-treating the Sudeten Germans and acting provocatively towards Germany by assembling troops on the border, and also for good measure to crank on extra pressure by suggesting it mistreated its Slav citizens. This last group reacted as Hitler had hoped by also increasing their demands for independence. Then, on 28 March 1938, Hitler instructed the leader of the Sudeten German Party to increase his demands for concessions and independence to the Prague government.

On 20 May, alarmed by all these sabre-rattling moves, the Czech government mobilised its troops in the expectation that Germany was about to attack. It was a false alarm, but Hitler advised the *Wehrmacht* that he wanted to invade Czechoslovakia if necessary and they should be ready to go by 1 October.

Europe looked towards Britain in the hope that she would act as mediator, but Chamberlain's government was sticking to its policy of appeasement. Chamberlain felt it was better to try to deal direct with Hitler rather than organise pacts against him behind the scenes. So, on 15 September 1938, Chamberlain flew to the Obersaltzberg to try to resolve the Sudeten question. A week later, the two leaders met again at Bad Godesberg, but this time Chamberlain said that his government was happy for self-determination for the Sudeten Germans and the cession of that territory to Germany. However, Hitler now wanted to move his troops in prior to any vote, and also to encourage Poland and Hungary to make their own territorial claims on Czech territory. Chamberlain left the next day – even he felt unwilling to agree to these new demands. He asked Mussolini to intercede with the hope of avoiding a European war. A conference was arranged for 29 September, to be held in Munich. At this meeting, Mussolini put forward the proposal that the European superpowers would guarantee Czech independence once the territorial concessions had been made. This was agreed on the following day, enabling Chamberlain to return to England, waving a piece of paper stating that this was Herr Hitler's last territorial demand and would ensure "peace for our time".

The BBC put it as follows:

> The British Prime Minister has been hailed as bringing "peace to Europe" after signing a non-aggression pact with Germany. PM Neville Chamberlain arrived back in the UK today, holding an agreement signed by Adolf Hitler which stated the German leader's desire never to go to war with Britain again.
>
> The two men met at the Munich conference between Britain, Germany, Italy and France yesterday, convened to decide the future of Czechoslovakia's Sudetenland.
>
> Mr Chamberlain declared the accord with the Germans signalled "peace for our time", after he had read it to a jubilant crowd gathered at Heston airport in west London.
>
> The German leader stated in the agreement: "We are determined to continue our efforts to remove possible sources of difference and thus to contribute to assure the peace of Europe."
>
> But many MPs are bound to criticise it as part of the Prime Minister's "appeasement" of German aggression in Europe.
>
> And Mr Chamberlain's personal pact will be little comfort to the Czechoslovakian Government which has been forced to hand over the region of Sudetenland to Germany, despite not being present at the conference.
>
> After greeting members of the public at the airport, Mr Chamberlain appeared in front of another rejoicing throng on the balcony of Buckingham Palace with the King and Queen, and again later outside 10 Downing Street.

Duly sorted, Hitler ordered his troops into the Sudetenland on 1 October 1938 and also began plans to expand the German Navy's surface fleet to a size capable in time of matching the Royal Navy. However, this did not mean the end of Hitler looking longingly at the rest of Czechoslovakia. On 15 March 1939, having approved the independence of Slovakia and bullied elderly Czech President Doctor Emil Hàche into agreeing to his demands, he sent German troops into the rest of Czechoslovakia to create the Reich Protectorate of Bohemia and Moravia.

Hitler commented:

> The creation of this heterogeneous republic after the war was lunacy. It has none of the characteristics of a nation, whether from the standpoint of ethnology, strategy, economics or language. To set an intellectually inferior handful of Czechs to rule over minorities belonging to races like the Germans, Poles and Hungarians with a thousand years of culture behind them, was a work of folly and ignorance. The Sudeten Germans have no respect for the Czechs and will never accept their rule. After the war the Allied Powers declared that Germany

was unworthy to govern blacks, yet at the same time they set second-rate people like the Czechs in authority over 3½ million Germans of the highest character and culture.

In honour of Hitler's 50th birthday on 20 April 1939, a large parade was held in Berlin, and amongst those invited was Czech President Hàche. It is said he had been invited just to be overawed by the massive display of military muscle; it is reported that over 50,000 troops took part in the parade.

By now Britain and France had come to see exactly what Hitler's promises meant. To try and keep Hitler in check, they formed military pacts with Poland, Romania, Greece and Turkey – which meant that if they were invaded by Hitler, Britain and France would come to their aid - and entered into talks with the Soviets.

Hitler was also concerned with his eastern border and from about October 1938 onwards had been asking his diplomats to persuade Poland to enter into an anti-Soviet alliance in return for rewards of Ukrainian territory. But the Polish government would have none of it, and on 26 March 1939 finally rejected any ideas of entering into an alliance with Germany against Russia. Ideologically, Germany and Russia were poles apart and would one day be at war with each other, but the problem now was that Germany would have to invade Poland to get at the Soviet Union.

To try to persuade Hitler to enter into a general peace agreement, on 31 March 1939, Britain guaranteed Polish independence. In an attempt to make Hitler see sense, Britain also tried to enter into an alliance with the Soviet Union. Chamberlain was wrong-footed by developments, as Stalin opted for an alliance with Germany instead. In spite of their ideological differences, this was a shrewd move by Stalin, as he knew that Russia was not ready for war, and an alliance with Germany, however unpalatable, would buy him some time to sort out his armed forces. A formal German-Soviet Non-Aggression pact was signed in Moscow by von Ribbentrop and the Soviet Foreign Minister, Molotov, on 23 August 1938. This gave the Germans the benefit of oil, raw materials and grain supplies from Russia, and also the opportunity to invade Poland without having to fear a Russian reaction.

A few months earlier, on 28 April 1938, Hitler made a speech before the Reichstag that was reported around the world. In this he condemned the "British change in foreign policy", claiming that it breached, and thus negated, the 1935 Naval Treaty, and carried on by also declaring the non-aggression pact with the Poles null and void, the reason for this being "Polish transgressions". In one afternoon, Hitler had basically torn up two international treaties in front of the whole world.

Additionally, on 22 May, Germany and Italy signed the Pact of Steel, bonding them to mutual aid and efforts in time of war. The next part of the plan was to persuade Japan to join the Pact of Steel. The following day, Hitler announced to the Heads of the Armed Forces that he intended to invade Poland. He also told them that some secret clauses of the proposed non-aggression pact with the Soviets gave them a clear area of operations as far as line of the Narva, Vistula and San rivers. All that was needed now was an excuse.

The excuse for invasion was manufactured by the Germans under the code name Operation Himmler. This was a staged incident in which a German radio station just inside the Polish-German border at Gleiwitz was "attacked" and taken over by a group of supposedly armed "Poles" on the evening of 31 August. One of the "Poles" started broadcasting anti-German slogans and called for conflict. To add credence to the ruse, a number of condemned prisoners from a concentration camp were dressed up in Polish Army uniforms and given lethal injections, before being shot and then scattered around the radio station as if they had been killed in the attack. Additionally, on 25 August, Germany had sent a series of demands to the Polish Government, which encompassed the following: the return of Danzig to Germany; rail and road access across the corridor between Germany and East Prussia; the cession to Germany of any Polish territory, part of Germany before the Great War, that contained 75 per cent or more ethnic Germans; and an international board to discuss the cession of the Polish Corridor to Germany.

2

September 1939 - The Opening Shots

The outnumbered and outgunned Polish Army put up a brave fight against the German invaders, but the result was never really in doubt. Only about 600,000 Polish troops out of the potential 2.5 million had been mobilised when the Germans attacked, and they were severely lacking in armour, anti-tank guns, artillery support and transport. The Germans, meanwhile, had deployed 1.8 million men to attack Poland, with 2,600 tanks to the Polish 340 and over 2,000 aircraft to the defenders' 420.

Hitler had ordered his generals: "Kill without pity or mercy all men, women and children of Polish descent or language ... only in this way can we achieve the living space we need." Mobile killing squads, *Einsatzgruppen*, would follow the main body of troops, shooting PoWs and any Poles who might organise resistance.

At 0445 on 1 September 1939, the German Army crossed the border to "prevent further Polish aggression".

German forces and their Danzig and Slovak allies attacked Poland across many sectors of the border. In the north, they attacked the Polish Corridor (the strip of land between Germany and its outlying territory of East Prussia which gave Poland access to the Baltic Sea). In southern and central Poland, Nazi armoured spearheads attacked toward Łódź and Kraków. In the skies, German planes commenced terror bombing of cities and villages. Nazi armies massacred civilians and used women and children as human shields. Everywhere there were scenes of savage fighting and unbelievable carnage. Polish forces defending the borders gave a good account of themselves, and the battle in the Polish Corridor was especially intense.

Where the Poles were in defensive positions, they usually got the better of the fighting, but because of the delay in mobilisation, their forces were too few to defend all sectors. German mechanised forces bypassed Polish strong points, cutting them off, using a new type of warfare, which they called blitzkreig or lightning war. They probed for weak spots, using armour and air power to keep blasting more holes in the Polish defences, pushing on and letting follow-on troops mop up. This caused great confusion in the rear areas as nobody could be sure where the Germans would turn up next.

Britain and France had guaranteed Polish independence, and diplomatic moves were afoot to make the Germans pull back. On the morning of 1 September, the British Ambassador in Berlin met with the German Foreign Minister and passed on his government's demands. Two days were given for the Germans to respond to the demands, but nothing was forthcoming.

At 1115 on 3 September, British Prime Minister Neville Chamberlain broadcast to the nation:

I am speaking to you from the Cabinet Room at 10 Downing Street. This morning the British Ambassador in Berlin handed the German Government a final note stating that, unless we heard from them by 11 o'clock that they were prepared at once to withdraw their troops from Poland, a state of war would exist between us.

I have to tell you now that no such undertaking has been received, and that consequently this country is at war with Germany.

With these words, Britain entered its second major conflict of the twentieth century. But this was of little comfort to Poland, whose forces were unable to contain the Nazi breakthroughs and German tanks drove on toward Warsaw. German aircraft systematically targeted Polish civilians, especially refugees. Bombing and shelling sent tens of thousands of people fleeing for their lives, crowding the roads and hindering military traffic.

The effects of the Poles' lack of mobility and the decision to position forces closer to the border now began to tell. A Polish counter-attack came to nothing. The Germans' superiority in tanks and aircraft allowed them to regroup and halt the Poles, for whom the counter-attack turned into a battle of encirclement, with the bulk of the Polish forces destroyed.

By the middle of September, Polish losses had been severe and the German advance had captured half of the country. However, Polish defences were stiffening and German losses began to rise.

Polish hopes were extinguished, however, on 17 September, when Red Army forces crossed Poland's virtually unguarded eastern border as Stalin moved to assist his German ally and seize his share of Polish territory.

Polish defences in the south-east of the country fell apart as formations were ordered to fall back across the relatively friendly Romanian and Hungarian borders to avoid capture. On 28 September, Warsaw capitulated and other Polish forces were overcome by the first week in October.

During the first two-and-a-half weeks of September, while Germany threw her entire air force, all her panzer forces and all her frontline infantry and artillery against Poland, the border with France was held by a relatively thin screen of second and third-string divisions. The French Army, from its secure base behind the Maginot Line, had overwhelming superiority in men, tanks, aircraft and artillery. A concerted push into western Germany would have spelled disaster for Hitler. Yet the French stood aside and did nothing, due to their defensive mentality and fearful of losses like those they suffered in the Great War. The British were equally inactive, merely sending RAF bombers to drop propaganda leaflets over German cities.

Both remained largely idle while Poland desperately requested the French Army to advance into Germany to tie down German divisions, and also asked Britain to bomb German industrial targets. Field Marshal Wilhelm Keitel, head of the Supreme Command of the Armed Forces (OKW), later commented that had France reacted with a full-scale invasion of Germany, the Nazi regime would have fallen immediately.

The British Expeditionary Force, which had been formed on paper in 1938, started to gear up for action, but far too late to stop the Germans in Poland. Commanded by

Lord Gort, the first deployment of troops was completed by 11 October 1939, at which point 158,000 men had been transported to France.

There were immense pressures to produce the equipment necessary for the BEF, which led to a serious ramping up of output. To give some idea of how badly Britain was prepared, in the early months of the war clothing items were being produced at up to 50 times the normal peacetime rates. Twenty-five years' worth of greatcoats were produced in six months and 18 months of army boots were turned out in one week.

By 19 October, the BEF had received 25,000 vehicles and the majority of its troops were stationed along the Franco-Belgian border and behind the Maginot Line. For those troops along the Maginot Line, the inactivity and an undue reliance on the fortifications, which it was believed would provide an unbreakable defence, led to what was labeled "Tommy Rot" – as portrayed in the song *Imagine Me on the Maginot Line*. Morale was high amongst British troops, but the lack of activity led to this period becoming known as the Phoney War.

Over the next few months, troops, materials and vehicles continued to arrive in France and Belgium, and by 13 March 1940 the BEF had doubled in size to 316,000 men. Most British eyes were therefore fixed on France as the likely location for a German attack. However, Hitler had other ideas.

Norway did not possess a large standing army at the outbreak of the Second World War. After more than a hundred years of peace, her government considered that effective national defence against a major power was impossible. King Haakon VII was Commander-in-Chief of a basically territorial army, which when fully mobilised, would have had a strength of about 100,000 men. A small cadre of regular officers and NCOs was responsible for running the army and for the training of conscripts.

The country was divided into six military districts or commands, with their headquarters in Halden, Oslo, Kristiansand, Bergen, Trondheim and Harstad. Each command was initially expected to field a brigade, later to be expanded to a division, besides garrison and ancillary troops.

An infantry division comprised a staff, two or three infantry regiments and either a field artillery regiment or a mountain artillery battalion.

The 2nd Infantry Division in Oslo included the Royal Guard and a cavalry regiment. The 5th and 6th Infantry Divisions had, in addition, a pioneer and a flying battalion.

An infantry regiment had a paper strength of 3,750 men, armed with Krag-Joergensen M1894 rifles. Some regiments had a bicycle company for reconnaissance duties, which in winter became a ski troop. Perhaps the most glaring weaknesses were that the troops had no sub-machine guns or anti-aircraft guns, very few anti-tank guns and no tanks.

The Norwegian Air Force was organised in three flights (one each of fighters, bombers and reconnaissance aircraft) with a total of 76 aircraft and 940 men, and was intended to play a ground-support role.

In 1940 there were 5,200 officers and men serving in the Norwegian Navy and its Air Service, but the bulk of its vessels were obsolete. The navy had 113 vessels, comprising: two small armoured cruisers; 10 minelayers; seven destroyers; three large Trygg class torpedo boats; 14 torpedo boats; nine submarines; eight minesweepers; nine patrol boats; and 49 vessels converted into patrol boats.

In addition to the fleet there were coastal fortifications armed with guns of various calibres at Oscarsborg, Oslofjord, Kristiansand, Bergen and Agdenes, which were manned by 308 officers and 2,095 other ranks. The Naval Air Service was again small in size and limited to flying from land bases.

On the Western Front in France, both sides endured one of the coldest winters for many years and a state of *Sitzkreig* ensued, but Germany was planning to strike in the spring of 1940. Norway did briefly enter the minds of the senior commanders in 1939. After some years in the political wilderness, Winston Churchill was recalled to the government on the outbreak of war and given the job of First Lord of the Admiralty. One of his first acts was to try to get his colleagues interested in the neutral port of Narvik in Norway. In spite of Norway's neutrality, it was one of the main outlets for exports of iron ore, of which a great deal ended up in Germany. Churchill wanted to stop the flow of iron ore from this port, but his suggestion fell on deaf ears as the Foreign Secretary, Lord Halifax, did not want to impinge upon Norwegian neutrality and was supported in this by Chamberlain.

But things were about to change in northern Europe, as amid much international condemnation the Soviet Union attacked Finland on 30 November 1939. The main reason for its attack was the Soviets' desire to extend their influence over the Baltic States. Lithuania, Estonia and Latvia had all been made to sign treaties of mutual assistance that allowed the Soviets to establish military bases there: Finland was undoubtedly next in line. This also had the effect of pushing Britain and France closer to Sweden and Norway, who had offered to support the Finns. Although stopping short of actually sending troops, Britain was happy to let volunteers go to fight, and offered supplies and logistical support. The RAF managed to scrape together 150 aircraft from its limited supply to go to Finland. Given that its main priorities were the defence of the United Kingdom and supporting the BEF in France, only some of the older and second-line aircraft were allocated for the Finnish expedition.

Diplomatic efforts were not slow in coming. By the middle of December, the League of Nations had excluded the Soviet Union, and on 18 December the Secretary-General requested that every member give assistance to Finland in any form they felt fit. France was one of the first to act, and felt this might also be an opportunity to cut or hinder the supply of Swedish iron ore to Germany. They proposed a joint action with Britain, which involved naval operations at Petsamo or Murmansk. Additionally, on 31 December the French loaded 30 of their Morane MS 406 fighter aircraft on a Finnish merchant ship at Dunkirk to be "loaned" to the Finnish Air Force. In Britain, these plans were greeted with scepticism as no one welcomed the prospect of war with the Soviet Union. However, Churchill sniffed an opportunity and stated: "If Narvik was to become a sort of Allied base to supply the Finns, it would certainly be easy to prevent the German ships from loading ore at the port and sailing down the Leads to Germany."

He also suggested that mines be laid inside Norwegian waters, but the Chief of the Imperial General Staff (CIGS), General Sir Edmund Ironside, went even further and suggested that a large expeditionary force be sent to the Scandinavian countries to occupy the iron ore mines. In line with much of the pre-war years, there was a lot of talking but not much action. Various schemes were put forward for stopping

A panorama of Narvik Fjord. (The National Archives)

the iron ore traffic by sea without impinging upon Norwegian neutrality or for the longer-term goal of garrisoning Norway with Allied troops. These discussions did not achieve anything, but in February 1940, at one of the regular Supreme War Council meetings between Britain and France, the French finally recognised that the British were not going to take on board any idea of invading the Soviet Union in any of its vast territories. Instead, Chamberlain suggested an expeditionary force to land in Norway under the banner of the League of Nations and advance towards Finland. The French Prime Minister, Édouard Daladier, readily agreed to this and the creation of such a force was approved.

However, on 23 February –to the Allies' annoyance – an agreement was concluded between Norway and Germany, which allowed for exports from Norway to Germany not to exceed the levels of those of 1938. Norway, wishing to remain neutral and trying to please both sides, then negotiated an agreement which capped British imports to Norway at the same level as in 1937-1938. This agreement was signed on 11 March.

The expeditionary force plan was for two or more Allied brigades to be in action on the Finnish front by mid-March. As part of this plan to rescue the Finns, the main part of this force would land at Narvik in Norway and advance along the railway line to Kiruna and Gällivare, two important Swedish mining centres and therefore crucial for German exports. From there it would continue on to the Baltic port of Lulea. A second force of five British territorial units would occupy three ports in southern Norway, with the intention of providing bases for the defence of Scandinavia, providing an alternative route towards Finland and – more importantly – denying these ports to the Germans.

The British Government initially decided to hold back two divisions intended for France to be part of the new expeditionary force, but it was hoped that the British element would ultimately be about 100,000 strong, with the French contributing around 50,000. It was felt that at least 40 destroyers would be needed for convoy duties and other tasks, plus an assortment of larger ships. The RAF contribution was planned to be at least seven squadrons, made up of three fighter and four bomber squadrons. The Chiefs of Staff believed that an intervention in Scandinavia was the "first and best chance of wresting the initiative and shortening the war".

One of the divisions considered for the Norwegian expedition was the 49th (West Riding) Division, a territorial unit commanded by Major General Pierse Mackesy, which had been mobilised on the outbreak of war. The HQ of the division was at Bedale Hall in North Yorkshire, with its units spread out around the county, from Thirsk to Scarborough and Malton to Ripon. As its commander commented, they "were like every other Territorial Army division doing their best to fit themselves for war in spite of a great shortage of clothing, of equipment, of arms, of ammunition, of transport, of indeed adequate supply of every military necessity except a fine spirit".

Towards the end of January 1940, Major General Mackesy, received an order to attend a meeting at the War Office the following Monday, 29 January, to see the CIGS, General Ironside, and General Ronald Adam, Director of Military Operations and Plans. Mackesy was due to preside over a court martial on that day, so it was agreed that he would just see General Adam on 31 January. He was instructed to take his Chief of Staff and Chief Administrative Officer with him to the meeting, where Mackesy learned he was to take command of a force called Avonmouth. With the consent of the Norwegian and Swedish governments. he was to land these troops at Narvik, seize iron ore mines at Lulea and deny ore supplies to Germany for at least a year. The original 5,300-strong fighting force was to consist of the 24th Guards Brigade – the 1st Scots Guards, 1st Irish Guards, 2nd South Wales Borderers and 5th Scots Guards (a specialist ski unit) - together with a French demi-brigade (three battalions) from the *Chasseurs Alpins*. Mackesy commented that the force was overloaded with headquarters and administrative units amounting to a further 3,000 men, but no anti-aircraft artillery, field or light artillery. The actual fighting force of just over 5,000 men was intended to defend Narvik, protect hundreds of miles of very vulnerable lines of communication, protect advanced depots in Sweden and hold the Lulea area for as long as possible.

In addition to Avonmouth, a force named Stratford was also planned. This was to have three elements:, the first, planned to be of battalion size, was to go to and hold Trondheim; the second, consisting of two battalions, was to do the same at Bergen; the third group, also of two battalions, was to secure Stavanger. Again it was felt that no supporting arms and services were needed. The final element of this early planning stage was the despatch of a force known as Plymouth. This was to consist of up to three divisions and to be transported to Sweden via Trondheim, with the aim of assisting the Swedes against a German invasion which, it was anticipated, might follow a British seizure of the iron ore mines in northern Sweden. With the benefit of hindsight, it is probably for the better that none of these proposed moves actually came into being. Apart from the chances of Sweden and Norway, two neutral countries, agreeing to such an armed incursion, the British Government simply could not make a decision and any German reaction would have probably caused the under-equipped Anglo-French force many casualties. There was also talk of Avonmouth Two, an enlarged version of the previous force, that was to proceed to the aid of the Finns and fight the Russians in the Kemijarvi region. It was recognised that the previous level of troops might be slightly outnumbered, so the number was increased, with the proposed addition of a second demi-brigade of *Chasseurs Alpins*, two battalions from the French Foreign Legion and a brigade of Polish troops.

According to comments from Major General Mackesy, the politicians in London, having thought long and hard over incursions across neutral territory, advised him that they had "persuaded themselves that the arrival of Avonmouth Two at Narvik would rally local sympathisers with Finland to our cause". Other advice given by London included: "It is the intention of His Majesty's Government that your force should land provided it can do without serious fighting ... If the Norwegians or Swedes open fire on your troops a certain number of casualties must be accepted. Fire upon Norwegian or Swedish troops is only to be opened as a last resort ... It is not the intention of the Government that the force should fight its way through either Norway or Sweden. None the less, should you find your way barred by Swedish forces, you should demand passage from the Swedish commander with the utmost energy."

To make the situation clear to the soldiers under his command, Mackesy issued the following observations:

> It is possible however that active hostility may be encountered. His Majesty's Government earnestly desires to fulfil their moral obligation to assist Finland without any serious fighting with Norway or Sweden. It is the intention of His Majesty's Government that the force should fight its way through. But hostility, if it is shown, may prove to be neither widespread nor serious. It is to be hoped that it would disappear in the face of a good humoured but determined attitude on the part of all ranks of the force, and that our object will be achieved by moral persuasion and without warlike action. Should fire be opened on your troops, a certain number of casualties must be accepted and your counter-action should, within limits, rest upon the use of weight, discipline, the rifle butt and fist.

In a bid to try clarify things even further, instructions were issued to all platoon commanders, which included: "So long as you act with good intent within the above limitations, you can count on the complete support of your commanders."

Then, in February 1940, a minor incident occurred which ratcheted up the tension.

3

The *Altmark* Incident

Just before and just after the outbreak of war in September 1939, several capital ships of the German Navy had slipped out of their home ports, with the intention of wreaking havoc on British merchant ships in both the North and South Atlantic oceans. One of these capital ships was the *Deutschland* class heavy cruiser (but often known as a pocket battleship) *Admiral Graf Spee*. She was named after Admiral Maximilian von Spee, commander of the East Asia Squadron that fought the battles of the Coronel and the Falkland Islands in the Great War. She was laid down at the *Kriegsmarinewerft* shipyard in Wilhelmshaven in October 1932 and completed by January 1936. The ship was nominally under the 10,000 tons limitation on warship size imposed by the Treaty of Versailles, though with a full load displacement of 16,020 tons, she significantly exceeded it. Armed with six 11in guns in two triple gun turrets, *Admiral Graf Spee* and her sister ships were designed to outgun any cruiser fast enough to catch them. Their top speed of 28 knots meant there were only a handful of ships in the Anglo-French fleets able to catch them and then be powerful enough to sink them.

The ship conducted five non-intervention patrols during the Spanish Civil War in 1936–1938, and participated in the Coronation Review for King George VI in May 1937. *Admiral Graf Spee* was deployed to the South Atlantic in the weeks before the outbreak of the Second World War, to be positioned in the sea lanes used by merchant shipping once war was declared. Supply ships were also sent to try and make sure that maximum value was extracted from these patrols. So the *Graf Spee* with her supply ship, the *Altmark*, slipped though the English Channel on 6 August 1939 and moved down into the South Atlantic where, for the next three months, she supplied the *Graf Spee* with oil and provisions, allowing the battleship to make continued forays against merchant shipping. She also became a prison ship, taking aboard survivors from the ships sunk by the *Graf Spee*.

Between September and December 1939, the ship sank nine vessels totalling 50,089 gross register tons (GRT). But on 13 December 1939, the *Graf Spee* was found in the South Atlantic off the coast of Uruguay and attacked by the cruisers HMS *Exeter*, *Ajax* and *Achilles* in the Battle of the River Plate, entering Montevideo harbour to avoid destruction. As Uruguay was neutral, warships were only allowed to stay for 72 hours for repairs, following which they would be interned. Convinced by false reports of superior British naval forces approaching his ship, Hans Langsdorff, the commander of the ship, ordered the vessel to be scuttled. The ship was partially broken up in situ, though part of the ship remains visible above the surface of the water to this day.

On 17 December 1940, a message was sent to the *Altmark* from German Navy High Command which read: "Announcing with regret that *Panzer* ship *Admiral Graf Spee* has been scuttled in the face of superior enemy forces. *Altmark* to return to home waters. Observe total radio silence." As the ship's position was not exactly known, the route for their homeward passage was not clear. However, they were advised to avoid the Cape Verde Islands and the Azores, and head for the southern point of Greenland, then use the Iceland–Shetland Islands gap to head for Scandinavia and then southwards to Germany and the port of Wilhelmshaven.

By now the *Altmark* had around 300 British and Commonwealth seamen on board. They were kept in primitive conditions in the holds, with little exercise and not much in the way of food or water. These men came from the merchantmen SS *Ashlea*, SS *Doric Star*, SS *Huntsman*, SS *Newton Beach*, SS *Tairoa* and SS *Trevanion*.

The men were not that happy with being incarcerated and many of them were thinking of ways of getting away, or at least alerting friendly forces of their predicament. One of the first attempts occurred on 18 December 1939 after one of the *Altmark* officers had inadvertently given away their position. The following message was written: "SOS 18.12.1939. We are 300 seamen of British ships sunk by *Graf Spee*. We are now on the *Graf Spee* supply ship *Altmark* of Hamburg and somewhere south of the Cape of Good Hope. It is possible that we shall be moving towards Germany soon but we are not sure. We are quartered in holds forward and aft. The *Altmark* has sufficient oil and provisions for the voyage."

This message was wrapped in tinfoil and put into a tin can to which a short stick of wood was attached and a tiny Union Jack was donated by one of the captured crew members. The tin was dropped overboard the next morning, but unfortunately it was spotted and the *Altmark* retraced its course to pick it up. In spite of several interrogations of the men, no one would admit to anything. The result was that Heinrich Dau, the *Altmark*'s captain, decided that exercise periods would be further curtailed.

By 23 December, the *Altmark* had reached the Roaring Forties, but the chief engineer reported to Dau that the engines were running rough and needed attention. So over the next few days the *Altmark* was basically drifting whilst these repairs were carried out. It took until 19 January 1940 to effect all the required repairs. This obviously was bad news for the captured sailors. As the captain of the now-sunk SS *Huntsman*, Captain Brown, commented, "We'll soon be off to Germany."

The question was how to avoid any Allied warships. From their starting position in the northern South Atlantic, there were several ports with an enemy presence. These included Freetown, Britain's main base in the central Atlantic, and Dakar, a major French base in Africa. On the western side of the Atlantic, there were Allied bases in Trinidad, Barbados, Martinique and Guadeloupe. With a bit of luck, helped by the fact that the *Altmark* remained in strict radio silence and made good progress (about 15 knots in daylight but speeding up to over 20 knots during darkness), by 7 February she was approaching Iceland. During the voyage, the *Altmark* had sighted at least six enemy vessels but ploughed on unscathed. From Iceland, they were helped by bad weather and heavy seas as the *Altmark* steamed for the Norwegian lighthouse at Halten. From there they hoped to use the protection of The Leads to make it to German waters. They hove to off the lighthouse on 12 February and requested a pilot. This was now a dangerous time for the *Altmark*, as the chances of her passing through Norwegian waters without her presence being reported to the British were remote. Captain Dau perhaps hoped that the fact that he was holding prisoners would be kept from the Norwegians, and that the length of time it would take for the British to react might mean his ship could slip through.

Meanwhile, around 400 miles away at the Royal Navy base at Rosyth in Scotland, the cruiser HMS *Aurora*, was being fitted with degaussing equipment. This was a protection against German magnetic mines, which the *Luftwaffe* was starting to drop around the coast of Britain. The crew were hoping for a few easy days, but things changed very quickly. Around 1800 on February 13, groups of 21 names were called out over the tannoy system to report to the quarterdeck. These groups were told to report back at 1930, together with basic kit, as they were being seconded to other ships of the 4th Flotilla for a short-term loan. One of the groups was sent to HMS *Cossack*, the flagship of flotilla commander Captain Vian. Upon reporting in, they were told the ship would soon be leaving for a an "ice reconnaissance in the Skagerrak". The flotilla had been hit hard by an outbreak of influenza and needed reinforcements.

The group who joined the *Cossack* arrived just before 2200, carrying rifles, bayonets, steel helmets and webbing. In addition to *Cossack*, the cruiser HMS *Arethusa* and the destroyers *Sikh*, *Nubian*, *Ivanhoe* and *Intrepid* were also under sailing orders.

Despite the official line of an ice reconnaissance in the Skagerrak, the men felt they were going to look for a German prison ship. The fact that several of the groups from *Aurora* were given instruction on boarding procedures once they were aboard only reinforced the rumours. At midnight, the ships, led by *Arethusa*, sailed out into the North Sea and set course due east. They then split up to sweep a wide area in a predetermined pattern.

On the morning of February 14, *Altmark* was stopped by the Norwegian patrol torpedo boat *Trygg*. A Norwegian officer boarded and requested to search the ship. He was conducted to the bridge and shown the navigating cabin but, when the German captain insisted that the ship was an unarmed tanker, the Norwegian officer surprisingly seemed satisfied and left.

This action has to be taken in the context of the times. Norway was a neutral country and, although made aware of Britain's view that the *Altmark* was carrying British prisoners, which therefore breached her neutrality, she was also in fear of being invaded by Germany. Norway therefore did not want to create an incident which could be used to precipitate such action.

Captain Dau of the *Altmark* had requested a pilot, but as none was available, until they reached Alesund *Trygg* lent them a seaman who knew the waters well. At Alesund, two pilots boarded, together with another Norwegian officer who asked for the ship's details, looked around, but again did not search the ship. It was said by the Norwegians that ships were not allowed to pass close by the fortified base of Bergen in darkness. One of the captured seamen had seen the Norwegians board the ship and started to make a commotion in the hope of being heard, but the Germans switched on the *Altmark*'s winches to drown out the noise. Whether by accident or design, the Norwegians ignored the noise and left the ship. A notice was given to the prisoners in the holds: "Notice to Prisoners. On account of today's behaviour of the prisoners there will be bread and water only tomorrow instead of regular meals. Further I have given the order that neither prison officer nor doctor will make their regular rounds. Any severe case of sickness can be reported on occasion of handing down the food. At sea, February 15, 1940. Dau, Commander.'"

In spite of the Norwegian presence on the *Altmark*, the fact that there were prisoners on board went undiscovered. The pilots tried to stop the *Altmark* moving during the hours of darkness, but Captain Dau insisted and steamed off. To avoid a large number of Norwegian fishing vessels, the *Altmark* steered away from the coast and put on speed. This caused the *Trygg*, shadowing her, to drop back, but then out of the darkness came the flash of a signal lamp. It was another Norwegian Navy vessel, the *Snøgg*, who stated she had orders to question the captain. Comments that he had already been questioned were cut short and a small party of Norwegians again boarded, but soon left. To the Germans' disgust, it was soon discovered that the *Trygg* was back in her shadowing position. The *Altmark* was still well north of Bergen when she was again stopped, this time by the Norwegian destroyer *Garm*, and another small party went aboard to search the ship. Captain Dau refused to allow this and was therefore told to leave the Bergen fortified area. The pilots refused to stay aboard and also departed. Captain Dau was invited aboard the *Garm* to discuss the proposed text of a message to the German Embassy in Oslo. After fruitless talks, Captain Dau returned to the *Altmark* with the feeling that the Norwegians were quite happy to delay him and let him run into a British warship.

Word got to the British Embassy at Oslo from a friendly coastal watcher and the Naval Attaché signalled the Admiralty: "*Altmark* steaming two miles off the Norwegian coast north of Bergen." The fortuitous ice reconnaissance being undertaken by Captain Vian's flotilla put them south of *Altmark*. Winston Churchill, the First Lord of the Admiralty, gave clear instructions to the First Sea Lord for transmission to Captain Vian. Find her, edge her into the open sea, board her and liberate her prisoners." The signal Captain Vian received also gave the rough position of the *Altmark*.

The first problem, however, was to find the *Altmark*, and Captain Vian's force was split up to search the Leads and offshore islands. Nobody had a clear idea what the *Altmark* looked like, so every supply ship was investigated – a procedure which took some time if the vessel was close inshore against a background of snow and rock.

By around 0800 on 16 February, the *Altmark* had covered around 100 miles in a leisurely, peaceful night-time cruise, reaching a position just north of Stavanger. There were now only about 100 miles to go to the deep waters of the Skagerrak, and it was hoped that the *Altmark* would be in a position that night to attempt a high-speed dash towards the Danish coast and, eventually, German waters.

Just before this, the RAF tried to help find the *Altmark* by sending two Hudson aircraft on a reconnaissance mission from RAF Thornaby near Durham. The crews had been told that somewhere along the coast of Norway, either in the North Sea or the Skagerrak, a German tanker was making for Kiel or Hamburg; their job was to locate the tanker, identify her, photograph her and give her position and direction as speedily as possible.

One of the aircraft sent back a message around 1300. They had found a tanker steaming southwards, following the Norwegian coast. The Admiralty relayed this information to HMS *Cossack* but she was too far south to act and so asked HMS *Arethusa* to investigate. *Arethusa* closed on the position and found a tanker by the name of *Baldur*; she was carrying iron ore and the crew scuttled her before a boarding party from the *Arethusa* had even got into their boats.

```
                                    0230/1⁷ ꜰ...

   SECRET.              MESSAGE.              IN.

   From Capt. (D) 4th D.F.          Date.  17.2.40.
                                    Recd.  0250.

                NAVAL CYPHER (A) BY W/T.
   ─────────────────────────────────────────────────────
   Addressed Admiralty.  Repeated C. in ᶜ. Home Fleet.

   MOST IMMEDIATE.

             My 0150.    Boarding effected by laying

   H.M.S. COSSACK alongside.   Fighting followed resulting

   in one British casualty and several German.   I am

   steering for Rosyth with my force.   H.M.S. SEAL remains

   but is not aware of situation, nor of remote possibility

   of ALTMARK being refloated unassisted.

             I have no German prisoners on board.   H.M.S.

   COSSACK is somewhat battered.   Prisoners state that

   Norwegians search of ship at port of call was most

   perfunctory and their efforts to discover themselves

   unmarked.

                              0230/17.
```

Signal from HMS *Cossack* regarding the *Altmark*. (The National Archives)

Meanwhile, also about 1300, the other aircraft, piloted by Pilot Officer C. McNeill, found a ship of about the right tonnage steaming south at approximately 8 knots. Sweeping around her, the crew were able to make out the name of *Altmark*. The problem now was although McNeill had been told to report any sightings in code, it would soon be dark and a message going through the normal channels might take too long to reach the Royal Navy ships in the area. McNeill took a calculated risk to send a message in a self-evident code that the *Altmark* had been found steaming at 58° 17' N and 06° 05' E.

This message was picked up by RAF Leuchars in Scotland. Other aircraft were quickly despatched to the area as McNeill was running short of fuel. The message was also picked up by HMS *Cossack*, and Captain Vian ordered all his ships to intercept at top speed. In the growing darkness, at about 1445 lookouts on the *Altmark* spotted ships approaching which looked suspiciously like warships. As they neared, *Arethusa* sent out signals that "suggested" the *Altmark* steer westwards and out of Norwegian territorial waters. These messages were ignored and she continued to hug the Norwegian coast in a southerly direction.

In London, a Cabinet meeting was called to discuss the position of the *Altmark*, particularly with regard to Norwegian neutrality and the effect that any attack on the

```
                        M E S S A G E      0625/17 February.

      SECRET                                    IN

      From Capt. (S) 2 S.F.              Date 17.2.40
                                         Recd., 0851


              Administrative Code (E) (by T/P)


      Addressed H.M.S. SEAL, Polish Subm. ORZEL, H.M.S. TRIAD,
      repeated Submarines on Patrol.


      IMPORTANT


              Own force left Josing Fjord with recovered

      prisoners about 0100 proceeding westward.  ALTMARK still

      there but probably unseaworthy.  Resume normal patrol

      H.M.S. SEAL as in my 1931 10th February.  Polish Sub.

      ORZEL H.M.S. TRIAD as in company orders.  Polish Sub.

      ORZEL proceed now submerged by day.  H.M.S. TRIAD after

      sunset on 17th February.

                                         0625/17
```

A further signal about the *Altmark*. (The National Archives)

ship would have on Germany's attitude to Norway. *Altmark* was in Norwegian territorial waters, but her voyage was quite legal if she was a genuine merchant ship. Against that were the reports that she was carrying 299 British merchant seamen, taken by the *Admiral Graf Spee* from the prizes she had sunk or captured. If the reports were correct and the *Altmark* tried to carry these internees through Norwegian territorial waters, it would be an infringement of Norway's rights. In this case *Altmark* must therefore release the internees or she herself must be interned, or she must sail outside Norwegian waters – where she could be intercepted by the Royal Navy. Of course, if she were a genuine merchant ship then the Royal Navy had no right to enter Norwegian territorial waters to stop her. It was legally doubtful whether the Royal Navy could enter Norwegian territorial waters even if the *Altmark* was a regular warship, packed with prisoners, and was there illegally herself. In spite of these questions, aboard HMS *Intrepid* (who had now joined in the chase) a boarding party was detailed off and a boat made ready to be lowered. A signal flag was hoisted asking the *Altmark* to "heave to", but again this was ignored and Captain Gordon from the *Intrepid* ordered a shot to be fired across her bows. No doubt much to the chagrin of the *Intrepid*'s gunnery officer, the shot landed on Norwegian soil. Another was fired, which landed in front of the *Altmark*. This action caused one of the shadowing

The *Altmark* in Jøssing Fjord. (Imperial War Museum HU27803)

Norwegian ships, the *Skarv*, to approach *Intrepid*, shouting out warnings and hampering efforts to force the *Altmark* out of their territorial waters.

To try and seek sanctuary (of a sort), the *Altmark* slipped into Jøssing Fjord - a narrow inlet almost covered in places with quite thick ice. By this time there were three Norwegian warships in the area: the two torpedo boats *Skarv* (which had taken over from *Trygg*) and *Kjell*, and the patrol boat *Firern*.

Captain Vian in *Cossack* arrived at dusk to confer with the Norwegians. A Norwegian officer explained that the *Altmark* had been searched at Bergen and nothing amiss had been found. Captain Vian reported to the Admiralty and awaited their reply. Presently, orders arrived direct from the First Lord of the Admiralty, Winston Churchill. Captain Vian was to offer to help the Norwegians escort the *Altmark* back to Bergen to be searched again. If they refused, then *Altmark* must be boarded. If the Norwegians interfered, they must be warned off. If they opened fire, it must not be returned unless necessary, and then only as few shots fired as possible.

For a while there was a stand-off until, nearing 2200 in the cold night, Captain Vian ordered the *Cossack* towards Jøssing Fjord. It was not an easy voyage; the ice seemed to have increased as the temperature fell. As the *Cossack* neared the fjord, a message rang out in the darkness from the *Kjell*: "You are requested to leave Norwegian territorial waters."

Captain Vian replied: "My orders are to ask you to join us and take the *Altmark* to Bergen for inspection. Come on in with me."

The captain of the *Kjell* declined to do so, saying – possibly for diplomatic reasons – that his ship did not have any ice-breaking equipment. Vian ordered half speed ahead and his boarding parties to stand by. At 2312, *Cossack*, with a boarding party of three officers and 30 ratings ready, approached *Altmark*. The big tanker switched on her searchlights to dazzle *Cossack*'s bridge personnel and tried to crash her heavy stern into the destroyer's thin plates. Expert handling saved *Cossack* from damage. As the two ships brushed together, some of the boarding party leapt across. One of those was Paymaster Sub-Lieutenant Craven, who leapt from the torpedo davit just moments before it was demolished by contact with the *Altmark*. *Cossack* closed again, the rest of the boarding party followed and *Cossack* backed clear.

Four Germans were killed and five wounded in a brisk action before the *Altmark* was seized. Only one of the boarding party was injured. Two British officers dived into the icy water to rescue a German who had fallen overboard, but he was dead when they picked him up. Other Germans escaped across the ice floes and reached the shore.

Meanwhile, the boarding party had secured *Altmark*'s bridge and stopped her engines, but the tanker's momentum carried her on and she ran aground. Then the search for prisoners began and a hold was opened up.

One of the boarders shouted: "Are there any Englishmen down there?" The reply came ringing back: "Yes, we're all English down here." "Come up. The Navy's here." In all, 299 captives were released and moved across to the *Cossack*. Captain Vian had a decision to make as to what to do with the German crew, and decided it would be best to leave the Germans behind. At 2355, Vian and *Cossack* sailed out of Jøssing Fjord, heading out of Norwegian territorial waters.

The force returned to the UK, covered by the Home Fleet, and the released prisoners were landed at Leith. HMS *Cossack* suffering minor damage from collisions with the *Altmark*, but these were soon repaired.

This is the post-action report from the officer in command of the boarding party:

Report on boarding of *Altmark*.

Plan. Some 45 officers and ratings were detailed as boarding party. They were organised into four sections:

(1) My own party to secure the Bridge and interrogate the Captain.

(2) Under Lieutenant Parker to secure the Bridge structure.

(3) Under Mr Smith to secure the after part.

(4) Under Petty Officer Atkins to secure the fore part.

The boarding parties, under their leaders, mustered on *Cossack*'s forecastle, and were ordered to jump on board *Altmark* as opportunity offered. In actual fact only 33 managed to get across.

Orders given to Boarding Party. To get *Cossack* secured to *Altmark*, and then to follow their leaders. To use sufficient force to overcome opposition but not to fire unless fired at (as a safety measure magazine cut-offs were closed and the chambers of rifles were not loaded). Leaders to report to the bridge as soon as their sections of the ship were under control.

Execution. *Altmark* manoeuvred to try and prevent *Cossack* coming alongside, and also tried to ram stern into *Cossack*. At the first contact Petty Officer Atkins and myself managed to get across and secured a manila from *Cossack*'s forecastle to *Altmark*'s quarter. Ships then came together again and most of the rest of the party scrambled across. We met no immediate opposition. Leaders gathered their parties and rapidly gained command of the ship. There was some opposition aft and the Germans opened fire, to which the after party replied. Elsewhere we were met with sullen obedience. My own party reached the bridge fairly quickly and cornered most of the officers. The telegraphs were at Full Ahead and we put them to Stop; as the ship had considerable sternway on at the time she went aground stern first; rudder and screws were probably damaged and put out of action. Mr Craven interrogated the German officers and the Captain and Prison Officer agreed to show us the prisoners' quarters. Mr Craven remained on the bridge with two guards while I went away with a sentry and the two German officers to arrange the release of the prisoners. The latter were in four parties:

(1) Two Captains in a double cabin aft;

(2) About 150 white officers and ratings forward;

(3) All Lascars forward in a separate compartment;

(4) Remainder of white ratings aft. Some difficulty was found in releasing the prisoners as the German sentries aft had fled with the keys, and the forward access door had been so securely lashed with wire that it took 10 minutes to open. The ex-prisoners were sent to the fore part of the ship to await *Cossack*'s return (she had shoved off clear after disembarking the boarding party). At about 2330 Mr Craven sent a message that he had discovered that time bombs had been placed set for 0030; this may well have been bluff but the report had to be acted on. *Cossack* came alongside the fore part of *Altmark* and embarked the released prisoners. The Germans who had been held in various cabins, etc, by sentries were then driven on to *Altmark*'s forecastle, where they could be covered from *Cossack*'s left. It is regretted that the W/T Office was not found and put out of action.

Remarks. I got the impression that *Altmark* was settling slowly while we were on board, but saw no water in the Engine Room. The time bombs, if they were placed, were probably rendered safe after our departure. The *Altmark* should be easily salvageable, but it is thought that her rudders and screws will be out of action. I believe that the Captain of the *Altmark* intended to damage and even sink *Cossack* by manoeuvring his ship, but did not intend to use firearms; the firing which started on the German side was probably the act of individuals. The Surgeon of the *Altmark* (said to be a Naval Officer) treated Mr Smith's wound very well, and on our part our men carried two wounded Germans into their sick bay.

The *Altmark* Incident was definitely an infringement of Norway's neutrality by both Britain and Germany, and the ramifications of the incursion were at first mainly diplomatic.

Shortly after the news had come out that Norwegian territorial waters had been "invaded", a war of words began. Not satisfied with a mere protest, Norway demanded the

Members of the 1st Airborne Reconnaissance Squadron in Norway in 1945 with the captured *Altmark* sign. (Airborne Assault Duxford)

return of the British prisoners and that damages be paid. Winston Churchill commented in the House of Commons: "What kind of people do they think we are?"

The President of the Norwegian Parliament, Carl Joachim Hambro, stated that it was "an insolent and impetuous intrusion on the sovereign rights of this small country which by tradition is the best friend of England."

The Germans complained that it was an unheard of violation of international law, and even accused Norway of not giving sufficient protection to the ship. Professor Halvdan Koht, the Norwegian Foreign Minister, stated that their authorities were unaware that British prisoners were held on the *Altmark*. Perhaps it is best to leave the final word to Neville Chamberlain, who commented in the House of Commons: "Considering that the fact was published in newspapers throughout the world, I can only regard this as a surprising statement. According to Professor Koht, the Norwegian Government see no objection to the use of their territorial waters for hundreds of miles by a German transport ship for the purpose of escaping capture on the high seas and of conveying British prisoners to a German prison camp. Such a policy for a neutral country is at variance with international law as the British Government understands it and the abuse of neutral waters by German warships is unacceptable."

But things rumbled on and the Norwegians tried to put the blame on Britain. The Norwegian Parliament, the Storting, met in a tense atmosphere to hear a report from Professor Koht on the events in Jøssing Fjord and the actions of their navy. Additionally, the Norwegian representative in London, Erik Colban, was instructed to go to the Foreign Office and hand over to Lord Halifax a protest at "this grave violation of Norwegian neutrality". Norway also requested that Britain should "hand over the prisoners and make due compensation and reparation". All of this fell on deaf ears in London. Norway, in

The *Altmark* sign before it was liberated. (Airborne Assault Duxford)

grave danger of being invaded by Germany, felt she was in a tricky position. As Germany was hugely dependent on Norwegian iron ore for her war effort, she knew that an interruption of the supply would be catastrophic. Hitler had in fact decided as far back as 14 December 1939 on an invasion of Norway, and had told his planners to get on with the task. The *Altmark* Incident firmed up his view, and on 17 February he ordered that Operation *Weserübung* (the invasion of Scandinavia) go ahead.

On 15 March, Lord Halifax finally rejected all Norwegian protests in a note in which he outlined Britain's legal position and refuted Norwegian assertions that nothing was known of the presence of British prisoners on the *Altmark*. The Germans, for their part, tried to make some propaganda use of the incident, with Captain Dau broadcasting about the "act of British piracy". The *Altmark* was repaired in Jøssing Fjord and, with the help of some tugs, reached the open seas, arriving back in Kiel on 28 March. Captain Dau was relieved of his command and retired. The *Altmark* was renamed *Uckermark* and continued as a naval supply ship until November 1942, when she was in Yokohama harbour in Japan, having brought munitions from Germany. While she was being cleaned with chemicals she exploded, with the loss of 53 lives and many more wounded. Captain Dau committed suicide on the day of Germany's surrender in May 1945.

After they had conquered Norway, the Germans erected a commemorative board in Jøssing Fjord reading (in German): "Hier wuede am 16 Februar 1940 die *Altmark* von britischen seepuraten überfallen." (Here on 16 February 1940 the *Altmark* was set upon by British sea-pirates.) The sign, which was double-sided, was "liberated" by British

The *Altmark* board. (Airborne Assault Duxford)

airborne forces in 1945, and one side given to the then Admiral Vian. The other side was kept by the airborne forces and is now in the Airborne Assault Museum at Duxford.

Back in England, the BBC later interviewed some of the newly released sailors. Their comments included:

> We tried to break out of our cell as we knew we were sailing along the Norwegian coast, but we were beaten back by the Germans using hoses and cudgels on us. Then at 1800 we stopped dead in a fjord, we heard several shots being fired and the crew seemed to be running around in a bit of a panic. Then I heard a voice shouting down, "Are you British prisoners?" We replied, "Yes." The voice then said, "You are safe now, we have come to save you." The hatch was opened and we all went up on deck and across to the destroyer which I now know was the *Cossack*. We all felt mightily relieved.

Meanwhile, in England public opinion started to call out for some action against the Germans' continual breaching of Norwegian neutrality . The British and French agreed on the following actions:

On 1 April a diplomatic warning was to be sent to Norway and Sweden on the lines that the Allies reserved the right to stop German iron ore traffic.

On 5 April, Operation Wilfred would commence. Although it was only a small operation, it had the potential to have a great effect. It was decided to start the operation on 5 April with the laying of two small minefields off the Norwegian coast and the simulated laying of another. One of the two actual minefields was in the waters off Narvik and the other was between Alesund and Bergen, further south. The simulated minefield was to be "laid" off Molde. All of these were to try to stop shipping moving down The

An aerial view of the *Altmark* holed up in Jøssing Fjord. (Imperial War Museum CS24)

Leads. The important point is that these mines were to be laid whether the Norwegians agreed or not. Obviously, once the mines were in place and it was known they were there, it was difficult for the British to gauge the consequences of their action. Either the Norwegians would make some sort of protest or the Germans would move into Norway to protect their vital iron ore routes. With remarkable naivety, the government in London thought that there would be a pause to assess the reactions of Norway and Germany, during which countermeasures would be developed to these reactions. It was assumed that everyone was going to move to a timetable set down by London!

The main countermeasure planned for any German reaction, and of course all in slow time, was Plan R4. The idea was that an expeditionary force would be ready to go to Norway, but was on no account to sail until the Germans were clearly about to violate Norwegian territory. It was intended that the force should occupy Narvik and guard the railway line to Sweden, together with forces in Bergen and Trondheim. The final part of the plan was for a small element to go to Stavanger, where the only decent-sized airfield in central Norway was located. On 5 April, notes were handed to the Norwegian and Swedish governments, warning them of some sort of action in the very near future. This was leaked to the press in both countries and soon headlines speculated about an impending Allied invasion. Hand in hand with this, the start of Operation Wilfred was put back to 8 April. But what was the detailed plan on the other side of the fence?

4

Invasion, April 1940

The Germans had been thinking about an invasion of Norway for several months, but their planning was dominated by questions arising from their naval strategy after the Great War. In 1929 Admiral Wolfgang Wegener's book *Die Seestrategie des Weltkrieges* was published. This looked at Germany's geographical situation compared to the fighting in the Great War. Wegener's idea was that the main function of a navy was to open, and keep open, a country's trading routes. His main point was that in the Great War, Germany had ended up defending "the dead angle of a dead sea". By this he meant that the main German North Sea ports had languished under the effects of a Royal Navy blockade. This would not have been eased even had neutral Denmark been occupied. Further, he wrote:

> The Norwegian position was certainly preferable. England could then no longer maintain the blockade line from the Shetlands to Norway but must withdraw approximately to the line of the Shetlands–the Faeroes–Iceland. But this line was a net with very wide meshes. Moreover, this line was hard for England to defend: for in the first place it lay comparatively near to our bases; but above all, we should considerably outflank the English strategic position to the north.

The Royal Navy tried during the early months of the Second World War to replicate the crippling blockade they had achieved 20 years or so before, but it did not have the same effect. Hitler is said to have looked on Wegener's work as his "bible for sea warfare", and in October 1939, Grand Admiral Raeder further sowed the seeds for an invasion when he advised Hitler how important it would be for submarine warfare to obtain bases on the Norwegian coast, such as at Trondheim. Raeder backed this up a couple of months later by pointing out that a German occupation of Norway was the best method of blocking trade between Norway and Britain, and that a British occupation of Norway would effectively bottle up the Baltic. Free passage through this water was the foundation on which the German Navy's strategy depended.

A study for a potential invasion of Norway and Denmark was given the green light on 14 December 1939. It was to be a joint service study, but under the chairmanship of the Supreme Command of the Armed Forces (OKW). The *Altmark* incident basically changed the study from a theoretical one into a full-blown preparation for an invasion, and towards the end of February 1940, General von Falkenhorst was appointed commander of the invasion forces. Hitler signed an order on 1 March 1940, which included a strategic aim for Operation *Weserübung*. This was to "prevent British encroachment in Scandinavia and the Baltic; further, it will guarantee our ore base in Sweden and give our navy and air force a wider start-line against Britain".

It was felt that the German Navy would not be able to carry out a sustained campaign against the Royal Navy in Norwegian waters, so *Weserübung* would have to include elements of speed and deception. Also, for reasons of security it was necessary to keep the number of troops taking part in the invasion to a minimum, so von Falkenhorst was given a limited list of objectives. The minimum force judged necessary for holding the country was six divisions. On his list were the occupation of Oslo, the capital, Kristiansand on the south coast of Norway, Stavanger, Bergen and Trondheim - the main west coast ports – and, for reasons already explained, Narvik in the north. The main problem facing the Germans was how to move over 100,000 troops and all their equipment from their port of embarkation to Norway without the British and French finding out. In theory this would have meant transporting the troops in the normal manner, using a large number of ships. The Germans believed they would be unable to assemble their Armada without the Norwegians – and indeed their enemies – spotting a relatively slow-moving fleet, long before it reached Norwegian territorial waters. So the German plan called for the first wave of troops to be taken to Norway in warships rather than troop transports. This had the advantage of getting the men to their objectives fairly quickly, but if the German warships were engaged by hostile forces they would be handicapped by their extra guests. An additional disadvantage was that the warships would be unable to carry the vital stores and equipment the troops would need on landing. A gamble was taken to move the leading elements' essential and heavy equipment by a series of elaborate and carefully executed side operations One such operation sent seven merchantmen, carrying military stores, as a "normal" convoy on its way to Murmansk in Russia. Another had ships travelling on their own and trusting to luck to escape investigation. The Germans also planned to take advantage of "Trojan horse" ships disguised as coal ships arriving in Norwegian ports some days before the actual invasion, giving a variety of reasons why they were at anchor and couldn't leave.

British plans, in the form of Operation Wilfred, had now got the green light to take place on 8 April, and so on 6 April the four mine-laying destroyers detailed for the task (*Esk, Express, Icarus* and *Impulsive*) set sail. All under the command of Vice-Admiral W. Whitworth, additional ships including the battle cruiser HMS *Renown* and eight escorting destroyers accompanied the minelayers. On the morning of 7 April, at the port of Rosyth in Scotland, troops were boarding ships as part of the Plan R4. Two battalions from the 148th Brigade, intended to go to Stavanger, and two battalions from the 146th Brigade, heading for Bergen, were split amongst three cruisers. Also present were the Trondheim force (a battalion from the 146th Brigade) and the Narvik element – the 24th Guards Brigade: these were to be transported in the cruiser HMS *Devonshire* and two transport ships from the Clyde.

The Germans for their part thought that the initial wave of troops would be enough for the task and planned the first serious numbers of reinforcements to come in three and five days after the first landings. These would be directed to the Oslo area and redistributed to wherever was thought necessary by land, sea or air. The ships that brought the invaders to Norway and the escorting warships (with the exception of two destroyers, which

Hitler especially ordered should remain at Trondheim), were to make for German ports as soon as possible. Again, this plan assumed that the Allies would not be able to block the Skagerrak, or interfere with the passage of stores and men from Germany to Norway. Meanwhile, the staff of Group XXI had completed "Operations Order No. 1 for the Occupation of Norway", which was issued on 5 March and concerned the landings and consolidation of the beachheads. Two possibilities were envisioned: (i) that the desired objectives of a peaceful occupation could be achieved; and (ii) that the landings and occupation would have to be carried out by force. If the first possibility materialised, the Norwegian government was to be assured of extensive respect for its internal sovereignty, and the Norwegian troops were to be treated tactfully. If resistance was encountered, the landings were to be forced by all possible means, the beachheads secured and nearby mobilisation centres of the Norwegian Army occupied. Complete destruction of the Norwegian Army was not considered possible as an immediate objective because of the size of the country and difficulty of the terrain, but it was believed that the localities selected for landings comprised the majority of the places needed to prevent an effective mobilisation and assembly of Norwegian forces and to control the country in general. Attempted Allied landings were to be fought off, unnecessary losses were to be avoided and, if the enemy proved superior, the troops were to withdraw inland until a counter-attack could be launched.

General von Falkenhorst, commander of the land forces, had served in Scandinavia before, in 1918, when German troops landed in Finland to support General Carl Gustav von Mannerheim's White Guards in their fight against the Russians. However, it is said that he had never been to Norway and that, upon being told he was in command, he went into town to buy a Baedeker guidebook to learn more about the country and where the main ports were! A few days before the orders were issued on 21 February, Hitler had a meeting with von Falkenhorst and quizzed him about co-ordination between the army and navy during the Finnish operations in 1918. Hitler also revealed to von Falkenhorst that he had information that the British were going to land in Norway and had reached an agreement with the Norwegians in this respect. Von Falkenhorst later commented: "I could feel the sheer nervousness caused by the Jøssing Fjord affair." Later that afternoon, von Falkenhorst reported back with a broad outline of his thoughts and Hitler instructed him to carry on and finish, for there was no time to lose. As von Falkenhorst later commented: "He seemed preoccupied by the idea that our undertaking might be compromised by an English operation."

From 26 February, plans started to move forward rapidly. As well as an invasion of Norway, the OKW approved von Falkenhorst's idea to invade Jutland in Denmark, to help seal up the Baltic. This was extended by Hitler, who suggested landings at Copenhagen. Hitler also decreed that the invasion of Norway and Denmark should be planned independently of *Fall Gelb* (Case Yellow - the attack on France and the Low Countries) in terms of schedule and forces employed. This meant that von Falkenhorst would not get the better troops earmarked for the western European campaign and would have to make do with what he could get.

For the first phase of the assault, troops would land at what were considered to be the top six strategic locations, plus two secondary objectives (Arendal and Egersund, mainly because of their cable stations) in a series of seaborne and airborne landings. In phase two of the operation, further troops and equipment would arrive in Oslo by sea, and move overland to link up with the first wave, including those at Narvik, more than 800 miles away.

On 29 February, a few days after the final plans for Case Yellow had been issued, a revised plan for the Scandinavian enterprise was shown to Hitler, who gave his approval. Denmark and Norway were to be occupied to anticipate Allied action in the region, to secure supplies of ore from Sweden and to provide the *Luftwaffe* and *Kriegsmarine* with bases to operate against Britain. Hitler stated: "The forces employed will be as small as possible having regard to our military and political strength in relation to the northern nations. Weakness in numbers will be made good by skilful action and surprise in execution."

Amid signs of growing Allied concern, Hitler decided to launch his Scandinavian expedition, but the start had to be delayed a few days as the ice took longer to thaw in the area than expected. On 1 April, the senior commanders of all three services were called to a meeting with Hitler in Berlin. The following day, at a high level conference with all the senior commanders, after receiving favourable reports on the melting of the ice and weather conditions, it was decided to launch the attack on all the selected objectives in Denmark and Norway at 0515 on 9 April. It was also intended that the German Ambassador in Oslo deliver a formal note advising of the invasion at 0520, the same time as his counterpart in Copenhagen was delivering a note to the Danish government.

Amongst the forces earmarked for the Norwegian operation were the 2nd and 3rd Mountain Divisions, plus the 69th, 163rd, 181st, 196th and 214th Infantry Divisions. Two divisions – the 170th and 198th Infantry Divisions – were selected to go into Denmark. Also chosen to take part were the German airborne forces – the *Fallschirmjägers*. The initial seaborne landing force of 8,850 men was to be carried in six groups of warships: these going to Narvik, Trondheim, Bergen, Kristiansand, Oslo and Egersund.

The naval assets were allocated to each group as follows:

Group 1, Narvik - ten destroyers.
Group 2, Trondheim - one cruiser, four destroyers.
Group 3, Bergen - two cruisers, two support ships, two torpedo boats, one flotilla of motor torpedo boats.
Group 4, Kristiansand - one cruiser, one support ship, three torpedo boats, one flotilla of motor torpedo boats.
Group 5, Oslo - three cruisers, three torpedo boats, one flotilla of minesweepers.
Group 6, Egersund - four minesweepers.

Also accompanying Group 1 were the battleships *Gneisenau* and *Scharnhorst*, which were to escort this fleet as far north as Mo and then head off northwards to act as a diversion.

No major reinforcement of the landing teams at the beachheads was contemplated until contact had been established overland with Oslo, where the main force was to disembark – 16,700 men (in addition to the 2,000 landed on W-Day) to be brought in by three sea transport echelons during the first week, with another 40,000 to be transported

German troops approaching the shore at Oslo 9th April 1940. (Imperial War Museum HU128788)

in shuttle movements thereafter. An additional 8,000 troops were to be transported to Oslo by air within three days of W-Day.

Several "Trojan horse" ships had been sent with essential supplies, including artillery, heavy equipment and anti-aircraft guns, while the warships transported the troops. Seven such ships left Hamburg between 3 and 7 April, with three bound for Narvik, three for Trondheim and one for Stavanger. All were timed to make their entry into their respective ports late on 8 April. This would hopefully stop any customs inspections until the following day, when it would be too late. The Germans thought of all eventualities; also despatching three tankers carrying not only fuel for the army and air force operations, but oil for the warships. These all sailed independently, with an arrival date at their destination of invasion day – 9 April. The *Skagerrak* went to Trondheim, the *Kattegat* and *Jan Wellem* headed for Narvik. Other smaller tankers were due to arrive on W+1, with two going to Oslo and one each to Bergen, Stavanger and Kristiansand.

Following slightly behind was the first wave of additional stores and equipment needed to bring the bulk of the troops to southern Norway, in readiness for the breakout and hopeful link-up with the forces that had landed in northern Norway. This consisted of 15 ships leaving on 6 and 7 April: three ships heading for Bergen, three for Stavanger, four for Kristiansand and five for Oslo. This small armada would carry in total 3,761

German troops just after landing with one of their JU52 transport aircraft in the background.
(Imperial War Museum HU128789)

troops, supported by 1,377 vehicles and 672 horses. Perhaps the most important cargo consisted of four tanks and 5,935 tonnes of stores and equipment. This was followed on W+2 by a further fleet of 11 ships, and on W+6 with 12 more ships, both of these groups going to Oslo.

A final – and novel – aspect was the use of air power. It was intended for Stavanger, for example, to be taken by air assault alone. *X Fliegerkorps*, with 500 transport aircraft, was tasked with bringing in 3,000 airborne troops in the early hours of W-Day. Other objectives for the first wave were for *X Fliegerkorps* to fly two battalions to Oslo on W-Day, another two battalions on W+1, three battalions on W+2 and a further two battalions on W+3. Most of these aircraft were JU52s, the *Luftwaffe's* transport workhorses, but some other aircraft such as floatplanes and a number of bigger four-engined transports were also involved. It was hoped that these lifts would bring in around 8,000 men.

For more offensive operations, *X Fliegerkorps* had around 350 aircraft, with 220 bombers (HE111s, JU87s and JU88s), 100 fighters (ME109s and ME110s) and the balance being reconnaissance aircraft.

For the Danish end of the operation, the principal objective was Aalborg at the northern tip of Jutland. Its two airfields were to be taken at W+2 hours by a parachute platoon and an airborne battalion. Full control of the airfields and the lines of communication from Germany would be secured by the 170th Infantry Division and the 11th Motorised Rifle Brigade, in a rapid advance across Jutland from the German border. Five warship groups - consisting of light naval craft, merchant vessels and the Great War battleship *Schleswig-Holstein* - were organised to stage landings on the west coast of Jutland and the Danish

German airborne reinforcements, a good method when you look at the terrain. (Imperial War Museum HU128790)

islands. Command of operations in Denmark was given to XXXI Corps under *General der Flieger* Leonard Kaupisch.

In detail, the Norwegian plans were as follows:

Narvik Group:
Ten destroyers with about 2,000 troops from the *Gebirgsjäger-Regiment 139* were to leave from Wesermünde around midnight on 6 April, escorted by the battleships *Gneisenau* and *Scharnhorst* for part of their journey.

Trondheim Group:
One cruiser and four destroyers would sail from Cuxhaven at midnight on 6 April, moving the three battalions (less one company) of the *Gebirgsjäger-Regiment 138*, accompanied by one company of engineers and one battery of mountain artillery: in all about 1,800 men. They were to rendezvous with the ships going to Narvik until they reached the area of Trondheim, when they were to turn north as a diversion before doubling back and going to Trondheim.

Bergen Group:
This group, consisting of two cruisers, two support ships, two torpedo boats and five motor torpedo boats, was to sail at midnight on 7 April from the ports of Wesermünde and Cuxhaven. They were mainly transporting the staff of 69th Infantry Division and Infantry Regiment 159, together with two battalions from the latter formation (less one

9 April 1940: At Oslo airport the first German troops landed. In the background is the smoke of a shot down Norwegian aircraft. (Bob Gerritsen Collection)

company) and two companies of engineers: around 2,000 men. This group was to be reinforced on W-Day by 5. Company of Infantry Regiment 159, brought in by aircraft, while three transports would bring in more elements of the 69th Infantry Division.

Stavanger Group:
This was a particularly important objective for the Germans as Stavanger possessed the largest airfield in Norway and was the only one to be initially attacked by airborne troops. The initial force only consisted of one company (about 130 men) from *Fallschirmjäger Regiment 1*, who were due to jump on to the airfield on the morning of W-Day. After they had hopefully secured the airfield, JU52s would then bring in the Regimental Staff and two battalions from Infantry Regiment 193: around 1,400 men together with 9,000 litres of fuel. Meanwhile, three transports were nominated to enter the harbour shortly after the airborne landings, bringing in more elements of Infantry Regiment 193 together with their equipment ,and heavy weapons such as artillery and anti-aircraft guns. On the next day, W+1, aircraft were due to bring in the remainder of Infantry Regiment 193.

Kristiansand Group:
This group consisted of one cruiser, one support ship, three torpedo boats and seven motor torpedo boats. These all left from Wesermünde at 0500 on 8 April. They carried one battalion and staff from Infantry Regiment 310, about 1,000 men in total. Another

element of the group – one of the torpedo boats – was to land a party about 100-strong at Arendal, to cut the telephone link that left Norway there and ran across to England. This was an excellent strategic target and would, if cut, hinder communications with the outside world. Another four ships of this group would also land another battalion from the Infantry Regiment 310, more equipment, and artillery and anti-aircraft guns at Kristiansand.

Oslo Group:
Oslo was the capital city, so more resources were sent here. Three cruisers, three torpedo boats and a flotilla of minesweepers left Swinemünde at 2200 on 7 April. This force was to land two battalions from Infantry Regiment 307, one battalion of *Gebirgsjäger-Regiment 138*, a company of engineers, parts of the 163rd Infantry Division and of *Gruppe XXI*, in all about 2,000 men. Also heading towards Oslo were two companies from *Fallschirmjäger Regiment 1*, who were tasked with dropping on the airfield at Fornebu, near Oslo, and securing it. Once the airfield had been taken, the first wave of transport aircraft would fly in, bringing two battalions of Infantry Regiment 324, one company of engineers, more elements of staff from the 163rd Infantry Division and *Gruppe XXI*. This would more than double the number of troops and further reinforcements and equipment would land from five transport ships on W-Day, including artillery, anti-aircraft guns, aviation fuel and a few tanks.

Egersund Group:
Tacked on almost as an afterthought were four minesweepers, heading for this port on the south-western coast of Norway. They left Cuxhaven at 0530 on 8 April with around 150 men from the 69th Infantry Division. Their first task was to cut the telephone cable to Peterhead in Scotland.

The German Navy also cut back on Atlantic patrols to support the invasions, so that nine U-boat groups were deployed in the North Sea and off Norway and Denmark. There were some naval actions, which will be analysed later, but the majority of the German ships arrived at their destinations unscathed.

Meanwhile, Britain and France still had friends around Germany and received information in almost a constant stream, alerting them that troops seemed to be concentrating in northern ports and that many ships of the German Navy were steaming past Denmark on a northerly course. Some of these rumours were confirmed on the morning of 7 April, when RAF Hudsons from Coastal Command reported a German cruiser, escorted by six destroyers, sailing due north. They were located about 130 miles south of Cape Lindesnes, the most southerly point of Norway.

This information was passed to Bomber Command and 12 Blenheims were despatched to attack the ships. They were spotted about 80 miles off Cape Lindesnes and were attacked, but without success. The aircraft had been told to keep a radio silence and it was when they returned in the late afternoon that they discovered that as well as this first group, a second, larger, German armada had been spotted, consisting of at least two battle cruisers, three cruisers and 12 destroyers, heading north-west. These were the German ships heading for Narvik and Trondheim.

HMS *Berwick* in heavy seas. (The National Archives)

In London, the senior commanders at the Admiralty were confident that these ships were heading for the Atlantic to attack British convoys, and an invasion of Norway was not on the agenda. German naval ships were still a target, whatever their objective, so the British Home Fleet under the command of Admiral Sir Charles Forbes was ordered to get steam up and intercept them. The force from Scapa Flow in the Orkneys comprised three battleships (HMS *Repulse*, HMS *Rodney* and HMS *Valiant*) and two cruisers (HMS *Penelope* and HMS *Sheffield*), together with an escort of ten destroyers. A second, smaller fleet sailed from Rosyth, consisting of two cruisers (HMS *Arethusa* and HMS *Galatea*), with an escort of four destroyers. Additional resources were called for in the shape of two cruisers (HMS *Manchester* and HMS *Southampton*) and four destroyers, which were diverted from escorting convoy ON25, and the French threw into the mix an additional cruiser (*Emile Bertin*) and two destroyers. At Rosyth, four cruisers (HMS *Berwick*, HMS *Devonshire*, HMS *Glasgow* and HMS *York*), which had already taken on board a number of troops and their equipment, destined for Norway, were told to join the fleet, summarily dumping men and material on the quayside.

The British had decided to lay mines in Norwegian waters, and this operation was duly carried out in the early hours of 8 April in Vestfjord off Bodø. Later that morning, the British and French ambassadors delivered notes to the Norwegian Foreign Minister stating that minefields had been laid in her territorial waters the previous night. There were a number of naval actions, which will be considered in a later chapter.

On the evening of 8 April, the Norwegian Minister of Defence told his parliament that a German merchant ship, the *Rio de Janeiro*, had been sunk in the Skagerrak that

Destroyers in Ofotfjord. (The National Archives)

morning. It had been carrying German troops, and some of those rescued said they had been told they were going to Bergen. The ship had also been carrying artillery and horses. The survivors also claimed that the main reason for their operation was to assist the Norwegians, who had invited them into their country. So both sides claimed they were planning to invade a neutral country to protect it from the other. Perhaps because of the messages received from Britain and France about laying minefields, the Norwegian government seemed more concerned with the threat from the west, rather than that from the south. It was only in the early hours of 9 April, when news came in of German ships approaching Bergen, Oslo and Stavanger, that they decided to issue mobilisation orders to four brigades stationed in southern Norway.

The heads of the Norwegian Army had been advocating this measure for a number of days. Some time between 0400 and 0500, the commander-in-chief of the Norwegian Army, General K. Laake, was told to mobilise the 1st, 2nd, 3rd and 4th Brigades.

But as this was happening, around 0500 on 9 April German ships had entered Norwegian territorial waters and prepared to execute Hitler's orders. The objectives from north to south start at Narvik. Nine out of the ten destroyers intended to arrive here slowly steamed up the Ofotfjord. The tenth arrived about three hours late because of damage suffered from heavy seas. The Ofotfjord is about 50 miles long, and at the end furthest away from the sea lies the port of Narvik, the place that planners on both sides of the North Sea had spent so much time thinking about. Three destroyers from the group (*Lüdemann*, *Schmitt* and *von Roeder*) landed troops at Ramnes, about 20 miles west of Narvik, with the intention of capturing Norwegian gun emplacements believed to be located there, but on arrival no trace of them could be found. Three other destroyers

(*Zenker*, *Künne* and *Koellner*) moved up a side fjord – the Herjangen - to head for Bjerkvik, about six miles north of Narvik, and from there to go to Elvegärdsmoen, where a Norwegian Army depot was located. The final three destroyers (*Heidkamp*, *Thiele* and *Bernd von Arnim*) headed for the prize objective: the port of Narvik. Two of the largest ships in the Norwegian Navy were by coincidence anchored in Narvik harbour. These were the so-called ironclads, *Eidsvold* and *Norge*.

Eidsvold had been built in England by Armstrong Whitworth on the Tyne around 1900, and remained, along with her sister ship *Norge*, the backbone of the Royal Norwegian Navy for just over 40 years. She was named after the town of Eidsvold, the site of the drafting and signing of the Norwegian Constitution on 17 May 1814. Considered to be quite powerful ships for their time, with two 21cm (8¼in) guns as their main armament, these two ships were soon outclassed by the new Dreadnought battleships. They were armoured to withstand battle with ships of a similar class to their own, with 6in (15.24cm) of Krupp cemented armour in the belt and 9in (22.86cm) of the same armour on their two turrets. *Eidsvold* and *Norge* were the largest vessels in the Royal Norwegian Navy at 4,233 tons gross and crews of up to 270 men.

It had been intended to augment the Norwegian fleet with the two ships of the *Bjørgvin* class, ordered in 1912, but after these were confiscated by the British Royal Navy at the outbreak of the Great War, the *Eidsvold* class and the older, two-ship strong *Tordenskjold* class were forced to soldier on long after they were obsolete. As well as the 21cm guns, these ships had six 15cm guns, and for anti-aircraft defence two 76mm guns, two 20mm cannons and six machine guns.

As Norway was still in theory a neutral county, the leading German ship, the *Heidkamp*, hove to, lowered a small boat and sent an officer across with a message that they had arrived in Norway as "friends" who had come to protect them against the British. After a short while, the Germans returned to their ship and the skipper of the *Eidsvold*, Captain Willoch - sent a message to his superior, Captain Askim, on the *Norge* explaining what has happening and asking for instructions. Captain Askim ordered the *Eidsvold* to open fire, but perhaps still playing by a set of outdated rules, the Germans were invited aboard the *Eidsvold* to be told that any further incursion would be treated as a hostile act and the Norwegians would resist. The Germans departed and Captain Willoch ordered the port-side battery to open fire, but before the Norwegians could act, the *Eidsvold* was hit by at least three torpedoes fired from the *Heidkamp*. She quickly broke into two pieces and sank: only six sailors were rescued from the cold waters of the fjord.

At around 0445, the *Norge* spotted two German destroyers calmly tying up amidst other ships in Narvik harbour. The *Norge* opened fire with her larger guns. The Germans were slicker in their drills and the *Bernd von Arnim* was able to get a number of torpedoes in the water before the Norwegian fire became effective. At least two of these struck the *Norge*, and she sank in less than a minute. Around 90 men – nearly half the crew –were pulled alive from the icy waters.

The German soldiers from the *Gebirgsjäger-Regiment 139* were thus able to land virtually unopposed, much to the bewilderment of the local civilian population. The Norwegian garrison was too stunned to do anything. The Germans moved quickly off

The German destroyer *Bernd von Arnim* lying scuttled at Narvik. (The National Archives)

the quayside and occupied strategic locations in and around the harbour and town. Soon after, the commander of the 3rd Mountain Division, General Dietl, arrived ashore and met the local garrison commander, Colonel Sundlo. Sundlo was outraged and said he was giving the Germans 30 minutes to leave or he would order his men to open fire on them. General Dietl convinced him that this would be a futile gesture, and so at about 0615 Sundlo surrendered and handed over Narvik to the Germans. However, not all his men were happy at this decision. A battalion of around 250 men took exception to this and disappeared eastwards in the confusion to fight another day.

Meanwhile it was becoming apparent that only one of the three Trojan horse ships which should have been moored in the harbour had made it. The one that arrived was the *Jan Wellem*; a converted whaling ship which had arrived the day before. The Captain had told the Norwegian port authorities that he was on his way to Germany from Murmansk in Russia and wanted a short stopover in Narvik. Of the three ships that should have been there, the *Bärenfels* had been diverted to Bergen, and the *Rauenfels* and *Alster* were still steaming towards Narvik. In fact neither made it, as the *Rauenfels* was sunk on 10 April by HMS *Havock* close to Narvik, while the *Alster* was boarded and captured off Bodø by a party from HMS *Icarus* on the same day.

The tanker *Kattegat*, which had accompanied the force to refuel the destroyers, also suffered a mishap. She had been intercepted by the Norwegian patrol boat *Nordkapp* in the entrance to the Ofotfjord, and her captain decided to scuttle her without a shot being fired. This prevented the 10 destroyers being refuelled as planned, so they could not leave that evening for Germany as intended. It was not altogether bad news for the Germans, as the destroyers could be refuelled – albeit slowly – by the *Jan Wellem* but it took about eight hours to fuel two ships. This would eventually have consequences for the Germans. Five of the destroyers (*Heidkamp, Lüdemann, Schmitt, von Roder* and *Künne*) moored for the night

On the runway at Trondheim German infantry sort themselves out. (Bob Gerritsen Collection)

in Narvik harbour, while three (*Zenker, Giese* and *Koellner*) went to Bjerkvik at the head of the Herjangsfjord, around six miles north of Narvik, while the remaining two (*Thiele* and *Bernd von Arnim*) sailed to Ballengen Bay on the south side of the Ofotfjord, some 15 miles west of Narvik. At Trondheim, the armada of ships met little resistance from the coastal batteries on their journey to the port. Although some shells were fired, the German cruiser *Hipper* returned fire, producing a cloud of dust and smoke so great it obscured the Norwegian gunners view until the battle group had slipped past. Three destroyers broke off to land troops to capture these positions while the *Hipper*, escorted by one destroyer, steamed into Trondheim harbour. The troops were successfully unloaded and again the occupation of the town was achieved before most residents were aware that the Germans had invaded. Again, none of the Trojan horse ships had arrived: the *Main* had been sunk by a Norwegian torpedo boat on 9 April and another, the *Sao Paulo*, sank after striking a mine off Bergen on 10 April. The tanker *Skagerrak*, which was detailed to sail here, was delayed, ran into HMS *Suffolk* and ended up being scuttling on 12 April. So only one of the reinforcement ships, the *Levante*, finally arrived at Trondheim on 13 April.

At Bergen, the naval force under the command of Admiral Schmundt came under fire from Norwegian coastal batteries situated on the approaches to the port. Troops were landed to neutralise the Kvarven forts but in order to reach Bergen in line with the timings of the plan, the ships could not wait for the capture of the guns and so ran the gauntlet of fire from them. Two of the ships – the *Bremse* and *Königsberg* – were hit and damaged by fire from these guns, the *Bremse* receiving two hits and the *Königsberg* three. However, this did not stop the landing of two battalions from the 69th Infantry Division, which, as planned, successfully occupied the harbour and town with minimal resistance being put up by the few Norwegian troops. It was a different matter at the Kvarven forts, which held out for nearly 24 hours before falling, enabling seaplanes to start moving in more troops. Again the resupply ships meant to arrive here suffered problems, and only the *Marie Leonhardt* arrived. Other ships had been sunk – in the case of the *Rio de Janeiro* by a Polish submarine, the *Orzel*, on 8 April whilst in transit. The *Curityba* was delayed by running aground near Helsingborg, and after being refloated was diverted to Oslo. To try and assist the troops in Bergen, the *Bärenfels*, originally going to Narvik, was diverted to Bergen, although she was sunk there on 14 April during an air raid.

The German warships in Bergen harbour felt exposed, even more so after several RAF aircraft flew over the area. The commander of the task force here, Admiral Schmundt, was advised that large British warships were at sea and at least one battle group had been seen off western Norway. At the same time, a force of several cruisers and destroyers appeared to be heading for the approaches to Bergen, and to Schmundt the risk of meeting superior forces when leaving the fjords seemed a clear danger, especially as some of his ships were damaged. The fleet engineer, sent to the *Königsberg* to assess the damage, reported that in his opinion she could be made ready for sea relatively quickly, but was uncertain whether her inexperienced crew would be able to cope. Her captain, Ruhfus, was more circumspect: he suggested 24 to 48 hours was needed. She could sail that evening but would be limited to 20 knots, and the patch over the hole in her starboard side would hamper her handling in the rough seas expected. Ruhfus proposed a joint departure for the following afternoon, 10 April. But Admiral von Schrader (in command of Norwegian West Coast naval forces) suggested that all ships should remain in Bergen for the time being. Schmundt disagreed with both of these comments, so signalled Group West at 1145 on 9 April stating: "*Königsberg* damaged. Length of repair not yet known. Intend break out 2200–2300 hours with *Köln*, *Leopard* and *Wolf*. Exit route depends on enemy position." *Königsberg* was to complete what repairs she could and plan for an independent return to Germany whenever possible. Schmundt considered sending her into the fjords as some protection against air assaults but eventually decided to keep her in Bergen, where her guns could supplement the shore batteries in case of an attack. As a further precaution, Ruhfus was told to make sure *Königsberg*'s Arado aircraft maintained a patrol off the coast during daylight hours.

The RAF had already appeared over Bergen. Bombers first arrived around 1815, when 12 Wellingtons from 9 and 115 Squadrons launched an attack on the German ships. The aircraft from 9 Squadron made the first attack around 1830, dropping 500lb bombs on the cruiser *Köln* from a height of around 3,000 feet. Some failed to go off and all missed their target. Shortly afterwards 115 Squadron had a go, but this time aiming at the *Königsberg*. Again their aim was not accurate, and although a hit was claimed on her stern this was an error. However, three German sailors were killed and five wounded on the *Köln* by machine gun fire from the Wellingtons, attempting to suppress the anti-aircraft barrage coming up during the 9 Squadron attack. It is reported that all aircraft made it back safely, albeit some with minor damage.

Shortly after the second attack, *Köln*, *Leopard* and *Wolf* left Bergen, accompanied by some of the torpedo boats which lead the way, towing their mine-sweeping gear. This was a wise decision, as several mines laid by a Norwegian minelayer, the *Tyr*, the night before were cut loose. In a final effort by the RAF, 12 Hampdens from 50 Squadron arrived around 2000, attacking the harbour and dropping bombs on the departing warships, but with negligible results. Schmundt then received further intelligence from Germany that there were a number of cruisers and destroyers in his area. He took the decision to hide in the network of small fjords, planning to attempt a break-out the following night when his weathermen had suggested conditions would be more suitable. *Köln* dropped anchor in the Maurangerfjord around 0200 on 10 April, with her escorts close by.

Their arrival here did not go unnoticed. Norwegian Lieutenant Stansberg and his crew, flying a MF11 seaplane on a reconnaissance flight, spotted two of the patrolling German torpedo boats in the Maurangerfjord, decided they were friendly and would land to ask if they had local intelligence. He then saw the *Leopard,* landed nearby and started taxiing towards her. *Leopard* then started signalling at Stansberg and, realising his mistake, he did a quick U-turn while his rear gunner opened fire. Fortunately they managed to get away with only minor damage.

Later that morning Lieutenant Hansen, in command of the Norwegian torpedo boat *Stegg*, was advised by local fishermen that there were several German destroyers in Maurangerfjord. He had the report confirmed and, using a telephone from the shore, advised Admiral Tank-Nielsen (commander of the 2nd Sea Defence District) at Voss what was happening and planned an ambush at dusk. But as dusk approached, the *Wolf* and *Leopard* steered away and joined the *Köln*, as Schmundt had decided it was time to try and return home.

The German ships followed The Leads south towards Haugesund and moved into the North Sea around midnight, with no British interference. They reached Wilhelmshaven without incident just after 1900 on 11 April. In his report on the operation, Schmundt commented that while he and his staff had done all they could to ensure success, luck had played a major part in his operation. Fog had disguised their outward journey, and they were fortunate that *Köln* had not been hit during her skirmish with the Kvarven coastal batteries and that the RAF bombs on the whole had failed to explode. His ships had also for the most part been hidden under low clouds while they were in the Maurangerfjord on 10 April.

Meanwhile, the *Königsberg*, with a variety of other German ships, was left at Bergen. These escorts consisted of a gunnery training ship, the *Bremse*, a depot ship, the *Carl Peters*, and some smaller auxiliary ships, including the *Hans Rolshoven* (a seaplane tender), *Bernhard von Tschirschky*, four S-boats and *Schiff 9* and *Schiff 18*. *Schiff 11* also arrived on 10 April with a cargo of mines underneath a cover of wood, but like her other sister schiffs she had no real combat ability apart from the mines she was carrying. This force was now under the overall command of von Schrader, and after consulting with the land force commander, General Tittel (commanding the 69th Infantry Division), they were both of the opinion that if they came under a serious attack from a British-Norwegian combined assault they would be hard pressed, especially as at that time the Kvarven and Hellen batteries were not yet in a fit state, having been damaged in the initial assault. With hindsight, neither of them should have worried too much about a ground action, as the idea of the British arriving in strength was still very much a pipe-dream. Nevertheless,

Fleet Air Arm Skuas and a Swordfish pictured at their base in Scotland 1940. (Imperial War Museum A8279)

the *Königsberg* was positioned so that her aft guns could engage any hostile forces coming from the south, while her forward guns and port torpedo tubes could take care of the northern approaches. Artillery forward observer parties, with radios, were sent to positions overlooking the western fjords, should it be necessary to use indirect fire on this approach. Additionally, the *Bremse* moored at a position from where she could cover Puddefjord and the *Carl Peters* moored north of Marineholmen.

Some of the merchant ships were moved to try and block off blind spots, but positioned in such a way that the warships' fields of fire were not obscured. Several of the serviceable torpedo boats patrolled the approaches to the harbour, but the main threat was not going to come by sea but from the air.

Further reconnaissance flights by the RAF on the evening of 9 April confirmed that there were still warships in Bergen and that the previous raids appeared to have caused little or no damage. Bomber Command thought it would be best if they concentrated their efforts in the Heligoland Bight area and suggested that targets in Norway be given over to the Fleet Air Arm. A raid on Bergen was proposed and Blackburn Skuas of 800 and 803 Squadrons, based at Hatston in the Orkney Islands, were given the 550-mile or so round trip. This was just about at the limit of their endurance and left very little leeway for navigational error. The Blackburn Skua was a pre-war low-wing monoplane dive-bomber with a distinctive "greenhouse" cockpit. The Skua was constructed as an all-metal aircraft, which diverged from the Royal Navy tradition of fabric-covered aircraft. It was also the Fleet Air Arm's first naval dive-bomber and their first deck-landing aircraft to have flaps, retractable landing gear and a variable-pitch propeller. Advanced in concept, it was nevertheless nearing obsolescence when it entered service. It had a maximum speed of around 230mph at 6,700ft and just over 200mph at sea level. Around 0500 on 10 April, 16 Skuas took off from Hatston for the raid. Each was armed with one 500lb SAP (semi armour-piercing) bomb. Seven Skuas came from 800 Squadron, led by Captain R. Partridge, while the other nine, from 803 Squadron, were led by Lieutenant W. Lucy. One aircraft lost contact with the rest of the formation but decided to carry on independently. After about two hours' flying time, landfall was made just south of Korsfjord. Captain Partridge later wrote:

> Ahead of us was Bergen, looking quiet and peaceful in the sparkling early morning sunlight. To port were three large fuel storage tanks and ahead and to starboard ships, but merchant ships only – no cruiser. There was no sign of activity of any sort, no enemy fighters and no anti-aircraft fire. We were almost down to 8,000 feet when we spotted her, a long thin, grey shape lying alongside a jetty. I pulled away to port in order to make a great sweep up to the mountains and over the town of Bergen itself and so attack out of the rising sun.
>
> Now I was heading back towards the German cruiser and concentrating hard to get my Skua and those following me into the correct position for starting our dive. Having reached a suitable position I did a 90 degree turn to port, eased back on the stick, flaps down, further back on the stick, a half stall turn to starboard and then I was in a well-controlled dive with the cruiser steady in my sights.

It was around 0720 and for once luck was on the British side. The cloud base was quite high, visibility was good – no mist or fog – and the *Königsberg* was not moving. The two squadrons had an ideal opportunity to make a concentrated attack. Matters had probably been helped when the air raid warning had been triggered about half-an-hour previously, when a RAF Hudson from 233 Squadron, sent as an "evidence gatherer" for the Skua attack, had arrived over the area and started circling. Apparently the Hudson was identified as a German HE111 and so the alert was cancelled. When the Skuas arrived, again circling at a relatively high altitude, it was assumed they were also German. Then just before the attack, some *Luftwaffe* personnel on board the *Rolshoven* realised the aircraft were hostile and the alarm was sounded again, but it was too late.

The *Königsberg* opened fire with some of her anti-aircraft guns but not all of them could bring their fire to bear. Because she was tied up close to a jetty, some of the guns positioned at the rear of the ship could not fire because of cranes and buildings restricting their field of fire. Then the bombs starting finding their target. One of the first hits knocked out some of the electrical systems of the *Königsberg*, making the 88mm guns with their electrically powered mountings virtually useless and causing the crews of the 37mm guns to hand-crank them. However, a fair amount of fire came up from the *Rolshoven*, causing some of the Skua crews to refer to it in their post-action reports as a "flak ship". Captain Partridge continues:

> I was attacking the ship from bow to stern and the only resistance being offered was coming from a light Bofors-type anti-aircraft gun on the fo'c'sle, which kept firing throughout the engagement, tracer bullets gliding past on either side. My

dive was still firm and controlled with the ship held steady in my sights, and I could see water and oil gushing out of her below the waterline and guessed she had already been damaged. Down to 3,500 feet now and beginning to watch my height, at 1,800 I pressed the release button on the stick and let my bomb go, turning violently away to starboard and then down to water level when clear.

After releasing their bombs, the Skuas headed west across Askøy, gaining altitude for the return flight. The attack was all over in about 10 minutes: the last attack was made by the Skua flown by Lieutenant Taylour, who had lost contact with the formation shortly after take-off. On the return journey, the aircraft flown by Lieutenant Brian Smeeton with his gunner Midshipman Fred Watkinson was seen to go into a spin and crashed into the sea about 40 miles west of Bergen. Their bodies were never found. Fred Watkinson was just 18 years old.[1]

All the other 15 Skuas made it back to Hatston after a flight of nearly five hours. Two of them had suffered damage from flak. At their debriefing, the aircrew felt that significant damage had been caused to the *Königsberg* but they had been lucky, as there had not been a significant amount of flak or fighters opposing them.

The damage caused to the *Königsberg* was a matter of speculation in the Orkneys, but at Bergen the Germans were counting the cost of at least six 500lb bombs hitting or near-missing the cruiser. One of the first bombs dropped actually missed the *Königsberg* but ricocheted off the pier she was tied to and hit her starboard side. The bomb caused damage to the No. 1 boiler room. A second bomb entered the port side and ended up exploding in one of the ship's generator rooms, which caused a massive drop in power. This bomb had entered below the waterline and so water started to pour in into the generator room. This spread to the adjacent No. 4 boiler room, then into the command and control centre, radio room and gunnery control room. The amount of water flooding into the *Königsberg* started to cause a list to port. A third bomb struck towards the rear of the *Königsberg* and exploded in the 'tweendeck auxiliary boiler room. All of these hits caused a number of fires which, together with the rising waters, hampered the damage control parties.

Two final bombs exploded in this 'tweendeck area, causing further damage. The last bomb impacted the cruiser's port side but only caused further leaks. All four of the *Königsberg's* boiler rooms were now taking on water, and a decision was taken to close down all the generators. The back-up diesel generators, which had been damaged by artillery fire from the shore batteries, were started up, but soon gave up and refused to restart. All of this meant that the fire-fighting capability of the *Königsberg*, plus any pumping resources, were severely limited. The bombs that missed had mainly impacted on the pier she was tied to and burst the water mains, so no water could be got from them. The fires began to spread, and the crew were unable to stop them spreading. Captain Ruhfus concluded that his ship could not be saved, and ordered it to be abandoned. The weight of water flooding in caused the list to increase, and around 1000 she capsized.

---

1   As Lee-on-the-Solent, Hampshire, was principal base of the Fleet Air Arm, it was chosen as the site for the memorial to almost 2,000 men of that service who died during the Second World War and who have no known grave. Brian Smeeton is on Bay 1 Panel 2; Fred is on Panel 3.

Eighteen men were killed and 23 wounded. A number of members of the *Königsberg*'s crew were sent to the gun batteries at Kvarven and Hellen, where their expertise was put to good use. Ruhfus was made harbourmaster and kept other members of his crew as a port guard force, freeing up two companies of soldiers to be reallocated as mobile reserve. Most members of the *Königsberg*'s crew did not make it back to Germany until late May. At the time, the significance of the action of this small group of Skuas was not recognised – it was the first time in war that aerial bombing had sunk a major warship. Air power would in fact be the death knell for capital ships. The wreck was raised on 17 July 1942, and after being righted in March 1943 was used as a pier for U-boats. The wreck capsized again on 22 September 1944, and was broken up in Bergen after the end of the war.

A further air attack by Skuas was planned for the afternoon of 12 April, but the Germans were learning their lessons and felt it was dangerous to try and unload the large transport ships during daylight; on this day three merchant ships were dispersed at various locations around Bergen harbour. These were the *Bärenfels*, the *Bremse* and the *Carl Peters*. Twenty Skuas from 800, 801 and 803 Squadrons based at Hatston again headed towards Bergen. A number of smaller vessels moored in the harbour bore the brunt of the attacks from the Skuas, but apparently no bombs hit their intended targets. The bombing attack was followed up with some machine-gunning attempts and S-boat *S24* was damaged, killing nine sailors and wounding another eight. Slight damage from bullets was caused to the *Bremse* and the *Carl Peters*, and also some of the warehouses. One Skua had to ditch because of damage from flak but the crew were helped by local civilians and eventually made it back to Britain.

Towards dusk the *Bärenfels* (whose load included around 150,000 litres of aviation fuel) was on the quayside but the local dock workers, almost to a man, had disappeared or refused to unload her, partly because they did not want to work on a German ship and also because of the dangerous cargo. The next day, the Germans rounded up groups of men and sent them on board with promises of money and alcohol if they worked for them. Just over half of the aviation fuel was unloaded, but there was still around 60,000 litres (13,215 gallons) on board. The *Bärenfels* was still alongside the quayside when dawn broke on 14 April, and at 0715 800 Squadron returned. One of the bombs dropped missed the *Bärenfels*, but blew up a stack of drums carrying aviation fuel on the quayside. This blew a hole in the side of the *Bärenfels* and started a fire on board. which quickly got out of control. About an hour later, further Skuas arrived, this time from 803 Squadron, but only three out of nine got through because of bad weather en route. Nevertheless, at least one of the three bombs dropped hit home, causing more damage towards the stern and starting further fires. One of the three Skuas, that of Captain Eric McIver, was shot down. McIver was a Royal Marine officer,aged 24. He was awarded a Mention in Dispatches for this attack. His body was recovered from the water and he now lies at Bergen Mollendal Church Cemetery in the Commonwealth War Graves Commission plot, grave B2. The body of his crewman, Petty Officer A. Barnard, was not recovered and he is commemorated on the Fleet Air Arm Memorial to the Missing at Lee-on-Solent, Bay 1, Panel 3.

The fires on board were getting out of control, and as well as the aviation fuel there was the danger posed by around 150 tons of ammunition. At 0900 a series of explosions on *Bärenfels* damaged nearby cranes and warehouses. Eventually she keeled

A typical method of transport for the German Army in 1940. (Bob Gerritsen Collection)

over to starboard and sank, stern first. The bow section remained afloat, and when the fires died down, it was found that the forward holds were virtually undamaged. Some valuable loads were salvaged, including three 15cm field guns, one 10.5cm anti-aircraft gun, trucks and ammunition. *Bärenfels* was later refloated and repaired, and was back in German service by May 1942, but was again sunk in Bergen harbour on 14 April 1944 by a British midget submarine, *X24*. After the war, she was again salvaged but sank for good when on tow south of Bergen.

On 16 April, the Skuas visited Bergen again, this time damaging a U-boat, *U58*. and a captured Norwegian torpedo boat, the *Brand*. On the next day, *Bremse* was attacked but no real damage was inflicted. The Skuas of 800, 801 and 803 Squadrons were then sent to two aircraft carriers, HMS *Ark Royal* and *Glorious*, for operations off Norway. Bergen was left unmolested until 806 Squadron launched a series of attacks between 9 and 16 May. These attacks were mainly focusssed on oil tanks at Askøy. As a result of the raids, approximately 19 million litres (over 4 million gallons) of petrol and oil were burnt, in fires that lasted for about a week.

In early April 1940, *Hauptmann* G. Capito, commander of a JU52 transport squadron, was invited to a meeting with *Oberleutenant* O. von Brandis, commander of 3. Company of the *Fallschirmjäger Regiment 1*. At this meeting, in an otherwise empty room, he was shown by von Brandis a model of a coastal scene including beaches, hills and woods, and in the middle was an airfield. Von Brandis admitted he had not been told where the location was but that it would be the objective for his men within a few days, and Capito and his crews were to fly the paratroopers there. Over the next few hours, the two commanders worked out the best method of approach and the exit route. On the evening of 8 April, after he and the crews had been put in a sealed camp at Stade near Hamburg, Capito

German armoured car being loaded on a train. (Imperial War Museum HU104677)

found out that the model was of the area around Sola airfield near Stavanger in south-west Norway. He would be flying the *Fallschirmjägers* there the next day. Sola-Stavanger airfield, which had only been opened in the late 1930s, was also only about 300 miles from Scapa Flow in the Orkneys, where much of the Royal Navy's Home Fleet was based. It was felt that a blockade of the northern entrances to the North Sea by the British would be almost impossible should the Germans control Sola, while British control of one of the few airfields in Norway would endanger Operation *Weserübung*. It was a high priority target that needed to be secured at the very start of the operations - an ideal objective for the *Fallschirmjägers*.

In common with other aircraft flying to Norway on the morning of 9 April, Capito and his men found themselves flying through thick fog. The commander of the escorting Messerschmitt ME110s, *Oberleutenant* Gollob, decided it was not feasible to carry on and turned round, intending to land at Aalborg airfield in Denmark – which he hoped would be in German hands by the time he landed – and wait for the fog to lift. He was under strict radio silence, so when he turned round he hoped the rest of his crews would see this and follow him. One started to turn but must have collided with another, which had not seen what was happening: both planes crashed into the sea. The other two ME110s missed the manoeuvre completely and carried on through the banks of fog, trusting their instruments and heading towards Sola.

Hauptmann Capito was in a similar position. His 12 JU52s had taken off from Stade airfield, each loaded with 12 paratroopers, faced with an uncomfortable flight of about three hours to Norway. It was planned that the JU52s would arrive just after the supporting aircraft had subdued the defences, but in time to capture the airfield before the bulk of transports carrying the reinforcements arrived.

By the time his group was flying over the Skagerrak, Capito could barely see the wings of his own aircraft. He later wrote:

> It was very difficult. The whole squadron was swallowed up and despite the closest formation, the nearest plane was like a phantom. Even if the soldiers had parachutes, they would land in the sea if they managed to get out and none had a lifebelt. And what if the fog extended over land? It would be certain suicide. On the other hand it was our first war effort, and the paratroopers were as eager as I to succeed. If we turned, those coming behind would have nowhere to land. The mission would have to be completed! I was only 27 at the time and the decision was based as much on youthful light-headedness as bravery.

So the aircraft flew on and after about 30 minutes the fog bank came to an end. The aircraft were in clear skies about 60 miles from the coast of Norway, which was just about visible on the horizon. Capito put his plane into a slow bank and one of his crew counted all but one of his wing emerging from the fog. The others formed up on him and they went down low to avoid detection for the last leg of their journey. Not far behind, the advance wave was being followed by around 100 JU52s carrying the 1. and 2. Battalions of the 193rd Infantry Regiment.

There had been a few RNAF (Royal Norwegian Air Force) aircraft stationed at Sola, including their bomber wing, with four Fokker CV biplanes and four Caproni CA310s, all under the command of Lieutenant H. Hansen. A couple of weeks earlier, it had been decided by the High Command that the bomber wing and scout wing at Kjeller should swap bases, and the advance party from there had only just arrived at Sola in early April. Also in the area were two MF11 and one HE115 aircraft based at the Sola seaplane station. These were operated by navy pilots and were used for coastal patrol duties. Lieutenant Hansen was convinced that the British mine-laying operations were only the precursor to more serious events, and suggested to his commanders that the runway be prepared for demolition, but this was rejected. The news of events at Oslo made him order that the machine-gun posts be manned, and he prepared his few aircraft for action. He reported back around 0200 on 9 April that his aircraft were fuelled and bombed up, ready to go. To his frustration, he was told there was no use for them at the moment and no further orders. The navy crews at the seaplane base had received orders to carry out a dawn patrol, but little else. Hansen arranged with the civilian airport manager to close off as much of the airfield as possible, and rolls of heavy wire were placed across the runways about 100 metres apart. A small section was left open should the bombers need to take off.

At 0500, one of the navy pilots, Lieutenant Stansberg, took off in his MF11. Off Feistein Island, south of Sola, he spotted the German freighter *Tübingen* and returned to the airfield, dropping a message advising of its position before resuming his patrol. More than 12 other ships were seen, a U-boat and several German aircraft. He returned to Sola about 0800. Meanwhile, Hansen ordered up one of the Fokkers. It had a massive bomb load of four 50kg bombs, but soon after it had left, Hansen received orders from SDD2 not to bomb anything until further orders arrived. This was passed on to the airborne Fokker, which returned to the airfield.

There were other Norwegian forces in the area that the Germans may have to face. In late March 1940, around 800 men from the Ranger Battalion of Infantry Regiment 2, normally based in Oslo, were sent to defend Sola and the Stavanger peninsula. These men were supposed to have received between 60 and 80 days of military training, and were supposedly amongst the better-trained units of the "Neutrality Watch". They were based mainly at Madlamoen, situated between the airfield and the city. The commander of the garrison positioned one rifle platoon and one machine gun platoon at Sola to defend it. They were on a weekly rotation, with a similar force in reserve. Just nine machine guns were available to defend the large area, with three anti-aircraft guns available. One bunker had been built on the airfield, with another under construction. There was little in the way of firepower or men to repel any incursion.

It was against this background that the Germans intended to launch an attack. Just before 0800, orders arrived for Lieutenant Hansen from Oslo: he was to move all available aircraft east as soon as possible. Just as the few aircraft left were taking off, eight JU88s attacked the airfield with machine guns and cannon fire. One Caproni was hit and had to make an emergency landing, but the others escaped safely. The Norwegian infantry on the ground fired back, mainly using machine guns, but in their inexperience fired too-long bursts and the guns overheated. Morale amongst the defenders plummeted and it seems some of them deserted, not expecting to end up in a shooting war during their national service. To add to the confusion, the two ME110s appeared. Most of the Norwegian soldiers regrouped at the one completed bunker, which had been disguised as a shed. Flying in from the south-east, the coast was virtually clear for the 11 JU52s carrying the paratroopers. Capito had approached using the cover of nearby hills. A few minutes before reaching the airfield, he climbed up to about 100 metres and the aircraft doors were opened. Capito commented later:

> I had a brief glance at the airfield and thought it looked just like the model. As we had discussed, I aimed for the hangar and saw that the other aircraft were following me as planned. Back with the throttle, green light on. The troopers were gone in seconds and we dived back down to pick up speed and avoid any anti-aircraft fire and headed away. Our mission was completed.

Von Brandis and his 134 men were floating down, to the amazement of the Norwegian soldiers, who had probably never seen paratroopers before. Perhaps more seasoned troops might have been less in awe and acted quickly, as the first few minutes after exiting the aircraft are the most dangerous for a paratrooper. It was not against the Geneva Convention to fire at descending paratroopers, and the Germans were basically unarmed as they floated down. Although they were equipped with a knife and pistol, their rifles, other weapons and ammunition were dropped in containers, which had to be located and opened before they were really ready for combat. However, the Norwegians were

German at an airfield in Norway 10 April – A member of the *Luftwaffe* pictured in Norway soon after landing. (Imperial War Museum HU104689)

probably unaware of this, and now that their machine guns had cooled down they continued to expend most of their remaining ammunition on the aircraft. One of the few Norwegians to keep cool under pressure was Johansen, a soldier who was in the bunker east of the runway. He was able to keep a large portion of the *Fallschirmjägers* who landed in his field of fire pinned down. Their containers had landed some distance away and it would have been suicidal to try and get to them. Fortunately for the Germans, some landed out of his arc of fire. Collecting their weapons, they approached the bunker from behind. His resistance was soon ended and he was taken prisoner. This allowed the group of *Fallschirmjägers* previously pinned down to collect their weapons and start to mop up what was left of the opposition. Lieutenant Tangvald, who had been an intelligence officer on the base, and was one of the few officers left, saw that carrying on would lead to a massacre of his inexperienced troops, and arranged a ceasefire with von Brandis. Shortly after 0900, Sola airfield was in German hands. Johansen suggested later that German casualties were around 40 wounded, but German sources stated three dead with 10 wounded, four seriously. Only three Norwegian soldiers were wounded, with none killed, and around 80 were taken prisoner. Some, showing remarkable initiative after what they had been through, managed to slip away in the confusion on the ground after the ceasefire. Within minutes, the wire barricades had been cleared away and between 50 and 60 JU52s started to land in quick succession, nearly all of them moving on to the grass by the side of the runway to disgorge their passengers and cargo.

Some of the first aircraft to arrive contained signallers and communication equipment, with which an air-traffic system was set up, thus aiding the arrival and departure of the transports. The Germans intended to turn the aircraft round as soon as possible. Some of the returning JU52s took the *Fallschirmjägers* back to Germany, their work done. By the early afternoon, more than 2,000 men had arrived by air at Sola, plus ground crews, anti-aircraft guns, ammunition, aviation fuel and other equipment. The gamble of carrying on through the fog and mist had paid off, but it must be said the Norwegians did not put up as much resistance as they could have done.

While the *Fallschirmjägers* were dropping on Sola, 12 HE59 seaplanes landed at Hafrssfjord and taxied towards the base. The handful of Norwegian soldiers and ground crew there were quickly overwhelmed by the 40 or so soldiers who leapt out of the seaplanes. Within a couple of hours, this site was also operational and was used by HE115 seaplanes as a station for reconnoitring out into the Atlantic.

Once the airfield and its environs had been secured, the Germans moved towards Madlamoen and Stavanger. Lieutenant Tangvald was apparently forced at gun-point to walk in front of the leading German infantry, carrying a white flag. The local population looked on in stunned silence and within a few hours key points in Stavanger, such as the radio station, police station and telephone exchange, were secured without a single shot being fired.

One of the German officers from the 193rd Infantry Regiment later recalled:

> Equipment and ammunition were hurriedly unloaded from the aircraft and stacked on the grass next to the runway. 5th Company headed for the Madla camp, between Sola and Stavanger. They encountered no opposition, as all units there had withdrawn towards Sandnes; hence the way to Stavanger was free. *Oberleutenant* Christ captured a bus and the driver was ordered to take us to town. We secured the port and there *Oberleutenant* Weissenberg appeared with several maps that he had bought in a nearby bookshop – a strange war!

As with other objectives, the Germans needed to get additional forces into the area but another of the Trojan horse ships heading for Stavanger – the *Roda* – also suffered problems. At around 0100 on 9 April, Norwegian customs officers went aboard the modern Norwegian Navy destroyer *Æger* (which had entered service in 1936) while she was at anchor in Stavanger, and reported their suspicion that the 6,780-ton cargo ship *Roda*, anchored near Ullsnes, was probably carrying a different cargo than the 7,000 tons of coke stated in her cargo documents. The German vessel was riding far too high in the water to carry such a cargo. Adding still more suspicion was the fact that the Germans claimed they were bringing the coke to the Norwegian company Sigval Bergesen, which the customs officers knew had never before taken deliveries of coke. Although the situation was unclear, the Norwegian destroyer's commander, Captain Niels Bruun, decided to take *Roda* as a prize.

When the Norwegian destroyer found the German ship in the Byfjord near Stavanger and signalled that they were going to seize the vessel, the crew of the *Roda* resisted. Captain Bruun decided to sink the cargo ship. After the German crew had abandoned their ship, *Æger* fired 25 10cm rounds into both sides of the vessel, sinking her in deep waters. A short while after the sinking of *Roda*, Luftwaffe aircraft started appearing overhead. At 0830, the first three of a total of 10 JU88 bombers from *III/Kampfgeschwader 4* began attacking *Æger* at low altitude. Responding with her single 40mm Bofors gun and two 12.7mm Colt anti-aircraft machine guns, *Æger* managed to shoot down two of the attacking bombers while zig-zagging to avoid the stacks of bombs being unleashed at her. However, while trying to avoid an attack by three aircraft from different directions, *Æger* was hit amidships by a 250kg bomb, tearing up the deck of the destroyer and blowing out its sides. Seven members of the crew were killed outright, one died later of his wounds and three were lightly wounded. The ship was left dead in the water. As seven more German aircraft continued to attack the crippled destroyer, another bomb hit and buckled the mast, but it bounced off into the sea without exploding. Yet another bomb hit amidships, but did not explode. All the time the attacking aircraft were pelting the crippled vessel with machine gun fire. As all of the ship's anti-aircraft weapons were by now knocked out, Captain Bruun ordered his crew to abandon ship. The entire surviving crew managed to get ashore without further casualties. The cargo of the *Roda* had been heavy anti-aircraft guns, intended for the defence of Sola, and their loss was a major blow to the Germans. Another three ships - *Tübingen*, *Tijuca* and *Mendoza* - arrived during the afternoon of W-Day. Then as planned on the following day, transport aircraft flew in more elements of the 3. Battalion of the 193rd Infantry Regiment.

The Kristiansand force, under the command of Captain Rieve, arrived somewhat later than planned, owing to thick fog. It was spotted by coastal batteries and came under fire, but suffered little damage. Nevertheless, the first troops did not get ashore until about noon. The Germans seized two Norwegian Navy vessels in the harbour, but again there was no serious opposition and the Germans started to set up defensive positions. The fog that delayed this group also delayed the *Greif*, which did not reach Arendal until the late morning, so the telephone line to England was also cut later than planned. The follow-up transports suffered problems too: one of them, the *Kreta*, was torpedoed in the Kattegat on 9 April, but the other three – the *August Leonhardt, Westsee* and *Wigand* - all reached Kristiansand.

At Egersund, the small group entered the harbour without interference. The landing party was put ashore and cut the cable to Scotland.

The most important objective for the Germans was the capital city, Oslo. After the mobilisation order, the Norwegian Navy had put out patrol boats at the mouth of Oslofjord on the night of 8-9 April. The Germans, aware of this, planned to try and hoodwink them by sending the following message: "Am putting in with permission of Norwegian Government. Escorting officer on board." However, the Norwegians were not fooled. They sent a message back to their HQ requesting that the lighthouses in the fjord be switched off to confuse the Germans. Around midnight, one of the patrolling Norwegian boats, the *Pol III*, spotted the advance units of the German Navy and fired warning shots across the bows of the intruders. The commander of the German fleet ordered one of his torpedo boats, the *Albatros*, to deal with her. Whether by accident or design, the *Pol III* rammed the *Albatros;* when the two vessels separated, the *Albatros*

The embarkation of the garrison for Narvik begins. (Bob Gerritsen Collection)

opened fire. The *Pol III* was hit and started to sink, not all the Norwegian crew could be rescued (the Captain, L. Olsen, was among the dead) and the 14 survivors became the first prisoners of the campaign.

The German commanders realised that any element of surprise was now lost, and the captain of the *Lützow*, Thiele, suggested that they crank up their speed towards Oslo before the Norwegians got word out to all the lighthouses and the journey became more dangerous. But the senior commander, Admiral Kummetz, did not agree. He decided to carry on with the illusion of being a peaceful force and not to increase speed. The most dangerous point for the invasion fleet was where the fjord narrowed to about 600 metres wide, near Drøbak. As this was a bottleneck, several defensive positions had been constructed. One of the largest was at Oscarsborg, which was located on an island in the fjord and contained three 280mm guns. These monsters had been made by Krupp's of Germany in 1892, and fired shells weighing 600lbs. As well as this fort, there were two forts on the eastern bank, one with 150mm guns and the other with two 57mm guns. On the western bank at Nesset was another fort, again with two 57mm guns.

As the *Blücher* led the German fleet into the fjord, they were seen by the Oscarsborg fort, whose commander, Colonel B. Eriksen, gave the order to open fire. There were only enough men to man two of the guns, but according to German sources, fire was opened by the Norwegians at 0521. Two of these massive shells hit the *Blücher* at around 500 yards, with devastating effects. One shell penetrated a locker containing fuel for the ship's seaplane and started a large fire. The other hit the ship's anti-aircraft control centre. The 150mm shells fired from the Kopäs battery on the eastern bank caused further damage, but the *Blücher* pressed on. However, she was heading into further trouble, as there was a bank of torpedo tubes on the Nordre Kaholmen island. Several were launched at the *Blücher* and at least two struck, causing severe damage with the ship starting to list to starboard. The damage was too great for the *Blücher*'s crew to contain, and the order was given to abandon ship. Around 1,500 of those aboard escaped safely. The majority either struggled to an island in the middle of the fjord or to the eastern bank. At about 0630, one of the fires reached a magazine and caused a huge explosion, This resulted in the *Blücher* rolling over and sinking within about an hour. The loss of life was considerable – around 130 crew and nearly 200 soldiers who had been due to land at Oslo. Faced with this setback, Admiral Kummetz decided not to press on but to turn around and disembark troops at alternative landing spots. At around 0700, the *Lützow* and *Albatros* started to offload troops on the eastern side of the fjord at Son and Moss.

A couple of hours earlier, around 0430, Kurt Bräuer, the German Ambassador, delivered to the Norwegian Foreign Minister a 13-point ultimatum, which basically demanded total capitulation and free access into Norway for the Germans. Foreign Minister Koht requested a small pause to allow the Norwegians to consider their options. After about 30 minutes, Koht advised Bräuer that the Norwegian government would not be taking up the German offer. However, this delay did help King Häkon, Crown Prince Olav and most of the government to board a special train from Oslo and go to Hamar, a town around 90 miles north of the capital.

One of the main thrusts of the German assault on Oslo was made with the use of their airborne troops. For a paratrooper stuck in the back of an aircraft there are many things that can go wrong, including bad weather. On the morning of 9 April, dense fog covered most of the Skagerrak and caused most of the 29 JU52s carrying men from *Fallschirmjäger Regiment 1* to divert to Aalborg in Denmark, which had already been captured by that unit's 4th Company. There were just a few JU52s still heading towards Oslo, escorted by a small number of Messerschmitt 110s that were to support the assault on the city.

Oberleutnant Wilhelm Metscher, one of the pilots flying to Oslo that day, commented:

> Our mission this morning was on the edge of what I felt we were capable of. I was quite tense and I am sure many of the others were as well. After taking off, we received two radio signals: the first saying that Denmark had surrendered, the second, which came a little later, over the Skagerrak, said there was opposition in Norway. Flying north, the weather gradually worsened and we encountered fog. Eventually, it was just one grey soup. *Hauptmann* Walther protested strongly at Drewes's decision to turn back. The other paratroopers later said the two argued loudly, shouting at each other. Walther meant the conditions were far from impossible. Here and there, openings in the fog could be seen. Drewes, however, had made up his mind and as senior commander enforced his decision. Walther was deeply disappointed.

Walther was the overall commander of the two companies of *Fallschirmjägers* due to take Fornebu, and Drewes was the pilot in charge of the first wave of transport aircraft taking the airborne troops.

While Metscher banked his aircraft away, Drewes ordered the radio operator in his aircraft to advise the others in his group of his decision, and also to send a signal back to Hamburg that his formation was turning back because of poor weather conditions. In spite of this, some aircraft either did not receive the signal or chose to ignore it and carried on to their objective.

Hauptmann Wagner, in command of the second wave, received a recall signal from the *X Fliegerkorps*, but as it was not specifically addressed to him and conditions over the Skagerrak seemed to be improving, he decided the signal did not apply to him and he continued towards Oslo as planned.

The Norwegian Air Force had also been put on alert earlier in the day, and some of their Gloster Gladiator fighters based at Fornebu were in the air when the first German aircraft arrived in the area soon after 0730. Although the Germans looked on the Gladiators as old-fashioned, obsolete biplanes, a number of the transports and escorting fighters were shot down. However, enough of the escorting ME110s got through unscathed, attacked the ground defences at Fornebu airfield and destroyed a number of Norwegian aircraft on the ground. It was not looking good, though, to those ME110 pilots in the area as the bulk of the JU52s seemed to have disappeared. It had been assumed that the ME110s could land once the airfield had been taken, and refuel using captured supplies. Many of the aircraft pilots were looking anxiously at their fuel gauges and virtually flying on fumes. Then three JU52s appeared at about 0820 and the lead aircraft lined up for a landing, although the ME110s had expected the *Fallschirmjägers* would exit the aircraft whilst it was still in flight. In the lead JU52 was *Hauptmann* R. Wagner, commander of the first wave,. He was hit by machine gun fire from the ground and killed, together with several *Fallschirmjägers*. The pilot then decided to abort and fly back to Denmark. Fornebu was a key objective for the Germans. As well as the theoretical 340 *Fallschirmjägers* being transported in 29 JU52s, another 900 men from the 324th Infantry Regiment of the 163rd Infantry Division and their light equipment, together with other support troops, were due to be flown in. A potentially dire situation for the Germans was salvaged by the actions of the commander of the escorting fighters, *Oberleutnant* W. Hansen. He ordered *Leutnant* Lent to try and land, while he and the others would attempt to keep the Norwegian machine gunners quiet. Lent was apparently so low on fuel that he had already shut down one of his engines to conserve what fuel he had, and so landed on one engine. Machine gun bullets struck Lent's aircraft but none hit the cockpit. His ME110 careered on down the runway, running off the end and down a bank when the undercarriage broke off. His aircraft slithered to a halt in the fence of a house bordering the aerodrome, and both crew were shaken but not seriously hurt. The other ME110s then took their chances and also landed, most relatively unscathed. They gathered at the northern end of the runway – as far away as possible from the enemy fire. Lent and his navigator, Kubisch, managed to join them, and as a temporary measure some of the rear-facing machine guns from the ME110s were taken off and used to set up a defensive position.

Some of the JU52 pilots, seeing the fighters land, believed the aerodrome was now captured and started to land. A German report credits the first JU52 to land being that carrying *Hauptmann* P. Ingenhoven, who was second-in-command of the troops.

Although his plane was hit by machine gun fire, he started to organise things on the ground with those who survived the landing, although some had been killed or wounded by the Norwegian fire.

At 0833, the aircraft carrying the staff of the 1st Battalion, led by *Oberleutenant* Götte, arrived overhead and seeing aircraft on the ground, ordered the rest of his aircraft to land, so no *Fallschirmjägers* actually jumped on to Fornebu that day. Meanwhile, the German Air Attaché, Spiller, arrived at the aerodrome after avoiding the Norwegian defences, found the "air commander", Hansen, and suggested that a signal be sent in his name (Spiller) that Fornebu was now under German control. Also not one to miss an opportunity, Hansen went to the "communications" Junkers that had recently arrived and sent a signal to Aalborg, who forwarded it to Hamburg, which read; "Fornebu in own hands. Hansen. *1 Staffel Zerstörergruppe 76.*"[2]

The order to turn back from Fornebu was rescinded and all aircraft advised to go back to Oslo if possible. Some, thinking they had enough fuel, turned round again, hoping to get their tanks topped up with captured supplies, while others took off from wherever they had landed in places scattered around Denmark. Over the coming hours, they started to arrive at Fornebu at random intervals. It was a difficult landing for many, with no real air traffic control to help them in. Around 15 transport aircraft crashed at or near Fornebu on 9 April, with casualties sustained in many of these landings. As more men landed, and the Norwegians were overwhelmed or ran out of ammunition, order of a sort was established. To all intents and purposes, the airfield was in German hands. During the morning, follow-on troops from the 1. and 2. Battalions of the 324th Infantry Regiment, a pioneer company, other administrative troops and some of the 3. Battalion of the 159th Infantry Regiment landed. Also arriving, having flown from Aalborg in Denmark, was Walther, the commander of the *Fallschirmjägers*. The overall commander, *Oberst* Nickelmann of the 324th Infantry Regiment, could then start contemplating a move towards Oslo. A member of von Falkenhorst's staff, Pohlman, sent a message from the German Embassy at 1215 which read:

> Just back from Fornebu. Five companies with *Oberst* Nickelmann have landed. Only 12 *Fallschirmjägers* arrived. Eight transport machines from 6th Group crashed due to ground fire. Few losses. Anti-aircraft machine gun fire suppressed by landed troops. Embassy secured by guards. Entry to Oslo by Group Nickelmann imminent. No news of the warships.

Pohlman had been sent to Oslo, ostensibly as a diplomat, a few days before the invasion, and had been able on this morning to move about relatively freely.

At Fornebu, three ME110s were refuelled from captured Norwegian stocks and were able to maintain a combat air patrol around the airfield, not that there was much sign of Norwegian aerial activity.

---

2   Of the Germans involved, Helmut Lent went on to become a *Luftwaffe* night fighter ace with 110 kills to his credit. He was killed in a landing accident in 1944 and was given a state funeral, presided over by Reichsmarschall Hermann Göring. Werner Hansen was shot down and killed by "friendly fire" in 1941.

Around 1730, a Sunderland flying boat was reported over the inner Oslofjord. It was flown by Flight Lieutenant P. Kite from 210 Squadron, who had been sent on an impromptu reconnaissance flight as no other aircraft were available. The aircraft was on a volunteer mission, a special operation to find out what was happening in and around Oslo. The crew left on 8 April in Sunderland *L2168*, flying north from Pembroke Dock on the south-west tip of Wales to Holyhead in north Wales and stayed there overnight. The next morning they flew to Invergordon in Scotland where, for what was believed to be a mechanical problem, they changed to another Sunderland, *L2167*. They took off at 1300 and opened sealed orders to learn of their destination: Oslo, Norway. The mission was general reconnaissance. The crew had no knowledge that Germany had invaded Norway on that day. The Sunderland was first hit by flak over Oslo harbour, and then intercepted by Hansen and Lent and shot down. Out of the 10-man crew, only one survived –radio operator Sergeant Ogwyn George, who apparently fell out of the aircraft when it broke apart in mid-air.

The nine dead who now all lie in Sylling churchyard in Buskerud, Norway, are: AC2 G. Eveson (grave 2); AC1 R. Millar (grave 3); AC1 G. Maile (grave 4); LAC D. Upham (grave 5); LAC F. Morrison (grave 6); Sergeant J. Barter, observer (grave 7); Sergeant J. Carpenter, co-pilot (grave 8); Pilot Officer A. Lemaitre, co-pilot (grave 9); Flight Lieutenant P. Kite, pilot (grave 10).

The nine RAF airmen who lost their lives on 9 April 1940 were the first Allied servicemen to die in the defence of Norway. They are remembered with a special ceremony each year at their graves in the Sylling churchyard. The one survivor, the Welsh radio operator George, fell 3,000ft without a parachute, hitting trees and landing in unusually deep snow. He was discovered and rescued by a local, Johan Brathen, but spent the rest of the war in prisoner-of-war camps.

Many civilians had watched the dramatic events, including Johan, who worked as a forester. He and two of his friends tried to walk up the hillside. They met another forester who was close to the crash site and was able to give them an idea of where to go, but it proved impossible to make their way through the seven feet of snow without skis. Dusk was falling and the party was forced to return. Later that night, in his bed, Johan was unable to sleep. Might there be people in the forest who needed help? At 0200, he got up, put his skis on his bicycle and set off. It was still dark when he started climbing up the steep hillside. There was a strange atmosphere in the forest. Unfamiliar scents and 30 tons of burning wreckage had scared away the local wildlife. After a while he could smell aircraft fuel, and then he heard a human voice.

Ogwyn George was falling in and out of consciousness. He could feel something sniff his body and was concerned it might be a wolf (he later learned it was probably just a fox). With his serious injuries he started to hallucinate; he thought he could see the picture of Jesus on the wall of his home in Wales, and called out: "Jesus, if you want me, take me now!"

Johan didn't understand English, but could hear Ogwyn's voice. As Johan approached, Ogwyn tried to get up but Johan realised he was unable to get the severely injured man to the village on his own. He told Ogwyn by signs that he would go for help and, wrapped him in his jacket and returned to the village.

Orders are given just before landing. (Bob Gerritsen Collection)

For a second time that night, Johan climbed the 1,500ft, accompanied by Herbrand Mushaugen and Kristian Tangen. Reaching the area of the crash site in daylight, the marks in the snow showed how Ogwyn tumbled down the steep hillside for several hundred yards. Where he landed after a fall of 3,000ft without a parachute, there was a cavity through the seven feet of snow, exposing the heather on the frozen ground.

The British sergeant could hear them breaking twigs from the spruce trees to make him a bed on the sledge. They got him down to the valley and then he was transported by car to the hospital in Drammen, where he was to remain for five months.

Meanwhile around 25 German HE111 bombers, had been sent to make a "demonstration" over the Norwegian capital, followed by another dozen or so HE111s, all intended to scare the local population into accepting that resistance was futile. The original intention had been for them not to bomb, but they did carry bombs. Their orders were changed during the flight, when it was realised that the Norwegians were offering some resistance. The bombers were given orders to attack Fornebu, Oscarsborg (a large fort situated on an island in the Oslofjord) and any other targets spotted.

The German forces that had landed earlier moved towards Oslo, and at around 1400 Nickelmann was able to convince the local commander, Schnitler, to surrender. He had been put in charge when the rest of the High Command had been evacuated, but was able to contact the Prime Minister, Nygaardsvold, who was at Hamar. He received permission

German troops waiting to land just off the Norwegian coast. (Bob Gerritsen Collection)

to surrender the city to avoid bloodshed. The German cause was probably helped by the sight of many of their aircraft flying into Fornebu, whilst the Norwegians showed little by way of bold offensive spirit. German initiative also once again came to the fore. The commander of the 163rd Infantry Division, General Engelbrecht, who had been detailed to take control of all the troops in Oslo, had failed to arrive. He had been a passenger on the *Blücher* and had managed to struggle to shore, but was captured by Norwegian soldiers. However, his other senior commanders stepped up to the plate and were aided by local diplomats, led by Bräuer.

By nightfall on 9 April there were probably less than 1,000 Germans in Oslo. They had nearly all come by air and lacked heavy weapons. On the next morning, two of the warships, the *Lützow* and the *Emden*, which were planned to arrive the previous day, finally made it past the defences. Most of the transport ships did not arrive until 12 April. It would take about a week before the Germans felt securely established in the Oslo area and could consider taking the rest of eastern Norway. However, by 13 April the 163rd Infantry Division had reached its objectives, pushing the secure area out as far as Hønefoss, Drammen and Kongsberg.

Although some people jeered them, most Norwegians were in a state of shock as they witnessed the Germans marching into Oslo on the afternoon of 9 April. There was no organised opposition because the local commander had surrendered to avoid bloodshed.

Those who might actually have been able to resist the invasion were still some hundreds of miles away.

General von Falkenhorst arrived at Fornebu a day late at 1600 on 10 April, with Admiral H. Boehm, who had been designated as the Commanding Admiral Norway. Boehm was apparently not to report directly to von Falkenhorst, but orders had been given that the two were to collaborate. Boehm later reported to the then head of the German Navy, Admiral Raeder, that "upon arrival I found a chaos I was not prepared for". It seems in these early days nobody had any idea which areas were under German control. Personnel from disparate services were deployed as soon as they arrived, not necessarily in their original role, and much had to be improvised. When the *Emden* arrived, her commander, Captain Lange, was instructed to make his radio facilities and staff available for use by the senior commanders, as communication back to Germany had been difficult or non-existent. Things slowly started to take shape for the Germans, but there was still a problem facing the military commanders.

The Norwegian government had fled, leaving behind a void, so the Germans contacted the leader of the Norwegian Fascist movement, Vidkun Quisling, and said they would ask Berlin if he could form a cabinet and exercise power, Vidkun Quisling's name would soon become known around the word.

In keeping with many European countries in the 1920s and 1930s, a right-wing or fascist movement came into being in Norway. The party was called the *Nasjonal Samling* (National Unity) and was formed on 17 May 1933. Despite their leader Quisling having been in the Norwegian military, diplomatic service and the Minister for Defence between 1931 and 1933, his party never attracted mass support and was little more than an interested onlooker in April 1940. Even though he was virtually an outsider in Norway, he had tried to attract the attention of senior Nazis in Germany by sending Hitler a 50th birthday message in April 1939 and telling those who would listen that he felt it unlikely Norway would be able to remain neutral during the anticipated conflict. His messages seemed to impress the Nazi hierarchy, and in the summer of 1939 he was invited to Germany for meetings and returned with promises of financial aid to hopefully increase the visibility of and support for the *Nasjonal Samling* party. For the next few months this proved fruitless, the party still being very much on the periphery of Norwegian politics. However, Quisling was invited to Germany in December 1939 and indeed held a meeting with Hitler on the 14th. Prior to this meeting, Quisling's advisers suggested that his best course of action would be to ask for Hitler's assistance in a pro-Nazi coup in Norway which would allow the Germans to use Norway as a forward naval base with easy access to the North Atlantic. During this meeting, Hitler promised to react to any British invasion of Norway but felt some of Quisling's other ideas, such as a *Nasjonal Samling* coup d'état and the notion of an Anglo-German peace treaty, were unlikely to actually happen. Things were not helped by Quisling being ill for long periods between December 1939 and March 1940 and the fact that he relied on a translator at these meetings.

The *Altmark* Incident ensured that the German Supreme Command's planning for intervention in Norway moved forward at speed. Hitler remained in two minds over whether an occupation of Norway should require an invitation from the Norwegian Government. In late March 1940, Quisling was invited to a meeting with German

Mountain troops go ashore in inflatable boats. (Imperial War Museum HU86082)

intelligence officers in Copenhagen. During the meeting on 31 March, Quisling was asked for information on Norwegian defences and the likely deployment of its forces during the proposed invasion. Quisling was back in Norway by 6 April; on the afternoon of 9 April, he was told by German liaison officer Hans Wilhelm Scheidt that should he set up a government it would have Hitler's personal approval.

Quisling quickly drew up a list of potential ministers to serve in a new government, and although it had merely relocated some 30 miles north from Oslo to Elverum, he accused the legitimate government of having "fled". He was greatly helped in getting his message across as the Norwegian broadcasting service had been temporarily suspended around 1730 on 9 April at the Germans' request. However, around two hours later, with German permission, Quisling was on the airwaves announcing the formation of a new government and revoking an earlier order to mobilise against the German invasion. In spite of this, requests in his broadcast – to the military to arrest the government at Elverum, and to the Oslo chief of police - were ignored. However, from this small beginning, as more and more Germans arrived in Oslo, Quisling's position strengthened. With Hitler's support, the new Norwegian government under Quisling was officially recognised on 10 April.

In the late afternoon it was realised that the senior members of the government had flown the nest. It was believed they had moved to Hamar. The German Air Attaché, Hauptmann E. Spiller, commandeering some *Fallschirmjägers* and four buses, set out north in the hope of intercepting or capturing them. However, around 1930 the senior politicians and heads of state at Hamar were alerted of this threat, so they moved about 20 miles further to the north-east to Elverum. To protect this move, Norwegian forces set up road blocks on the road between Hamar and Elverum; around midnight, the German convoy ran into one of these at Midtskogen. The *Fallschirmjägers* opened fire but the Norwegians had dug in well, and the Germans were forced to withdraw after suffering heavy losses. The Air Attaché was killed in this skirmish, and when his body was later searched an arrest list of prominent Norwegians was found. The *Fallschirmjägers* on the return journey, surprised a Norwegian battalion moving north and took them prisoner.

Quisling's broadcasts caused some alarm amongst the civilian population of Oslo and many people decided to leave the capital, fuelled by a rumour that an Allied bombing raid was expected. It was agreed after some negotiation that the Oscarsborg fort would surrender on the morning of 10 April. which would leave the way open for German ships to sail unmolested up Oslofjord and allow vital reinforcements to land. By around 1045 on 10 April, the *Lützow*, the *Emden* and their supporting ships had arrived in Oslo and started to unload their cargoes. General Engelbrecht had managed to engineer his own release after his temporary capture, and took command pending the arrival of General von Falkenhorst, who was due the following day.

Three of the supply ships – the *Itauri*, *Muansa* and *Neidenfels* – with reinforcements from the 196th Infantry Division, arrived on schedule on 11 April, but the *Antares* and the *Jonia* were sunk en route by British submarines. The second group of 11 transports did not fare much better: two – the *Friendenau* and the *Wigbert* – were sunk by HMS *Triton*, but the others reached Oslo unscathed.

Apart from the losses in ships, the Germans could be satisfied with the way the invasion had gone. Losses among the land and air elements were small, and nowhere had the Norwegians put up any real resistance.

On the political front, on 10 April, Bräuer travelled to Elverum where the Nygaardsvold government now sat. On Hitler's orders, he called for King Haakon to appoint Quisling as head of a new government, securing a peaceful transition of power. Haakon refused and intimated that he would rather abdicate than appoint a government led by Quisling. The government unanimously supported the King's position, urging the people to continue their resistance. Having no popular support, Quisling was of no use to Hitler. Germany retracted its support for his rival government, opting to create an independent governing commission. Quisling was thus manoeuvred out of power by Bräuer and a coalition of his former allies, including Hjort, who now thought of him as a liability. He was even deserted by his political allies, including Prytz, with whom he had worked since the 1920s.

Hitler wrote to thank Quisling for his good faith, to prevent him from losing face (to the extent that he could become a future Norwegian leader) and promising him a position in the new government. The transfer of power on these terms came about on 15 April, with Hitler still confident that the King would support the Administrative Council he had instigated.

5

The Norwegian point of view

Whilst Norway was aware that she was being looked at enviously by the major belligerents, the invasion still came as a shock. In the early hours of 8 April, the air raid sirens were sounded in Oslo and the street lights were turned off. Foreign Minister Koht telephoned his ministry and was advised that German warships had entered the Oslofjord and that the Prime Minister had called an emergency cabinet meeting for 0130.

Just a few hours earlier, around 2300 on 7 April, a signal arrived at the Ministry of Defence in Oslo from SDD1 (Sea Defence District 1) in Horten, advising that there were warships in the Oslofjord. It was thought the ships were German, but it was suggested they might be trying to escape from superior Allied forces rather than being an invasion force. Around 0100, the British Naval Attaché, Admiral Boyes, went to the Ministry of Defence with a list of German ships he thought were either on their way to Norway or already in Norwegian waters. The situation became a little clearer when SDD2 at Bergen advised that seven warships had entered The Leads. Then coastal forts started reporting that they had opened fire, and around 0415, SDD3 reported warships off Narvik. There could be no doubt now that Norway was under attack. The cabinet met at around 0130. Prime Minister Nygaardsvold later wrote:

> It was an ominous night. I understood that we faced a war game between the belligerents. It was not we, but the powers at war that would fight over Norway. We however, would pay the price. A call was made to the British Minister in Norway, Dormer, to find out if he had any information from his government, but he was asleep and knew nothing. England slept.

It was Foreign Minister Koht who had called Sir Cecil Dormer, and suggested that Oslo's defences might succeed in repelling the German ships. When Dormer asked if the Norwegian government intended to remain in Oslo, Koht said they did as it was felt the defences were strong enough and it would be unnecessary to evacuate the capital.

Inevitably there was a certain amount of chaos and uncertainty. The mobilising of the armed forces was a protracted affair. The Norwegian Army was not really fit for combat against a modern army. For example, although Norway had quantities of rifles and artillery pieces in store, vital components such as bolts and breech-blocks had been placed in different locations, so the weapons were useless until the pieces were put together. The overall commander of the Norwegian Army was General K. Laake. He suggested mobilisation of the field brigades in southern Norway around 0230 on the morning of 8 April, but it was becoming clear to some politicians that he was not the right man for

Til det norske folk!

De tyske tropper er ikke kommet for å kjempe mot Norge, men for å beskytte landet. De kom først etter t engelskmennene stadig hadde krenket Norges nøytralitet på en meget graverende måte.

Engelskmennene ville ved Norges okkupasjon trekke Skandinavien inn i krigen mot det tyske folk. Negre, anamiter, indere skulle ved siden av bare noen få engelskmenn føre krig mot oss i Deres fredelige land. Dere skulle blø for engelskmennene i en håpløs kamp. Kongen av Danmark og hans folk har gjennomskuet dette perfide spill og forstått at Tyskland handler i nødverge og har derfor overdratt beskyttelsen av sitt land til Tyskland.

Gjør det samme så at også Dere får fred!

Vi tyske soldater hadde ventet at Dere ikke ville skyte ved vår ankomst.

Men nå opphisser den engelske kringkaster Dere stadig til sabotasje og franktirørkrig, som vi aldri vil tåle. Dere selv skal vareta beskyttelsen av Deres verdifulle bygninger og magasiner. Det er en feiltagelse å tro at slik sabotasje nytter kongen og landet. Dere varetar derved bare Englands interesse. Vi ønsker ikke kamp mot Dere, mens engelskmennene ville misbruke Dere i kampen mot oss. De lover Dere hjelp, men kommer ikke til å holde sitt løfte og vil la Dere gå til grunne som de alltid har gjort med de små nasjoner i historiens løp.

De kan ikke sende Dere noen nevneverdig hjelp.

Derfor la være å yte motstand, la være å øve sabotasje, ellers er vi tvunget til å gå fram med skarpe forholdsregler.

Gjør dette klart for de opphissede og den uerfarne ungdom. Vi ønsker å leve i fred med Dere. Hold også fred med oss og hjelp oss å lempe på de hårde vilkår av en krig, som vi ikke ville,

Den tyske øverstkommanderende
von FALKENHORST
General-der Infanterie.

German propaganda leaflet dropped to the Norwegians. (The National Archives)

the situation. A report on the 65-year-old general later stated that he held there were no reports of any landings, and that he never considered "mobilising the whole lot". Anyhow, the Norwegians mobilised their forces by mail or telegram, a process that might take a minimum of three days! The politicians were appalled by this and thought there should be a full mobilisation, with the news broadcast over the radio for speed. The decision to mobilise was actually taken around 0400 on 9 April. Orders were drafted and taken to the main telegraph office in Oslo by an officer at 0530, but no one had thought to warn the civilian staff. The office was closed and did not open till 0800, by which time it was virtually meaningless to send the telegrams.

Around 0430, the German Ambassador, Bräuer, arrived with the German demands, which amongst other things stated that:

> Germany had against its wishes been drawn into a war with the Allies. As they did not dare to attack Germany on mainland Europe they had shifted the theatre of war to neutral territory and Norway was neither able nor willing to oppose the Allied pressure. The German Armed Forces had therefore commenced certain military operations to take over the protection of the Kingdom of Norway. The sole purpose of the operation was to prevent the intended occupation of

bases in Norway by Anglo-French forces. All military installations would have to be surrendered, but there would be no hostile intentions. If opposition was met, however, all necessary means would be employed. To avoid unnecessary bloodshed, an immediate military and administrative co-operation was advised and information therefore sent to the Armed Forces, with orders to avoid friction or difficulty.

Most of the Cabinet was in a nearby room so an answer was quickly forthcoming in the rejection of any German "help". Bräuer returned to the German Embassy and sent a message to Berlin which read:

> Have presented the Foreign Minister at 0520 German time with our demands in firm, insisting manner and explained the reasons for them as well as handed the memorandum to him. The Minister withdrew for consultations with the government, after a few minutes he returned with the answer: We do not willingly give in; the war has already started.

Most of the Norwegian government left on a train for Hamar to the north. Other moves were also afoot that would not please the Germans. Norway, fearing that a conflict was looming, had in 1938 and 1939 sent most of her gold reserves to the USA, but it is said around 120 million kroners worth of gold was still in the vaults of the Norges Bank in 1940. Plans had been put in place to move this should an emergency arise. During the night, the head of the Norges Bank was awoken by a call from one of the Finance Minister's aides with instructions to put the evacuation plan into place, and so about 50 tons of gold and other valuables escaped the clutches of the Germans. It first went to Lillehammer, and eventually to Britain, Canada and the USA.

At the British embassy in Oslo, after receiving the call from Koht, Ambassador Dormer issued instructions to his staff that they should start destroying documents and files. This was particularly important for those who worked in the Passport Control Section, which was basically a not very good cover story (in those days) for those who also worked for MI6. The head of the MI6 team was Frank Foley, nominally an assistant to the chief passport officer. His secretary was Margaret Reid, who wrote a few weeks later:

> I slept soundly while the Germans were sailing up Oslofjord until the telephone brought me leaping from my bed. "Come to the office at once, will you – and be ready to go!" The taxi exchange refused to send me a car, but fortunately I hailed one on the main road and reached the office. Foley and Newill were tearing files out of their drawers in the open safes. We drove in a taxi to the Legation by the back way to avoid being seen from the German Legation, which faced onto ours. We saw a great bonfire before we reached the grounds and were soon frantically rending code books and files to feed the flames.

Just before 0400, a brief telegram from Dormer arrived in London, which simply said: "Am burning cyphers archive." It was followed about 30 minutes later by the request:

"Can you give me any information helpful in deciding direction of eventual evacuation from here?"

This question was answered to some extent by the Norwegian Foreign Office, which advised that a train would be leaving Oslo at 0700 and that any members of the diplomatic corps who wished to stay with the government could go to Hamar. Dormer thought this was a good idea and advised his team accordingly.

Meanwhile, the Norwegian Army was in a state of total confusion. The General Staff was normally based in a barracks at Akershus, but it was felt this was would be a prime target for the Germans, so the decision was taken to move to the Slemdal Hotel, situated in one of the northern suburbs of Oslo. With typical disregard for the growing seriousness of the situation, General Laake told his aides that he would go home first and arrive at Slemdal around 1000. At the same time it was decided to dissolve the General Staff and establish a Supreme Army Command, the *Haerens Overkommando* (HOK). This was a sensible decision as most of the officers allocated to the General Staff had other roles upon mobilisation. Army officers arrived at the Slemdal Hotel to find it still full of guests; nobody from the hotel was expecting them. The Chief of the General Staff, Hatledal, decided they should continue towards Eidsvoll (about 40 miles north of Oslo). However, no one remembered to leave word or wait for General Laake, and when he turned up at the hotel, nobody could tell him anything. After trying desperately to find out what had happened, Laake eventually discovered where his staff had moved to and joined them in the early afternoon. Then the Defence Minister, Ljungberg, passing through on his way to Hamar after a brief situation report, ordered Laake and Hatledal to come with him to join the government there, thus separating the two top generals from their key decision-makers.

In London, one of the senior figures in the Army, Major-General Hastings Ismay, commented on the events of 9 April:

> The Twilight War ended for me in a most unexpected and dramatic way. In the early hours of 9 April, I was wakened out of a deep sleep by the telephone bell. It was the Duty Officer at the War Cabinet Office: his report was brutal in its simplicity. The Germans had seized Copenhagen, Oslo and all the main ports of Norway. The gathering that assembled in my office at 0630 was not exactly inspiring. I had hoped that one or other of the Chiefs of Staff would have a plan of action, but so far as I can remember not a single constructive suggestion had been put forward by the time that we had to break up the meeting and join the War Cabinet at 10 Downing Street.

Further intelligence on the situation in Norway was received in London from Dormer, whose staff had had the foresight to bring a portable wireless set with them and strung a makeshift aerial up a flagstaff while they were at Hamar. Prior to his first message, Dormer had received a request from the Norwegian Government for "immediate military and aerial assistance". The first message sent by Dormer arrived at the Foreign Office in London around 1630. This stated:

A typical scene of German troops on the move near Oslo. (Imperial War Museum HU104703)

Oslo has capitulated. Government are at Hamar, 15 kilometres north of which I and several members of staff are staying. United States Legation has taken charge of His Majesty's Legation. Reported one German ship sunk by fire from Droebak; Tonsberg, Bergen, Trondheim, Narvik occupied. Lillestrom bombed and in flames. French Minister and I would be grateful for any reassuring news as Government anxious and are subject to strong pressure to declare a war on His Majesty's Government.

This was followed by two more pleas, which stressed that Norway needed strong and quick assistance before the Germans established themselves, and that strategic airfields, such as Sola and Fornebu, had been taken by the Germans.

In the ensuing chaos, it appears that as early as 0700 on that day a message was sent to Dormer indicating that Britain was going to support Norway, but this message never got through. This was followed by a more detailed response timed at 1255, which said:

You should at once assure the Norwegian Government that in view of the German invasion of their country; His Majesty's Government has [sic] decided forthwith to extend their full aid to Norway and will fight the war in full association with them. You should at the same time inform the Norwegian Government that His Majesty's Government are taking immediate measures to deal with the German occupation of Bergen and Trondheim and will be glad to learn what the

Picture taken after the battle in Elverum. (Author's Collection)

Norwegian Government's own plans are, so that subsequent British dispositions may be in conformity with them. His Majesty's Government would in the meantime suggest that the Norwegian Government should if possible destroy the Stavanger aerodrome should they be unable to hold it.

This news was relayed to the Norwegian Government, which received some comfort from it, but the good news did not last long. Word had got out to the Germans that the Government was at Hamar, and the German Air Attaché, Spiller, with some *Fallschirmjägers*, had decided to try and capture them. Those at Hamar learned that the Germans were on their way, causing another move, this time to Elverum. Meanwhile, word was passed to the diplomats and in the chaos Dormer ended up heading towards Lillehammer. Somewhere in the next few hours the wireless set and its operator were separated from Dormer, so very little information reached London for the following few days. The main part of the Norwegian leadership set up in a school at Elverum around 2130, and news reached them that the German Ambassador, Bräuer, wished to meet with them. It was decided, against the advice of Carl Hambro (the president of the Norwegian parliament – the Stortings), that the Foreign Minister, Koht, and three MPs should meet Bräuer and at least hear him out. The feeling was that unless Bräuer had something new to offer, and potentially a way out of this apparently serious situation for Norway, then the previous decision to go to war would stand. They knew that Quisling had broadcast to the Norwegian people, and it was felt that any solution involving him would be totally unacceptable. Given the fact that further moves might be necessary over the coming days, it was felt it would be difficult for the parliament to discuss and agree any options, so Hambro suggested that a "constitutional prokura"

Pictures taken after the battle in Elverum. (Author's Collection)

should be given to the government, allowing it the authority to "attend to the interests of the nation and make those decisions deemed necessary until such times as it is possible to convene formally again". There was no formal vote, but no voices were raised in objection and the Norwegian Parliament would not formally meet again for over five years. An agreed statement was read out over the airwaves next day, confirming that the Nygaardsvold administration was the only legal authority of the country that had been endorsed by the King.

Bräuer met with the Norwegians early in the morning of the 10th; he suggested he should meet with King Häkon alone, whilst it was counter-offered that Koht and some MPs should sit in. Bräuer initially maintained his position, but the King wanted witnesses to what was said. He argued that, as a constitutional monarch, he had no real authority to make political decisions without his government agreeing, and as he did not speak German an interpreter would be required. Outmanoeuvred, Bräuer gave in and agreed that Koht could be present. The meeting was a tense affair. Bräuer suggested again that the Germans had come as friends and been forced to react to British provocation. He added that the "Norwegian forces had not laid down their weapons as had been agreed". Further points included that the Norwegian Government had ordered a futile resistance, that the Nygaardsvold administration would have to go and be replaced by the Quisling one, which the King would have to recognise, and he should return immediately to Oslo to endorse him.

King Häkon said very little during all of this, except to say that he could not support a "government that was not the people's choice". No solution was agreed on, except that Bräuer would telephone Koht during a stop on his way back to Oslo. After he had left, the King told Koht that he could not accept Quisling as Prime Minister. He would have no option but to abdicate if his present government wanted to accept the German demands to avoid bloodshed.

The King then travelled to Nybergsund, where most of the Cabinet was located. News of the earlier meeting was recounted and he repeated that he could not approve Quisling, who had no public or parliamentary support. However, if his government wanted to accept Germany's demands in order to avoid a war, so be it: he would abdicate. One of the ministers present later wrote:

> This made a great impression on us all. We had through the five years in government learned to respect and appreciate our King and now, through his words, he came to us as a great man, just and forceful; a leader in these fatal times to our country.

Meanwhile, the politicians looked to the military men to come up with a plan to sort out the mess. Having travelled to Hamar with the Defence Minister, Ljungberg, two of the top military men, Laake and Hatledal, were expecting a conference with senior politicians, but were left waiting outside. A message then arrived from the HOK that several bus-loads of Germans were on their way, which resulted in the prompt move to Elverum None of the politicians had much to say to the Army chiefs, apart from demanding that they stop the German advance; nor were they invited to join the politicians on their bus. After a few hours doing their best to control the situation by issuing orders over the telephone, Laake and Hatledal travelled to Elverum, about 70 miles from Oslo, where they met the rest of the HOK and eventually arrived at Rena, where they arrived in the early hours of 10 April.

Information was scarce in the general chaos. In the early afternoon of 10 April, Laake gathered his core team for a conference, and upon hearing that the Minister of Justice, Wold, was nearby, took the fateful decision to invite him over to share intelligence. Laake then started to present a somewhat negative assessment of the situation. It seemed that key storage depots and barracks had been taken over by the Germans, and those units which had managed to mobilise were low on ammunition and other vital stores. None of his officers expressed any criticism of their leader To the civilian Wold, the officers appeared to have given up already; and while under the surface it appeared Hatledal was trying to bring some order out of the chaos, Wold believed them all to be "weak and not the right men for the situation".

Wold returned to the seat of government and recounted his version of events in strong words. He did not paint General Laake in a good light. The consensus was that he was not the man for the job and "his resignation would be accepted". Thoughts turned to his successor and the spotlight fell on the current Inspector-General of the Army, Otto Ruge, then 58 years old. It seems that without even asking if he wanted the job, he was promoted and appointed as Laake's successor. Defence Minister Ljungberg did defend Laake to some extent, but his support was overwhelmed by the opposition of others. Laake was asked to come to Nybergsund, where he arrived with an aide in the early hours of 11 April. He was taken into a room where Ljungberg broke the news to him. Laake spoke to his aide and advised him what was happening. Apparently he was "unhappy, but also somewhat relieved". The official line, announced to the Norwegian public, was that he had volunteered to step down on the grounds of age. It seems that no one had thought to tell Ruge of his new appointment and he first heard of it in a telephone conversation with the Minister of Trade and Supply, T. Lie, on the evening of 10 April, but dismissed it as a misunderstanding. The next morning he was officially informed by Ljungberg and asked to come to Rena. At the subsequent meeting, the head of the Navy, Admiral Diesen, agreed to accept orders from Ruge, so the Norwegians effectively had a supreme commander. Ruge's first plan was to establish a series of blocking lines, to slow the German advance while mobilisation continued and Britain and France arrived. This was followed on 13 April by orders to blow up all road and railway bridges near Oslo and to cut the telephone wires. His maxim for these early days was: "Fight we shall and we must fight with what we have." Perhaps inspired by this, many men, young and old, tried to join up and so the army's strength grew, but there was a shortage of experienced leaders and weapons such as machine guns and field, anti-tank and anti-aircraft guns.

The government had relocated to Nybergsund, where, on the afternoon of 11 April, the *Luftwaffe* appeared, with several *HE111* bombers. They bombed the town, just missing killing the King, Prince Olav and senior members of the government. The Prime Minister, Nygaardsvold, was visibly shaken by the bombing and suggested that perhaps they should consider going to Sweden, but it is unclear whether this was to be a temporary move or as a government-in-exile. Other ministers persuaded Nygaardsvold to stay in Norway and move to Rena, where Ruge was setting up his headquarters, and from

A German infantry commander consults with the leader of his armour support in a Kl.Pz.Bef.Wg command tank. (Imperial War Museum MH2621)

there – if necessary under German pressure – to go to Gudbrandsdal. The Norwegians did, however, ask politely what might happen if members of the royal family entered Sweden temporarily for a "rest". The reply was that they ran the risk of being interred. Upon hearing this, King Häkon refused even to consider any suggestion of going to Sweden. He and his family would remain with their people, at least for the time being.

Sir Claude Dormer and the Assistant Air Attaché, Dore first met Ruge on the morning of 11 April. Dore later described him as having the "reputation of being a soldier and a man of outstanding quality. The subsequent relations of the other attachés and myself with him at the GHQ fully confirmed this." At this meeting Dormer learnt that the Norwegians were happy that Allied support was coming and had rejected out of hand any negotiations with the Germans. After the air attack on Nybergsund, it was decided not to let many people know the whereabouts of the government. When they moved from Nybergsund, it was to a secret location, and it took a while for the diplomats to find out where they were. Dormer eventually travelled to meet them at Drevsjø, near the Swedish border, about 180 miles north-east of Oslo in central Norway. He later said: "With the exception of the Crown Prince, who looked none the worse, they were all very exhausted, and I urged that, if possible they should take it in turns to sleep a night or two in peace across the border." He also commented to Lord Halifax, the Foreign Secretary, of his experiences in Norway:

His Majesty and his Government were called upon to decide at a moment's notice in a [state of] more or less complete unpreparedness and physical exhaustion. I

After landing a company of *Fallschirmjäger* assemble in Björnfell close to the Swedish border. (Bob Gerritsen Collection)

was in touch with them most days, but there was no time for conversation. When they asked me to come to them it was invariably to discuss on a particular question, in a crowded room, standing up; in the kind of conditions that might be described as chaos and confusion. And yet, although they had no administrative machine to deal with – since everyone became scattered – they have succeeded in establishing some semblance of government in districts free of the Germans.

Back in Oslo, Quisling was trying to get some kind of government up and running, but his efforts were fraught with difficulties. The King had refused to deal with him to the point of abdication. When Quisling appointed ministers to his new government, few of them accepted his invitation, and he had little popular support. On 13 April, the Germans banned Quisling from broadcasting on the radio, and by 15 April, after reports from Bräuer and others on his incompetence had gone back to Berlin, Hitler had decided his time was over. On this day Bräuer informed Quisling that Hitler had decided he could no longer be leader and was to be replaced by a German. His "government" had lasted five days and achieved nothing. However, Quisling later came back into favour and left a lasting legacy – a new word, his surname, which became another word for traitor and collaborator.

6

HMS *Glowworm* and other naval engagements

In late March and early April, the Allies had been slowly planning an intervention in Norway, with the main idea still being an expedition based around the port of Narvik. Admiral Sir Edward Evans was appointed as commander of the naval side of the operation and hoisted his flag on 4 April on the cruiser HMS *Aurora*. The plan was that HMS *Aurora*, together with another cruiser, would move the advance guard of troops across to Narvik. Hand-in-hand with this was a plan for four battalions to move in another four cruisers to Stavanger and Bergen. These four battalions were the 5th Leicestershire Regiment, in HMS *Devonshire*; the 4th Lincolnshire Regiment, in HMS *Berwick*; HMS *York* had the 4th King's Own Yorkshire Light Infantry; and the 8th Sherwood Foresters were to go in HMS *Glasgow*. All of these were territorial battalions, not first line troops. In more comfort, moving on two troopships which were pre-war liners, were the Hallamshire battalion of the York and Lancaster Regiment on the *Chrobry* (a Polish ship) and the only regular unit allocated, the 1st Scots Guards in the *Batory*.

It was also decided to send the battle cruiser HMS *Renown* to guard these ships and prevent any Norwegian interference. Additionally, 19 submarines, including two French and one Polish were sent to the Kattegat and Skagerrak area of the southern North Sea, to protect against any German naval forces which would have to cross this area. As planned, the Allies also laid minefields off the Norwegian coast. The RAF had seen a number of German ships steaming for Norway, so several Royal Navy ships based around Scapa Flow put to sea. It was thought that these German warships were going to try and break out into the North Atlantic and disrupt the Allied convoy system. At 1730 on 7 April, Admiral Forbes, the commander of the Home Fleet, ordered every available ship to raise steam, and around 2000 a force of two battleships, one battle cruiser, two cruisers and ten destroyers sailed from Scapa Flow. About an hour later, two cruisers and ten destroyers left Rosyth. They steamed in a north-easterly direction for the rest of the night, but dawn on 8 April brought no sight of any German ships. However, around 0800 messages were received of a contact by HMS *Glowworm*, some 300 miles to the south of the main fleet.

HMS *Glowworm*, a G-class destroyer built for the Royal Navy in the mid-1930s, spent part of 1936 and 1937 in Spanish waters, enforcing the arms blockade imposed by Britain and France during the Spanish Civil War. After the outbreak of the Second World War, *Glowworm* was transferred home from the Mediterranean Fleet, with the role of escorting shipping in the South Western Approaches and later with the 22nd Destroyer Flotilla in

HMS *Glowworm* pictured before the outbreak of the Second World War. (Author's Collection)

the North Sea. In March 1940, she joined the 1st Destroyer Flotilla of the Home Fleet at Scapa Flow. *Glowworm* displaced 1,350 tons, had a length of 323ft, a beam of 33ft and a draught of 12ft 5in. Her Parsons geared steam turbines, driving two shafts, developed 34,000 shaft horsepower and gave a maximum speed of 36 knots (about 40mph). A full fuel load of 470 tons provided a range of 5,530 nautical miles at a speed of 15 knots (17mph). In peacetime, her complement was 137 officers and men. *Glowworm* had four single 45 calibre 4.7in Mark IX guns. She had two quadruple Mark I mounts with 0.5in Vickers Mark III machine guns for anti-aircraft defence, and was the test ship for the new quintuple torpedo tube mounts for 21in (533mm) torpedoes. She was fitted with one depth charge rail and two throwers; 20 depth charges were originally carried, but this was increased to 35 after the outbreak of war.

On 5 April, Glowworm was part of the escort force for the battle cruiser HMS *Renown*, together with her sister ships HMS *Greyhound*, HMS *Hero* and HMS *Hyperion*, covering mine-laying operations. During this period, one of her crew was washed overboard and, after receiving permission to look for him, *Glowworm* lost contact with the rest of their group. After retrieving the lost man from the sea, they steamed northwards in the hope of rejoining the other ships, but because of bad weather they failed to make contact. By the morning of 8 April, *Glowworm* was a little north of the latitude of Trondheim when her lookouts sighted two German destroyers. These were the Z11 *Bernd von Arnim* and Z18 *Hans Lüdemann*, part of the German forces heading for Narvik, which had lost contact with the capital ships they were meant to be escorting – the *Scharnhorst* and *Gneisenau*. In spite of being outnumbered, the commander of the *Glowworm*, Lieutenant-Commander Gerard Broadmead Roope, had no hesitation in attacking. *Glowworm* opened fire and the German destroyers attempted to disengage, signalling for help. One German vessel suffered considerable damage in the running battle, which went on for an hour

Captain Roope of the *Glowworm*. (Author's Collection)

or more. Both sides sent messages asking for support, but other German forces were much closer. The cruiser *Admiral Hipper* was only a short distance away, off Trondheim, and quickly headed to the area. The *Hipper*, skippered by Captain Helmuth Heye, was armed with 8in guns, which easily out-ranged those on the *Glowworm*. Making for the area at full speed, the *Hipper* spotted the *Glowworm* at 0950. The *Hipper* initially had difficulty in distinguishing *Glowworm* from the *Bernd von Arnim*, but opened fire ten minutes later at a range of about 9,000 yards, her 8in guns firing a shell weighing around 250lbs. *Glowworm* was hit by the *Hipper*'s fourth salvo and started giving off smoke. In an attempt to break visual contact with *Hipper*, she turned into her own smoke, but the German cruiser's radar-directed guns were unaffected by this. When the *Glowworm* emerged from her smoke, the range was short enough that the *Hipper*'s 4.1in guns could also range in. *Glowworm*'s radio room, bridge and forward 4.7in gun were destroyed, and she suffered further hits in the engine room, the captain's day cabin and to the mast. As the latter came crashing down, it short-circuited the wiring, setting off the ship's siren. At 1010, Lieutenant-Commander Roope gave an order for five torpedoes to be fired at a range of about 1,000 yards, but all missed their target as Captain Heye had kept *Hipper*'s bow pointing towards *Glowworm* throughout the battle to minimise the risk from such an attack. The *Glowworm* fell back through her smoke screen to try to launch a second torpedo attack, but Heye followed her to finish her off before she could fire any further torpedoes. The ships were very close when *Hipper* emerged from the smoke and Heye

HMS *Glowworm* pictured as she is turning to try to ram. (Imperial War Museum FL1973)

ordered a hard turn to starboard to reduce the range and possibly ram the destroyer. *Hipper* was slow to answer her helm and *Glowworm* struck the cruiser near the anchor. *Glowworm*'s bow broke off in the collision, and the rest of the ship scraped along *Hipper*'s side, gouging several holes in her hull and destroying the forward starboard torpedo mounting. One German sailor was knocked overboard in the collision. *Hipper* took on some 500 tons of water before the leaks could be stopped, but otherwise was not seriously damaged. *Glowworm*, now ablaze, drifted clear and her boilers exploded at 1024. She soon sank, with the loss of over 100 of her crew.

The *Hipper* hove to in a bid to rescue her man overboard and the survivors from *Glowworm*. The German sailor was not found, but 40 of the British crew were recovered, although at least six later died of their wounds. Lieutenant Ramsay, who was the senior surviving officer, told his rescuers that *Glowworm*'s turn towards the *Hipper* was probably accidental as neither the helm nor the emergency rudder were manned when the ships collided. German accounts mention only four torpedoes being fired by *Glowworm*, but according to the British all ten were fired. The British accounts were confirmed by photographic evidence from after the collision which showed all of her torpedo tubes empty.

Roope, who drowned when he could no longer hold on to a rope whilst being pulled up the side of the German cruiser, was posthumously awarded the Victoria Cross, becoming the first VC recipient of the Second World War. The award was in part justified by the recommendation of Captain Heye, who wrote to the British authorities via the

Red Cross, telling of the valiant courage Lieutenant Commander Roope had shown when engaging a far superior ship in close battle. Lieutenant Ramsay was also awarded the Distinguished Service Order. Petty Officer Scott, Engine Room Artificer Gregg and Able Seaman Merrit were awarded the Conspicuous Gallantry Medal; all awards being made after the end of the war.

The Victoria Cross citation was as follows:

The London Gazette, Tuesday 10 July, 1945 - (From the Admiralty, Whitehall, SW1)The King has been graciously pleased to approve the award of the Victoria Cross for valour to:

The late Lieutenant-Commander Gerard Broadmead Roope, Royal Navy.

On the 8th April, 1940, HMS *Glowworm* was proceeding alone in heavy weather towards a rendezvous in West Fjord, when she met and engaged two enemy destroyers, scoring at least one hit on them. The enemy broke off the action and headed north, to lead the *Glowworm* on to his supporting forces. The Commanding Officer, whilst correctly appreciating the intentions of the enemy, at once gave chase. The German heavy cruiser, *Admiral Hipper*, was sighted closing towards the *Glowworm* at high speed and an enemy report was sent which was received by HMS *Renown*. Because of the heavy sea, the *Glowworm* could not shadow the enemy and the Commanding Officer therefore decided to attack with torpedoes and then to close in order to inflict as much damage as possible. Five torpedoes were fired and later the remaining five, but without success. The *Glowworm* was badly hit; one gun was out of action and her speed was much reduced, but with the other three guns still firing she closed and rammed the *Admiral Hipper*. As the *Glowworm* drew away, she opened fire again and scored one hit at a range of 400 yards. The *Glowworm*, badly stove in forward and riddled with enemy fire, heeled over to starboard, and the Commanding Officer gave the order to abandon her. Shortly afterwards she capsized and sank. The *Admiral Hipper* hove to for at least an hour picking up survivors but the loss of life was heavy, only 31 out of the *Glowworm*'s complement of 149 being saved.

Full information concerning this action has only recently been received and the Victoria Cross is bestowed in recognition of the great valour of the Commanding Officer who, after fighting off a superior force of destroyers, sought out and reported a powerful enemy unit, and then fought his ship to the end against overwhelming odds, finally ramming the enemy with supreme coolness.

It is recorded that Roope was one of those who survived an icy ordeal in the water but, in the throes of holding on to a rope thrown to him from the *Hipper*, his numbed fingers lost their grip. His body was never found; he is commemorated on the Portsmouth Naval Memorial to the Missing, Panel 36, Column 3.

The *Hipper* sustained some damage in the engagement, including losing around 130ft of armoured belt and her starboard torpedo tubes, but was able to make it to Trondheim harbour. After the campaign, repairs to the damage caused by *Glowworm* took several months, so *Glowworm*'s sacrifice was not in vain.

Glowworm's desperate signals had been picked up by ships around 150 miles away to the north, under the command of Admiral Whitworth. He ordered his group to turn south, but it was a hopeless gesture, as heavy seas prevented the escorting destroyers from keeping up and progress was slow. By the time *Renown* and the others could have reached the area, the action was long over. Meanwhile, after completing their task, the destroyers sent to lay the northernmost minefield were ordered by the Admiralty in London to join the Whitworth force. Faced with this slight change of plan, Whitworth changed course again to rendezvous with them. This move meant that the Vestfjord, on the way to Narvik, was basically unguarded, allowing the Germans to slip in unscathed.

Members of HMS *Glowworm*'s crew later gave their accounts of the events surrounding the sinking of their ship.

Bert Harris had joined the Navy in Portsmouth on 14 February 1938, together with his elder brother. He recalled:

I was 18 years old, my brother was 20. We did six months training and then I was sent to HMS *Glowworm* in Portsmouth. From there we went out to the Mediterranean at the time of the Spanish Civil War. I was there at the start of the Second World War in 1939. In November 1939 we were ordered back to England where we started patrols in the Channel, bringing contraband ships back and also convoy duties. We were based at Harwich for a time when the magnetic mine scare first started. We saw many a ship sunk by this method. Things stayed like this until March 1940 when we went to Scapa Flow. After a short spell there we were ordered to proceed to sea.

It was on 5 April 1940 that the *Glowworm* with three other destroyers made up the escort for HMS *Renown* and steamed across the North Sea, although we never had any idea what the operation was for at that time. It was a rough and very cold journey. All that day rumours kept going around about the German Navy being at sea, and we were hoping it was true so we would get the chance to meet them, as we felt pretty sure of ourselves being with the *Renown*. My brother and I were both young stokers on the *Glowworm*. We both lived on the same mess deck and of course we thought a great deal about each other, as we had joined the Navy together and had been together all the time. As we rolled and pitched our way across the North Sea he told me to be very careful whenever I had to go on watch and hang on tight as the sea was washing over us. And so it went on until the morning of 6 April when the alarm went out that a man was washed overboard, he was a torpedo man. A signal was made to *Renown*. We were told to turn and search for him, it was hopeless in such weather but our skipper turned the *Glowworm* and began the search. That left us all alone as the rest of the group carried on course. We never saw them again. Needless to say the man was never found. We steamed around all that day hoping to make a rendezvous with the *Renown* again, but no luck.

The following morning on 7 April our luck seemed to be right out when another man was reported over the side. A search found him tangled in ropes which were trailing over the side. When they pulled him in he was badly injured and there was no hope for him. Well, that was a bad omen indeed. For two consecutive mornings, something nasty had happened and we were all asking what the third morning would bring. We were still on our own in the great North Sea, or at least it seemed that way.

And so I come to the morning of 8 April 1940. I was asleep in my hammock when suddenly the loud ring of alarm bells sounded and all the off-watch men scrambled to their action stations; mine being in the after part of the ship, in the magazine supplying shells for the gun crews. Not a very nice place to be in.

As I made my way along the upper deck I saw another destroyer in the distance and wondered who it could be. After a short while I soon found out. Our Captain, Lieutenant-Commander Roope, sent a signal asking her nationality as she flew no ensign. The next moment she answered us with a salvo from her guns. Then the fun started. After exchanging round for round with her she turned and steamed away with us in pursuit. After a while we were told we were chasing her into a squadron of our own fleet who could be seen in the distance. However, we soon found out our mistake as it was a German squadron that we were being led into. But instead of turning and running for it, our Captain took the *Glowworm* into action against the German cruiser *Admiral Von Hipper* and her escort of four destroyers. While we kept hard at it supplying the guns it seemed as if all hell broke loose. The *Hipper* opened up with her big guns and started to knock us about. She seemed to be hitting us hard as we were chasing around in the heavy seas getting into position.

All our guns were firing, but our torpedoes which we fired missed the *Hipper* although they went very close to her. Our Captain was a good seaman and he knew how to handle his ship. By now, we were badly damaged but he kept manoeuvring the *Glowworm* so that it was easier for the gun crews, but this could not go on much longer as we had a very bad list to the starboard side. Most of the guns were soon out of action. I was still in the magazine when the *Glowworm* gave an extra thrust forward and there was a crash and a shudder. The lights went out, the ship rolled and tossed and suddenly seemed to settle well on her starboard side. Then came the order to abandon ship. We had just made our last big play. Our Captain had done all he could and what was right to the last. He had turned the *Glowworm* and drove her straight at, and rammed the *Hipper*, causing quite a bit of damage to her.

By this time I and others had made our way to the upper deck. As I passed the place where my brother's action station was, I called to him but there was no answer, so I went to look for him. I got to the hatchway and looked down, it was pitch black, water swirled around. I kept calling but had to get out as we were well over on our side by now. I reached the upper deck and was shocked by the mess we were in. The Germans had shot us to pieces and were still doing so. Only one of our guns was firing now and it seemed strange to me as it was the aftermost gun. He must have been a very brave man as the ship was sinking and men were jumping over the side, but he kept that gun going for quite a time.

As I reached the upper deck I got my first look at the *Hipper*. She seemed to be such a huge ship with her Swastika painted on her foremost deck. They were still firing at us with their big guns and machine guns. I crawled on my hands and knees along the deck to a lifebelt locker and was lucky to find some there. I passed some to others and strapped one around me although I was in two minds whether to jump or stay where I was, as it was a big thing to leave the ship and jump into the North Sea. So I waited and talked to a stoker who had his leg blown off. Another young stoker locked himself in the galley.

One thing struck me as funny at the time; yet another stoker had jumped over and had got washed back again. As he picked himself up he said he would rather stay put as it was too cold in the water.

I remember a young officer shouting "Open all sea cocks", although we were sinking fast now. I never saw him again. Then the Captain came and told us to get off as soon as we could. That was the last time I saw Lieutenant-Commander Roope. By this time the ship had turned over onto her starboard side and the siren was blowing and smoke was belching from the funnels.

I scrambled down the port side and then onto the bottom of the *Glowworm*. She turned right over in the water. All the time the Germans were pumping shells into us. At last I decided to take the plunge and jumped into the sea and swam as hard as I could from the sinking ship. After what seemed a long time I stopped swimming and just let the lifebelt keep me afloat. I watched the end of HMS *Glowworm*. The Germans finished her and she began to sink below the waves with men still standing on her. I felt lost and just could not realise that my ship had gone. I didn't know what to do next; one minute I was tossed onto the top of a huge wave and the next down into a steep valley of water. I was just drifting, swimming made no difference. Then suddenly right in front of me I saw the German ship. I was being carried towards her. I could see some of our chaps being pulled up the side of her. I swam as fast as I could, because I thought if I never reached her I would be lost forever. It was at this moment that I felt the underwater explosion and a kick like a mule. It must have been some depth charges on the *Glowworm*. I was nearly all in but I managed to look up and see some German sailors who threw a rope. I grabbed it and that was the last I knew for a long time.

I finally came to my senses to find a group of Germans standing around me. When I moved, one of them gave me a cigarette and asked me if I felt alright. I was under a cradle of electric light bulbs which they had put over me to keep me warm. My first words were for news of my brother, but there was none. I felt sick and stunned as it was weeks before I could realise that he had gone with all the others. All that was left were 29 survivors of that grim and terrible day. The following day only 27, two having died of oil fuel poisoning. They were buried at sea.

I must say that they were the best German sailors I ever knew. They looked after us the best they could. Their Captain came to us and told us that our Captain had been a very brave man.

We were all locked below decks with armed sentries. We were there until the

Some of the few survivors from HMS *Glowworm* being picked up. (Imperial War Museum HU104705)

following Friday. The *Hipper* was on her way to Norway, where she discharged the troops she was carrying. Her mission completed, she made for the open sea again.

Bert "Ginger" Lowman was a 19-year-old stoker mechanic on the *Glowworm*. He remembered:

On the morning of 8 April 1940 at a quarter to eight the alarm bells went for action stations. I was supposed to be on watch at eight o'clock but once you go into action you stay where you are. I went to the Petty Officers' Mess as an ammunition supplier, where the number two gun support was situated. It was those 15 minutes that saved my life because I know my boiler room got blown out of the ship. If I had been on watch at the time I wouldn't have been here now. I often think of the poor devils that was down where I should have been.

A shell exploded in the Petty Officers' Mess but luckily it exploded on the other side of the gun support. The concussion knocked me out. When I came to, I found that the back of my left hand was gone and I had shrapnel in my left arm and leg. The floor of the Petty Officers' Mess was covered in blood. It looked like a butcher's shop. I felt the ship listing over. She was going down. I began sliding down with it. I managed to crawl to the other side and up on deck. I remember seeing one of our stokers running along by the lifebelt lockers. He didn't seem to be injured. I didn't know what happened to him but he didn't get picked up.

Just as I got in the water she heaved right over and I got caught up in ropes and wires underwater. I thought to myself "I've had it now". I struggled and struggled and all of a sudden my head popped out of the water. I could see she was about to go down so I swam as hard as I could to get away from her as I didn't want to get sucked down. I could feel myself being drawn back. Eventually I managed to get away from her. I was swimming with one leg and one arm heading towards the *Hipper*. I think I was one of the last to leave the *Glowworm*.

I was lucky that I didn't swallow any oil when I was in the water. There were about three or four inches of oil on the surface of the sea. I know a lot of chaps swallowed it. But as my mouth and nose became blocked with it, I put my head underwater below the layer of oil and cleared it. I kept doing this until I got picked up. The Germans put a rope over the side with a loop in it. At first I grabbed it with my good arm but halfway up I didn't have enough strength to hang on, so I let go and went back into the water. They put it down again. So this time I put my right arm through the loop and I tucked it under my left armpit. As they pulled me up like that, I could feel my arm coming out from under my armpit. I thought that I would let go again before they could get hold of me. Just at the last minute as I began to let go I could feel hands on me and blacked out.

The next thing I remember I woke up in a bunk in the German sickbay and there were a couple of German sailors rubbing me down with towels getting all of the oil off of me. They congratulated us on a good fight. I didn't realise we had rammed the *Hipper* until the other chaps told me later on. We must have injured a lot of them in the battle as I looked to another part of the sickbay which was full of German sailors. Somebody told me that during the action the Captain's dog was sitting between his legs and was killed by shrapnel, but he wasn't touched.

Duncan Blair, who in 1940 was a 19-year-old Able Seaman on the *Glowworm*, recalled:

The *Glowworm* was with the *Renown* to screen the minelayers that intended to mine the entrance to Narvik. On the morning of 7 April 1940 we lost a man overboard by the name of Ricky. Able Seaman Ricky, who was a lifebuoy sentry. We were ordered to turn around and search for him. Well this we did, and we did it for hours and hours, and unfortunately he was never recovered. We turned to rejoin the unit. After steaming for what seemed hours and hours we were unable to find them. We did however run into some very heavy weather. In fact it was force 10 on the Richter scale. Believe me it was really terrible weather. I've never experienced anything like it in my life before nor since.

On the morning of 8 April, as we were steaming in the hope of picking up the rest of the unit, we came across two German destroyers which we immediately engaged. We were fortunate enough to inflict some damage on one of the destroyers and they both turned and fled immediately back into the squalls that were blowing across the ocean. When we appeared on the other side of the squall, lo and behold in front of us was this bloody great German ship, the *Hipper*. The Captain ordered smoke to be laid so we had a smoke screen, and we turned around and went back into it. When we came back out of it the next thing was to fire torpedoes at her, which was done. But unfortunately none of them found their mark, which may have made a big difference to the whole episode.

In the meantime we had received many hits. We had dived back into the smoke screen. When we came out the Captain said "stand by to ram" and that is what happened. We turned around and we ran straight into the *Hipper* - smashing into her side and tearing a gaping hole in her. I believe this was instrumental in disabling her water desalination plant. As we turned away we received many hits, some of them very serious. In fact one of them ripped a hole in the engine room in the starboard side of the ship. The Captain, then realising that we were sinking, ordered us to abandon ship.

I was in the Petty Officers' Mess as an ammunition handler. When the order came I went through onto the starboard side of the fo'c'sle. There was a Carley raft there which was still intact. I believe it was the only one that was left in that condition. But to undo the lashings was impossible as the seawater had tightened the ropes up considerably. I could not undo it by hand. There was a young Able Seaman there by the name of Morris from Bournemouth. I asked him if he had a knife on him because I wasn't allowed to carry a knife being in ammunition supply. He produced a very small penknife that his girlfriend had given him. It had on it "Souvenir of Bournemouth" or something like that. I managed to cut the Carley raft free from its lashings. Morris and I heaved it over the side. There were two splashes, one as the raft hit the water and one as I hit the water alongside it. I managed to scramble aboard but what happened to Morris I'll never know because from that day to this I never saw him again.

The raft slid alongside the ship and me and the other men in the water managed to push off so that we weren't carried into the gaping hole in the starboard side. Eventually after we had cleared the ship I turned round and saw the ship sliding under. The last person to talk to our Captain was a Petty Officer named Townsend. Both he and the Captain used to play cricket for the flotilla. The Captain said to Townsend: "I don't think we'll be playing cricket for a long time yet." Then he proceeded to go to the wardroom where the sea cocks were situated to open them and sink the ship.

We were in the water for quite a considerable time before the *Hipper* returned and proceeded to pick up survivors. Among the survivors a few names have come to mind; Petty Officer Townsend, Petty Officer Walter Scott, Leading Seaman Smith from *Southampton*, Leading Seaman Shergold, Able Seaman Andrew Perry, Able Seaman Edgar Seeward, Able Seaman Bob Rainer, Able Seaman Mallett, Able Seaman Merritt and Petty Officer Gregg.

Eventually I was helped out of the water with a rope. From my waist down I was absolutely frozen. I never felt so cold in all my life and I don't think I've warmed up yet. We were taken to Wilhelmshaven and handed over to the military authorities where they proceeded to interrogate us. Two of our ratings who were ASDIC operators had an immediate change of status by becoming torpedo men. After interrogation we were sent to a prison camp in a place called Spannenburg in Germany, where we were registered in an officers' camp of all things. I was given POW number 161. Then we were sent to a naval camp near Bremerhaven. Whilst there I met two Flight Sergeants who had been shot down over Germany on the day war was declared, operating a leaflet drop.

As the main group of warships steamed north on what might seem a wild goose chase, there were developments further south. A Polish Navy submarine, the *Orzel* (*Eagle*), was patrolling the Skagerrak, and around noon on 8 April her captain, Lieutenant-Commander J. Grudzinski, spotted an approaching merchant vessel. She was not flying any flag but he was able, using the maximum magnification on the periscope, to see the name *Rio de Janeiro* on her bows. This was one of the German transports destined for Bergen. Pre-war she had been a general cargo ship but did carry a few passengers, shuttling back and forth between Europe and South America. But for this trip to Norway she was loaded with military stores, including four 10.5cm guns, six 20mm anti-aircraft guns, over 300 soldiers, 73 horses, 71 lorries and nearly 300 tons of stores. Grudzinski ordered the submarine to surface and had a signaller flash a message to the *Rio* stating: "Stop engines. The Master with ship's papers is to report on board immediately." But instead of stopping, the *Rio* increased speed and turned towards the coast. *Orzel* gave chase, firing warning shots from a Lewis gun, which had the desired effect and the *Rio* stopped. A boat was lowered but made no real effort to row across to the *Orzel*. Meanwhile, the *Rio* was sending out radio messages, which although in code, were picked up by the *Orzel*. Grudzinski ordered another flash message to be sent, which instructed the *Rio* to abandon ship as he was about to fire a torpedo. This was ignored by the *Rio*, so at around 1145 the *Orzel* fired. This struck the *Rio* amidships and the *Orzel* disappeared under the surface. Through his periscope, Grudzinski saw smoke pouring from the *Rio*, and soon afterwards crowds of men in army uniforms appeared on the deck. They started to throw lifebelts and pieces of wood overboard and then followed them into the cold water. *Rio* listed and turned slowly over to starboard, but did not appear to be sinking. Fortunately for the Germans, a number of fishing boats in the area picked up some of the survivors.

As the *Rio* had been close to the coast, the coastguards had seen both the ship and the submarine. This had been reported to the military, and an aircraft was sent to investigate. Meanwhile, *Orzel* had stayed in the vicinity and around 1215 fired a second torpedo, which finished off the *Rio* and she quickly sank. Around 150 men were rescued from the sea, but nearly 200 were killed. Regretfully, none of the horses could be saved. Later, the Norwegian coastguards plotted the position of the wreck of the *Rio de Janeiro*, decided that it was just outside the three-mile territorial water limit and so was a legitimate target. The *Orzel* slipped away and later surfaced to send a report to London, the implications of which seemed to have been ignored.

Meanwhile, further east near the Svenner Lighthouse, HMS *Trident* (from the 2nd Submarine Flotilla) spotted the German tanker *Stedingen*, which was heading for the Stavanger area laden with a vital cargo of aviation fuel. The captain of the *Trident*, Lieutenant-Commander A. Seale, later wrote:

> A large tanker, laden, with no national marks or name on her side was sighted steaming west outside territorial waters. This vessel appeared most suspicious and was thought to be a German auxiliary. I decided to investigate and at 1215 surfaced on her port quarter and fired a blank shot. She turned to starboard for territorial waters and increased speed. I then fired two rounds of SAP (Semi Armoured Piercing), which fell just short in line with the bridge. This caused her to stop engines. I closed on her quarter with a "Do Not Transmit" pennant flying and made by lamp, "Abandon ship. I shall torpedo you in five minutes."

The *Stedingen* was still outside Norwegian waters and her crew started to abandon ship, but the sea cocks had been opened and she started to sink. Lifeboats had been launched and made for shore; *Trident* intercepted the boats and the captain, Schäfer, was detained. The *Stedingen* was finished off with a second torpedo before *Trident* headed off. The rest of the *Stedingen*'s crew made it ashore to Stavern. Later the same day, the *Trident* fired a torpedo at the *Kreta*, a supply ship bound for Kristiansand, but it missed and she escaped into Norwegian territorial waters.

The German survivors from the *Rio* were taken ashore and were questioned soon after their arrival. They said that they had been on their way to Bergen to protect it against British aggression. This news filtered out via the *Reuters* network around 2000 and was flashed around the world, but for unknown reasons this was not forwarded to Admiral Forbes, the commander of the Home Fleet, until around 2300. Forbes had also received news earlier in the day that a German battle cruiser, escorted by two cruisers and two destroyers, had been seen north-west of Trondheim. The Admiralty in London advised that other "large German vessels" had been seen in the Kattegat and Skagerrak areas. This second group seemed to offer a better chance of being found, and so at around 2000 Admiral Forbes ordered a turn to the south. He also sent a patrol line of cruisers to sweep northwards. However, when the Admiralty heard of this they feared that the cruisers might be ambushed by German naval forces. Admiral Cunningham (1st Cruiser Squadron) and Admiral Edward-Collins (commander of the 2nd Cruiser Squadron) were ordered to join up and steer north towards the ships commanded by Admiral Layton (18th Cruiser Squadron). The intention was that they should all join the capital ships - *Repulse*, *Rodney* and *Valiant* - and then hopefully overwhelm the German ships. Yet most of the German ships were preparing to enter, or already in, fjords on the way to their objectives, and matters were not helped by rough seas and poor visibility.

But if some German ships were still heading for the northern Norwegian port of Narvik, there might be an opportunity for the ships of the Whitworth group (*Renown* and her escorting destroyers) to intercept them. The *Renown* had joined up with more escorting destroyers off the Skomvaer lighthouse, about 70 miles west of Bodø, at around 1700 on 8 April. After considering his options, Whitworth decided not to enter Vestfjord while the storm was raging and moved out westwards towards open seas, perhaps with the hope of intercepting the German ships reported to be in the area. Whilst doing this, Whitworth received orders from London that he was to "concentrate on preventing any German force proceeding to Narvik". London also ordered the *Repulse* group to join Whitworth. These manoeuvres did not stop the German destroyers bound for Narvik escaping the trap that had been laid for them. There were snow showers on and off throughout the night, but in the couple of hours before dawn weather conditions improved. Whitworth's ships turned and headed south-east towards the Norwegian coast. When the *Renown* group was about 50 miles west of the Skomvaer Lighthouse, in the growing light a lookout reported a battle cruiser and a cruiser to the south. It was the *Gneisenau* and the *Scharnhorst*.

At 0350, a contact aft on the port quarter was reported from the radar room to the bridge of the *Gneisenau*. The radar had not performed well over the previous days, probably due to the bad weather, and Captain Netzbandt wanted visual confirmation before alerting Admiral Lütjens. He joined his senior gunnery officer at the rangefinder to try and verify the contact. At 0359, the foretop lookout reported a shadow in the direction of the contact, at less than 20 kilometres; it was initially identified as a tanker and then as a *Nelson* class battleship. The alarm was sounded and the ship went to action stations.

The Whitworth group movements in the early hours of 9 April were recorded as follows:

At 0100, the *Renown* force changed course to 180¼.

At 0337, in position 67-22N, 09-36E, when steering 130¼, *Renown*, with destroyers *Greyhound, Icarus, Ivanhoe, Esk, Impulse, Hardy, Hunter, Havock* and *Hotspur* in company, sighted two unknown ships at a distance of 10 miles through a snowstorm, approaching from port, bearing 070¼. The ships were identified as a battle cruiser and a heavy cruiser, but were in fact the German battle cruisers *Gneisenau* and *Scharnhorst*. At 0359, *Renown*, having now positively identified the ships as German, turned on 305¼, parallel to the Germans.

At 0405, *Renown* opened fire against the *Gneisenau* with her main armament at a range of 18,600 yards, and with her 4.5in AA battery against the *Scharnhorst*. The destroyers also joined in with their 4.7in guns. On board the *Gneisenau* they realised that large-calibre shells had been fired at them from the size of the water splashes.

HMS *Renown* carried six 15in guns in three turrets, two at the front and one at the stern, each with two guns. She fired a shell weighing 1,920lbs to a maximum range of 32,500 yards – about 18½ miles.

The *Gneisenau* and *Scharnhorst* were basically similar. Each had nine 28cm guns, in three turrets like the *Renown*, but in groups of three, not two. These guns fired a shell weighing about 700lbs to a maximum range of 30,000 yards – about 17 miles. In an extreme range shoot-out, the *Renown* ought to hold the upper hand.

The following extracts are from the log of HMS *Renown*:

At 0416 hours *Renown* had a 28cm shell hit on her foremast, probably fired by *Gneisenau*. *Hardy* and *Hunter* were able to keep up with *Renown* for a time in the heavy weather, but the other destroyers fell behind. Also at about this time *Renown* suffered damage to her starboard anti-torpedo bulge from a combination of vibration and the weather.

At 0417 hours a hit from *Renown's* 16th salvo put *Gneisenau's* fire control out of action and *Gneisenau* turned away on to 30¼. *Scharnhorst* moved between her and *Renown* and attempted to obscure *Gneisenau* with smoke. Admiral Whitworth commented later that he found the fire from both German ships "ragged both for line and range and the spread was very variable".

The range at which the *Renown* opened fire was about 10 miles. The seas were very rough and the *Renown* had to slow down to allow her front turrets to operate; at speed, the waves breaking over the bow were hindering the crew's ability to fire. *Renown* was hit three times, but in spite of being less heavily armoured than her German opponents, she suffered no major damage.

Scharnhorst returned fire at 0410 and *Gneisenau* a minute later, although the logbook entry for *Gneisenau* states she was not battle ready until 0416. Admiral Lütjens had orders to avoid battle with superior opponents if possible and believing this was the situation, gave orders to steer away. Visibility improved after a while and a *Renown*-class battle cruiser was correctly identified as their main opponent. However, as some of the destroyers also opened fire, the flashes from their guns made Lütjens believe he was facing more than one capital ship.

Lütjens ordered a 40 degree course to starboard, steering to 350 degrees, even if this meant that only the after turrets could fire. As speed was increased up to 27 knots, heavy seas crashed into the *Gneisenau*, making observation difficult. Netzbandt, the captain of the *Gneisenau*, suggested a course more to port, which Lütjens agreed with. This allowed all the main gun turrets to come into use.

In spite of the somewhat derisory comment by Whitworth, at least one of the German ships found the range, and around 0415 *Renown* was hit by two 28cm shells. One hit the foremast and destroyed some of the radio masts, the other towards the rear of the ship, damaging some storage lockers and causing some flooding but inflicting no serious damage. Then at 0417, the *Renown* got the range, and a 15in shell hit home on the port side of the foretop, causing 15 casualties. Six were killed, including the senior gunnery officer. This caused the *Gneisenau* to stop firing for a few minutes until an alternative fire control director could be bought into action. Then 4.5in shells from *Renown* hit home, causing damage to a rangefinder in A turret. It was after this that the *Scharnhorst* laid down a smoke screen and *Renown* concentrated its guns on her.

Gneisenau turned away to the north-east, with the *Scharnhorst* following, and *Renown* gave chase. The German ships were a few knots faster and, more importantly, better at handling the heavy seas. *Renown* shipped tons of icy-cold water over her bows, some of which entered the front turrets and turned to steam when it came into contact with guns hot from firing. An additional problem was water flowing down the barrels when the breeches were opened to reload. The poor visibility and large sheets of spray obscuring the optics of the fire control systems also hampered support personnel. Due to all these factors, the fire from *Renown* became intermittent.

The Germans fared little better. They returned fire from their aft turrets, and *Scharnhorst* turned occasionally to fire a broadside at *Renown*, but no hits were achieved. Lütjens commented in his war diary:

Speed 27 knots. Course 30 degrees. It became clear that after the last change of course the enemy had come in an unfavourable position for the efficient use of his guns. As he followed the turn, he could only apply his two forward turrets and the firing from these became very erratic and inaccurate. The smoke we were making due to the emergency engagement of the idle boilers also hampered his observations. The battle range was increasing rapidly and rain showers made it impossible for both parties to maintain covering fire. On the other hand, our own observation improved, although with only one turret bearing per ship and a narrow target, the chance of a hit was small.

The log of the *Renown* continued:

At 0419 hours *Renown* scored a hit on *Gneisenau's* A (Anton) turret and also hit the after flak deck.
At 0420 hours *Renown* now shifted her main armament to *Scharnhorst*. It was during this phase that *Renown* received a further hit near the stern; it was superficial but killed a crew member.

Around this time *Scharnhorst's* radar malfunctioned and she could not track the target, so both German ships turned away to the north-east and increased speed, disappearing from view occasionally in the snow squalls sweeping over the dark seas.

Renown followed, but could only manage 20-23 knots without swamping A turret: the wind was force 7 from the NNE. The German ships thus slowly pulled away. They were also later forced to reduce speed, but not before *Scharnhorst's* A turret had been damaged by the heavy seas crashing over her bow. She also suffered damage to her starboard turbine, which reduced her speed to 25 knots.

As she came back into range because of her reduction in speed, *Renown* briefly opened fire on *Scharnhorst* at 0515 but without hitting the target; for the next hour or so *Renown* chased the two German ships. Then, owing to their superior speed, at 0615 *Renown* lost contact with the enemy ships and her escorting destroyers.

During the action, *Renown* had fired 230 15in shells and 1,065 rounds of 4.5in. *Scharnhorst* fired 195 rounds of 28cm and *Gneisenau* 54 of 28cm. Of the latter's 54 rounds, 44 were high explosive, which would have had little effect on the thick belt of armour plate that made up *Renown's* outer skin.

As both sides drew further apart in distance, Lütjens began to question his decisions, and at 0507 sent a signal to *Scharnhorst* asking her how many ships she had seen and identified. About 30 minutes later, *Scharnhorst* replied that she had only recognised one. Later that morning, there was a further exchange of signals, perhaps for the benefit of Lütjens, in case it was held that he hadn't shown enough aggressive spirit. These were recorded in his war diary:

0805 To *Scharnhorst*: Are you sure there was only one enemy ship? From here two were seen.

0817 From *Scharnhorst*: Have looked into matter, appears there were two enemies at the beginning of the engagement.

0829 To *Scharnhorst*: All shipboard aircraft unserviceable. Judging from shell fragment found on quarterdeck, enemy was firing 38cm guns.

0834 From *Scharnhorst*: A third enemy was seen aft of *Scharnhorst* at start of the battle.

The Germans sailed off to the north after an engagement that had been unsatisfactory for both sides. After pursuing for a few hours, the *Renown* group gave up. Around 0800, Whitworth turned his group westwards, in the hope that the Germans might turn south after disappearing, but the German ships did not do so for another day or so, by which time they were in the vicinity of Jan Mayen Island.

Whitworth later commented that the action against the *Scharnhorst* and *Gneisenau* "confirmed the experience of that off the River Plate, namely that the enemy has little liking for close action and his morale deteriorates rapidly if the ship is hit".

While this action was taking place, the Admiralty in London was doing its best to interfere. The log records the following: "At 0626 hours Vice Admiral Whitworth ordered Captain D2 in *Hardy* to proceed with all the destroyers to patrol the entrance to Vestfjord."

At 0918, Admiral Whitworth received further orders from London. He was to concentrate his ships off Vestfjord to prevent German ships heading for the vital port of Narvik. He turned his force round once again. The *Repulse* group was also contacted and told to meet up with the *Renown* group south-west of the Lofoten Islands. This junction was effected around 1400 and was recorded as follows: "At 1400 hours *Renown* RVed with the battle cruiser *Repulse*, cruiser *Penelope* and destroyers *Bedouin*, *Kimberley*, *Punjabi*, *Eskimo* and *Hostile*." *Penelope* was then detached to patrol the entrance to Vestfjord and the rest of the force moved to patrol 30 miles to the west of *Penelope*.

By then the Admiralty in London had been informed that German ships were already in Narvik harbour.

The situation now was that there was a relatively large force of British ships heading towards Narvik, with further ships coming across the North Sea and other forces further south.

The commander of the Home Fleet, Admiral Forbes, decided to get the 18th Cruiser Squadron under the command of Admiral Layton to attack Bergen, where it had been reported that there were German ships. His force was due to meet these at around 0630 (while the *Renown* was still involved in the skirmish with *Gneisenau* and *Scharnhorst*). Shortly afterwards, Forbes received orders from the Admiralty that he was to "prepare attacks against German warships and transports in Bergen and if possible Trondheim". He was also advised that the coastal defences were still believed to be in Norwegian hands. However, the proposed attack on Trondheim was cancelled by London around noon to avoid undue dispersion of the ships, in case the German capital ships were located. Forbes did give the go-ahead for ships to go into the fjords north and south of Bergen once definite orders had been received. At 1130 a force of four cruisers and seven destroyers under Layton was sent towards Bergen. The plan was that the destroyers would enter the fjords to destroy the German ships whilst the cruisers remained in support at the entrances.

The 18th Cruiser Squadron at this time consisted of five cruisers: HMS *Manchester* (Layton's flagship), HMS *Birmingham*, HMS *Glasgow*, HMS *Sheffield* and HMS *Southampton*. For this operation, HMS *Birmingham* was not present. The destroyers acting as escorts were HMS *Afridi*, HMS *Gurkha*, HMS *Matabele*, HMS *Mashona*, HMS *Mohawk*, HMS *Sikh* and HMS *Somali*. These destroyers came from the 3rd and 6th Destroyer Flotillas. On this day the RAF had carried out a number of reconnaissance flights over Norway, and reported back that "two German cruisers" had been spotted at Bergen. This information was reported to the Admiralty and to the commanders at sea. Admiral Layton, for one, began to have doubts about the venture up the narrow fjords, which seemed to be becoming more risky, coupled with the thought that the Germans might also control the shore batteries. Orders came from London to cancel the attack by the destroyers, and substitute it with one by torpedo bombers from the aircraft carrier HMS *Furious*. The *Furious*, although part of the Home Fleet, had been on the Clyde after finishing a refit in early April and was initially overlooked by Forbes in the general mobilisation of the fleet. This was rectified around 1630 on 8 April when a staff officer in London thought that aircraft might be a useful addition to Forbes's armoury. So *Furious* was ordered to re-embark her aircraft, which had been dispersed to naval air stations ,and prepare to join the fleet at sea. It would be around 24 hours before her two Fairey Swordfish squadrons (Numbers 816 and 818) had landed on board and the ship could get under way. However, her squadron of fighter aircraft (Number 801), flying Blackburn Sea Skuas then based at RNAS Donibristle in Fife, failed to arrive in time and *Furious* sailed without them.

From about 0800 on the morning of 9 April, the British ships had been shadowed by German aircraft. A series of attacks from enemy bombers started at about 1345. The first attack went in against Admiral Layton's group, returning from the area of Bergen. The attacking aircraft included around 45 JU88s and 40 HE111s, flying mainly from captured Norwegian airfields. In spite of the ships putting up a heavy anti-aircraft barrage, two of the cruisers, *Glasgow* and *Southampton*, were slightly damaged by bombs; five of *Southampton*'s crew were casualties, including two killed. The ships protected themselves by acting in conjunction with each other, but heavy seas made life particularly difficult for the smaller destroyers and tons of water broke over the forecastles. Commander A. Buzzard, captain of HMS *Gurkha*, was becoming increasingly frustrated at the lack of effective fire his ship was putting up, and so without any orders from the flotilla commander, Vian, he turned *Gurkha* out of the wind and sea to give his gunners and fire-control officers a better chance of hitting something. This manoeuvre took *Gurkha* towards the rear of the screen and Vian did not interfere. She was becoming an isolated target and attracted a lot of attention from German aircraft. Neither could she put up as much fire as the cruisers. Commander Buzzard wrote later:

At 1507 when about five miles on the quarter of the cruiser squadron, steering 290°, one of the several enemy aircraft then in sight, a four-engined bomber, was seen to be approaching on a steady course from the starboard quarter, at about 10,000 feet. Course was altered to bring the aircraft on the beam so that all guns could bear, but after a few rounds were fired the angle of sight became too great for the limited elevation of the 4.7in guns. The target was, however, kept abeam so that the pom-poms were able to bear in the event of the aircraft starting a dive-bombing attack. It was soon clear, however, that a high level bombing attack was being made and the rudder was then put to "hard-a-starboard" in an attempt to take avoiding action. A stick of six bombs fell on the starboard side abreast the gear room. The gear room quickly filled, followed by the engine room and by the majority of the after compartments.

These bombs caused severe damage and as well as the inrush of water the stern caught fire and the after magazine had to be flooded. Soon the stern was awash and *Gurkha* had a 45 degree list to starboard. All the lights were out but the wounded were brought up and laid on the fo'c'sle. Many were blinded by fuel oil and everyone had to cling to the guard rails or anchor chains to keep from falling overboard. In spite of this the forward guns were still operational and were able to keep some further aerial attacks at bay. The radios had been knocked out of action in the first attack but an emergency aerial was rigged up and about an hour after the first attack requests for immediate help were broadcast. After some difficulties with the aerial, contact was made with the cruiser HMS *Aurora*, who replied, "Am coming to your assistance."

HMS *Aurora* was heading in the direction of the Home Fleet. She had not left the Clyde (her home port) with the rest of the 2nd Cruiser Squadron, but now set course for the *Gurkha*. On board *Gurkha*, Commander Buzzard ordered the firing of shells to help guide the *Aurora* to them, and at 1855 she was sighted on the horizon.

Aboard *Gurkha*, with it was now getting dark and cold, the list was getting worse as more and more water entered the stricken destroyer. *Aurora* closed with the *Gurkha*, then stopped and lowered boats. About half of the 215 men on board *Gurkha* had moved across to *Aurora* when Commander Buzzard decided it was becoming too risky to stay on board: at 2045, he gave the order abandon ship. A few minutes later, *Gurkha* rolled over and sank, about 35 nautical miles west of Karmoy Island, in position 59°13'N, 04°00'E. Of the ship's company, 16 members died in this incident and the other 199 were rescued – 194 by the *Aurora* and five by the *Mashona*, who, accompanied by other destroyers, had been sent back to look for the *Gurkha*.

Gurkha was the first Tribal class and first British destroyer to be sunk by air attack, although as the Second World War dragged on, she would not be the last.

The following is the report on the loss of HMS *Gurkha*, written by Commander Buzzard:

Subject: Sinking of HMS *Gurkha*
From: Commanding Officer, HMS *Gurkha*
Date: 11th April 1940
To: Captain (D) 4th Destroyer Flotilla
Copies to:

Secretary of the Admiralty,

Commander in Chief, Home Fleet,

Vice Admiral Commanding, 18th Cruiser Squadron,

Rear Admiral (D), Home Fleet,

Commanding Officer, HMS *Aurora*

1. When the air attacks on the cruiser and destroyers under Vice Admiral Commanding 18th Cruiser Squadron, started at about 1430 on 9th April 1940, some thirty miles to the west of Kors fjord, HMS *Gurkha* was in company with Captain (D), 4th Destroyer Flotilla, and HM Ships *Sikh* and *Mohawk*, two miles on the starboard beam of the cruiser squadron – course 025 degrees. Wind force 5 from the northward. Sea about 32.

2. The destroyers broke formation early in the attack and became somewhat separated. Gurkha's courses were adjusted as necessary to bring the guns to bear on enemy aircraft. Control of fire and fighting of guns being very much facilitated when steering down wind. Ground was first made to leeward and later towards the rear of the cruiser squadron for which position Captain (D) 4th Destroyer was seen to be making.

3. At 1507 when about five miles on the quarter of the cruiser squadron, steering 290 degrees, one of the several enemy aircraft then in sight, a four-engined bomber, was seen to be approaching on a steady course from the starboard quarter, at about 10,000 feet. Course was altered to bring the aircraft on the beam so that all guns could bear, but after a few rounds were fired the angle of sight became too great for the limited elevation of the 4.7 inch guns.

4. The target was, however, kept abeam so that the pom-poms were able to bear in the event of the aircraft starting a dive-bombing attack. It was soon clear, however, that a high level bombing attack was being made, and the rudder was then put to hard-a-starboard in an attempt to take avoiding action. Speed had been reduced to 15 knots on going into a head wind, so that avoiding action actually taken was small.

The policy of giving prior consideration to control of fire was deliberate.

Soon after the rudder had been put to "hard-a-starboard" a "stick" of six bombs fell on the starboard side abreast the gear room, from about 150 yards to right alongside.

5. The gear room quickly filled followed shortly by the engine room, and by the majority of the after compartments. The steering compartment remained intact. What appeared to be an oil fuel fire started in or under the after superstructure, and the ship listed to starboard bringing the upper deck to within about two feet from the waterline amidships, and one foot aft.

6. The wireless installation and large signal projectors failed immediately after the explosion, and efforts were made to attract the attention of the remaining destroyers and cruisers with the 6in Aldis lamp, siren, flag signals, and "Not under Control" balls, but without success. *Gurkha* was about five miles on their quarter and they were busily engaged repelling aircraft.

7. During the subsequent five and a half hours that the ship remained afloat

the HA director, TS, foremost guns, and supply parties remained in action in primary control and engaged approaching enemy aircraft on about twelve separate occasions. This fire was sufficient to deter them from making further attacks except one which, like the first, carried out a high level bombing attack at about 10,000 feet. A "stick" of about six bombs missed ahead by about 200 yards.

8. The remainder of the men were employed on placing the collision mat, jettisoning all weighty articles and fittings on the starboard side and high up in the ship, preparing boats and rafts for lowering, preparing to tow forward, and baling out boiler room bilges.

Unfortunately, the torpedo tubes were jammed fore and aft so that the torpedoes could not be placed overboard.

9. Attempts were made to deal with the fire after, but no fire main pressure being available, and access being impossible, due to dense fumes, the after compartments were battened down. The risk of fire spreading to the after magazines were accepted, it being considered undesirable to surrender further buoyancy by flooding them.

10. The technical details of action taken in the engine room and boiler rooms were not available without further enquiry from the ratings concerned. The Engineer Officer reported at the time that the engine room could not be cleared by the main circulators and that the Downton pump could not be usefully employed.

After discussion with the Engineer Officer, it was decided to clear the foremost oil fuel tanks on the starboard side (Nos. 1–3) and this was done.

11. Meanwhile, Telegraphist rigged jury aerials, provided spare batteries from the fore store, repaired fuses, etc., and about 1600 were able to transmit on 366 kc/S (low power) a message stating that Gurkha was in danger of sinking from bombs, giving her position 60-29 degrees North, 3-20 degrees East (Based on Vice Admiral Commanding 18th Cruiser Squadron's reference position at 1300).

No reply was received for some time, but after altering settings and length of aerials, at 1715, Aurora answered saying "coming to your assistance."

12. A signal was then made stating Gurkha's position would be indicated by firing HE bursts. This was done at about 1830, and the bursts were apparently observed by Aurora who was thus able to make contact. She was sighted at about 1855.

13. It was, at first, decided to continue preparations for towing forward, while disembarkation of personnel proceeded with Aurora's boats, but as the fire aft developed into a blaze, and the ship was clearly sinking, these preparations were discontinued.

14. Boat work was slow and difficult in the prevailing wind and sea, and only about half the ship's company had been taken off when the ship sank at 2045. The remainder jumped from the forecastle and nearly all were able to swim or paddle in rafts to Aurora, who was brought close abreast of them to windward. The accurate placing of Aurora in this position at the correct moment was responsible for the large number of men able to reach her.

15. When *Aurora* was lying to windward of *Gurkha* while operating boats, *Gurkha* swung round so that the wind was brought from port to starboard, causing her to right and then list over to port. When finally foundering she listed right over on her port side and then went down stern first, bows vertically in.

It is feared that some officers and men remained on the forecastle a few seconds too long and were probably sucked under.

16. Ships of the 6th Destroyer Flotilla appeared just after the ship had sunk and assisting in searching for survivors in the failing light. HMS *Mashona* picked up six.

17. Of the 215 officers and men originally on board, 199 were picked up alive; five officers and ten ratings are missing. One rating was picked up dead.

The three ratings injured in the original explosion were successfully rescued.

18. Confidential and secret books were taken below and stowed at the bottom of the ship before sinking.

19. The behaviour of officers and men as a whole was excellent. I wish to commend Lieutenant-Commander (E) I. Howden, Royal Navy, unfortunately among the missing, for the untiring efforts made by him in endeavouring to save the ship, and Acting Petty Officer Telegraphist Rainer for the determination and resource shown by him in successfully repairing the damaged wireless installation, without which assistance would not have been forthcoming in time to save life. (signed) A.W. Buzzard

Commander

It is worth noting that the only four-engine bomber that Germany possessed at that time was the *Kondor 200*, but they were supposedly not in service in Norway for another week or more, so perhaps the report in point 3 is wrong.

What follows below is further correspondence on the loss of HMS *Gurkha*:

Secret
Loss of HMS *Gurkha*
(HMS *Gurkha*'s letter dated 11 April 1940)
No. 819/H.F. 490
Admiralty
copies to:
The Rear Admiral (D), Home Fleet
The Captain (D) 4th Destroyer Flotilla
Forwarded for information

1. At 1100 on 9th April 1940, the Battle fleet was in position lat. 60-05 degrees N., long. 02-57 degrees E. steering 180 degrees at 20 knots. The 1st, 18th, and 2nd Cruiser Squadrons were spread in pairs 7 miles ahead to form an AK line.

2. At 1100 the Vice Admiral Commanding the 18th Cruiser Squadron received my 1045/9 ordering the 18th Cruiser Squadron in company (the *Manchester*, *Southampton*, *Glasgow*, and *Sheffield*), and the 4th and 6th Destroyer Flotillas

(consisting of Captain (D) IV in the *Afridi*, the *Mohawk*, *Sikh*, and *Gurkha*, Captain (D) VI in the *Somali*, the *Matabele* and *Mashona*) to proceed and attack Bergen when ordered. This force was ordered to proceed at 1125 and the 18th Cruiser Squadron and destroyers altered course at 025 degrees, speed 20 knots, at 1140. This speed was subsequently reduced to 16 knots as destroyers could not keep up on account of weather.

3. At noon the course of the Battle fleet was altered to 360 degrees, speed of advance 16 knots. The weather at this time was wind NNW. force 5, sea 33. Sky, broken cloud, visibility very good.

4. At 1410, the Vice Admiral Commanding 18th Cruiser Squadron, received Admiralty message 1347/9 cancelling the operation against Bergen and altered course to rejoin the Battle fleet whose position at 1410 was lat. 60-20 degrees N, long. 02-53 degrees E, course 360 degrees, speed of advance 16 knots.

5. At 1425, heavy air attacks on the 18th Cruiser Squadron and destroyers in company developed and air attacks on the Battle fleet were also made. The 4th and 6th Destroyer Flotillas had dropped astern of the 18th Cruiser Squadron during the attempt to make high speed towards Bergen and were further scattered by their alterations of course during the air attacks.

6. When *Gurkha* was damaged by bombs at 1507, she was about five miles on the quarter of the cruisers and in the heat of the action the fact that she was damaged was not observed by the cruisers or destroyers.

7. Captain (D) IV in paragraph 1 of minute II has generously accepted the responsibility for allowing *Gurkha* to become detached, but his minute was written on the 22nd April by which time all or most of us had realised that to remain concentrated was the best defence against air attack, whereas on the 9th April, when the attack took place this was not generally realised. Destroyers escorting Norwegian convoys when under air attack had often been out of supporting distance from each other and no harm had come to them. I knew this and had issued no instructions on the matter. I do not, therefore, consider that Captain (D) IV, is any more to blame than I am, except for the omission to notice that the *Gurkha* had detached herself completely as opposed to taking independent avoiding action.

The Commanding Officer of the *Gurkha* was unwise in his decision to steer down wind in order to facilitate gunfire and thus become totally detached from his Captain (D). Unless definite orders to scatter had been given he should only have taken individual avoiding action whilst remaining in company.

8. I concur in the remarks of paragraph 3 of minute II and consider that *Aurora* did extremely well to pick up the *Gurkha*'s W/T signal, find her, and rescue nearly all her crew.

9. I do not consider either a Board of Enquiry or a Court Martial is necessary.
(signed) C.M. Forbes, Admiral of the Fleet
HMS *Rodney*
15th May 1940

Secret

Sinking of HMS *Gurkha*

(Commanding Officer, *Gurkha*'s report dated 11th April 1940)

II

No. 73/169

To Rear Admiral (D) Home Fleet

1. *Gurkha* was in the hands of an inexperienced Commanding Officer and became detached; he should not have been allowed to have become detached; the responsibility for failure to call him in is wholly mine; I have not, I regret to report, any explanation worth recording to account for this omission.

2. I endorse the commendations contained in the final paragraph of Commander Buzzard's report, and have noted the name of Petty Officer Telegraphist Rainer for further action.

3. The discipline and steadiness in adversity of the ship's company of *Gurkha* reported by the Commanding Officer, HMS *Aurora*, in his letter 00291 of 10th April 1940, reflects credit on Commander Buzzard, and provides a pleasant feature in an incident which was otherwise regrettable.

(signed) Philip Vian, Captain (D), Fourth Destroyer Flotilla

HMS Afridi

22nd April 1940

Thus the matter of the loss of the *Gurkha* was put to bed. Perhaps the Royal Navy was still trying to adhere to peace-time procedures in this period at the end of the "phoney war".

While the *Gurkha* was facing its final test, the rest of Layton's group steamed off, and most joined up with the bulk of the Home Fleet. The Germans could now turn their attention to this seemingly tempting prize. The group consisted of the battleships HMS *Rodney* and HMS *Valiant*, and the cruisers HMS *Berwick*, HMS *Devonshire*, HMS *Galatea* and HMS *York*. These bigger ships were escorted by a number of destroyers – HMS *Codrington*, HMS *Electra*, HMS *Escapade*, HMS *Griffin* and HMS *Jupiter*. Also in attendance from the French Navy were one of their cruisers, *Emile Bertin*, with two destroyers, the *Maillé-Brézé* and the *Tartu*. For once in recent days the sky was clear and the ships were going to face a severe aerial examination. The German bombers pressed home numerous attacks but were largely kept at bay by intense anti-aircraft fire. Some ships fired off around 40 per cent of their ammunition that afternoon – not an ideal state of affairs, as resupply would be tricky. However, in spite of this barrage a few steep dive-bombing attacks were successful. Around 1530, a JU88 scored a hit with a 500kg bomb on *Rodney*'s deck, but it hit a section of 6in-thick armoured plate and so the damage was not as bad as it could have been. Several other bombs fell close to the *Rodney* and other ships, including the *Berwick*, *Devonshire* and *Valiant*, but caused no damage. Four JU88s were shot down. The attacks continued sporadically until around 1800, when the growing darkness curtailed German aerial interference.

Admiral Forbes ordered his fleet to steam north for some hours, then west, before making a final change to the east at around 0500 on 10 April. He was heading for a position from which it was deemed suitable to launch aircraft from HMS *Furious* for an attack on the ships in Trondheim harbour. At 0730, another battleship, HMS *Warspite*, accompanied by HMS *Furious*, joined up with the main group of ships. They were accompanied by a number of destroyers, which took over escort duties as many of the original vessels needed to return to port for refuelling. The group now consisted of *Rodney*, *Valiant* and *Warspite* – three battle cruisers - with one aircraft carrier, *Furious*, three cruisers - *Berwick*, *Devonshire* and *York* - and 18 destroyers. Forbes now made a strategic decision, perhaps recognising the value or danger of air power, in that his group would try to operate outside the area that the Germans could cover with aircraft. He also felt that Bergen could be taken care by "Skuas from Hatston" (RNAS Hatston near Kirkwall on the Orkney Islands) and that he would concentrate his ships so that they could operate against Narvik. On the way there he could get aircraft from *Furious* to raid Trondheim. The Admiralty fell in step with this plan and told Forbes: "Recapture of Narvik takes priority over operations against Bergen and Trondheim while interference with communications in southern area is to be left mainly to submarines, air and mining, with intermittent sweeps when forces allow." Winston Churchill added in an additional signal to Forbes, that he considered the Germans had "made a strategic error in incurring commitments on the Norwegian coast, which we can probably wipe out in short time".

Meanwhile, the 2nd and 18th Cruiser Squadrons were sent to the Bergen area on the orders of the Admiralty, with instructions to watch the German forces there and prevent any reinforcements and supplies reaching them. On the night of 9/10 April, HMS *Glasgow*, HMS *Sheffield* and the 6th Destroyer Flotilla were positioned at the entrance to Korsfjord, while HMS *Manchester* and HMS *Southampton*, accompanied by the 4th Destroyer Flotilla, patrolled off Fejeosen. HMS *Aurora*, after saving most of the crew of HMS *Gurkha*, joined the *Glasgow* group, but didn't stay long as she went back to Scapa Flow the following morning to offload the *Gurkha* survivors. During the early hours of the morning, Admiral Layton split his forces into two. He took some ships back to meet up with the main fleet, while *Glasgow*, commanded by Captain F. Pegram, together with some escorting destroyers, headed off on a patrol some distance south, before turning north-west. There were no incidents to report, except for one from HMS *Manchester*, which attempted to ram a U-boat she sighted on the surface. She reported that she caught the submarine a glancing blow, as it was probably undertaking an emergency dive, but no depth charges were fired and no real search instigated.

At the rendezvous spot, the cruiser squadrons found HMS *Codrington* with Captain D (1) G. Creasy, the commander of the 1st Destroyer Flotilla, awaiting them. He had orders from Admiral Forbes that all the ships were to return to harbour for a resupply of fuel and ammunition. The destroyers were to go to Sullom Voe in the Shetlands and the cruisers to Scapa Flow. Both groups made it back by that evening and started topping up their stores.

The Germans, aware of these movements, sent around 20 JU88s to bomb Scapa Flow in the late afternoon. The British picked them up on radar and the anti-aircraft defences were ready for their arrival, together with several fighter aircraft. Two German aircraft were shot down.

On 10 April, the *Luftwaffe* came looking for the Home Fleet, again positioned in northern waters, but the attacks did not come in with the ferocity of the previous day. The only ship to suffer any real damage was HMS *Eclipse* from the 12th Destroyer Flotilla, hit in the engine room, causing severe damage and flooding. The *Eclipse* had to be towed back to Lerwick in the Shetland Islands by HMS *York*.

From the point of view of the German Navy, Operation *Weserübung* had gone well as far as troop-landings went, but several German ships had been sunk or damaged and Lütjens noted that things were not quite going to plan. But during the afternoon the Germans received good intelligence. At 2100, Lütjens wrote in his diary that he thought that there were two groups of British capital ships at sea, one off Vestfjord, consisting of *Repulse* and apparently another battleship (one *Nelson* or *Barham* class); and one north of the Bergen–Shetlands Narrows, consisting of "three heavy ships with three heavy and five light cruisers". He also concluded that French ships were entering the area.

Lütjens did consider attacking the ships off Vestfjord to relieve some pressure on the German ships at Narvik, but abandoned the idea because it was considered that it might be difficult to locate the British ships on terms favourable to the Germans. It was impracticable to try to move his big ships into the narrow fjords leading to Narvik, and Lütjens thought that his destroyers and cruisers should be able to slip back to German ports on their own. Buoyed by bad weather forecasts for the coming days, he decided that his two capital ships would linger off the Norwegian coast, repairing what damage they could, before attempting to slip through into German waters on the night of 11/12 April.

Like the Admiralty in London, German Naval Group West Headquarters had limited knowledge of what was happening in northern waters. Lütjens had picked up signals on the morning of 10 April, asking for information. He did not want to break radio silence and possibly give his position away, so the requests were ignored. However, he did have an ingenious plan. Around noon, an *Arado* seaplane was launched from the *Scharnhorst*. The crew had been told to set course for Trondheim (around 600 miles away), and when in the vicinity to transmit a report, including the battleships' positions and Lütjens' intentions. A flight to Trondheim was just about at the limit of the range of the seaplane, so almost certainly this was a one-way trip.

At 1500, a signal arrived from Group West: "All available cruisers, destroyers and torpedo boats to proceed to sea tonight. Narvik destroyers are to concentrate with the Commander-in-Chief. It is left to your discretion whether *Hipper* with three destroyers joins you or breaks through and proceeds direct to home port." Lütjens assumed that the *Arado* had not yet made it to the Trondheim area, and when its message was received further orders would be issued. This is precisely what happened. At 2238, a cancellation message was received, with the additional news that the British Home Fleet, including the aircraft carrier HMS *Furious*, was somewhere north of the Bergen-Shetland Narrows. The capital ships were ordered to keep on heading west but the destroyers were to remain close to the Norwegian coastline.

The *Admiral Hipper*, after being damaged in the action with HMS *Glowworm*, had entered Trondheim harbour. The orders sent to him gave her captain independent choice of action, but with the proviso that he was to leave Trondheim as soon as possible, even if this meant going without any escorting destroyers. Lütjens was not unhappy with these orders and altered course south-westward, aiming for an entry into the North Sea near the Shetland Islands. All the Allied capital ships except the *Warspite* and the French

Dunkerque were north of him, and the fact that carrier aircraft had mounted an attack on Trondheim meant that these assets were north of Trondheim. In his eyes this favoured the idea of the *Gneisenau* and *Scharnhorst* slipping southwards in the coming hours. Provided the *Admiral Hipper* could leave Norwegian waters safely, she would also have a fair chance of getting through unscathed.

Around noon on 11 April, when the *Gneisenau* and *Scharnhorst* were about 75 miles to the north of the Faroe Islands, the seas abated a little and both ships cranked up to around 28 knots. Assisted by rain and fog, both ships slipped unnoticed into the North Sea and were joined by *Hipper* on 12 April. The voyage did not go entirely to plan, as the ships were spotted by British reconnaissance aircraft, but no attacks developed. Later on that morning, friendly aircraft, in the form of HE111s and later ME110s, arrived as air cover, and two destroyers also met the *Gneisenau* and *Scharnhorst* as further escorts. By 2230 on 12 April, the ships had reached the port of Wilhelmshaven. *Hipper* and *Scharnhorst* were both in need of repair, and for all practical purposes were out of service for the rest of the month. Lütjens' reputation was enhanced as a result of his Norwegian exploits, and in July 1940 he was appointed as C-in-C of the Fleet. However, in May 1941, he went to sea on board the *Bismarck*, a voyage from which he would not return.

Meanwhile, after the skirmish with the *Gneisenau* and *Scharnhorst*, Admiral Whitworth's group was heading in the direction of Narvik as he had been advised that "we shall probably want to land a force there". To back this up, Admiral Forbes had, on the morning of 10 April, instructed the commander of the 2nd Destroyer Flotilla, Captain (D) 2 B. Warburton-Lee, to "send some destroyers up to Narvik to make certain no troops land there". The message also included the news that Norway was at war with Germany. Then at 1200, London sent a further signal to Warburton-Lee:

> Press reports one German ship arrived Narvik and landed small force. Proceed to Narvik and sink or capture enemy ship. It is at your discretion to land forces if you think you can recapture Narvik from number of enemy present. Try to get possession of battery, if not already in enemy hands. Details of battery to follow.

This signal was copied to Admirals Forbes and Whitworth, but was essentially taking control away from both of them.

The 2nd Destroyer Flotilla headed towards Narvik. It consisted of five H-class destroyers - HMS *Hardy* (Warburton-Lee's ship), HMS *Havock*, HMS *Hostile*, HMS *Hotspur* and HMS *Hunter*. The "details of battery" followed shortly afterwards and described "three 12 or 18 pounders mounted on Framnes and facing north-west. Guns 4 inch or less may be in position on both sides Ofotfjord near Ramnes." None of this information was true, but as it turned out had little influence on matters.

The *Hardy* – a typical H-class destroyer - displaced 1,455 tons at standard load, had an overall length of 337ft, a beam of 34ft and draught of 12ft 9in. She was powered by Parsons geared steam turbines, driving two shafts, developing a total of 38,000 shaft horsepower and providing a maximum speed of 36 knots.. She carried a maximum of 470 tons of fuel oil, providing a range of 5,530 nautical miles at 15 knots. The *Hardy's* complement was 175 officers and men.

Narvik Fjord. (The National Archives)

The ship had five 45-calibre 4.7in Mark IX guns in single mounts. For anti-aircraft defence, there were two quadruple Mark I mounts for 0.5in Vickers Mark III machine guns. *Hardy* also had two above-water quadruple torpedo tube mounts for 21in torpedoes, one depth charge rail and two throwers; 35 depth charges were carried on active service.

Warburton-Lee, who had a number of destroyers under his command, decided to take the five H-class destroyers to Narvik, leaving the others under the command of Captain (D) 20 Bickford in Vestfjord. These were HMS *Esk*, HMS *Greyhound*, HMS *Icarus* and HMS *Ivanhoe*. Other ships supporting the operation included HMS *Penelope*, positioned south of the Skomvaer Lighthouse. The capital ships HMS *Renown* and HMS *Repulse* were further west and screened by a number of destroyers – HMS *Bedouin*, HMS *Eskimo*, HMS *Kimberley* and HMS *Punjabi*.

Around 1600, in the growing dark, the 2nd Destroyer Flotilla arrived at the pilot station at Tranøy in the inner Vestfjord. Two officers from HMS *Hardy* went ashore to seek intelligence about any German ships that had passed recently on their way to Narvik. In spite of a few language problems, it was learned, with help from the local pilots, that six German destroyers, all "larger than your ship", and a submarine had already passed that point earlier in the day, presumably heading for Narvik. One of the Norwegian pilots, who spoke a little English, apparently asked the officers how many ships they had, and when advised of the number, suggested not to attack until they had twice as many, as Narvik was very strongly held. One of the British officers, the *Hardy*'s torpedo officer,

HMS *Eskimo* pictured in February 1939. (Author's Collection)

Lieutenant G. Heppel, was not convinced that anyone at Tranøy had actually seen any German vessels.

Heppel and the other officer, Paymaster Lieutenant G. Stanning, Captain Warburton-Lee's secretary, returned to HMS *Hardy*. Once on board, Warburton-Lee held an O Group meeting with his senior officers, and in the face of this information had to determine what to make of the orders he had been given by London. His hands were tied to some extent by the direct order from the Admiralty, and after considering his options he advised his commanders that they were going in. At 1751, he sent a "most immediate" signal to the Admiralty, copied to Admirals Forbes and Whitworth, which said: "Norwegians report Germans holding Narvik in force, also six repetition six destroyers and one submarine are there and channel is possibly mined. Intend attacking at dawn, high water."

Admiral Whitworth was not happy with the situation and considered sending additional assets to Warburton-Lee when he received the decoded signal just after 1830. He even contemplated sending a signal to one of his cruisers, HMS *Penelope*, together with four destroyers – HMS *Bedouin*, HMS *Eskimo*, HMS *Kimberley* and HMS *Punjabi* – to move at high speed up the Vestfjord to support the attack, but decided against it. He later wrote: "I have always regretted that I did not intervene and order Warburton-Lee to postpone his attack until *Renown* could join him. Now that I know that the Admiralty had no special intelligence not available to myself, this regret is all the more poignant."

The first Battle of Narvik might have turned out very differently if Whitworth had followed his instincts.

Meanwhile, a surfaced German submarine, *U51*, had spotted, in their words, "five British destroyers heading on a south-westerly course", i.e. away from Narvik. The commander at Narvik, Commodore Bonte, drew the conclusion that the ships were on a routine patrol and posed no danger. Shortly afterwards, the ships reversed their course and headed for Narvik, but by now *U51* had submerged and took no action against the destroyers.

It was well after midnight and conditions were poor as the destroyers passed Barøy. The weather report described "continuous snow storms with visibility seldom greater than 1½-2 cables"(900-1,200ft). The fjord they were sailing up was fairly narrow and it was a very dark night, which taxed the skills of the flotilla navigation officer, Lieutenant-Commander Gordon-Smith. Lieutenant Stanning later commented that the navigation was by "dead reckoning, Asdic and echo sounding, as we never saw each side of the fjord – except early when we nearly hit it". Keeping station was difficult and speed was reduced to 12 knots. Things were made worse when a local ferry loomed out of the darkness: HMS *Hostile* had to steer away to avoid a collision, and lost touch with the other ships. Her captain, Commander J. Wright, decided to make his own way towards Narvik, relying on the skills of his own navigator.

An Admiralty signal to Warburton-Lee, received just after 0100, suggested that the Germans might have arrived in Trojan horse ships which, although appearing to be ore carriers, were troop carriers. These were suggested as priority targets. Around 0130, a final signal arrived, copied to Forbes and Whitworth, reading: "Norwegian coast-defence ships *Eidsvold* and *Norge* may be in German hands. You alone can judge whether, in these circumstances, attack should be made. We shall support whatever decision you take."

Shortly after 0230 on 10 April, the destroyers slipped through the narrow part of the fjord and increased speed. They were lucky to remain undetected, as there were apparently two U-boats in the fjord, but neither spotted their presence.

Further up the fjord in Narvik harbour, the Germans had kept one destroyer out, acting as picket. At 0300, the *Roeder* relieved the *Schmitt*, which returned to a position amongst the many merchant ships in the harbour. Conditions were just as bad for German Navy lookouts as their British counterparts, with driving snow, low visibility and bitter cold – which probably helped Warburton-Lee's group to slip up the fjord unnoticed.

It appears that the orders Commodore Bonte gave to his destroyer commanders were, at best, ambiguous. Two commanders thought that Bonte intended one destroyer to patrol the harbour entrance, another believed there was to be a patrol line within the narrows, whilst a further commander felt he was to patrol off the harbour mouth, as U-boats would cover further down the fjord. When *Roeder* took over sentry duty from *Schmitt*, no other ship was detailed to take over from her when they considered their turn was over. This would have repercussions later that morning. The commander of the *Roeder* later claimed that on his way out he received word from the *Schmitt* that he was to: "patrol against submarines outside the harbour entrance until daylight". So at around 0420 – a short time before dawn, when no submarines had been detected – her commander, Holtorf, considered his tour was over and took *Roeder* back into harbour.

Further down the fjord, the reunited group of five British ships were approaching Ankenes, and around 0400 land could be seen to starboard amid a gap in the snowstorms. Warburton-Lee halted the flotilla and got Gordon-Smith to work out a firm bearing towards Narvik harbour. The *Roeder* was probably only about a mile away but neither side detected the other. At around 0420, Warburton-Lee ordered HMS *Hostile* and HMS *Hotspur* to take care of the batteries on Framnes should they open fire, and also to protect the exit route from any German ships positioned to the north.

The attack on Narvik - HMS *Hardy* firing torpedoes. (The National Archives)

The time was now approaching 0430 and visibility was improving as dawn approached – around half a mile being one estimate - while the snowfall had abated a little. HMS *Hardy* entered the harbour, while HMS *Havock* and HMS *Hunter* stood ready in support. Warburton-Lee wanted to open the attack by using torpedoes, and after consulting with his torpedo officer, Heppel, he decided to enter the harbour along the south-western shore off Ankenes, turning to port once inside to bring one of his torpedo banks to bear on enemy shipping. Two merchantmen were spotted first, one of which was grounded, but these were ignored in favour of trying to find warships for the *Hardy* to fire torpedoes at. A German destroyer was then seen between some freighters, and as *Hardy* commenced a slow turn to port, Heppel gave the order to fire three torpedoes. As they were fired, speed was increased, and when two more destroyers came into view a further four torpedoes were fired (two at each target). Shortly afterwards, the main guns of *Hardy* joined in. It seems the first of the salvo of three torpedoes fired missed its intended target, the destroyer *Heidkamp*, and hit a freighter behind it, but one of the other two struck *Heidkamp*'s port side near the stern. This caused the aft magazine to explode and killed around 80 men, including Commodore Bonte and most of his staff. The second salvo of four torpedoes appeared to have missed their intended targets, but detonated upon hitting the quays to the north-east, causing great damage. On board the *Heidkamp*, the explosion lifted the three aft turrets into the air. Shortly afterwards the ship was hit by shells fired from the *Hardy*. In spite of his ship sinking by the stern, the commander of the *Heidkamp*, Captain Erdmenger, managed to secure her to a nearby ore carrier.

Following close on the heels of HMS *Hardy* was the *Hunter*, whose commander, Lieutenant-Commander L .de Villiers, selected a number of targets, engaging them with his 4.7in guns and torpedoes. He fired four torpedoes at what he believed was a destroyer and another salvo into a "traffic jam" of berthed merchant ships. He hit several of the merchantmen and the destroyer *Schmitt* with several shells and a torpedo, which hit the forward engine room. The captain of the *Schmitt*, Böhme, was awakened from his bed by these explosions and found that his cabin door was jammed, so he was temporarily trapped.

Bringing up the rear was HMS *Havock*, but by now the Germans were starting to react with some fire of their own. This, together with smoke from the gunfire and explosions and a smoke screen put down by *Hardy*, made accurate target identification difficult. However, *Havock* did exchange a few inconclusive rounds with the *Künne* before the *Schmitt* came into her sights. *Havock* fired a number of torpedoes, at least one of which hit home, causing further damage. The *Schmitt* then started to sink. Böhme had managed to wrench open his cabin door and gave the order to abandon ship. He, together with a few members of his crew, slid down the deck and endured a freezing cold swim to the shore.

On the *Roeder*, Captain Holtorf realised the British ships had virtually followed him into Narvik harbour. He had just ordered the anchors to be dropped when gunfire rang round the harbour. His crew, scrambling to their posts, opened fire, using the flashes from the British ships as an aiming point, but thick snow added to their visibility problems. The *Roeder* also fired blind a salvo of eight torpedoes towards the harbour entrance. At short range, lookouts on the Royal Navy ships spotted the wakes of these, but all either missed or passed underneath the ships without exploding.

Panic and confusion set in amongst the German ships. Two of them, the *Künne* and *Lüdemann*, had been refuelling from the *Jan Wellem* when the first shots were fired. To their credit, the crew of the *Künne* reacted very quickly, even if they didn't cast off all the fuel pipes and mooring ropes before getting under way. But when the *Havock* emerged from the smoke and hit the *Schmitt*, *Künne* was only about 40 yards away. She suffered severe engine damage from the blast, which stopped her dead in the water: as a result she drifted out of control into the submerged wreck of the *Schmitt* and remained there for the rest of the engagement. Some of her crew jumped overboard, taking their chances in the freezing water.

As *Havock* was leaving the harbour, she came under fire from the *Roeder* and the *Lüdemann* but the Germans' gunnery was ineffectual and no hits were scored. *Havock* successfully returned fire from her rear turrets, knocking out one of *Lüdemann*'s forward guns and also causing damage aft. This started a fire, caused steering problems and flooded a magazine. With loss of control and starting to list heavily, her captain, Friedrichs, had no choice but to try and hurry away to safety.

The two guard ships, *Hostile* and *Hotspur*, hearing the explosions and gunfire from Narvik harbour, headed there, not having come under fire from the shore or having met any enemy ships. Upon reaching Framnes, they saw the other three ships coming out and laid a smokescreen to assist in their escape. Warburton-Lee then asked *Hotspur* to fire blind a salvo of four more torpedoes into the harbour, in the hope of preventing any chase, but they were lucky and hit and sunk at least two more merchant ships. HMS

The ensign from the *Hans Lüdemann* captured after the Second Battle of Narvik. (Imperial War Museum)

Hostile was allowed to probe forward and engaged the *Roeder* with her main armament. At least five shells hit home, causing damage to her steering, guns and boiler room, and thick black smoke to blanket the *Roeder*. Her anchor could not be raised but Captain Holtorf turned his ship, using the engines to steer back towards the piers, dragging the anchor with them. *Roeder*'s stern was eventually secured to a pier in the harbour by a cable, while the anchor held her bow off at an angle. The fires were bought under control but the ship was effectively out of the battle.

At 0530, when Warburton-Lee's group of five destroyers was outside Skjomnes, he called a brief halt for a quick situation report. Even though it was daylight, there were still occasional snow showers and it was misty, so it seemed a reasonable gamble. His ships reported that none had received any significant damage from German fire, but more worrying was the lack of torpedoes. A check amongst the ships revealed that 24 had already been fired from the total of 40 carried by all ships. *Hardy* had one left, *Havock* three and *Hotspur* four, while *Hostile* had a full load of eight. *Hunter* had fired all of hers. It was also found that even though the Norwegians at Tranøy had suggested six German warships were at Narvik, only four or five had been positively identified in the harbour, so there ought to be others around somewhere. In fact, there were five inside the harbour and another five outside.

Warburton-Lee decided that it would be worth another incursion towards Narvik harbour as it was thought there were a number of undamaged merchant ships there, which would be easy targets. Some of them were British ships, which were in Narvik harbour on the morning of the German invasion. However, these were considered to be commandeered German ships and so a legitimate target.

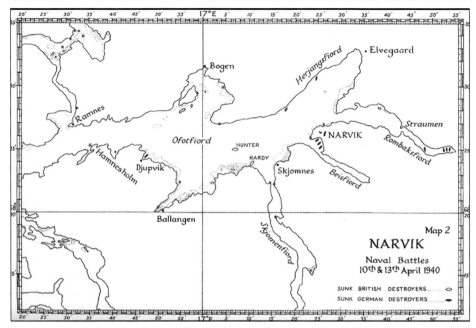

General view of the Narvik area. (The National Archives)

Back in Narvik, the Germans had managed to sort themselves out somewhat. At 0515, the *Lüdemann* sent a signal to the five other destroyers of the group, advising them that they had come under attack. On the *Jan Wellem*, which was undamaged, the captain decided to move his ship towards Malmkaia in the hope that they might gain some protection, should there be any further attacks. Also on board were a number of British seamen who had been present at the time of the German invasion. Their senior officer, Captain Evans (from the *North Cornwall*), suggested to the Germans that he and his men should be given an opportunity to get away to safety: to his surprise they were allowed to have a lifeboat and proceeded to row ashore to Ankenes.

The returning five British ships, in a line astern formation, cruised past the harbour, although visibility was still poor and few targets could be identified. The *Lüdemann* fired a salvo of four torpedoes towards the British ships, but again these either missed or passed under their targets. HMS *Hostile* went in closer, looking for some targets for her torpedoes, and in doing so was hit towards the bow, but again only minor damage was caused.

After completing this second pass, Warburton-Lee did not have to face the decision of whether to try and put landing parties ashore (as had originally been suggested) as three German warships could be seen heading down Herjangsfjord at high speed. HMS *Hardy* opened fire first when the Germans were about four miles away and the Germans soon returned fire. Warburton-Lee called for his ships to accelerate to 30 knots and sent a signal to Captain (D) 20, reading: "One cruiser, three destroyers off Narvik. Am withdrawing to westward." This was also picked up on board the *Renown*.

The detached group of three ships from the German 4th Destroyer Flotilla (*Zenker*,

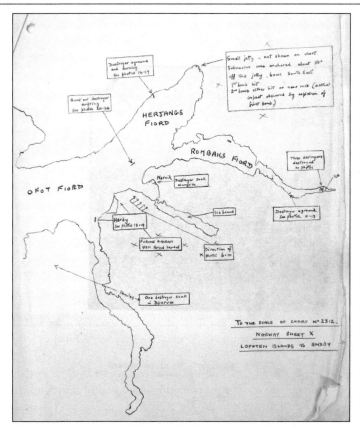

A brief summary of events around the early days at Narvik. (The National Archives)

Giese and *Koellner*) under the command of Captain Bey had spent the night at anchor in Herjangsfjord. Once the warning signal had been received from Narvik, the ships were brought to action stations and headed south. All three ships were low on fuel, which would hinder their movements, but their guns had a longer range than their British counterparts, giving them a slight advantage. At first the weather was clear in the Herjangsfjord, but mist started to appear as the ships approached Narvik. Then the British ships were spotted and they opened fire. German reports say the range was about five to six miles. A running battle down the fjord ensued as Warburton-Lee's ships headed west. He also ordered the ships to make smoke to hinder the German fire. A second signal was then sent from *Lüdemann* to Captain Bey: "*Heidkamp* sunk. Bonte killed. Three destroyers ready in harbour as protective batteries." Then, as the Germans were slowly closing on the British ships, they all had to take evasive action to avoid three torpedoes coming out of Narvik harbour, fired by *Lüdemann*, thus losing any advantage they had gained.

There were two more German warships in the area at Ballangen, the *Thiele* and the *Arnim*, under the overall command of Captain Berger.

They had also heard the messages from *Lüdemann*, and in spite of the apparent urgency of the situation, Berger waited until about 0545 before moving, possibly due

HMS *Hardy* aground in Narvik Fjord. (The National Archives)

to snowstorms. Within minutes they were approaching Ofotfjord, with the visibility improving all the time. At 0550, five warships were seen ahead and were recognised as H-class destroyers from the Royal Navy. It appeared the British were sailing into a trap. At a range of about three miles, the *Thiele* opened fire on HMS *Hardy*. The two German ships held an advantage, because although outnumbered, they could initially fire broadside on. Also, only two British ships – the *Hardy* and the *Havock* – could see their enemy because of the smoke screen. It was briefly thought that these two ships might be a couple of cruisers sent to support the withdrawal, but this was soon corrected. *Hardy* steered away so that her rear guns could fire back. Warburton-Lee sent a signal to the rest of the flotilla at 0555, which simply instructed them: "Keep on engaging enemy."

The third salvo fired by the *Thiele* is thought to have straddled the *Hardy*. Shortly afterwards she was hit several more times; her two front turrets were put out of action and the bridge, wheelhouse and superstructure were also badly damaged. Captain Warburton-Lee was severely wounded, having been hit in both legs and the head. Many others on the bridge were killed or wounded, leaving the ship was temporarily leaderless. One of the few survivors was Warburton-Lee's secretary, Lieutenant Stanning, who had been at the rear of the bridge, making notes on what was happening. One shell-burst threw him into the air, he struck the gyro compass housing and was knocked unconscious. Coming to some moments later, he thought he was the only one left alive on the bridge, having

The German destroyer *Hans Lüdemann*. (The National Archives)

sustained wounds to his legs and back. He assumed command as *Hardy* sped down the fjord, dangerously close to the shoreline. Stanning struggled down to the deserted wheelhouse, where he took the wheel for a time before he was relieved by Able Seaman Smale and was able to return to the shattered bridge. The *Arnim* now also joined in the attack and scored several hits, including some on the boiler room. With all power lost, *Hardy* started drifting. Stanning decided he had to try to save as many of the crew as possible, and shouted "hard-a-port" to Smale, with the intention of beaching the *Hardy*. Around this time, Lieutenant Heppel, the torpedo officer, arrived on the bridge and at first cancelled this order. However, he soon agreed to reverse it when he realised the severity of the *Hardy's* situation. Coasting along, the *Hardy* ran aground on the south side of the fjord at Vidrek, around three miles east of Ballangen.

The First Lieutenant, Lieutenant-Commander Mansell, who had not been on the bridge when it was hit, then appeared and gave the order to abandon ship, as the fiercely burning wreck was still under fire from the Germans. The *Hardy's* last remaining torpedo was fired at one of the German ships but missed, and one of the guns continued to fire after the beaching, but soon ran out of ammunition. The crew struggled ashore as best they could. Lieutenant Stanning collected the confidential books and codes, and dropped them over the stern in the weighted bag kept ready for such an occasion. He then slid into the water and struggled ashore. He later recorded that his watch stopped at 0712. It has been suggested that the Germans later recovered the bag and were able to dry out the books and documents and use them as valuable intelligence tools.

The commander of the *Hardy*, Warburton-Lee, was briefly conscious as he was bought ashore on a raft, but died soon afterwards on the icy shoreline. His efforts around Narvik did not go unnoticed and he was posthumously awarded the first Victoria Cross of the war. His citation read as follows:

HMS *Hardy*. (The National Archives)

For gallantry, enterprise and daring in command of the force engaged in the First Battle of Narvik, on 10th April, 1940. On being ordered to carry out an attack on Narvik, Captain Warburton-Lee learned that the enemy was holding the place in much greater force than had been thought. He signalled to the Admiralty that six German destroyers and one submarine were there, that the channel might be mined, and that he intended to attack at dawn. The Admiralty replied that he alone could judge whether to attack, and that whatever decision he made would have full support. Captain Warburton led his flotilla of five destroyers up the fjord in heavy snow-storms, arriving off Narvik just after daybreak. He took the enemy completely by surprise and made three successful attacks on warships and merchantmen in the harbour. As the flotilla withdrew, five enemy destroyers of superior gun power were encountered and engaged. The captain was mortally wounded by a shell which hit the bridge of HMS *Hardy*. His last signal was "Continue to engage the enemy".

One of the crew of HMS *Hardy*, F. Mason, commented about his experiences at Narvik on 9 and 10 April:

I was a Leading Seaman and Leading Torpedo Man (LTO for short) and my job on board was the care and maintenance of the after set of quadruple torpedo tubes. I was classed as Number One on the Tubes. This was my action station, cruising station and general work station. The Tubes Crew also formed part of the Depth Charge Watch Keepers. We could change positions very quickly.

Later on that evening (9th April) Lieutenant Heppel had it broadcast that anyone interested could congregate in the forward mess deck and he and other officers would explain to us what to expect at Narvik and our course of action. They had drawn up a fairly good chart of the area on a blackboard showing the harbour and where we expected to find German warships. Surprise was the keyword of success and we hoped to sneak close into the harbour at the very first light of day and blast away. Thinking of it afterwards, I was amazed to realise how accurate they had been with their predictions.

Since the previous sea action, on training our after-tubes, I noticed they had become exceedingly stiff as if seizing up. The training numbers were having a hell of a job getting them to move. I had searched underneath for any grease nipples and applied a grease gun where I could use it. I called on the Chief EA to see what he could make of it but he was useless! All I got was some sarcastic remarks that we did not know our job. Throughout that long night it was a constant worry to me that if we got a quick order to train starboard, we were in trouble.

On we steamed through the dark arctic night; closed up at action stations; huddled around our weaponry; foremost tubes trained to starboard; after tubes trained to port; firing cartridges inserted but "ready" pushes withdrawn. No noise, no talking - just the gentle swish of water against the ship's side. Above us and aft No. 4 gun crew closed up and as silent as the grave. Then somewhere near a flicker of sparks and we immediately jumped into action. Below in his little galley our Captain's Maltese cook Giuseppe was endeavouring to cook his master's supper. In seconds his "charley noble" chimney was dismantled amid a deck plate screwed over the hole. The next minute he was out through the after door wondering why his galley had so suddenly choked up with smoke and fumes and his captain's supper in ruins. Just too bad for "the old man".

Occasionally we sighted a jut of land in the middle of nowhere; now and then a tiny blue flash of a signal for the next ship astern; otherwise total blackness.

It was now 0400 on the 10th April 1940 and a whispered message came though - "We are within 15 minutes of Narvik". Nerves were getting tensed up and straining our eyes we could just make out a snow covered shore line, and what looked like a scuttled merchant ship partly lying on its side.

Then suddenly the order from the bridge "All tubes ready starboard". This was the dreaded moment and I knew we were in trouble. Our four training numbers were struggling desperately to get the tubes around 180 degrees; at the same time the foremost tubes were firing and all their torpedoes were gone. With that, all hell broke loose as our five 4.7 inch guns opened up on targets that became visible.

With our communication man screaming his head off "Ready starboard - ready starboard!" I felt completely helpless, but then the men from our other tubes saw

Abandoned and burnt out German destroyer. (The National Archives)

our predicament and quickly set to pushing like hell to get those obstinate tubes into position.

A split second before they locked into position I was knocking in the "ready" pushes; the TL in the torpedo control had his fingers on the firing switch and the first torpedo shot out causing the tubes to whip and the "fish" to slightly graze the protecting stanchion. Then the tubes locked and two more missiles followed, leaving us with one.

The destroyer then turned to port picking up speed, but we still could not see much of our target area as it was shrouded in smoke from direct torpedo hits. Later we were told by some escaped merchant seaman that we had made a terrible mess of German naval ships lying alongside the wall in the harbour; some of them had received more than one direct hit. Perhaps our torpedoes should have been spread out a bit more.

In a matter of minutes we were well clear and out in the open fjord and had a chance to assess any damage the *Hardy* had received. There were no casualties as far as we knew but we noticed a few small shell holes in the after funnel. Tansy Lee, one of our number, picked up a small shell lying nearby; he quickly dropped it and kicked it over the ship's side as it was red hot!

For us, the torpedo men, we thought it was all over as we retreated down to the entrance to the fjord. I was wishing we could have got rid of the last "fish" so that we could stock up a complete new outfit when we got back to base. It was not to be! Our captain had decided to go back in again, leading the others in the flotilla to give them a chance to fire their torpedoes. This time it was quite different as

guns up to 6in calibre.

Havock and *Greyhound* spent much of the late morning and early afternoon patrolling the outer Vestfjord. It was fairly quiet until around 1530, when they obtained a sonar contact; and shortly afterwards the conning tower of a submarine, *U64*, could be seen breaking the surface. Apparently its depth-controlling system had broken and she shot to the surface. The two ships raced towards the position as the U-boat went into a crash dive. Many depth charges were dropped and an oil slick appeared on the surface, but *U64* was only slightly damaged and survived to fight another day.

Earlier in the day, Captain Yates had taken *Penelope* and several of the accompanying destroyers into the fjord, with the objectives of preventing German reinforcements reaching Narvik and stopping any of the ships bottled up there escaping. Admiral Whitworth sent instructions in a signal timed at 1116:

> Enemy forces reported in Narvik consist of one cruiser, five destroyers and one submarine. Troop transports may be expected to arrive through Vestfjord or through Inner Leads disregarding minefields. Your object is to prevent reinforcements reaching Narvik. Establish a destroyer position between positions 67° 47' N, 14° 20' E and 68° 2' N, 13° 40'E, one destroyer also to patrol north east of minefield during daylight. Enemy submarines may operate in West Fjord. Establish warning and anti-submarine patrol 30 miles north eastward of your patrol line.

Some of the captains wanted to press on to Narvik, but Captain Yates would not do this and decided to remain in the Vestfjord. In the evening, however, Yates received a signal from the Admiralty asking him to consider taking his available destroyers in the Narvik area and attacking the enemy either that night or the following day.

Whitworth, once again sidelined, pointed out this would weaken the patrol line in the Vestfjord area and might enable the Germans to slip through with reinforcements. Yates also suggested that it might be best to wait for more ships and thought that an attack on the morning of 12 April would be a suitable alternative. London agreed with this.

At 1904 on the evening of 10 April, the Admiralty sent the following signal to Admiral Forbes, copied to Admiral Whitworth:

> As enemy is now established at Narvik recapture of that place takes priority over operations against Bergen and Trondheim. Expedition is being prepared as quickly as possible. It is of primary importance to prevent Narvik being reinforced by sea. The possibility to seize and hold a temporary base near Narvik with a small military force is under urgent examination. In the meantime, you will presumably arrange for a temporary refuelling anchorage in north. As Narvik must also be of primary importance to the Germans, it seems possible that battle cruisers may turn up there.

A "temporary refuelling anchorage" had already been sorted out in the Lofoten Islands, and in time a minor repair facility was also established there. Two destroyers, *Eskimo* and *Bedouin*, patrolled the mouth of the fjord for much of the day without incident until about 1900, when close to the Barøy lighthouse, around 250 yards in front of the patrolling ships, two explosions occurred one after the other. The two captains consulted and agreed that there might be a remotely controlled minefield up ahead, so decided to turn away towards Tranøy. The explosions actually came from torpedoes fired by a German U-boat, *U25*, which had exploded prematurely.

We now turn to the British reaction to the German invasion of Norway and the military moves that followed.

The badge awarded to German troops for the Narvik action. (Imperial War Museum)

7

Further air and naval actions

As well as Narvik, the Germans also had forces ashore and afloat at other important harbours, namely Bergen and Trondheim. On 9 April, Admiral Forbes had been ordered by the Admiralty to prepare a plan for attacking German ships at both ports. He was also advised that his fleet should "take control" of the approaches to these two places – assuming that he thought he had enough resources to do this and that the coastal defences still appeared to be under Norwegian control. The aircraft carrier allocated to Forbes, HMS *Furious*, arrived on 10 April and he decided to use his newly acquired air power to attack Trondheim. *Furious* had two squadrons from the Fleet Air Arm, 816 and 818, both flying Fairey Swordfish aircraft. Forbes requested that Bergen be attacked by Skuas from the Orkney Islands.

A reconnaissance flight by a Sunderland aircraft from 228 Squadron on the afternoon of 10 April confirmed that there was German shipping in Trondheim, so Forbes gave the go-ahead for the air attack. Around 0400 on 11 April, 18 Swordfishes took off from *Furious* about 90 miles off the Norwegian coast, in what would be the first aerial torpedo attack of the Second World War. The first aircraft from 816 Squadron arrived over Trondheim around 0515, to find the harbour obscured to some extent by cloud. Undaunted, the squadron commander, Lieutenant-Commander Gardner, led the aircraft through the clouds with the intention of attacking the German ships in the harbour. To their dismay there were no ships to attack, so Gardner led the aircraft towards Skjorenfjord. On the way they sighted a German destroyer at anchor. Their target was the *Riedel*, which had been temporarily grounded in the shallow fjord. All nine 816 Squadron Swordfishes launched their weapons but four exploded prematurely and others ran into rock formations and detonated harmlessly. The frustrated airmen returned to the *Furious*.

Meanwhile, 818 Squadron found another destroyer, the *Eckholdt*, heading towards Trondheim after leaving the *Admiral Hipper* as she had been unable to keep up. Lieutenant-Commander Sydney-Turner ordered his squadron to attack. Again the torpedoes did not work well. Two went off early and the *Eckholdt* was able to avoid the other six that were dropped, so the aircraft returned to *Furious*, which they reached around 0630.

When war broke out in September 1939, the Swordfish was virtually obsolete. The design dated back to the early Thirties, when the British Air Ministry issued specification S.9/30 for a "fleet spotter reconnaissance aircraft". The Fairey Aviation Company submitted a privately financed design. Later design improvements led to the designation: "Torpedo Spotter Reconnaissance". It was a large, slow biplane with a low wing loading, ideal for actions off carrier decks. The structure was largely metal, covered with fabric. The first version was powered by a Bristol Pegasus IIM air-cooled, nine cylinder radial engine, developing 635hp. This was severely underpowered. The next, much-improved, prototype used a Pegasus IIIM3 with 775hp. First flown in 1934, this aircraft exceeded the government's demands, so an order was placed for the first 86 production examples in 1935. The first deliveries were made in the following year, further orders continuing to be placed well after the beginning of the war.

The three-seater airplane could easily lift off a carrier deck with a standard 18in 1,610lb torpedo slung between the wheels under the fuselage. Its ungainly looks gave it the nickname "Stringbag".

In spite of its apparent lack of sophistication, the Swordfish was to prove excellent in its intended role. Although highly vulnerable to attack by fighter planes, its low speed and stable stance made it easy to line up for a torpedo attack, coming in from a beam of a hostile vessel, while staying below the level at which the enemy ships could respond with anti-aircraft fire. Its slow flying speed made landings much safer on carriers: into the wind, the closing speed could be as little as 30 knots. A few were fitted with floats so they could be launched from a catapult on capital ships, and then land nearby and be lifted aboard to fly another day.

The performance was modest, with a top speed of 139mph and a cruising speed of around 110mph. It took 19 minutes to climb to 5,000 feet, with a maximum ceiling – presuming the crew in their open cockpit could bear it –of 15,000 feet and a range of 350 nautical miles. For offensive and defensive actions, it was armed with one fixed Browning machine gun firing forward, and a rear gunner with a similar weapon.

Its main weapon was either an 18in 1,610lb under-slung torpedo; one 1,500lb mine; three 500lb bombs; two 550lb and two 250lb bombs; three Mk VII depth charges; or eight 60lb rockets. The Swordfish remained operational until the end of the war, gaining the distinction of being the last biplane to see active service.

The low speed of the Swordfish and the necessity of a long straight approach made it difficult to deliver an aerial torpedo against well-defended targets. An approach at 5,000 feet was preferred, followed by a dive to the torpedo release altitude of 18 feet. The maximum range of the early Mark XII torpedo was 1,500 yards at 40 knots and 3,500 yards at 27 knots The torpedo travelled 200 yards forward from its release to water impact, and required another 300 yards to stabilise at its preset depth and arm itself. The ideal release distance was 1,000 yards from target, if the aircraft could survive to get that close.

Following the initial unsuccessful sorties, a proper reconnaissance of Trondheim harbour was ordered to be carried out. Two Swordfish risked a lengthy flight up the fjord and around the harbour. They reported that just a few seaplanes had been seen in Trondheim harbour, with the only ship a "small enemy warship". This was actually a Norwegian minelayer, the *Frøya*, which the two aircraft attacked her with the bombs they were carrying. In spite of not being fired at, the Swordfishes missed the target with all their bombs and no casualties ensued. Both aircraft returned to *Furious*, although on their return they were shadowed by a German aircraft. In the late afternoon the *Luftwaffe* struck at *Furious*, but the high-level attack was not pressed home with any enthusiasm and the ship was undamaged.

During the morning of 11 April, the Admiralty issued orders to Admiral Forbes to investigate reports of German merchantmen off Trondheimsfjord. Two destroyers, HMS *Ilex* and HMS *Isis*, both from the 3rd Destroyer Flotilla, were sent to investigate but initially found no ships. Splitting up, *Isis*, under the command of Commander J. Clouston, steamed towards Trondheim, while *Ilex* went north towards the Stjørnfjord. Around 1315, as *Isis* was approaching Hysnes, she came under fire from a shore battery at Brettingen Fort about two miles away. *Isis* returned fire, but neither side achieved any hits. Commander Clouston ordered a smokescreen to be laid and that both destroyers should get out of the fjord at high speed. Upon reporting the incident, both destroyers were ordered to join the 1st Cruiser Squadron in a continued search for German shipping in the fjords north of Trondheim, but again nothing was found. By now, Admiral Forbes was being focused by London towards Narvik. He decided there was little to gain by chasing non-existent German ships in central Norway, and ordered his ships north.

As there were few airfields in Norway, it was realised that either controlling them or denying their use to the enemy was key. The Germans brought in fighters, dive-bombers and anti-aircraft guns, and the British did their best to knock them out. At Sola, a solitary Blenheim from 254 Squadron of Coastal Command strafed the airfield. It reputedly destroyed one JU52 transport aircraft and damaged another at the main base, and destroyed one HE59 at the seaplane base. But more than pinprick attacks were needed, so the area was given as a target to the RAF, and in particular Bomber Command. On 11 April, two directives arrived at its Headquarters. The first read:

> Aircraft have general permission to attack without warning any ships, merchant or otherwise, under way within ten miles of the Norwegian coast, south of latitude 61° 00'N and anywhere east of longitude 06° 00'E, as far south as latitude 54° 00'N. Ships at anchor may be attacked if definitely observed to be enemy.

The second directive was:

> Confirming conversation between AOC-in-C and DHO [Directorate of Home Operations] today, guerrilla bombing operations against Stavanger aerodrome and seaplane anchorage should be carried out as soon as possible and continued until further orders with the object of destroying aircraft installations and runways. Effort should not exceed one Wellington squadron a day. Attacks should be carried out by small formations or single aircraft spaced out in time best to avoid fighter defences.

Bomber Command was also instructed to start looking at operations on the German lines of communication in and around Kiel, the Kattegat and Skagerrak. However, their chief, Air Vice Marshal C. Portal, was not very keen on diverting resources to what he considered a sideshow, and, like many others, favoured concentrating resources on the Western Front. He commented that in his opinion his men were being asked to undertake a "role for which they were neither trained nor suitably equipped". But having received orders, he grudgingly agreed that four squadrons, already based in Scotland and normally carrying out maritime operations, could also look after Norway. These four squadrons were the Wellington-equipped 9 and 115 Squadrons, and 107 and 110 Squadrons with Blenheims. These squadrons were based at Kinloss and Lossiemouth, both near Inverness in northern Scotland. He also gave permission for squadrons based further south to be involved, but this of course would mean longer flights and potentially lighter bomb loads.

In the first RAF bombing raid of the Norwegian campaign on a mainland target, six Wellingtons of 115 Squadron targeted Stavanger airfield on the evening of 11 April. It was intended for two Blenheims from 254 Squadron of Coastal Command to act as fighter escort. The Blenheims would also strafe the airfield, hopefully to deter any anti-aircraft fire. However,, the two groups never met and they both went in separately. The Blenheim attack was ineffectual and probably only served to alert the defences, so when the Wellingtons arrived, several ME110s were airborne and prevented any bombs from falling on the airfield. During evasive action, the aircraft flown by Pilot Officer F. Barber was hit by flak and crashed into Stavanger town centre, killing all the crew and several civilians.

The six-man crew were buried together in Stavanger's Eiganes cemetery. They were: Pilot Officer F. Barber – grave Z42 (pilot); Pilot Officer D. Rankin – grave Z43 (second pilot); Pilot Officer P. Bull – grave Z41 (gunner); Sergeant G. Juby – grave Z40 (navigator); Sergeant A. Pearce – grave Z45 (observer); and Leading Aircraftsman L. Westcott – grave Z44 (gunner). Their date of death is given as 12 April 1940.

On the following day, when 12 Wellingtons from 38 and 149 Squadrons were on a maritime patrol looking for probably non-existent German battleships off Stavanger, they were attacked by JU88s and ME110s. Three were shot down. These and other losses meant that squadrons had to be rotated, so on 14 April the two Wellington squadrons were ordered south and replaced by further Blenheims, and 77 Squadron equipped with Whitley bombers. The Whitleys were earmarked to undertake raids against the Trondheim area because they were one of the few available aircraft with the necessary range. Most attacks, except those by Coastal Command Hudsons or Blenheims, were carried out at night, with the expectation that the aircrews would be able to find small targets using the skills of their navigators and dead reckoning. It was also believed more German aircraft would be on the ground at night, so the bombing would be more effective. While not decrying the bravery of the aircrew, finding precision targets at night, without proper navigational aid, was a tough ask for Bomber Command in 1940.

So the majority of the daylight air attacks fell to the Blenheim squadrons. The Blenheim had been designed and entered service in the 1930s, and the Blenheim Mk I outshone most biplane fighters in the late 1930s. But by 1940 it stood little chance against the German ME109 during daylight operations, as it had a top speed of only just over 260mph. Also, when attacking targets in Norway, the round trip was very close to its maximum range so very little leeway was left for navigation error or mechanical failure.

Between 15 April and 10 May, 35 attacks were carried out on Sola airfield, yet achieved very little. As well as the anti-aircraft guns that the Germans had flown in, fighters were also based there and made accurate bombing of the airfield difficult. An additional factor was that because 500lb bombs were the largest dropped, damage from these, if dropped close enough to the runways, was relatively easily repaired. Another factor that hampered the effectiveness of the attacks was the weather. For example, out of six aircraft sent on 16

April, only one made it to the target, the others turning back because of ice build-up on their aircraft. On 19 April, because of previous losses, the crews were told to abort if there was insufficient cloud cover, so seven out of nine aircraft turned back. Of the remaining two, one bombed "an airfield" somewhere – but probably not Sola – and the other failed to return. On the following days, aircraft were sent out on three occasions, but all turned back owing to bad weather. The RAF did its best in trying circumstances, but a number of factors, including poor aircraft and the lack of heavy bomb loads, meant the bombers failed to have any meaningful effect on German air operations in Norway.

The German Navy at Narvik had been given a bloody nose at the hands of a small number of British destroyers. As well as losing two ships, two more were extensively damaged and not fit for combat, so the men who were not required to assist with repairs were sent ashore and placed under the command of the Army in a composite "Naval Battalion". These men were led by Captain Erdmenger and came from four ships - the *Lüdemann*, *Roeder*, *Heidkamp* and *Schmitt*. They were used to secure the harbour and town area, freeing up troops for more important duties. At 1400 on 10 April, a signal arrived from Group West HQ advising that all combat-ready ships were to leave that evening and join up with the *Scharnhorst* and *Gneisenau*, acting as escorts for the voyage back to German waters. Bey reported back that only two ships – the *Giese* and the *Zenker* – would be ready to undertake this, as four others (*Arnim*, *Künne*, *Koellner* and *Thiele*) required repairs and refuelling. At 1830, a further signal arrived from Wilhelmshaven: "*Zenker* and *Giese* to depart with C-in-C at nightfall." Around 1930, the two ships left Narvik harbour, moving cautiously as it was felt highly likely that Royal Navy ships could still be patrolling the fjords leading to the open seas. This caution was justified, for when the two ships reached the area of Tranøy, HMS *Penelope* and two destroyers came into sight; Bey promptly turned his ships around and returned to Narvik.

Once back at Narvik, Bey sent a signal advising that he had run into superior forces. In his opinion, his breakout would have to wait for bad weather conditions so his ships could slip past the Royal Navy. He also requested that more U-boats be sent to the area to dampen down enemy activity. The response suggested that any ruse of war could be applied during subsequent breakout attempts, including the use of the British flag. The tanker *Skagerrak* had been redirected from Trondheim and would remain offshore as long as possible; if she could not be reached, fuel could be found in Bergen or Kristiansand. Trondheim was to be avoided, as there were already ships there, needing whatever fuel and repair facilities were available.

Koellner and *Künne* completed what repairs they could by 11 April, and also topped up their fuel tanks. As a bonus, *Lüdemann* reported that she was just about ready to sail, and crew members who had been sent ashore were recalled. In spite of his orders and banks of thick fog, Bey did not attempt a breakout that night, sending a signal to Group West that "breakout of destroyers as impossible tonight as last night". Bey then took the prudent measure of sending the *Koellner* to patrol off Ballangen, to avoid getting caught unawares by any British incursion. But around midnight she ran aground, causing significant damage to her hull. Although not in danger of sinking, she was leaking badly in several compartments and limped back to Narvik,. The *Zenker* also scraped the seabed and damaged one of her propellers, which limited her speed to 20 knots.

HMS *Warspite* coming into action off Narvik. (The National Archives)

One of the patrolling U-boats, *U48*, also ran into elements of the Home Fleet on 11 April. She fired two salvos of three torpedoes at some of the cruisers. Once again mechanical problems bugged the torpedoes; four exploded prematurely and the others missed. When this was reported back to U-boat headquarters in Kiel, an investigation was started, but no real solutions were found. It was, however, decided to use a mixture of contact and magnetic pistols in future; in later years the U-boat threat to her maritime lifeline caused the greatest danger to Britain. The Royal Navy had been lucky in that around half of the torpedoes fired by the Germans so far had exploded short of their intended targets.

There was a brief lull as both sides reassessed their options. This lasted until the evening of 12 April, when eight Swordfish aircraft from 818 Squadron of the Fleet Air Arm, flying off HMS *Furious* (positioned off the Lofoten Islands), launched an attack on Narvik. Following the abortive torpedo attack on Trondheim harbour the previous day, it was decided to use bombs, and each Swordfish was armed with four 250lb and four 20lb bombs. Flying conditions were very poor, with strong winds and snow, making life very difficult in the open cockpits of the Swordfishes. The Germans received early warning of their approach, and anti-aircraft gunners were waiting for the attack. The raid was pressed home but no ships were sunk immediately. However, two were damaged and later sank, eight sailors were killed and around 20 wounded from shrapnel and blast injuries. Two of the attacking Swordfish were shot down and crashed in the Ofotfjord. The crews were rescued by the *Penelope* and *Punjabi*.

Following closely behind 816 Squadron was 818 Squadron, but the weather conditions had by then deteriorated even further. They turned back before reaching

Narvik, and faced a difficult landing on the heavily pitching *Furious*. One Swordfish ended up in the water but the crew was rescued. In Narvik, Captain Bey had realistically given up all hope of achieving a successful breakout. His fears were confirmed when he received a signal in the early hours of 13 April telling him that patrolling aircraft had spotted a large vessel with seven or eight destroyers in Vestfjord. As *Koellner* was for all practical purposes dead in the water, Bey ordered her to move to Tärstad on the Ramnes Narrows, to act as an early warning and defensive fire ship. The water was relatively shallow here so she was in less danger of sinking, but as it was not thought good water for torpedoes, her remaining stock was offloaded and given to the *Thiele* and *Arnim*. The following message was received in the late morning: "Expect enemy attack this afternoon. *Repulse*, *Warspite*, five Tribals (a fast, powerful class of destroyer), four destroyers and probably carrier." On the basis of this information, Bey ordered that the remaining destroyers be ready to sail at 1300, regardless of their condition. Bey had the *Künne* fully operational with all guns ready for action and a full load of torpedoes; *Arnim* was in a similar condition but with only six torpedoes left. *Lüdemann* had four combat-ready guns and only a few torpedoes. *Giese* and *Zenker* were still undergoing repairs. The commander of the *Giese* suggested he might be capable of 28 knots, but *Zenker*'s captain thought 20 would be his top speed. The real problems were the *Thiele* – still needing a few more days of patching up – and the *Roeder*, which required about another week before she was seaworthy.

The German intelligence was correct. The Admiralty had issued orders to Admiral Forbes that he was to attack Narvik on a far heavier scale. The Forbes group had sailed north from the Trondheim area during the night of 11/12 April and met up with the Whitworth group at around 0730. Further instructions came from London that afternoon: "Clean up enemy naval forces and batteries in Narvik by using a battleship heavily escorted by destroyers with synchronised dive-bombing attacks from *Furious*."

A number of ships had been sent back to act as escorts for the troop convoys, so those available for this mission were the battleships *Renown*, *Rodney* and *Warspite*, together with HMS *Furious* and six destroyers as close escort. One ship unable to take part was the cruiser *Penelope*, which had run aground on the afternoon of 11 April off the Flenvaer Light north of Bodø while searching for German transports. She had been badly damaged: her hull had been holed, she had propeller and rudder damage and some of her engine and boiler rooms had been flooded. On the next high tide, she floated off and towed by HMS *Eskimo* to a repair facility that had been set up at Skjelfjord. Forbes had been advised to set up a temporary refuelling anchorage, and this had been positioned at Skjelfjord in the Lofoten Islands. HMS *Hotspur* was the first ship there and was setting up the repair facility. A German merchant ship, the *Alster*, which had been captured by HMS *Icarus* on the morning of 11 April whilst en route for Narvik, was taken there. Her cranes were later used to assist in repairs of other ships. The tanker SS *British Lady* was sent to the anchorage, escorted by two destroyers, HMS *Encounter* and HMS *Grenade* (from the 12th and 1st Destroyer Flotillas respectively). She arrived on 12 April and refuelled many ships over the coming days.

The following is taken from the war diary of the 2nd Cruiser Squadron:

HMS *Eskimo* after suffering damage at the hands of the Germans. (Imperial War Museum N233)

At 1500/11 *Penelope* reported being aground off Flenvaer Light with *Kimberley* and *Eskimo* standing by. At 1700 she reported being afloat in tow of *Eskimo* and proceeded to Skjelfjord at four knots. *Kimberley* had been instructed at 1630 to proceed to Bodø and deal with the enemy transport; *Bedouin* to detail two destroyers to deal with tanker in Tannholm Fjord. This latter instruction was subsequently cancelled.

At 1510/12 *Penelope* reported herself anchored in Vestfjord. Pumps had the damage under control, but should the diesel fail, the ship would have to be beached in Vestfjord.

The extent of the damage was reported by telegram to be: Keel, starboard, "A" and "B" strakes port and starboard and double bottom structure in vicinity buckled or fractured from stem to stern on both sides of the ship. Starboard forward and starboard after shaft "A" brackets fractured. Starboard outer, port outer, and starboard after inner propellers damaged, will require spares to be fitted. Rudder frame damaged, probably requiring renewal. (*Penelope*'s 0315/20 and 1446/25). She would probably be ready to sail on 8th May.

It took eight hours to get HMS *Penelope* to Skjelfjord. *Penelope* would have surely sunk and her crew been taken prisoner had it not been for the local Norwegians, who not only provided shelter and sustenance for the crew, but also organised pumping out, repairs

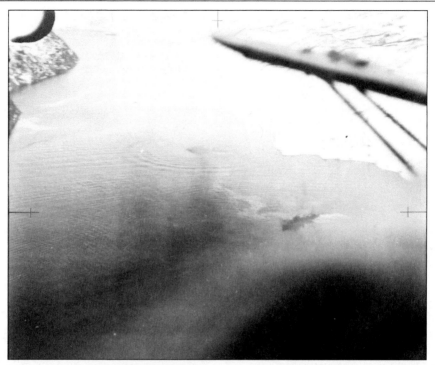

HMS *Eskimo* after torpedo attack. (The National Archives)

and supplies. The 1920s vintage salvage vessel *Skaerkodder* provided the much-needed equipment and expertise to make good temporary repairs, whilst essential supplies, information and transport were provided by the local fishermen in their "puffers" (60 feet long fishing boats). A young Norwegian, Hartvig Sverdrup (or "Snowdrop" to the crew), was above all others responsible for the success of the operation. Other damaged RN ships came and went during April, among them *Cossack*, *Eskimo* and *Punjabi*. HMS *Jupiter* arrived with pumping equipment from the UK. *Penelope*, however, was forced to stay throughout most of April until early May. To aid in maintaining the secrecy of her location, the crew had to paint her in a unique brown and white camouflage scheme to match the surrounding snow-covered slopes of the mountains. This had to be repeatedly altered, with more brown paint replacing the areas of white, as the surrounding thaw gained pace! A particular innovation that for some time was treated with suspicion by the Royal Navy sailors was the locals use of wooden plugs covered in sheep tallow to fill in bullet holes, but in time they proved to be first class and kept the seas out.

Admiral Forbes meanwhile ordered Whitworth to undertake "Operation DW" (as the attack was codenamed) on the afternoon of 13 April, with the following ships allocated: *Warspite*, *Bedouin*, *Cossack*, *Eskimo*, *Forester*, *Foxhound*, *Hero*, *Icarus*, *Kimberley* and *Punjabi*. His task as ordered was "the destruction of German warships, merchant ships and defences in the Narvik area". Admiral Whitworth moved his flag across to the *Warspite* and set off, picking up his destroyer support on the way. Admiral Forbes remained about 30 miles to the west of the Lofoten Islands with *Rodney*, *Renown*, *Furious* and five destroyers,

HMS *Eskimo* still fighting after the torpedo attack. (The National Archives)

with another four around Skjelfjord. It was considered that the biggest danger to the force would come from the shore batteries and mines. For once the air threat was believed to be negligible, as there were thought to be no German aircraft in the area and air cover for the British could be provided by *Furious*. One threat that was virtually ignored in the narrow waters was that of the U-boat – and there were five in the area.

Nevertheless, in the early morning of 13 April Whitworth's ships passed the Tranøy lighthouse doing about 20 knots. The weather favoured the attackers, overcast with a low cloud base, with visibility reduced at frequent occasions by rain and sleet showers. HMS *Eskimo* had been patrolling off Tranøy during the night and morning, hoping to secure the entrance to Ofotfjord. At around 1045, just as the main force was approaching this area, a submarine was sighted around four miles away in the path of the approaching fleet. The captain of the *Eskimo*, Commander Micklethwait, later commented: "It was a small boat and it flashed the letter 'U' to me as a form of recognition. I acknowledged this signal by light. He then made 'A A A' but receiving no answer and seeing *Eskimo* turn towards him, the submarine hurriedly dived."

Schultze, the captain of the *U48*, having realised it was not a friendly ship, dived. They remained undetected and undamaged in spite of several sweeps by the *Eskimo*, and several patterns of depth charges dropped in the narrow waters. Riding their luck, they apparently fired a salvo of torpedoes at *Warspite*, but without success. Further down the

HMS *Foxhound* heading towards Narvik. (The National Archives)

fjord, near Ramnes, another U-boat, *U46*, had managed to penetrate the escort screen and was around 750 yards away from the *Warspite*, when – to the good fortune of the *Warspite* – she ran on to a sandbank, and her bow and conning tower appeared above the fjord surface. Again this was missed by all the lookouts, but by the time she had backed off the sandbank, *Warspite* had moved out of effective range.

Admiral Whitworth was undoubtedly conscious of the fact that there were German ships in front of him, and wisely suggested to *Warspite's* captain that he launch his Swordfish to perform reconnaissance up the main and side fjords. Just before noon a Swordfish was launched. The pilot, Petty Officer F. Rice, later commented on the flight: "Flying in the fjords – particularly in the narrow ones – resembled flying in a tunnel between the steep sides of the fjord and the low cloud ceiling." Nevertheless, within minutes this sortie was paying dividends. Rice reported that an enemy destroyer was in the vicinity of Kjelde, and a few minutes later another was seen further up the fjord. Admiral Whitworth later commented: "I doubt if ever a ship borne aircraft has been used to such good purpose."

These two ships were the German destroyers *Koellner* and *Künne*. The Swordfish was spotted and fire directed at it, but Rice flew out of range. When the *Künne* was off Barøy, several ships were spotted on the horizon. The *Künne* increased speed in the expectation they might be friendly forces, but it was soon discovered they were undoubtedly British. There were now nine ships, so she hurriedly turned through 180 degrees and headed back towards Narvik, sending an alarm report. A few ineffective shots were exchanged between the destroyers, and *Künne* made good her escape. Back at Narvik, the Germans received the warning from *Künne* but they had thought the attack would come later in the day, so none of the destroyers had deployed to the side fjords as intended. Hurried orders were given to disperse at once, but the few U-boats in the harbour did not react with the same urgency as the destroyers. There was no co-ordinated thinking amongst the naval crews. One U-boat, *U25*, did not receive the warning and when it saw the Swordfish just dived out of harm's way; another, *U51*, believed the warning was for another air attack and also disappeared under the water; a third, *U64*, still trying to repair a defect in her periscope, remained at anchor. The offensive capability of some of these U-boats would be sorely missed in the coming hours.

Rice spotted *U64* stationary in the Herjangsfjord and decided to attack. Two 100lb bombs were aimed at her: one hit the bow and the second was a near miss close to the conning tower. Both bombs caused damage, and the near miss probably had the greater effect; the hull was cracked open, water started to pour in faster than the crew would get it out and she started to sink. Some fire was put up from the *U64* before she was abandoned and hit the Swordfish, damaging some of the control surfaces. Rice felt he could carry on with his mission provided that he flew slowly and manoeuvred gently. Flying back over Narvik around 1230, he discovered that none of the destroyers had yet left. This was reported back to *Warspite*.

The *Koellner* had orders to position herself at Tärstad, but she could not make it and so anchored parallel to and about half a mile off the shore near Djupvik, on the south side of the fjord. Her captain, Schulze-Hinrichs, hoped that he had not been spotted and that some British ships would emerge unsuspecting on to a broadside volley from his guns. But this was not to be, as Rice and his crew had seen her and signalled her position to *Warspite*. The *Koellner*'s masthead was also visible above the bank. Three British destroyers were in the lead – the Tribals *Bedouin*, *Eskimo* and *Punjabi* – and when they appeared just after 1300 there was a violent encounter. Fire was exchanged at a distance of just over two miles. None of the Tribals were hit but the *Koellner* was struck many times and one by one her guns disabled. The *Warspite* then hove into view and unleashed a few 15in shells into her at close range. Apparently some of these passed right through the ship and exploded on the shore. Within minutes the *Koellner* was a smoking wreck. She was finished off by at least one torpedo, and sank with the loss of 31 of her crew. The British ships carried on towards Narvik, where, around 1245, some of the German destroyers finally straggled out of the harbour. Captain Bey was on the *Zenker* and was followed out by *Arnim*. *Thiele* had already left a few minutes earlier, but *Giese* had not worked up enough steam and so stayed behind. The *Künne* could see her sister ships coming towards her, so once again reversed her course, and also laid down a smokescreen to try and hide them for as long as possible.

The Germans, although having a wider part of the fjord to operate in, were outgunned by the *Warspite*. The British were in a narrower section of the fjord and so could mostly only use their forward guns, while the Germans were able to criss-cross the space. There was much smoke and confusion during the early part of the engagement, and the gunnery from the British ships was not as accurate as it could have been. None of the German ships was hit, but some of the Royal Navy ships were straddled with firing that was later

Inner Rombakssfjord. (The National Archives)

recorded as "uncomfortably good". HMS *Cossack* had16 near misses. Her wireless aerial was shot away and shrapnel pierced the hull in several places, causing severe flooding. Pönitz, the captain of the *Zenker*, was able to position his ship for a torpedo attack on *Warspite*, but in doing so came under intense fire and the torpedoes he fired all missed. Then the *Arnim* was able to get in close enough to fire two salvos of three torpedoes at the destroyers. *Cossack*, *Forester* and *Kimberley* were able to avoid most of them, and one passed under the *Cossack* without making contact. The *U25* then entered the fray and fired torpedoes at the *Cossack*, but without success. The British did not realise the torpedoes had come from a submarine. The *U25* saw *Warspite* through her periscope but was too far away to fire at her. Her captain felt his best course of action would be to slip away and wait for the return trip of these prize targets at the Ramnes Narrows.

The Germans started falling back towards the Ofotfjord, and at around 1330 nine Swordfish from *Furious*, led by Captain A. Burch, flew over the British ships towards the Germans and commenced a dive-bombing attack. No hits were obtained on the warships, although the auxiliary *Kelt* was hit and later sunk. Two aircraft were shot down but the others made it safely back to *Furious*.

A critical problem now starting to affect all the German ships was lack of ammunition. Much had been expended that day and over the previous days, and at 1350 Bey gave orders to break off the engagement. A smokescreen was laid and he ordered his ships into the Rombakssfjord, on the basis that the big battleship could not follow them there.

Burning German destroyer taken from a Swordfish at Narvik. (The National Archives)

Künne either ignored or missed this signal and steered into the Herjangsfjord, where she was run aground near Bjerkvik. She had no ammunition left; even the star shells and practice rounds had been fired. Once all the crew had left, depth charges were rigged to go off. *Künne* had received no damage during this engagement, but was nevertheless now out of the fight. *Eskimo* and *Forester* had followed her into the fjord, and to make sure she was finished Commander Micklethwait ordered a torpedo to be fired at her, which broke off her stern.

Meanwhile, the *Giese* had finally raised enough steam ready to sail. Smidt, her captain, had heard via the radio that the other ships were heading for Rombakssfjord, and that he could be left on his own facing an unknown number of ships. Faced with this tricky situation, he recalled: "The proper duty of an officer and soldier is to inflict as much damage on the enemy as possible. We had about 10 minutes' worth of ammunition and all our torpedoes, so we could fight. But I had no hope that we would ever reach port again." He may have thought his prediction was coming true when one of the engines failed just as *Giese* was leaving the harbour, making it difficult to manoeuvre. *Bedouin* and *Punjabi* were bearing down on her. They loosed off five torpedoes, which all missed. *Giese* replied in kind, but with no more success. However, his 12.7cm guns were better aimed and scored at least six hits on the *Punjabi*, causing severe damage. Two of the shells entered just above the waterline on the starboard side, and others put most of the fire control and radios out of action, severed vital pipes and caused several fires. Seven men were killed and 14 wounded. *Punjabi's* captain, Commander Lean, was forced back and sent a signal to the flagship around 1400 which read: "Am damned sorry I have got to come out of it, main steam pipe and guns out of action."

Meanwhile, the engineers on *Giese* had managed to get the engines working again, and she left the harbour at her maximum speed of just about 10 knots. She was heading for disaster at this low speed, drawing the attention of five British destroyers. She suffered fatal damage from shells, although the torpedoes fired at her all missed. She fired back for a while but by 1415 was out of control and burning fiercely. Orders were given to abandon ship, but for 83 men it was too late. Eleven members of the crew were plucked out of the water by the *Foxhound*, and the remaining crew members struggled ashore as best they could. The abandoned hulk of the *Giese* drifted around the fjord until it sank just after midnight.

This still left the *Roeder* as a lame duck tied up in Narvik harbour and at least one of the torpedoes fired at *Giese* detonated against the pier to which she was attached. Using her forward turrets, she fired at targets when they passed within her arc of fire, aiming shells at *Bedouin*, *Punjabi* and even *Warspite,* achieving one hit close to the bridge on the latter target. The British initially thought this fire was coming from shore positions, but a message from the circling Swordfish revealed there was a destroyer tied up at the southern jetty. *Cossack* and *Kimberley* then moved into the harbour and both sides opened fire. *Cossack's* second salvo hit home, but she took seven hits herself and three holes were punched through the hull on the port side on or near the waterline. Shrapnel caused damage to the main steam pipe in *Cossack's* No. 1 boiler room and damage was also caused in the No. 2 boiler room. A fire in the lower mess deck led to the precautionary flooding of the forward magazine. Damage was also caused to the steering, and unable to control herself, she ran aground on the beach at Ankenes. In spite of this, the rear turrets of *Cossack* continued to fire at the *Roeder* and many hits were scored. *Warspite* weighed in with a couple of 15in rounds, and this was about the end for the *Roeder.* With the ammunition virtually exhausted, the gunners abandoned the ship. *Foxhound* approached her, with the intention of putting a party on board, but a small demolition party had stayed behind and set off a time-delay fuse before fleeing. Within a minute or so *Roeder* blew up and sank in the harbour.

Cossack's crew had suffered nine fatalities in this engagement, with another 21 wounded, of whom two later died. A cable was passed across from *Kimberley* and efforts made to pull her off the beach, but she was stuck fast and it seemed they would need to wait for the next high tide before being able to get her off. This would mean spending the night very close to the enemy, so Commander Sherbrooke gave orders that the codebooks and secret papers be destroyed. In preparation for a refloat, anything unnecessary was thrown overboard. The Germans did on the odd occasion go to investigate *Cossack*, but well-placed rounds from her main armament and pom-poms did much to deter such "sightseers".

The four remaining German destroyers, the *Arnim*, *Lüdemann*, *Thiele* and *Zenker*, had slipped into the Rombaksfjord. While they had escaped relatively unscathed so

German destroyer aground and on fire. (The National Archives)

far, they had little ammunition left, and preparations were being made to scuttle them should the grim situation deteriorate further. The only good news was that it was virtually impossible for the *Warspite* to follow the ships into the shallow waters. Both *Arnim* and *Zenker* were out of ammunition, so they sailed for the head of the fjord and were beached on sandbanks there. *Lüdemann* and *Thiele* did have some shells and torpedoes left, and intended to go down fighting. Five British destroyers were lurking around the entrance to the fjord – *Bedouin*, *Eskimo*, *Forester*, *Hero* and *Icarus* - and with the benefit of intelligence from Rice, flying above, they knew there were facing at least two enemy ships. The situation was rather confused as smoke floats had been dropped by the fleeing Germans, but nevertheless Commander Micklethwait took *Eskimo* inside the fjord at around 1445, closely followed by *Forester*. The others stood by to provide whatever support they could. The range was about three miles when the *Lüdemann* opened fire on *Eskimo* with her aft guns. All the remaining ammunition had been moved to these guns, and she also fired her four remaining torpedoes, but these all missed. Accurate fire from *Eskimo* started to fall on and around the three working turrets, putting them out of action. Captain Friedrichs decided that was his lot and beached *Lüdemann* close to the *Arnim* and *Zenker*. This only left the *Thiele*, and she still had four guns working. Her captain, Wolff, was determined to buy as much time as possible for his fellow captains to destroy their ships and save as many men as they could. He also had a few torpedoes left.

As *Thiele* was the last ship still fighting back, fire was concentrated on her. She was hit many times, starting several fires, but continued to return fire. Commander Micklethwait, perhaps wanting to finish off *Thiele* quickly so the group could gain booty from the other three ships beached further up the fjord, put his ship in danger. *Eskimo* manoeuvred herself into a position from which she intended to fire a broadside torpedo salvo, but *Thiele* struck first and fired three torpedoes at *Eskimo*. When these were spotted, Micklethwait was forced to order full speed ahead to avoid them. One of them was avoided in this way, but the coast was approaching very rapidly, so full astern had to be ordered. A collision with rocks was narrowly avoided but this placed the ship in direct line with one of the torpedoes, which exploded just below *Eskimo*'s No. 1 turret, taking away a large section of the hull. The remains of the bow section, with No. 1 turret just about attached, were left hanging vertically into the water. Fifteen men were killed in this attack, with 10 more wounded, of whom two later died from their wounds. In spite of this explosion and damage, the No. 2 turret kept firing and her last remaining torpedo was fired at *Thiele*. Micklethwait then decided to withdraw towards Straumen, stern first. Damage control parties were hard at work, and with the aid of *Forester* the ship was saved, ending up at the repair facility at Skjelfjord.

Hero and *Icarus* now entered the fjord, hopefully to finish off the job. However, *Thiele* had already taken a lot of punishment and with most of the officers dead, Captain Wolff ordered the ship to be run aground at Sildvik. His crew had suffered 14 killed and 28 wounded. His action gave time for some of the guns to be brought ashore from the other three ships, sea-cocks to be opened and demolition charges to be set.

Meanwhile, *Bedouin* signalled that both she and *Hero* had almost exhausted their ammunition. and that they believed the remaining three enemy destroyers were lurking round a corner of the inner fjord, out of sight. If they still had torpedoes this would be a position of great advantage.

Vice-Admiral Whitworth replied: "The torpedo menace must be accepted. Enemy must be destroyed without delay. Take *Kimberley*, *Forester*, *Hero* and *Punjabi* under your orders and organise attack, sending most serviceable destroyer first. Ram or board if necessary."

The destroyers cautiously entered Rombakssdjord, wary of an ambush, but were faced with the sorry sight of three abandoned destroyers. *Arnim* was listing very badly and had almost capsized, *Zenker* was turning turtle as the British ships approached, leaving only the *Lüdemann* almost upright as the demolition charges did not appear to have gone off properly. She was boarded by parties from both *Hero* and *Icarus*, but little in the way of intelligence was found: there were piles of ashes all over the ship. Other souvenirs such as binoculars and flags were bought back. As a parting gesture, shells were fired into the wrecks to ensure that no use could be made of them, and at 1655 *Hero* put a torpedo into *Lüdemann*. Apart from scattered parties of men strewn around the shores of the fjords around Narvik, the German Navy's presence here was now of little relevance.

About an hour earlier, *Warspite* had stopped off at Narvik, which finally allowed Rice to land his Swordfish and be recovered. His last act before landing was one more reconnoitre around Rombakssfjord, dropping his last bombs on the abandoned *Thiele*. Admiral Whitworth now paused to consider his options. He reported to Forbes that all German destroyers and a U-boat had been sunk. A landing by naval personnel was

HMS *Foxhound* approaching HMS *Cossack*. (The National Archives)

considered, but it would have to be a small one, as most would be required to man the ships and would not be able to venture far from the waterfront. Commander Sherbrooke apparently lobbied hard to put men ashore but, as Whitworth later wrote:

> A signal was then received from *Foxhound* that the officer prisoners taken had reported the presence of several German submarines in the fjord. At 1800 twelve enemy aircraft were sighted approaching from the westward. Apart from the above considerations. I felt that to place, at the end of a long and strenuous day, a party of less than 200 tired seamen and marines in the midst of a force of not less than 2,000 professional German soldiers, would be to court disaster, even allowing for the morale effect which the day's engagement must have had on the enemy.

With hindsight, it would appear that there were only around 200 German troops in the town itself, with a few hundred more spread out protecting a perimeter around Narvik. It is interesting to speculate what might have happened to the German plans if a body of British troops, perhaps a brigade, had been landed within hours, mopped up the Germans and taken control of the port. It would have been an isolated base with the Germans in possession of the rest of Norway, but the objective - to do damage to the export of iron ore to Germany - would have been achieved.

Nevertheless, Whitworth was now thinking that Narvik was a dangerous place in which to linger, and so saw no reason to keep *Warspite* stopped in the fjord, subject to submarine and air attack. Therefore, around 1830, he ordered *Foxhound, Icarus, Forester, Punjabi* and *Hero* to form up on him and they all headed back down the fjord towards the open sea. On the way, *U25* launched some torpedoes at the group, but no hits were

General view of Narvik Bay. (The National Archives)

achieved. Their wake was seen: *Foxhound* found *U25* on her Asdic, scared her off and she submerged deep. Whitworth, unaware at the time how many times he had been in danger on this day from U-boats, wrote later: "I have since come to the conclusion that a submarine navigating in the narrow waters of a fjord would find himself in a not very enviable position with anti-submarine destroyers overhead, and his desire to get out is therefore understandable."

Reinforcements for the Whitworth group (labelled as Force B) arrived in the afternoon in the shape of two more destroyers, *Hostile* and *Ivanhoe*. Their first role, together with *Kimberley* and *Bedouin*, two members of the original force, was to look after *Cossack* and *Eskimo*. *Cossack* of course was grounded, awaiting the next high tide when it was hoped she could be floated off, but *Eskimo* slowly sailed backwards down the fjord towards the repair facility, assisted by *Bedouin*. In spite of Whitworth's decision that *Warspite* should not remain in Narvik, she did not actually leave until just before dawn on 14 April. She had spent the previous hours accepting wounded from the destroyers, as she had better medical facilities than the smaller ships. In the early hours of 14 April, *Cossack* managed to free herself and, escorted by *Forester*, slowly sailed to Skjelfjord, arriving the next day. *Ivanhoe* halted briefly at Ballangen to pick up survivors from the *Hardy* and some merchant seamen who had made it there.

Some of the casualties from the attack on 10 April are buried in a small Commonwealth War Graves Commission cemetery there, including Captain Warburton-Lee in plot IV, grave B9. Another casualty there is the civilian NAAFI canteen manager from HMS *Hardy*, Joseph Mulligan, who is buried in grave A9.

When news of the withdrawal reached London, the Admiralty was not impressed, and at 2115 on 13 April sent a signal to Forbes to consider "the occupation of Narvik to ensure unopposed landing later".

Whitworth responded at 2210 to Forbes and the Admiralty:

My impression is that enemy forces in Narvik were thoroughly frightened as a result of today's action and that the presence of *Warspite* was the chief cause of this. I recommend that the town be occupied without delay by the main landing force. I intend to visit Narvik again tomorrow Sunday in order to maintain the moral effect of the presence of *Warspite* and to accept air and submarine menace involved by this course of action.

On the following day, after a request from London on his assessment of the German strength at Narvik, Whitworth wrote in a signal timed at 1027:

Information from Norwegian sources estimates 1,500 to 2,000 troops in Narvik. German Naval Officer prisoner states that there are many more than this, but I think this statement was made with intent to deceive. He also states that guns on shore are being positioned with the main object of opposing a landing, but *Cossack*, aground in Narvik Bay for 12 hours yesterday, was not seriously molested. I am convinced that Narvik can be taken by direct assault without fear of meeting serious opposition on landing. I consider that the main landing force need only be small, but it must have the support of Force B or one of similar composition. A special requirement being ships and destroyers with the best available AA armaments.

Warspite remained in Vestfjord in case a decision was made to go back and land in Narvik, but nothing happened on 14 April so on the 15th, when it was clear there would be no immediate landing, the ships moved back to a position off the Skomvaer Light. Later in the day, Forbes decided to head back to Scapa Flow with *Rodney* and *Renown*, escorted by *Esk*, *Forester*, *Icarus*, *Ivanhoe* and *Kimberley*. *Furious*, meanwhile, stayed in Norwegian waters, heading north of Tromsö to refuel.

For the Germans, losing so many ships at Narvik was a disaster. For those ashore at Narvik, the only good news was that the *Jan Wellem* (one of the transports) remained afloat. She had been beached and the sea-cocks opened when the Whitworth group approached on 13 April, but she remained unscathed. After the British left, the sea-cocks were closed and the tanker refloated, with much of her cargo undamaged by water. This included a large amount of food, which was invaluable to the soldiers ashore over the coming days.

Hitler was intrigued by what happened at Narvik, and sent a special envoy to interview General Dietl and others. He arrived by seaplane on 22 April and spent two days gathering information. When he returned to Berlin he was accompanied by Admiral Bey and his adjutant, Lieutenant Alberts.

German propaganda tried to label the fighting at Narvik as a "heroic defeat against vastly superior forces". A shield was awarded, and a new class of destroyer, the type 36A, was unofficially called the Narvik class.

The Narvik Shield was instituted on 19 August 1940, and authorised for all German forces that took part in the battles of Narvik between 9 April and 9 June. The shield was worn on the left arm of the uniform. Each recipient received three copies, and could purchase additional ones by producing the award document. The shield was hollow-backed and stamped from sheet metal, usually zinc, although some early examples were of brass, and had a cloth backing for attachment to the uniform. The shield was awarded in three versions: two silver and a gold. The gold shield was issued to members of the *Kriegsmarine*. This shield was issued on blue cloth backing. The two other versions of the Narvik Shield were for members of the *Luftwaffe* and the *Wehrmacht*. Both versions were silver, with the *Luftwaffe* one issued on a grey-blue cloth backing and the *Wehrmacht* one a field-grey cloth backing. The shield was worn on the upper left sleeve of the service, walking-out dress and guard uniforms of each recipient's arm of service. If the cloth backing was missing or not issued, it was attached to the upper left sleeve by four prongs on the back of the shield. If a second shield was awarded to an individual, both shields could be worn, one above the other, separated by a 5mm gap.

The first award was made to General Dietl by Hitler on 21 March 1941, with a total of 9,019 shields being presented. The *Wehrmacht* received 2,755 (96 posthumous, the *Luftwaffe* 2,161 (with 756 being awarded to the *Fallschirmjägers*) and the *Kriegsmarine* 3,661 (2,672 for destroyer crews, 115 to other crews and 410 being, posthumous). The German merchant navy received 442 (22 being posthumous).

A final fillip for the German Army was that around 2,500 sailors suddenly found themselves on land, and were gratefully received as additional manpower by General Dietl. Most of the sailors were formed into a unit commanded by Captain Berger (commander of the 1st Destroyer Flotilla) and used to guard the railway line to Sweden: engineers were used to maintain the rolling stock and lines. Survivors from the *Künne* and *Heidkamp* were attached to the 139th Regiment. The remainder were mainly used for security duties in and around Narvik, and some were armed with Norwegian equipment. Even though the Germans suffered a bloody nose at Narvik, the failure to follow the Royal Navy's success on sea with a landing would come back to haunt the British.

To keep up the pressure in other areas, attention was turned once again towards Stavanger and a plan was formulated to damage the airfield at Sola. The Admiralty in London suggested that it would be good to "inflict the greatest possible damage to the aerodrome so as to restrict the operation of aircraft therefrom". It was intended to be a naval operation and was codenamed Operation Duck. The heavy cruiser HMS *Suffolk*, with four escorting destroyers - HMS *Hereward*, HMS *Janus*, HMS *Juno* and HMS *Kipling* - were detailed to take part.

HMS *Suffolk* was a County class heavy cruiser, part of the Kent subclass. She was built at Portsmouth; launched on 16 March 1926, being commissioned on 25 June 1928. For much of her service life she was part of the Far East Fleet, but returned to home waters on the outbreak of war. She had a displacement of about 13,500 tons, was 630 feet long and had a main armament of eight 8in guns in four turrets, two at the bow and two at the rear, with secondary turrets containing 4in guns. The larger guns fired a shell weighing 256lb to a maximum range of about 17 miles. Mindful of the increasing threat of air power, more lighter guns were added during a refit in 1938 to bolster her anti-aircraft capability, including pom-poms and some 20mm and 40mm cannons.

For most of this operation the ships would have no dedicated air cover. It was intended for this to be a combined operation, with the RAF carrying out a bombing raid prior to the arrival of the ships. This, it was hoped, would provide a diversion and enable the ships to slip in, and also help identify the target by setting fire to hangars, aircraft and other buildings. After the naval bombardment, another attack by 12 Blenheims would be made to deter counter-attacks, whilst the ships made good their escape. To assist with reconnaissance and as flying forward observation officers, *Suffolk* carried two Walrus seaplanes. Coastal Command also offered to send some aircraft over the target. The First Lord of the Admiralty, Winston Churchill, was an enthusiastic supporter of this operation: another first for the Second World War in that it was the first time since the Great War that a large-scale bombardment of a land-based target had been undertaken from a relatively big warship. With hindsight, it is easy to add that the crew of the *Suffolk* had never done anything like this before and that there was only a limited availability of HE (high explosive) shells, which were ideal for causing maximum destruction.

Under the command of Captain J. Durnford, *Suffolk* and her escorts left Scapa Flow at 1625 on 16 April. After crossing the North Sea, they were guided towards their objective by the submarine HMS *Seal*, which was positioned off Skudeneshavn and signalled to them with a light. But from here on few things went well. Out of the 12 Wellingtons from 99 and 137 Squadrons (six from each) that were due to attack, only two managed to navigate to the correct area, and then failed to drop any bombs!

However, one of the Coastal Command aircraft allocated to the operation, a Hudson from 233 Squadron piloted by Flying Officer G. Edwards, arrived as planned at 0355. After circling to work out exactly where he was, he dropped small incendiary bombs and flares over the airfield. It was hoped that the presence of a naval officer, Lieutenant-Commander Fleming, on board the Hudson would help the gunfire be accurate. He started to transmit on the agreed frequency, but after a few minutes contact was lost and never again made. None of this helped the *Suffolk* group, which did not reach a position about 10 miles off the coast until about 0445, and then steered a course parallel to the coast. Meanwhile. the Hudson was attacked by a JU88, sent up from Sola itself, but in spite of shots being exchanged neither plane was damaged. The JU88 then disappeared. The first Walrus from *Suffolk* was then catapulted off, was able to see the airfield and from a height of about 10,000 feet had excellent views in the growing light. Once again, though, the plane was unable to contact *Suffolk*. Frustrated by all the static coming from his forward observer officers, Captain Durnford gave orders to open fire at 0513, but the firing was not very accurate. It appears that a snowy background made it difficult to identify where the shells landed, or where Edwards was dropping his ordnance. The first two salvoes from *Suffolk* did at least hit land, albeit to the north of the airfield. The next four landed in the sea before rounds started to fall in the area of the seaplane base within the perimeter of Sola airfield, starting several fires. The first Walrus was now at the limit of her time over Norway and needed to return to Scotland. The second Walrus now took over but the observer had difficulty seeing anything at all except smoke from around the seaplane base. At around 0550 it also had to return to Scotland. Crew members from both aircraft commented that the HE shells landing on the ground were difficult to observe because of the snow and lack of visible flash when exploding.

The *Suffolk* group made three passes along the coast. *Suffolk* fired over 200 rounds from her 8in guns until just after 0600, when Captain Durnford decided enough was enough and headed away from the coast at 30 knots. The sun was now rising behind the mountains overlooking the airfield, making observation even more difficult. Flying Officer Edwards and Lieutenant-Commander Fleming could see that most of the shells were not landing in the right place, but the continued lack of communication prevented corrections being given to the *Suffolk*; she was virtually firing blind. In spite of this, some damage was caused at the seaplane base – four HE59s and four HE115s were destroyed, together with an administration building. The main airfield was virtually untouched, except for minor damage caused by the bombs dropped by Edwards.

The original plan called for the *Suffolk* group to head pretty much due west under air cover provided by aircraft from Coastal Command, but the previous day a report had been received that several German destroyers was off the Norwegian coast near Stadtlandet, north of Bergen. A group of cruisers and destroyers from the Home Fleet was sent to look for them, and it was decided that the *Suffolk* group should join in this hunt. The Admiralty in London sent a signal to *Suffolk*, timed at 2300 on 16 April, ordering that the ships, on completion of Operation Duck, should "sweep to the northward to intercept enemy destroyers". Durnford was also advised that air reconnaissance was being sorted out, but inter-service communication was not all that it could have. This report of German destroyers was in fact spurious and all these ships were on a wild goose chase. When Blenheims of 254 Squadron turned up at what they thought was the rendezvous point, there were no ships to be seen. The *Suffolk* group had steamed westward until Durnford considered he was a suitable distance from the coast, and then steered to the north, looking for the non-existent enemy ships. The Admiralty was informed of their position at 0720, but this information was not forwarded to Coastal Command until about five hours later.

The Germans did not take punishment from *Suffolk* without getting in some retaliation of their own. Several DO18 seaplanes had been shadowing the *Suffolk* group for some time, so it was not difficult to call in the bombers. The first attack came in around 0830, when 10 HE111s from Sola arrived. Most of them bombed at a relatively high level, concentrating on *Suffolk*, and the other ships were mainly able to avoid the bombs. However, two 250kg bombs exploded close to *Kipling* and the shock wave caused cracks on her machinery mounts. This was followed by a pair of HE115s, which tried to launch a torpedo attack, but it was foiled by high seas. To his credit, Durnford realised that he was at severe risk from air attack, and with no sign of any friendly aircraft he scrubbed his search for the enemy ships, heading for safer waters. But the *Luftwaffe*, sensing an opportunity, sent out a general alarm and aircraft from Sola, Fornebu, Aalborg and Westerland were alerted to the presence of a "major British naval force off Stavanger". Aircraft from *Kampfgeschwader* (*KG*) *4*, *26* and *30* took part, with some of them first flying to Sola to refuel before joining in the attack. The men of *KG4* were the first to have a go. Some of their pilots did not find the group, and those who did were ineffective in their bombing attacks. *KG26* had no more luck. The real damage was going to be done by JU88s from *KG30*, who were rather more experienced in shipping attacks. Twenty-eight of them took off in small groups between 1000 and 1300. Their tactic was to attack en masse from different directions and heights in steep dives, a *modus operandi* to which the navy gunners did not really have an answer. On board the Royal Navy ships, having beaten off the somewhat ineffectual attacks by *KG4* and *KG26*, the crews had been confident they could see off further attacks. The first real blow came at 1037, when a 500kg bomb struck *Suffolk* just in front of X turret (at the rear) and passed through the wardroom, the warrant officers' flat and several other compartments before detonating on the port side of the platform deck, between the after engine room bulkhead and X shell room and cordite handling room. The blast also caused damage in the engine room and a sympathetic explosion amongst the cordite in the handling room. This found its way up the hoist into X turret and caused further explosions there, which lifted the roof off X turret. Other explosions put Y turret out of action too. The flash-over shot along passages, starting fires in other parts of the ship. These could not be easily controlled so most of the magazines had to be flooded to stop them blowing up. It is estimated the *Suffolk* had around 1,500 tons of water slopping around her – over 10 per cent of her weight: some of her oil tanks had also been ruptured and her radios were not working. Messages had to be sent to *Kipling*, mainly by signal lamp, for onward transmission, and her speed was down to about 15 knots.

A final bombing attack by the RAF had been planned to help the ships make good their escape. The original timing of this attack, at around 1200, would have been too late, but in the circumstances it was a good time. Twelve Blenheims from 107 Squadron, led by Wing Commander Embry, were heading for Sola when they saw British warships being attacked by the *Luftwaffe*, and decided to help. Although his aircraft were not really fighters, he ordered five to follow him whilst the other six went to the original objective. Embry bravely led his aircraft in a diving attack through the JU88s, which scattered. The Blenheims reformed and headed to Sola, but the defences were ready for them. Two were shot down by ME110s, while a third was damaged and crashed on landing back at RAF Lossiemouth in Scotland.

During this time a message was received from England that alarmed Durnford. He learned that *Repulse* and *Renown*, plus escorts, were leaving Scapa Flow for a patrol. He reported back via *Kimberley* that he did not think this was a wise decision and suggested they stay away unless they had adequate air cover. He also requested air cover for his group. Embry's intervention caused a brief lull in the attacks, but as *Suffolk* was leaking oil she was not hard for the *Luftwaffe* to find. More attacks came in from *KG30*. Suffolk's steering motors broke down because of mechanical failure, and for a while the ship was unable to take much avoiding action. At 1325, there were a couple of near misses on the starboard side from 500kg bombs very close to the damaged X turret. and these caused all the aft compartments of *Suffolk* to be completely flooded. The situation was becoming critical.

Soon afterwards, three Hudsons from 233 Squadron found the group, but the gunners had by then probably had enough. In spite of recognition signals, some sailors

HMS *Suffolk* pictured on her return to the UK, the extent of the damage caused to her stern is evident. (Imperial War Museum HU49677)

decided to shoot at them. A short while later, nine Skuas from 801 and 803 Squadrons of the Fleet Air Arm arrived as fighter cover. During the afternoon, a final bombing attack came in from *KG4* with 11 HE111s, but owing to the British air cover very few bombs fell near any ship. By around 1515 the attacks were over, and the crew of the *Suffolk* could now begin the fight to stop her sinking. *Suffolk* recorded that she faced 33 attacks (21 horizontal and 12 dive), but suffered only one direct hit and three near misses. However, these were enough to cause serious damage. The lookouts reported 88 misses during the seven hours that the ship was under attack. For all the ammunition expended, no German aircraft were shot down.

Suffolk reached Scapa Flow on 18 April after a tortuous voyage, with the deck only just clear of the water. The rudder had been wrecked, so she had to be steered using the engines. Thirty-two men had been killed and 38 wounded, the majority of these being burn injuries. Upon arrival at Scapa, Durnford ordered the ship to be beached at Long Hope to prevent her from sinking while temporary repairs were carried out. *Suffolk* sailed for the Clyde and proper repairs on 5 May: these would take the best part of a year.

This is the report from Captain Durnford on the operation (not all the enclosures mentioned in the report are included):

HMS *Suffolk*
26th April 1940
Sir,

Be pleased to inform Their Lordships that Operation Duck was carried out by HM Ship under command, and HM Ships *Kipling, Hereward, Juno*, and *Janus*, on 17 April 1940, in accordance with the Operation Orders issued by the Admiralty, Coastal Command Operations Instruction No. 14 dated the 15th April 1940, and such amendments to these instructions as were received by signal prior to the Operation.

Preliminary

2. On receipt of Admiral Signal timed 1935 of the 14th April, HMS *Suffolk* being then on passage from Thorshavn to Vestfjord after landing a Royal Marine Force for the protection of the Faeroe Islands and subsequent interception of the German tanker *Skagerrak*, altered course for Scapa. In reply to Admiralty signal timed 2203 of the 14th April, I informed the Admiralty by immediate signal that I expected to arrive at 1600 on the 15th April, provided that I could maintain high speed. HMS *Suffolk* arrived at the point of arrival at 1700 on the 15th April and anchored at 1820.

3. With reference to paragraph 5 of Coastal Command Operation Instruction No. 14, Lieutenant-Commander A. Fleming (Naval Observer) reported on board on arrival to establish contact and arrange details. As no Operation Orders had been received, full details of the co-operation could not be decided. It was necessary for Lieutenant-Commander Fleming to fly to Leuchars not later than a.m. the 16th April in order to arrange with RAF Leuchars details of the co-operating Hudson aircraft. As no Operation Orders had been received by 1000 on the 16th April, I directed him to proceed.

4. Soon after my arrival I was informed by signal by the Vice Admiral Commanding, Orkneys and Shetlands, that I should be required to sail about 1500 on the 16th April, that my second aircraft was to be embarked, and that detailed instructions were being flown from the Admiralty.

5. *Suffolk's* second aircraft, Walrus L2284, was embarked a.m. the 16th April, after being tuned. Details of tuning aircraft are given in enclosure 4 to this report.

6. At 0930 on the 16th April, it was learnt from the Vice Admiral Commanding Orkneys and Shetlands that the Operation Orders should arrive at Hatston by air at 1300. Arrangements were made for them to be delivered on board HMS *Suffolk* by drifter from Scapa, immediately on arrival, as it was then blowing hard. They were not received on board until 1430.

7. As I thought that local knowledge of the coast might be of some value, I asked Vice Admiral Commanding, Orkneys and Shetlands, if the services of a Norwegian pilot could be obtained. It so happened that Captain Ohlsen, Master of a Norwegian merchant vessel, was due to arrive at Lyness that forenoon. He volunteered for the service and was embarked before sailing. In the subsequent operation, although he was able to identify the navigational marks on the

coastline, his knowledge of the terrain and topography was not sufficient to assist in correcting the line of fire.

I regret to say that he received some minor facial injuries, being in the Ward Room ante-room when the ship was hit, and lost his personal effects in the subsequent flooding. His willing co-operation and the danger to which he was exposed seem worthy of recognition.

8. The Rear Admiral, Destroyers detailed HM destroyers *Kipling* (Senior Officer), *Juno*, *Janus* and *Hereward* to sail with HMS *Suffolk* at 1500 and ordered them to have steam and be completed with fuel by that time. He also ordered the Commanding Officer of HMS *Kipling* to report on board *Suffolk* at 1400. As the destroyers were exercising TSD Sweeps when these orders were received the Commanding Officer of HMS *Kipling* could not report before 1530, and the destroyers could not proceed, having completed with fuel and received their Operation Orders, until 1625.

Approach

9. Due to this late start, an average speed of 26 knots was required to reach Position "A" by 0355 on the 17th April. I therefore ordered the destroyers to make good 26 knots and accept parting of the sweeps. In fact, the sweeps of the two leading destroyers held until the completion of the bombardment, and the rear two destroyers formed an A/S screen after commencement of the bombardment.

10. Before dark, signalled instructions were passed to the destroyers that when the leading ship, HMS *Kipling*, obtained contact with *Seal*, she was to lead to the bearing on which *Seal* was sighted, without further signal, and leave *Seal*, if possible, on the starboard hand. They were also informed that speed would be reduced to 15 knots by signal at about that time on a course of 110 degrees. This would depend on the light conditions when contact was made with *Seal*.

11. Nothing was sighted on passage except at 2355 when course was altered to pass clear of lights presumed to be trawlers.

12. It was my intention to catapult my first Walrus aircraft immediately after sighting *Seal* and to catapult the second Walrus aircraft as soon as it was ready, i.e. about twenty minutes later and before opening fire with the main armament. Admiralty signal timed 1410 of the 16th April, received on board at 1512 just prior to sailing, directed *Suffolk* to use one Walrus as spotting aircraft and the other one as stand by spotting aircraft. It was calculated that the Walrus aircraft could remain in the air for approximately an hour in the vicinity of Stavanger and, if conditions were favourable and by maximum economy of fuel, have enough fuel to return to Scotland. Undercarriages were removed to improve their chances of covering the distance successfully.

13. Admiralty's signal timed 1410 of the 16th April also ordered HMS *Suffolk* to return to Rosyth. The Commander in Chief, Rosyth, was not included in the addressees as received in *Suffolk*.

14. See Track Chart No. 1. At 0414, *Kipling* was seen to alter course to port and a flashing light from *Seal* was observed at the same time. Speed was reduced to 15 knots and at 0418, Walrus aircraft L.2281 (Lieutenant H. H. Bracken –

Observer, Petty Officer V. Redgrave – Pilot, Naval Airman First Class D. R. B. Evans – Air Gunner) was catapulted. Speed was then increased to 26 knots as it was getting light, and course shaped to pass *Seal* to the starboard on a course of 110 degrees.

15. At 0420, in accordance with paragraph 14 of the Operation Orders, a signal was made to the Hudson aircraft to drop a flare at 0435.

16. At 0432, *Seal* was passed. At about this time warning rockets and anti-aircraft gunfire were observed fine on the starboard bow, presumably coming from the shore defences of Stavanger aerodrome.

17. The flare was not identified from the other pyrotechnic above the aerodrome. It was now getting fairly light; the land could be seen but with no detail. The sea was calm, sky clear, with a light easterly wind. At 0445, speed was reduced to 15 knots and at 0447, the force was turned to the bombarding course of 181 degrees, the second Walrus aircraft L2284 (Lieutenant (A) W. R. J. MacWhirter – Pilot, Petty Officer Observer T. W. Snowden – Observer, Naval Airman First Class R. P. Stanesby – Air Gunner) being catapulted as soon as the wind came on the port side. At this time fire was opened with the port 4 inch HA armament at an aircraft which had not identified itself.

18. Reports from the officer in charge of each aircraft from the time of flying off are forwarded as enclosures 2 and 3 to this report.

19. At 0505, a report was received that a torpedo had passed close astern from starboard to port, at an estimated distance of twenty yards. No destroyers obtained any submarine contact and no co-operating aircraft reported a submarine during the operation. Destroyers were warned that a submarine was in the vicinity and the position was given.

Bombardment

20. Technical details of the bombardment are given in enclosure No. 5 to this report.

Communication with the co-operating aircraft could not be established on 6650 kc/s and as the flare had not been seen, it was necessary to carry out the bombardment with such direct observation as was possible, assisted by any reports that could be given by the aircraft by V/S. As was made clear by the reports received from the aircraft after the operation, the conditions for observation [were] particularly difficult as a thin layer of snow covered the area, and the camouflage effect produced by these conditions was most noticeable to observers on board *Suffolk* though the reason was not apparent in the early light.

21. As a result of the delay caused by endeavouring to establish wireless communication with the aircraft, the bombardment did not commence until 0513 at a range of about 20,000 yards. The southerly course was maintained until 0523, when fire was checked on the turn to the northerly bombarding course. After the sixth, seventh, or eighth salvo, an explosion, followed by a heavy pall of smoke was seen. This may have been an oil tank or petrol dump.

22. Firing was continued on the northerly course from 0527 to 0548, when the course was again altered to the southward and the bombardment completed

from 0553 to 0604, when the sun had risen sufficiently to make observation impracticable. 202 rounds were fired.

23. The failure of wireless communication was most disappointing and inevitably had an adverse effect on the bombardment. Details of steps taken to tune and suggested reasons for the failure are given in enclosure No. 4 to this report.

24. From observation from the ship and from the verbal and written reports I have received from the officers in the three co-operating aircraft, I assess the damage resulting from the bombardment was as follows:

Seaplane Base. Two petrol dumps near the base and some aircraft were destroyed and material damage to the slipways would have been caused. At least 20 HE shells exploded in close vicinity of this base.

Stavanger Aerodrome. There is no doubt that some damage must have been done to the buildings around the northern edge of the airfield and I consider that some damage was done to the airfield itself and parked aircraft. Up to the time that the last aircraft left, on account of endurance, I do not consider that the fall of shot had crept sufficiently far right to hit the intersection of the runways, but this should have been achieved during the last few salvoes.

25. On conclusion of one hour in the air in the vicinity of the aerodrome, both the Walrus aircraft returned to Scotland, L2281, Lieutenant Bracken making a landfall at Rattray Head and thence to Aberdeen, and L2284, Lieutenant (A) MacWhirter, descending in a loch near Aberdeen and thence to Invergordon. The Hudson, Lieutenant-Commander Fleming, returned to Leuchars. The L2281 was in the air for 4 hours 35 minutes and L2284 for 4 hours 15 minutes, both machines having arrived almost at the limit of their endurance.

Withdrawal

26. At 0604, course was altered to 270 degrees, speed increased to 30 knots and destroyers formed on an A/S Screen. Destroyers were ordered to slip TSD Sweeps Two-Speed Destroyer Sweep set – a piece of kit carried for mine sweeping.

27. The original Operation Order had ordered HMS *Suffolk* to return to Scapa on completion of the operation, but this had been amended, immediately prior to departure from Scapa, to Rosyth, as stated in paragraph 13 of this report. Some fighter support had been arranged for the return passage to Scapa.

28. Subsequent to these orders, the Admiralty had given instructions in signal timed 2300 of the 16th April, received at 2340 during the approach, that *Suffolk* and destroyers were, on completion of Operation Duck, to sweep northward to intercept enemy destroyers.

This signal was repeated to the Air Officer Commanding, Coastal Command, the Commander in Chief, Rosyth, and the Rear Admiral, Submarines. The Rear Admiral, Submarines, in his signal timed 0057 of the 17th April had warned *Seal* to keep clear to the north eastward.

29. The fighter aircraft escort given in Coastal Command Operation Instruction No. 14 was amended by the Commander in Chief, Rosyth's signal timed 1958 of the 16th April, after the Force had sailed from Scapa, and further amendments were received by signal during the course of the operation.

30. At the commencement of the withdrawal therefore the following is the air support that I expected at various stages:

First escort of 3 Blenheims, originally at Point "A" at 0430, but now delayed and not expected until 0615.(CinC Rosyth's signal 0444/17)

Second escort of 3 Hudsons to take over at 0600 in position JSOX 5726 and remain while fuel permitted, approximately 0845. (CinC Rosyth's signal 0252/17)

As the first escort was delayed nearly 2 hours by weather, I expected the second escort to arrive later and remain longer. The third and fourth escorts had been cancelled. (CinC Rosyth's signal 0252/17th April)

31. At 0704, no air escort had been sighted. The Force was turned to the northward to comply with Admiralty instructions to intercept enemy destroyers, speed being reduced to 25 knots to conserve fuel. At 0720, a report was made to the Admiralty that Operation Duck had been completed, the course, speed, and position of the Force being given and repeated to the Commander in Chief, Rosyth, for the information of fighter escorts as well to the Senior Officers concerned in the new operation.

32. At 0810, fire was opened on enemy aircraft seen to be in a position to attack. The first attack took place at 0825 when an emergency air attack report was made. From then on, the ship was under continuous attack from High Level and Dive Bombing for 6 hours and 47 minutes. Details of each attack are forwarded as enclosure No. 1 to this report, positions of the air attacks being numbered and shown on the general track charge. From the commencement of the bombing, I had to keep the ship almost continuously under full rudder to avoid being hit and it was only on very rare occasions that a steady course could be maintained.

33. At 0934, I reported being attacked persistently by high and low bombing and at 0938, in view of the intensity of the attacks and that no air support had arrived, I decided to withdraw the Force at best speed to the westward, thus officering the best chance of obtaining air support as early as possible and avoiding being hit, which seemed to be ultimately inevitable.

34. At 1037, HMS *Suffolk* was hit by a heavy bomb from a steep dive bomber on the starboard side of the upper deck just forward of X turret. The bomber approached down sun and was expected to make a High Level attack. The ship was brought beam on to meet this attack, but on reaching an angle of sight of 65 to 70 degrees, at a height of about 10,000 feet, the aircraft dived on the ship releasing the bomb at an estimated height of from 4 to 5 thousand feet. The weight of the bomb is estimated at 500 kilos. Details of the damage sustained, action taken to keep the ship steaming and steering, the conspicuous services rendered by Officers and men, both on deck and below deck to achieve this end, will form the subject of enclosure No. 8 to this report.

35. The bomb passed through the Ward Room, Warrant Officers' Flat, and storerooms on to the Platform Deck, from starboard to port, and exploded in the inflammable store close to the Bulkhead of the After Engine Room. The effect of this explosion penetrated forwarded to the After Engine Room, and aft, through

X Shell Room to X Cordite Handing Room.

It is believed that a charge exploded in the Cordite Handing Room which penetrated the Cordite Hoist Trunk and vented into X Gun house. The empty cordite cage at the top of the hoist was broken and the charge in the Right Traversing Rammer caught fire. The roof of the Turret was lifted. X shell handing room and all Oil Fuel Tanks in the vicinity of the explosion were holed. The bulkhead of the After Engine Room was blown in, the Engine Room seriously damaged and flooded, and the force of the explosion vented up through the Engine Room Exhaust Trunks and up the hatches leading to the Ward Room Flat.

A column of flame was seen to reach the height of the gaff on the main mast, destroying the ensign. Fires started in the Ward Room Flat, the Warrant Officers' Flat, and the Storerooms underneath, and in the entrance to the Officers' Galleys.

The second W/T Office and the After Gyro Compass Room was wrecked. The Main W/T Office was unable to transmit as a result of the blast. The After 8 inch Magazine had to be flooded. About 1,500 tons of water entered the ship in about 20 minutes.

36. The immediate effect on the ship's fighting efficiency was a reduction of maximum speed to about 18 knots, X and Y turrets out of action and Main and Second W/T Offices out of action. A considerable volume of water had entered the ship aft. Signals had to be passed by V/S to *Kipling* for transmission.

37. At 1042, 1046, and 1052, I asked for fighters, giving the position. At 1050, HMS *Janus* also reported that *Suffolk* had been hit, giving the position. At 1102, I reported that the ship was heavily damaged, speed reduced to 18 knots, and that more air attacks were expected.

38. At 1050, *Kipling* reported a mine ahead. This mine was suspected as having been laid by a Flying Boat which had been observed flying very low across the horizon ahead of the mean course made good. The object passed close on the starboard hand. I cannot say with any certainty whether, it was, in fact, a mine but lookouts had reported that a low flying aircraft had been dropping something ahead of the ship.

39. At 1200, I received a signal from the Commander in Chief, Home Fleet, timed 1119 of the 17th April, directing all Skuas to be sent to my assistance, and at 1205, I received a signal from the Vice Admiral Commanding Orkneys and Shetlands, that Skuas were being sent. At 1214, I received the Commander in Chief, Rosyth's signal timed 1140 of the 17th April, informing me that 3 Blenheims and 3 Hudsons should be with me by 1230 and that air escort would be maintained. At this juncture, I knew also that HM Ships *Repulse* and *Renown* were ordered to my assistance though I did not know when they would arrive. As intensive bombing was still continuing, I reported by Most Immediate Signal to the Commander in Chief, Home Fleet, at 1216, that I had four destroyers with me, was making good 12 knots and that I only required air protection, as I thought the presence of further heavy ships in the area would only endanger them. At 1221, I made a further Most Immediate Signal to the Vice Admiral

Commanding, Orkneys and Shetlands, giving my position, course, and speed, hoping that this might expedite the arrival of the air protection. At 1312, the air escort of Blenheims and Hudsons, expected at 1230, not having arrived, I informed the Commander in Chief, Rosyth, of my position relative to Duncansby Head in the hope that this would assist the direction of the aircraft to me as soon as possible.

40. At 1305, both steering motors were out of action as both after sections of the ring main had been flooded. At 1328, No. 2 steering motor was again brought into action by means of an emergency lead direct from No. 3 dynamo to the emergency terminals on the after steering department. Between 1305 and 1328, it was necessary to steer the ship by the screws and it was not possible to alter course to take avoiding action. Three attacks took place during this period, the last one being a near miss under the starboard counter at an estimated distance of 5 yards. This bomb appeared to explode on the surface and did much damage.

41. The attacks continued. Near misses, which blew in the Lower Deck scuttles after and punctured the ship's side, in conjunction with flooding into the Warrant Officers' Flat from below, had caused further extensive flooding.

42. At about 1415, friendly aircraft were observed arriving. Difficulty was experienced in making them identify themselves, but at 1429, I was satisfied that nine were in company and reported accordingly to the Commander in Chief, Home Fleet, who had asked for a report of their arrival. At 1440, I asked the Admiral Commanding, Orkneys and Shetlands to send tugs as the steering gear might fail at any moment, giving my position, course, and speed. I later reported that more fighters were required as attacks were continuing. Bombing, however, continued until 1512 when the last attack took place. There were four attacks between 1430 and 1512, bombs falling extremely close, between 5 and 20 yards from the ship. It appeared that the fighters in pursuit of the enemy had left the overhead area unguarded. I ordered one fighter with whom we were in V/S touch to protect me from higher up, and keep a close patrol. With the exception of the hit, this series was the most dangerous and accurate experienced and it took place when the fighters were in company.

43. The majority of attacks were seen in time for the anti-aircraft guns to open fire. One aircraft was seen to alight on the sea after unloading the remainder of its bombs. Another is thought to have been hit during its second dive bombing attack as it flew away emitting black smoke from its port engine and losing height. This aircraft is considered to be the one which obtained a hit in its first attack.

44. At 1604, the emergency terminals to No. 2 steering motor were flooded finally, the emergency leads had to be cut in order to close the door of the after Capstan Flat, and the ship to be steered by the screws.

45. At 1620, identities were exchanged with HM Ships *Renown* and *Repulse*, who were sighted ahead. I reported my intentions to HMS *Repulse* of passing through the Fair Island Channel and down the west coast of the Orkneys. *Renown* and *Repulse* formed an escort ahead and astern and *Fury* augmented *Suffolk's* screen.

At 1718, I passed via *Repulse* a situation report for the Admiral Commanding, Orkneys and Shetlands, Commander in Chief, Home Fleet, and Admiralty. At 2026, *Renown* sent all destroyers to screen and at 2041, I requested the Admiral Commanding, Orkneys and Shetlands, to send necessary tugs to meet the ship off Torness at 0330 on the 18th April.

46. A speed of about 15 knots was made good during the night, the weather being good, and it was practicable to alter course without difficulty and maintain a fairly accurate course by keeping one shaft going at 240 revolutions and adjusting the revolutions on the other.

The constant succession of near misses had completed the flooding of nearly all the compartments abaft the forward engine room and up to the Main Deck level and the sea was lapping over the quarterdeck. A near miss on the port side had caused flooding of one bulge compartment, the Chief and Petty Officers' and Marines' Bath Rooms, so that the ship had taken a list of eight degrees to port.

47. By 0545, HM Tug *Bandit* had the ship in tow off Torness. The tugs *Imperious* and *Hendon* were made fast off Switha, with Mr MacKenzie of Metal Industries, in charge of the towing operations. Hoxa Boom was passed at 0708 and the ship anchored in A.5 berth at 0809. It was possible to assist with the engines. The distance steamed with the steering gear was 164 miles.

48. By this time, with the list to port, the top of the quarterdeck bollards were almost awash; it was apparent that the ship had settled after appreciably during the night and that she was still settling slowly. It was calculated that there was at least about 2,500 tons of water in the after part of the ship. A decision was reached to beach the ship in Long Hope. HMS *Suffolk* was aweigh at 1146 and was towed by tugs *Imperious* and *Hendon* under the direction of Mr MacKenzie, to the beaching site in Long Hope. The ship took the ground at 1415 when salvage operations commenced. It was no longer possible to use the engines from the Fleet anchorage to Long Hope, owing to the flooding of the port pipe passage and to the presence of fuel in the feed water.

49. I regret to report that, as a result of the explosion and continuous air attacks, a casualty list of 32 killed and 38 injured was sustained.

The majority of the casualties occurred in the After Engine Room, X Shell Room, Shell Handing Room, Cordite Handing Room, X Gun house and numbers 8 and 9 Fire Parties. Details are given in enclosure 8 to this report.

50. During the day, few deliberate attacks were made on the destroyers, but one attack was observed on *Kipling*, who afterwards reported that defects had occurred consequent to two near misses.

51. I commend the Commanding Officers of all destroyers for the handling of their ships during the operation and for the support they afforded me at all times. In particular, I wish to commend the good work of Commander A. St Clair Ford, Commanding Officer of HMS *Kipling*.

52. The conditions for enemy aircraft were very good in the forenoon and ideal in the afternoon when there was blue sky, a bright sun, and patches of white cloud at a height of about 8,000 feet.

The enemy aircraft made full use of these conditions and were evidently very highly trained. 33 attacks were carried out, 87 splashes were marked, some of which probably contained more than one bomb. The attacks lasted from 0825 to 1512. It cannot be stated with certainty what types of machines were engaged but it is believed that Heinkel 111s carried out the majority of the High Level bombing attacks, while the aircraft used for Dive Bombing Attacks were probably Junkers 88s.

53. The behaviour of the Officers and Ship's Company throughout the operation was exemplary. The ordeal was a severe one for those on deck who could see the near misses and see and hear the scream of the bombs, particularly during the period when the steering gear was out of action.

It was perhaps more severe for those below, who, engaged in keeping the ship steaming and steering, fighting fires, endeavouring to prevent flooding, and tending casualties, could feel the concussion from the explosion of bombs and the ship lifting to near misses.

As it seemed probable that the ship might be unable to survive another hit, and the state of affairs lasted for nearly five hours, I consider that their conduct is deserving of all praise.

I have the honour to be, Sir,

Your obedient Servant

(signed) J. W. Durnford, CAPTAIN

The Secretary to the Admiralty
Copies to: The Commander in Chief, Home Fleet, The Commander in Chief, Rosyth, The Vice Admiral Commanding, First Cruiser Squadron, The Rear Admiral (D), Home Fleet
HMS Suffolk
24th April, 1940
Report of Proceedings – Walrus L2281
Sir,

I have the honour to report on the preparation of Walrus aircraft for Operation Duck and my own proceedings in Walrus aircraft L2281 during the bombardment.

2. With reference to paragraph 5 of Coastal Command Instructions No.14, Lieutenant-Commander Fleming (Naval Observer) attended a preliminary conference on board HMS *Suffolk* on the 15th April. In the absence of any other instructions in the orders for the operations, which had not yet been received, it was agreed that the spotting should be carried out by Hudson aircraft with the ship's own aircraft only being used as a stand by. The operation orders however ordered *Suffolk*'s own aircraft to be the first spotting aircraft with the Royal Air Force Hudson as a standby.

3. In view of the recent changes in the catapult crew and aircraft handling personnel and modifications to the catapult, it was decided to devote the

forenoon of the 16th April to loading drill and firing light shots. Walrus aircraft L2284 was embarked at 1200 from Hatston.

4. For details of tuning Hudson and Walrus aircraft see Communication appendix.

5. Paragraph 18 of Duck ordered aircraft to fly back to Scapa. It was calculated that under average conditions Walrus aircraft could remain in the bombardment area for one hour before commencing the flight back.

6. The Commanding Officer, HMS *Suffolk*, ordered both aircraft to make their landfall at the nearest point on the coast of Scotland. The undercarriage and all equipment not actually required were removed to lighten the aircraft.

7. I was catapulted at 0418. The port float and hull of the aircraft struck the water a severe blow, due to an unexpected roll at the moment of launching. The pilot (Petty Officer V. Redgrave) succeeded in recovering. This was Petty Officer Redgrave's first experience in being catapulted from any ship and was performed in semi darkness. I consider he acted very creditably in this emergency and also during the subsequent operations.

8. The aircraft then proceeded towards Stavanger aerodrome, climbing to obtain a position for dropping flares. When approaching 5 miles from the objective, a Hudson was seen to drop flares and incendiary bombs at about 0435. I therefore returned over the ship and commenced taking ranges and bearings of the target, which was easily identified from my height of 13,000 feet, in spite of a recent fall of snow covering the ground.

9. No enemy activity was observed at this time except for anti-aircraft fire directed against the Hudson.

10. Throughout this period, continuous attempts were made by me to establish communications with *Suffolk* on 6650 kc/s. This ship was not heard at all. I was satisfied that my transmitter was working satisfactorily, range and bearings obtained were transmitted.

11. In spite of hearing no one else on the frequency I decided to continue transmitting the spotting reports in case reception in the ship was intact.

12. I did not observe *Suffolk*'s first two salvoes. This is attributed to the fact that they fell far to the left. *Suffolk*'s third salvo was observed falling in the sea and "SS 20 LF 20" was signalled. The next three salvoes were observed in approximately the same place and the following salvo went "up" considerably and hit the seaplane base. This seemed to confirm that at least part of my signals were getting through. This last salvo started a large fire, which judging by the bright flame and large quantities of black smoke I am of the opinion was a petrol fire.

13. Three subsequent salvoes were observed to fall, one starting a similar fire about 100–200 yards to the left of the first.

14. Spotting signals were made for all three salvoes using the naval method in preference to the clock code due to the large distances involved.

15. Although a tendency to go "right" on the target were observed, these spotting signals were obviously not being acted upon in their entirety; LF 20 was actually made.

16. The bursting of shells on the land was particularly hard to observe unless the observer is looking at the actual place at the time of burst. Even HE shells were practically impossible to see. In the opening salvoes, this is a very serious disadvantage.

17. At this state (0622), it was necessary for me to make my departure for the Scottish Coast. The ship had found the correct range, but was still "left".

18. My flight back was uneventful and nothing was sighted until I made landfall five miles south of Rattray Head at 0835.

19. In view of a northerly wind and shortage of petrol, I turned south and landed outside Aberdeen harbour, where damage due to the launching was repaired.

I have the honour to be, Sir,

Your obedient servant.

(signed) H. H. Bracken, Lieutenant.

The Commanding Officer,

HMS *Suffolk*

22nd April 1940

Report of Proceedings – Walrus L2284

Sir,

I have the honour to report on my proceedings in Walrus Aircraft L2284 during Operation Duck.

2. After being catapulted off at 0450 on the 17th April, I climbed to a position of 4,000 feet over the ship to stand by to take over observation of fire.

3. I observed HMS *Suffolk* open fire and listened for spotting signals which were not heard on 6650 kc/s, which frequency was partially jammed by a broadcasting station.

4. The fall of the first three salvoes was not observed and at this time I received a signal by V/S from *Suffolk* to spot by V/S. The ground round the objective was covered by a recent fall of snow, which made it almost impossible to locate the objective (the intersection of the white runways).

5. At 0515, it was still fairly dark, but I observed the result of the third salvo, which ignited what was, without a doubt, a petrol dump on the slip way close to the seaplane base.

6. The remaining salvoes, about 25 but most probably more, were observed to fall between the ignited petrol dump and the hanger, on the northern edge of the aerodrome. The spotting signals that I passed by V/S to *Suffolk* were all to inform to the ship to go right (i.e. south), which seemed to have the desired effect. The fall of shot had reached the northern edge of the airfield, when at 0548 I was obliged to leave due to the aircraft's endurance, and set course for Scotland.

7. The fall of shot was extraordinarily difficult to see due to snow and lack of flash of the shells landing. I was engaged intermittently by enemy anti-aircraft fire.

8. I observed the following aircraft operation near the bombardment area:

Suffolk's other Walrus about 8,000 feet above me.

One Hudson flying around the ship and somewhere over the aerodrome.

I saw no enemy machines in the air.

9. The flight across the North Sea was uneventful. The coast was sighted 0840 and I landed on a loch near Aberdeen to verify petrol at 0850.

10. As sufficient petrol remained, I proceeded to Invergordon, where I reported to Operations, Coastal Command, by telephone at 1000.

11. Invergordon was selected as the aircraft had been lightened as much as possible by removing the undercarriage.

I have the honour to be, Sir,

Your obedient servant

(signed) W. R. J. MacWhirter, Lieutenant (A).

8

The silent service

In early 1940, the commander of the Royal Navy's submarines was Vice Admiral Max Horton, normally known as VA(S). He felt that the best place for his submarines was in the North Sea, the Skagerrak and the Kattegat. He was also of the opinion that any Allied intervention in Norway would provoke a German reaction, and so decided in March that his submarines should be concentrated off the Norwegian coast. Informed of Operation Wilfred, he called his senior command group together for a meeting on 1 April. At this it was decided that all available vessels should be at sea by dawn on 5 April, to patrol the German Bight, Kattegat and Skagerrak, as well as likely German landing places in southern Norway. The Royal Navy's submarine assets had been bolstered by the addition of the Polish submarine *Orzel*, which had escaped in 1939 after the German-Russian invasion. On 1 April, *Swordfish* and *Triton* were off Skagen and *Trident* off Arendal. Over the course of the following few days, *Sealion*, *Sunfish*, *Unity* and *Orzel* sailed. *Narwhal* sailed on 2 April on a mine-laying mission to the Heligoland Bight. In those days of what has become known as the "Phoney War", the submarines had been told "not to compromise their positions by intercepting merchant vessels but to concentrate on warships".

Receiving intelligence that a large number of German ships seemed to be moving from their northern bases, Horton then ordered all of his remaining serviceable submarines to sea; there were now 20, including two French ones, ready to take part in any escalation in the conflict. The next day, when advising the Admiralty of his intentions, he was instructed to move the submarines positioned off the Norwegian coast and redeploy them in a line in the North Sea, south of Stavanger, to intercept German ships sailing to or from ports in Germany.

However, before these instructions could be carried out (and perhaps with some delaying tactics by Horton), information was received from Oslo that the German merchant ship *Rio de Janeiro* had been sunk east of Kristiansand, and that German soldiers had been on board. Horton therefore felt he had initially made the right decision and turned a Nelsonian eye to his new instructions. Over the next three weeks or so, British submarines either sank or severely damaged six German warships and 15 transport and supply ships, causing major disruption to German resupply plans. This is not to say, however, that all was plain sailing for the "silent service", as the shallow waters and narrow straits of the Skagerrak and Kattegat are a great help to anti-submarine assets. Masses of fresh water from melted ice and snow can cause also changes in the density of the sea, so submarines can find themselves either moving up or down in the water with no real warning. One of the submarine commanders, Lieutenant-Commander B. Bryant of HMS *Sealion*, who was on patrol in the Kattegat, wrote in his diary for 9 April:

A most unpleasant day. Glassy calm, surrounded by fishing boats and enemy aircraft being sighted continually flying low and close. It was not possible to go deep (owing to density) and continual action to avoid being trawled up was required. Boat was driven slow, shafts in series at 34 feet. The boat could not be driven below 37 feet without flooding or speeding up.

As intelligence had been received in the early hours of 9 April that Norwegian ports were being invaded by the Germans, Horton ordered *Thistle* to the Stavanger area and *Truant* to the Oslofjord. Until now, the submarines were only allowed to attack enemy warships and transports. This was difficult to put into practice in the confined waters of the Kattegat and Skagerrak, because of surface and air patrols, and it was not feasible to try surface interceptions. Therefore, in the late morning of 9 April, the War Cabinet in London agreed - under pressure from the Admiralty - that "all German merchant vessels in the Skagerrak east of 8° East could be treated as warships and sunk without warning", and this was sent to all submarines at 1324. These new orders arrived just in time for *Sunfish*, as her commander, Lieutenant-Commander J. Slaughter, had in his periscope sights a German merchant vessel, the *Amaisis*, just outside Swedish territorial waters off Lysekil. He wrote later: "Just as the sights came on, the last part of VA(S)'s 1324/9 was read out to me, so I fired. At least one of the torpedoes fired hit home and the ship sank, which with the success by the *Orzel* opened a series of actions by Allied submarines."

The Germans' Kristiansand force was under the command of Captain Rieve, on board the *Karlsruhe*. After he had got his transport ships there, his orders were that the escorts should return as soon as possible to Kiel in northern Germany. Having been at Kristiansand when an RAF reconnaissance Hudson had flown over, he knew he was within range of enemy aircraft and it could only be a matter of time before British bombers arrived. So on the afternoon of 9 April, Rieve, having overseen the unloading of his charges, decided that his orders gave him the opportunity to get out. With three escorting torpedo boats - the *Greif, Luchs* and *Seeadler* - they left about 1800. Once in open waters, mindful of a potential submarine threat, they started zig-zagging towards Kiel at about 20 knots. Rieve was right to be wary of the British underwater threat, as lurking somewhere off southern Norway were a number of submarines, including HMS *Truant* under the command of Lieutenant-Commander C. Hutchinson. This T-class submarine was laid down in March 1938 at Barrow-in-Furness, launched on 5 May 1939 and commissioned on 31 October 1939. She had a displacement of 1,090 tons surfaced and 1,575 tons submerged, was 275 feet long and had twin diesel engines each producing 2,500hp, whilst two electric motors each produced 1,450hp, giving a top speed of 15 knots on the surface and 9 knots submerged. The *Truant* had a crew of 59, carried 16 torpedoes - six in internal forward-facing torpedo tubes, with four external forward-facing torpedo tubes and six spares for the internal tubes - and had a 4in deck gun.

Truant had sailed from Rosyth on 6 April for a patrol in the Skagerrak. Inclement weather there, including many periods of fog, made identification of ships difficult, bearing in mind the limited rules of engagement, so it was not easy for Hutchinson actually to launch any attacks. Visibility improved on 9 April, and explosions and aircraft were heard at regular intervals throughout the day. Then in the early evening, around 1730, what were believed to be three torpedo boats were sighted coming from the north-west, heading south at an estimated 22 knots. Preparations for a torpedo attack were under way when it was decided the ships were Norwegian *Sleipner* class destroyers, It is most likely that they were three German minesweepers returning from Egersund, but in any case the attack was abandoned. This was fortunate as about an hour later a cruiser, escorted by three destroyers, was sighted on the horizon to the north. The range was decreasing, and at 1856 *Truant* fired 10 torpedoes from her bow tubes, leaving two for emergency use, at a range of about 2,500 yards. The first two torpedoes were set to run at 10 feet, the middle six at 12 feet, with the last two at a depth of 8 feet. The shallower setting of the last two torpedoes was intended to try to hit the escorting destroyers. After firing the last of the 10 torpedoes, *Truant* deep-dived, and after about three minutes an explosion was heard, closely followed by two more and the sound of grinding metal. Hutchinson took *Truant* up to periscope depth to see what had happened. To his horror, he saw one of the escorts heading towards his position. She dropped two depth charges, which exploded close to *Truant*. Over the next four hours, *Truant* was hunted by the escorts, and around 30 depth charges were dropped, exploding – as the log puts it – "nearly all of them unpleasantly close".

Truant dived deep, perhaps as low as 350 feet, which was 50 feet lower than she had been on her sea trials. Hutchinson wrote in the logbook about the attacks:

> After each attack, destroyers stopped to listen, used echo-sounding, but appeared not to transmit on any supersonic set. They appeared to drop some form of device which made a sound like gravel dropping on the hull of the submarine. Anti-submarine conditions were very good and the enemy appeared to be uncomfortably efficient at hunting and most persistent. I hoped forlornly that they would retire after dark on more important business.

Aboard *Truant*, the position was serious but not critical. One of the first depth charges dropped had caused the forward hatch to blow open and some water entered the hull; other depth charges knocked out the magnetic compasses and caused the after trim tank to burst, causing further leaks. The high-pressure air system also developed leaks, which caused the air pressure inside the submarine to rise. This made it difficult to breathe, because the air was becoming more stale as the time spent under water increased. Another pattern of depth charges temporarily jammed open the main engine water-cooling inlet values, resulting in further flooding. This caused *Truant* to adopt a bow-up position of 15 degrees. *Truant*, thanks to hard work by her crew, was still under control but it was decided not to use pumps as the noise of these might be heard by the German ships, and the water pumped out would probably contain traces of oil which would be a visible sign on the surface.

By around 2200, as it had been quiet for some time, Hutchinson decided to risk going up for a look through the periscope, but as they rose further explosions were heard, so *Truant* dived again. About ninety minutes later, conditions aboard *Truant* forced Hutchinson's hand and he ordered his vessel up again. By now the batteries were running low and the air was virtually unbreathable, *Truant* having been submerged for the best part of 19 hours. Fortunately everything was quiet and no enemy ships could be seen. All available hatches were opened and fresh air blew through the submarine. But their problems were not over. None of the compasses were working and for a time it was difficult to see any stars, so guesswork was used to steer hopefully towards open water. After a while, enough stars were visible for the navigator to work out which way was south-west, and friendly territory. At 0112 on 10 April, Hutchinson sent a signal, advising of his attack and that he was returning to Rosyth.

On board the *Karlsruhe*, several torpedo tracks had been seen coming from the starboard side just before 1900. Captain Rieve immediately ordered full ahead and hard-a-port, but it was too late. Even though those on *Truant* heard the sound of three explosions, only one torpedo hit the *Karlsruhe*. However this one hit, on the starboard side between the auxiliary machine room and the cruising turbine room, caused serious damage. The engines and steering gear were both affected, and she stopped dead in the water, listing around 10 degrees. Even more serious was the fact that most of the pumps would not work and water was flooding in. Most of the personnel from below deck were ordered up. *Luchs* and *Seeadler* came alongside and started taking members of *Karlsruhe*'s crew on board. When they had both taken on a large number of survivors, these two ships headed for Germany. *Greif* remained, with some survivors on board including Captain Rieve, who at 2010 was the last man to leave his sinking ship. It was decided to fire a torpedo to hasten her fate. Her bow was blown off but she still refused to sink, and it was only after another torpedo that she finally disappeared under the waves at 2142. These torpedoes were probably the noises heard when *Truant* was attempting to surface, causing her to dive again.

At a later inquiry into the sinking, Rieve was criticised for not trying to get a tow from the torpedo boats or calling Captain Thoma's minesweepers back to assist. It was also pointed out that it finally took two torpedoes to get the *Karlsruhe* to sink, so the damage may not have been as bad as was thought.

The following is from the log of HMS *Truant* for 9 April:

1833 hours - Sighted a cruiser hull down bearing 326 degrees. Enemy course was 146 degrees.
1852 hours - The cruiser was a "*Koln*-class". She was escorted by 3 "*Maas*-class" destroyers. Range was now 4,500 yards.
1856 hours - Fired a salvo of 10 torpedoes. 3 torpedo explosions were heard which were thought to be hits.
1900 hours - Returned to periscope depth. Saw one of the escorts approach at high speed. Went to 60 feet and altered course to 90 degrees from the firing course.
1902 hours - 2 depth charges exploded close. Went to 150 feet. Between this time and 2330 hours *Truant* was hunted by 2 of the escorts. In all 31 depth charges were dropped. Most of them unpleasantly close. *Truant* even went to 300 feet to escape damage.

Another ship anxious to get back from Norwegian waters to the safety of Germany was the *Lützow*, which had been one of the ships sent to Oslofjord. This battle cruiser had suffered damage from Norwegian shore batteries on the morning of 9 April, and Captain Thiele, whilst thinking that a meeting with Royal Navy ships would be unlikely, was wary of the threat from the air. At around 1500, *Lützow*, accompanied by the torpedo boat *Möwe*, sailed down the Oslofjord for the open sea. Whilst steaming down the Oslofjord, Captain Thiele received information that another of the torpedo boats sent to Oslo, the *Albatros*, had run aground on a shoal in the Gyrenfjord. Just before impact it was realised she was heading for some rocks, and her captain ordered the speed to be cut to five knots. However, it was too late and *Albatros* settled on the shoal with her stern well above the water line. The rocks caused a great deal of damage to the *Albatros*: the inflow of water caused most of the electrical systems to either fail or short-circuit, which in turn started several fires. Power was lost, more water poured in and the flames took hold. The German auxiliary *V707* carefully edged alongside and tried to assist with the fire-fighting, but it was an impossible task and eventually the crew was ordered to abandon ship. On hearing of the plight of the *Albatros*, Thiele decided that the *Möwe* should remain behind, while the *Lützow* continued alone. It appeared that Thiele had been advised of submarine threats, but believed that a speed of 24 knots would be enough to keep him safe. Intelligence had told the ships in the area that most British submarines were believed to be positioned near the Swedish coast, so Thiele took the *Lützow* on a westerly course, generally heading 138° but employing the usual anti-submarine drill of zig-zagging, heading for home using the Skagen in Denmark and the Paternoster Skerries gap. After midnight, radar operators on the *Lützow* reported a small radar return virtually dead ahead, at a range of about 10 miles. It was assumed that as the echo was a small one it was a fishing vessel, and Thiele gave orders to steer to port to give it a wide berth. Shortly afterwards, the radar operators reported that the contact had disappeared, so Thiele decided to resume his original course.

HMS *Spearfish*, of the 6th Submarine Flotilla, had sailed from her home port of Blyth on 5 April for her designated patrol area in the Kattegat, arriving on the morning of 7 April. Pending their invasion, there was a good deal of German activity both in the air and on the water in this bottleneck, and *Spearfish* spent many of the daylight hours under water. On 10 April, *Spearfish* was detected by German ships. She counted 66 depth charge explosions while trying to avoid destruction. However, some of these charges caused leaks in the casing, and also damaged the periscope and hydrophones. Nevertheless, *Spearfish* was able to avoid severe damage and eventually, by around 2330, the surface ships had moved on. *Spearfish* was brought to the surface to get some much-needed fresh air, having been submerged for over 20 hours.

The crew was recuperating when, about an hour later, the bow wave of a large ship was sighted to starboard at a range of about two miles. Lieutenant-Commander J. Forbes, the captain of the *Spearfish*, ordered course to port, thinking it might be one of the hunters back again, and manoeuvred the submarine so that it was stern-on to minimize the chances of detection. When the vessel got closer, it was believed to be the heavy German cruiser *Admiral Scheer*, but it was actually the *Lützow*. *Spearfish* stopped her engines and ordered six torpedoes to be fired, set to run at varying depths by line of sight.

HMS *Thistle* pictured before the war. (Author's Collection)

Immediately after firing, Forbes ordered a turn to a westerly course, still on the surface, and sent a sighting report back to Britain. After about five minutes, whilst doing his best to escape, the sound of a large explosion swept across the still waters.

Aboard the *Lützow*, there were no reports of torpedoes before the first impact, so the explosion came as a massive shock. Other torpedo tracks were seen in the water after the first impact, but ran past the *Lützow*. However, that single torpedo that did hit home caused severe damage aft, and the rudder was jammed at 20 degrees to starboard. Several compartments at the rear started to take on large amounts of water and the *Lützow* started to settle at the stern, with a list to port. Orders were given to rig emergency steering, but the damage control parties could not access the rudder room. Attempts to steer by the propellers did not work: it seems both propellers had been blown off by the exploding torpedo. At 0155, a message was sent from the *Lützow* to HQ Group East, which gave her position and stated: "Need immediate tug assistance." According to the log of *Spearfish*, the *Lützow* was attacked six nautical miles north of Skagen, Denmark, at 57°50' N, 11°00' E. A further message from *Lützow* was sent around 10 minutes later, saying: "Probable torpedo hit aft. Engines are OK. Rudder not operational. Submarine protection is required." There was a further message a short time later: "My position is 10 miles off Skagen. Ship is not manoeuvrable. Holding water. Both propellers lost."

Some of the leaks were plugged but most of the aft compartments and magazines were completely flooded. *Lützow* was drifting on the tide towards the Danish coast. It appeared to Thiele that the situation was serious. The lifeboats were swung out and the lower decks cleared, except for those on essential duties. Attempts were made to lighten the ship aft, including ditching all the ammunition for the rear turrets and pumping oil around the tanks. Help was on its way, however, with the 17th Anti-Submarine Flotilla, 19th Minesweeping Flotilla and 2nd S-boat Flotilla sent to the cruiser's position, while the torpedo boats *Jaguar* and *Falke* were ordered to sail from Kristiansand. Other ships such as the *Greif*, *Luchs* and *Seeadler* were ordered to the area from Kiel, and *Möwe* and *Kondor* from Oslofjord. Local attempts for help were made by an officer from the *Lützow* sailing in a cutter to Skagen to see what assistance could be found there. Another motorboat circled the *Lützow*, throwing demolition charges into the water at irregular intervals to simulate depth charges in an attempt to keep any submarines at bay.

After about three hours at the mercy of the waves, the rescue parties started to arrive and as many of the ship's crew as possible were transferred across to them. Three of the minesweepers that arrived – *M1903*, *M1907* and *M1908* – attempted to sort out a temporary tow, but the size and weight of the *Lützow* counted against the efforts of the smaller minesweepers to keep her heading in the right direction. *Möwe* arrived about 0830, and took charge of the tow from ahead. When daylight came, HE115 seaplanes provided much-needed air cover. The British were unaware of this lame duck prize in the Kattegat, and the opportunity to sink an important target was lost. In the afternoon of 11 April, two ocean-going tugs sent from Kiel, the *Wotan* and the *Seeteufel*, arrived to take over towing duties; and it seemed as though it might be possible to save the *Lützow*. It was feared that deteriorating sea conditions might break off the stern section, which appeared to be only held together by the drive shafts to the propellers, but the seas abated and she held together. It was a slow tug to Kiel, and keeping to shallower, calmer waters, the *Lützow* grounded on several occasions. However, by careful manoeuvring of the tugs and by flooding certain compartments in the bow, she was freed. *Lützow* arrived in Kiel late on the evening of 14 April. It was found she had around 1,300 tons of water in her stern area. Fifteen of her crew had been killed in the torpedo attack, and repairs to the cruiser lasted until well into 1941.

Despite the successful attacks on the *Lützow* and the *Karlsruhe*, not everything was going Admiral Horton's way or that of his crews.

In an aggressive move HMS *Thistle* (another T-class submarine), commanded by Lieutenant-Commander W. Haselfoot, which had been commissioned into the Royal Navy in July 1939, was ordered on the morning of 9 April to enter Stavanger harbour at the captain's discretion and attack opportunity targets there.

Haselfoot sent a signal back that he was on his way, intending to attack the following evening so long as enemy air activity did not prevent him. Haselfoot did add, however, that he only had two torpedoes left, having fired a salvo of six at a surfaced U-boat off Skudeneshavn at 59°00' N, 05°10' E, with unknown results. This was the last ever heard of *Thistle* until after the war, when it was worked out that the torpedoes she had fired were at the German U-boat *U4*. All the torpedoes were evaded, one passing less than 10 metres away. *U4* stalked the *Thistle* for the next few hours and eventually, in the early hours of 10 April, got into a favourable position. She fired two torpedoes at *Thistle*, the second of which hit home and sent her to the bottom with the loss of all of her 53 crew. *Thistle* was the first British submarine to be sunk by a U-boat in the Second World War: the first, but definitely not the last. The crew are commemorated on various Naval Memorials to the Missing at Chatham, Portsmouth and Plymouth. For most of the crew, the date of death is given as 14 April. Presumably this was the day the Admiralty decided the submarine was "missing in action".

After the initial wave of German forces had landed in Norway, the number of troops was considered to be insufficient should there be an Allied reaction, so reinforcements would need to be sent from Germany. Obviously the easiest method of doing this was by ship, as this would allow heavy equipment, artillery and transport to be moved. It was also intended for the bulk of the movements to be routed through Oslo, as this was the hub from which advances could be made to other areas of Norway. It was also recognised that the German Navy did not possess the same strength or experience as the Royal Navy, but it would need to dominate the waters off the Norwegian coast to facilitate the further build-up of ground forces. The Royal Navy in turn recognised that sea transport was a key element of the German logistics plan, and so on 10 April the Admiralty informed Horton that "interference with communications in southern areas must be left mainly to submarines, air and mining, aided by intermittent sweeps when forces allow". There were already several submarines in this area. One of them was HMS *Triton*, patrolling the Kattegat. Around 1630 on 10 April, she spotted a convoy of 15 ships off Gothenburg, probably just outside Swedish territorial waters, heading in the general direction of Oslo. It was the second group of resupply ships heading for Oslo. The sea was at this time very calm, and the periscope could only be used sparingly to avoid detection. Nevertheless, about an hour later *Triton* was in a good enough position to launch an attack. Her commander, Lieutenant-Commander Pizey, was at right angles to the convoy, and fired a spread of six torpedoes at a range of about 2,500 yards. Out of these six, three found targets - two merchant vessels, the *Friendenau* and the *Wigbert*, and one of the escorts, the *V1507* (an auxiliary patrol boat) - causing great confusion in the convoy. No instructions had been issued to the merchant vessels of what to do in the event of an attack. Some ships stopped to pick up survivors, while others carried on. The escorts eventually sorted out the situation by getting the transports to continue on their voyage, while some of the escorts stayed behind to rescue survivors. The three torpedoed ships sank within an hour, with some soldiers from the 340th and 345th Infantry Regiments – around 350 from both units – being lost, but around 800 were picked up, some by a Swedish destroyer which was keeping an eye on the convoy. Some of the escorts tracked the *Triton* and dropped around 80 depth charges in a bid to sink her, but she was able to slip away after about an hour of evasive manoeuvres. HMS *Sunfish* was also in the area and later successfully attacked the *Antares*, sinking her off Lysekil. Two other submarines, *Trident* and *Orzel*, had a go at ships in this convoy, but without success. The remnants of the second convoy arrived in Oslo on 12 April, followed by the third resupply convoy a few days later. From now on the success of the silent service led to a rethink in German plans. Larger transports were sent in small, heavily armed convoys, with air transport being the main means of moving troops. Those troops that could not be accommodated in aircraft were taken by train to Denmark, and then moved across using shorter ferry routes from Frederikshavn or Aalborg to Larvik or Oslo. These managed to ferry about 3,000 men a day across to Norway.

Also on 10 April, HMS *Tarpon* attacked what she thought was a German merchant ship off Jutland. She turned out to be a Q-ship. (A Q-ship was a name introduced by the British in the Great War to denote a decoy ship, especially an armed ship disguised as a merchantman to entice submarines to surface so that they might be attacked with gunfire.) *Tarpon's* torpedoes missed and the Q-ship, the *Schürbeck*, assisted by the minesweeper *M6*, pursued her for several hours. As nothing was heard from her again, it must be concluded that *Tarpon* was hit by depth charges and fatally damaged. She was sunk at about 57°43' N, 06°33' E.

In London, the War Cabinet agreed to extend the rules and area of engagement. Now all German ships, merchant or otherwise, under way within 10 miles of the Norwegian coast, south of 61° N and anywhere east of 6° E, could be attacked on sight. The Germans had also stepped up their game by sending more naval patrol ships, coupled with more air patrols, and in the narrow waters of the Kattegat the submarines were finding it more difficult to avoid detection and find safe areas to recharge their batteries. Nevertheless, HMS *Sealion* managed to sink the *August Leonhardt* and HMS *Triad* the *Ionia*, but after these initial successes – and in spite of eight submarines being positioned in the Kattegat and German Bight - only one ship, the *Moonsund*, was intercepted, by HMS *Snapper*, on 12 April. Lieutenant-Commander King, the commander of the *Snapper*, later wrote of this action:

> At 0340, as dawn was breaking, a small steamer was sighted to the north-eastwards, making for the northward. As it was getting light and aircraft were expected, it was desired to sink her quickly and two torpedoes were fired on a broad track. These missed astern. It was then seen that the steamer was smaller and nearer than at first estimated and that torpedoes were wasted on such a target as she could be chased and brought to. *Snapper* proceeded to chase and overhaul the steamer, which zigzagged and took no notice of the signal to heave to. After a chase of seven miles, she was brought to with a shot across the bows. She then broke the German merchant flag. The order was shouted to abandon ship and the reply was heard, "as you wish". No efforts appeared to be made to get the boats out. The Lewis gun was then fired over the masts but produced no results. One round of HE was then fired into the forepeak and the cargo of aviation spirit burst into flames and the crew jumped over the side. Six out of the seven were picked up; the seventh could not be seen. Two of these subsequently died of shock and exposure. The remaining four, including the captain, kept in good heart for the rest of the patrol.

Other successes came the way of the "silent service" when, on 13 April, *Sunfish* torpedoed the Q-ship *Schürbeck*, which forced her into Swedish waters, and so revenge of a sort was extracted for the loss of the *Tarpon* the previous day. Then on the following day, whilst in close proximity to "trawlers" of the 11th Anti-Submarine Flotilla, *Sunfish* managed to torpedo the *Oldenburg*, which later sank. However, the *Sunfish* was pursued for several hours by some of these trawlers but managed to escape unscathed. Also on 14 April, the gunnery training ship *Brummer* was in transit from Kiel to Frederikshavn in Denmark, where she took on board around 400 soldiers. She was going to move the troops to Oslo and would be accompanied by three escorts, the *Falke*, *F5* and the *Jaguar*. The troops quickly boarded the *Brummer*, which set off for Oslo that evening, arriving early on the morning of 15 April. The troops and their equipment were unloaded and, at around

1630, the vessel headed back to Frederikshavn for another load. By around 2300, when the convoy had reached the area of Jomfruland Island, a lookout on the *Brummer* spotted the tracks of three torpedoes. Two of them missed but the third hit home on the front section of the ship, virtually in line with the No. 1 turret. The resulting explosion caused the forward magazine to blow up, and the front section of the *Brummer* was effectively torn off. The three escorts circled round, trying to get a contact on what they supposed was a submarine. They fired a few depth charges, but without success. An attempt to take the *Brummer* under tow was planned for dawn, but before this could happen she sank just before 0700, about a mile off the Tvestinen lighthouse. There were over 50 casualties from this attack, of which 25 were fatalities. The submarine that attacked her was HMS *Sterlet*, whose fate is unknown. No messages were received from her and she was eventually reported "overdue". While it is possible she was sunk immediately after her attack on the *Brummer*, an "unknown" submarine attacked a convoy north-east of Skagen in the Skagerrak on 18 April. The German escorts reported that a submarine broke the surface and was then "heavily attacked". It is thought this was the *Sterlet*, and her likely position at the time of her loss was south of Larvik, Norway, at 58°55' N, 10°10' E. Her attackers were the German anti-submarine trawlers *UJ125*, *UJ126* and *UJ128*. Another theory is that she might have struck a mine whilst returning to base.

Other actions followed. On 15 April, HMS *Shark* fired a spread of five torpedoes at the German depot ship the *Saar* (although it was thought she was the *Brummer*) and two other merchant ships, but all missed or were avoided by the ships. Also on this day, HMS *Snapper* sank two minesweepers, the *M1701* and *M1702*, north-east of Skagen. Other ships tried to hunt her down, but she was able to escape. On 18 April, HMS *Seawolf* sank the transport ship *Hamm* north of Skagen., By now, however, the Germans were gaining experience and began to locate the submarines. On 20 April, *Swordfish* was attacked by an aircraft whilst at periscope depth. Shortly afterwards, when her commander, Lieutenant Cowell, heard engine noise, he decided to surface. *Swordfish* found herself in the middle of six enemy warships. Cowell immediately ordered a crash dive, but was depth-charged for the best part of the next two hours. Some of these exploded "uncomfortably close" to the submarine and caused leaks in the hull. To try to get away Cowell ordered the engines to be stopped to reduce all unnecessary noise, and somehow he managed to evade the six hunters. Within 30 minutes, when another group of ships was spotted – this time three transports and four escorts – she went in for another attack. A spread of six torpedoes was fired at the *Santos* about 20 miles south-east of Larvik, but again all either missed or were avoided. *Swordfish* was now not only being hunted by these three warships, but the original group joined in again, and a game of cat and mouse went on for about six hours before *Swordfish* was able to slip away and surface. She had no more success and was "pinged" by aircraft and anti-submarine patrols at regular intervals until Cowell decided that, as fuel was running low, it was time to call a halt and head back to base on 27 April.

Another submarine successful in these waters was HMS *Tetrarch*, which was being built as war broke out in 1939. She had been completed on 24 January 1940 and departed Barrow-in-Furness for Greenock. Several problems with the submarine necessitated a return to Barrow, but these were quickly resolved. After a few days at Greenock, she was ordered to Portsmouth for her sea trials. By 13 April 1940, under the command of

Lieutenant-Commander Ronald Mills, she was ordered to return to Rosyth. However, she was diverted en route to patrol in the Lister Light area, off the southern coast of Norway, in her first wartime patrol.

Lieutenant-Commander Mills recollected the latter part of that first patrol:

On 22nd April I was on the surface during darkness charging my batteries when we heard on the hydrophones four or five ships so I had to dive. At 1800 the following day I saw a small group of ships through the periscope passing from left to right. I thought it was three destroyers escorting a merchant ship. I closed in and ten minutes later I fired two torpedoes on a fairly broad track, and two minutes later I put up my periscope and saw the three destroyers steaming towards me so I ordered a crash dive to 300 feet. Some minutes later I heard their propellers and depth charges started to go off. This went on for about thirty minutes; I think about thirty depth charges exploded fairly close to me, but they were exploding in shallower water than I was. Around 2000 we heard the destroyers going away but other ships could be heard heading towards us. The air inside was getting worse and so I took the decision to surface. After the pressure had equalised I saw that the closest enemy vessel was about 1,500 yards away. I waited till it closed to within 500 yards before I crash dived to about 400 feet, deeper than I had intended. I over-corrected and we shot towards the surface, I again crash dived and stopped at about 350 feet. I ordered the main engines to be shut down and hoped that the Germans would go away. We stayed closed down and submerged for another twenty hours or so. So on the evening of the next day I gave orders to surface and we were in sight of land which was lit up like a Christmas tree. I realised we had drifted about thirty miles from the point of initial attack towards Sweden. I took the opportunity to recharge my batteries and report in to base, and was told to return to base. The whole of my pressure hull was rippled but after an inspection it was said I was OK to carry on. I later found out that we had torpedoed and sunk the German submarine chaser *Treff V* in the Skagerrak in position 58°21' N, 10°24' E.

For the rest of the month and into May, when other areas took priority, the activities of the British submarines were curtailed to a great extent by the longer days and the increasing patrols.

HMS *Tetrarch* went out on a second patrol on 12 May. These are the recollections of Lieutenant-Commander Ronald Mills:

We were again off the Lister Light and we had a mixed patrol. I missed sinking a U-boat on the surface. I was in the conning tower with the navigator when we saw a submarine on the surface. He said: "*Truant* has got lost and has come to join us."

I looked over and said "that's not *Truant* that's a bloody U-boat". He probably realised this at the same time as us and we both crash-dived and I tried to close to about 800 yards and fired four torpedoes, but they all missed. We then played a game of cat and mouse for about four hours until we lost contact, but in my post-operation report I didn't mention this. We did get two Danish fishing vessels though.

According to the records, these are the details of those successes:

23rd May 1940 Danish fishing vessel *Immanuel* is captured in the North Sea in position 56°59' N, 06°58' E and taken to Leith as a prize.
24th May 1940 Danish fishing vessel *Terje Viken* is sunk using scuttling charges in the North Sea west of Denmark in position 56°55' N, 06°50' E.

The "silent service" managed to sink or seriously damage a number of prize targets, such as the *Lützow*, and transports carrying valuable cargoes, but it came at a cost of four submarines lost. These included the *Tarpon*, *Thistle* and *Sterlet*, and also the *Unity*, which was rammed by a Norwegian freighter not far from her home base of Blyth as she was leaving for a second patrol towards the end of April.

In recognition of the efforts of the Royal Navy's submarines, the following message was sent to the submarine flotillas by the First Sea Lord, Admiral of the Fleet Sir Dudley Pound: "Please convey to all ranks and ratings engaged in these brilliant and fruitful submarine operations, the admiration and regard with which their fellow countrymen follow their exploits."

9

The Allied reaction

The British had intended to have a number of troops ready to land in Norway to achieve the aims of Operation R4, and by 7 April two battalions from the 148th Brigade (5th Leicesters and 8th Sherwood Foresters) were intended to go to Stavanger, with two battalions from the 146th Brigade (4th Lincolns and 4th KOYLI) heading for Bergen Also present were the Trondheim force (a battalion from the 146th Brigade – the Hallamshires of the York and Lancaster Regiment) and the Narvik element – the 24th Guards Brigade (1st Scots Guards, 1st Irish Guards and 2nd South Wales Borderers). The general perception was that Norway was for most of the year a country of ice and snow, and skis would be the best form of transport. Britain did not have any ski troops prior to the outbreak of war, but in early 1940 it was decided to form a "ski battalion": the 5th Battalion of the Scots Guards was formed and a request went out for volunteers to form a ski battalion to assist Finland in its resistance to the attack by Russia. Volunteers had to be either experienced skiers or mountaineers. In those days these pastimes were not the popular sport or holiday activity they are now, and it was mainly Army officers who answered the call. They had to resign their commissions and become guardsmen in this new unit. However, when neutral Sweden refused the British permission to cross their territory into Finland, and after training at Chamonix in the French Alps, the unit was disbanded.

Captain Alistair Mackenzie was one of the members of the 5th Battalion Scots Guards who had been formed to assist the Finns. He recalled:

In March 1940 I volunteered to join this ski battalion to be sent to help the Finns in the fight against Russia. Our commanding officer was Colonel Coates, who had been known before the war for doing the Cresta run. Virtually everybody else were young officers as they were the only people who had opportunity to go skiing before the war started. There were also a few civilians who had been to the Arctic and Antarctic. I was a Captain at the time, but had to become a Guardsman as virtually everyone was an officer. I was put into the "Right Flank" Company which consisted of people of six foot and over. We went to Chamonix in France, arrived in two trainloads and trained for about a week. We were paid at our "pre-joining" rank so in spite of being a Guardsman I was getting my officer pay. When we arrived it was in theory in the "closed" season but once word got round we had money, virtually the whole of Chamonix opened up again and we appreciated good food and drink.

After this brief spell of training we were hurried back in great secrecy to Glasgow, in theory to go to Finland. But by the time we got to Glasgow the

H. M. NEPTUNE
HEAD QUARTERS

I Neptune, God and King of the Icy Depths and Tropic Oceans Certify and testify with my signature that *Cpt. Marsh* *The Hallamshire Bn., The Yorks Lancasters Regt.* His British Majesty's Soldier Crossed the Arctic Circle on Board of a Troopship on this, the 14-th Day of April 1940.

I ask all my Vassal Gods and Nereids to protect Him and give Him the utmost Assistance in His Struggle with Our Enemies and Pirates of the Seas.

I order my subordinates, the Commodore of the Convoy and Master of the Troopship to testify that this Document be valid for ever.

Issued on the Arctic Circle this, the 14-th Day of April 1940.

NEPTUNE:

Commodore of the Convoy
Vice Admiral

Master of the Troopship

Hallamshire Neptune Crossing the line certificate belonging to Captain Marsh. (The National Archives)

Finnish War had virtually finished the day before. So we were sent back to southern England and the Battalion was disbanded.

Skiing in Chamonix was not downhill; it was langlauf (cross country). We formed up as patrols and we dragged all stores etc. on sledges. A patrol consisted of about 10 men. We did not do any training in tactical schemes and were instructed by NCOs who were more experienced in skiing. It was more about packing loads on sledges and tactical ways of getting them across country and downhill, so loads didn't run away, taking people with it. Patrols were up to about 15 miles across country.

If we had gone to Finland I think it would have been an absolute disaster. Perhaps something that was not appreciated at the time but would have had grave consequences was that most of us were young pre-war subalterns and we would have been taken prisoner. In the light of what was to come this would have been a disaster for the British Army as we were the hard core of the young officers and would have risen to higher ranks over the coming years.

Some weeks earlier, in February, the Allied Supreme War Council had decided that any operations in Scandinavia would be commanded by the British. Major-General P. Mackesy had been appointed to command the Norwegian expedition, but it would be a fractured command. The idea of having a supreme commander, as on the Western Front, did enter the mind of the politicians, but little came of it except this statement in the middle of April: "Once the Allies are in full control of the Trondheim area, a corps commander should be appointed to command all British, French and Norwegian forces in Scandinavia." So Mackesy was to lead the Scandinavian adventure. He later commented:

> At the end of March I took a few days' leave. Very late at night on Saturday 30th March I got a carefully worded telephone message to say that Avonmouth was on again. The Director of Plans drove from London to Suffolk on Sunday 31st March to tell me what was in the wind and early the next morning I went to London. The Chiefs of Staff instructions were that the force was to be prepared and embarked for a purely peaceful landing at an organised port. This time things moved quickly, except in one important point. Troops embarked on 5th, 6th and 7th April. I was due to leave Euston at 9.15 p.m. on Saturday 6th April and, as I had to embark in HMS *Aurora* with Admiral Evans, I would have a very short time at Glasgow to see my subordinate commanders, whom I could not expect to see again before reaching Narvik.

But the rumours of a German invasion caused the troops intended to go to Norway on the warships to be off-loaded. Two transport ships, the *Batory* and the *Chrobry*, were left behind, and Mackesy and his staff transferred to the *Batory*. Then on 10 April, new orders arrived, as follows, together with instructions and comments:

Instructions to Major-General P. J. Mackesy, CB, DSO, MC

1. His Majesty's Government and the Government of the French Republic have decided to send a Field Force to initiate operations against Germany in northern Norway.

2. The object of the force will be to eject the Germans from the Narvik area and to establish control of Narvik itself.

3. (a) You will command the troops including all units of the French Army and any RAF component which may subsequently be added to the force. The force will consist in the first instance of all troops now on board the SS *Chrobry* and *Batory*.

(b) Should you become a casualty or otherwise be prevented from exercising command of the force, command will pass to the next senior British officer, who will exercise command and, in the event of a French General officer being with the force, assume the acting rank of Major-General until another British officer can be appointed.

4. No information is available as to the strength of the Norwegian forces in the area but it is known that Harstad is normally the Headquarters of a mixed brigade and it is supposed that some troops are there now. Their attitude is not

known but it is believed that they will be ready to co-operate.

5. Your initial task will be to establish your force at Harstad, ensure the co-operation of Norwegian forces that may be there and obtain the information necessary to enable you to plan your further operations.

6. It is intended to reinforce you with a view to subsequent operations from such base as may be selected by you in consultation with the Senior Naval Officer. Salangen is the only neighbouring anchorage of which the Admiralty have full knowledge.

A timetable showing the time at which these reinforcements might be made available is attached as Appendix A.

7. It is not intended that you should land in the face of opposition. You may, however, be faced with opposition owing to mistaken identity; you will therefore take such steps as are suitable to establish the nationality of your force before abandoning the attempt.

8. The decision whether to land or not will be taken by the Senior Naval Officer in consultation with you. If landing is impossible at Harstad some other suitable locality should be tried. A landing must be carried out when you have sufficient troops.

9. You will appreciate the importance of the destruction of the railway leading from Narvik to the Norwegian-Swedish frontier should you be able to engineer it. This is the only known means of communication from Narvik into Sweden.

10. Your force will constitute an independent command directly under the War Office. You will keep in constant communication with the War Office and report as regularly as is practicable as to the situation.

11. A duplicate of these instructions has been handed to Brigadier Phillips.
E. Ironside,
General,
CIGS for Secretary of State,
The War Office,
10th April 1940.

Appendix A
Arrival Date
  (a) Remainder 24th Infantry Brigade (Regulars) a.m. 16th April.
  (b) Two TA Brigades (less two battalions) p.m. 16th and 18th April.
  (c) Transport for all above troops p.m. 19th April.
  (d) Remainder 49th Division a.m. 27th April.
  (e) Leading echelon *Chasseurs Alpins* between 21st and 25th April.
  (f) British formations ordered from the BEF twelve days between date of giving order for move and date of arrival of first brigade (without transport).

Copy of a message written out in manuscript by CIGS for General Mackesy 2330 hours 10th April, taken by Brigadier Lund.

High above skerries and fjords a German sentry patrols. (Bob Gerritsen Collection)

General Mackesy.

Brigadier Lund is bringing your instructions. Owing to naval difficulties in escorting, we have decided to send four Battalions together, the whole arriving 30 hours after the arrival of two Battalions. With a week's interval before the arrival of the other two Battalions.

Latest information is that there are 3,000 Germans in Narvik. They must have been knocked about by naval action.

You will have sufficient troops to allow you to make preliminary preparations and reconnaissance's. You yourself being some hours in front of your four Battalions with some men. You may be able to work up the Norwegians, if they still exist in any formed body in or around Harstad. Tell them that a large force is coming. There should be considerable numbers of ponies in the village and neighbouring ones. Let no question of paying trouble you. Issue payment vouchers and we will see that you get a paymaster as soon as possible. Don't allow any haggling over prices.

You may have a chance of taking advantage of naval action and you should do so if you can.

Boldness is required.

We will keep you informed of any action by the Germans giving them a chance

of getting men in via Sweden. At the moment they cannot reinforce Narvik.
Their first effort will be for reinforcing Bergen and Trondheim.
Good luck to you. We know your responsibility and trust you.
E. Ironside

Mackesy later commented:

A certain amount of difficulty ensued. The Hallamshire Battalion, which had been destined for a port hundreds of miles south of Narvik, had neither Arctic clothing nor maps. We were bound for an unknown destination of which we would have neither maps or knowledge. The Scots Guards had no mortar ammunition at all; we did what we could for the Hallamshires and transferred half their mortar ammunition to the Scots Guards.

Batory and *Chrobry*, with four escorting destroyers, sailed from the Clyde at about 0100 on 10 April, reaching Scapa Flow at about 0700 the following day, when the additional instructions from General Ironside were passed across. After the event, General Mackesy wrote of his thoughts from the time, and it is clear he was not happy. All he seemed to be getting was infantry, with no supporting weapons, aircraft or anti-aircraft guns. Both he and Brigadier Lund were confused by the comment: "Owing to naval difficulties in escorting, we have decided to send 4 Battalions together, the whole arriving 30 hours after the arrival of 2 Battalions. With a week's interval before the arrival of the other 2 Battalions." This was not the end of Mackesy's problems. Brigadier Lund also stated that the War Office in London did not know if there were any Germans at his proposed landing spot of Harstad, or indeed if Harstad was even suitable for the purpose. Nor did they know anything about any Norwegian forces, but thought there might be some at Bardu, which is many miles east of Harstad.

It is worth adding that the 148th Brigade from the 49th Infantry Division only had two battalions, instead of the normal three. At a meeting of the Supreme War Council on 9 April, Britain did offer to send a fourth brigade, the 147th, –the remaining brigade from the 49th Infantry Division. The French offered their original expeditionary force intended for the abortive Finnish operation, which had never been disbanded. This consisted of two battalions from the Foreign Legion, a brigade of the *Chasseurs Alpins* and four battalions of Polish troops. The force also included some of their 75mm field guns, anti-aircraft guns and one company of light tanks. It would appear the British also grudgingly advised that 12 25 pdr field guns could be stripped from home defence duties to go to Norway, along with a few anti-aircraft guns. The problem for the Allies was that they were pretty much at full stretch manning the Western Front, and any troops sent to Norway would have to be at the expense of that theatre. For the French, it was a fairly easy decision that they would form two light divisions, the manpower coming mainly from their Alpine troops and units in the process of formation from called-up reservists. The Alpine units stationed at the front were apparently told to lose about 25 per cent of their strength, and "adapt and overcome" if they complained. This allowed the French troops allocated to Norway to reach about 40,000, but the British would have to move them to Norway.

The British came up with the idea of forming 10 "Independent Companies" from volunteers from the Territorials on home defence duties. The volunteers came forward: there were around 3,000 men in these 10 large companies. It was also planned to try to divert to Norway units in the UK previously earmarked and under training for the BEF, or to move units already in France. The 126th Infantry Brigade, which was due to move to France on 17 April, was considered for Norway but allowed to join the BEF. A few days later, the 15th Infantry Brigade was brought back from France and moved via Scotland to Norway. Finally, two Canadian infantry battalions were also considered, but as it turned out never left the UK.

On the morning of 11 April, Major-General Mackesy's staff received a "mutilated" signal from the C-in-C Home Fleet to the Vice Admiral commanding the 18th Cruiser Squadron at Scapa Flow, to make available one cruiser to transport him and any staff he required, and take him to Norway at his convenience. At this stage Mackesy had not received further orders or instructions other than those already mentioned, but as a precaution, two companies of Scots Guards were ordered to be made available to go with him. As Mackesy commented, the staff and Scots Guards were "to be ready to tranship to some unknown cruiser of unknown troop carrying capacity at short notice". Later, Captain Maund, the chief-of-staff to the Senior Naval Officer, arrived, accompanying the "Avonmouth Force" (see Chapter 2). Mackesy asked when he would have to sail, either today or the next day, and was advised that tomorrow would be ample time. A message then arrived from the admiral in command of the 18th Cruiser Squadron, inviting him to a conference on board HMS *Manchester*, with a boat coming for him at 1330. The conference finished at 1315 and, as Mackesy said, he "swallowed a mouthful of food and had a long and rough trip across the anchorage". At this conference Mackesy learned that he was to sail on HMS *Southampton* at 1300 the following day. As soon as practicable, orders were issued to the Scots Guards to start moving across the 350 or so men with their equipment.

The advance element of the Scots Guards was as follows: Commander, Major H. Graham; Adjutant, Lieutenant D. Wedderburn; Intelligence Officer, Captain G. Taylor; Medical Officer, Lieutenant W. Burgess; First Reinforcement, Second Lieutenant H. Rose; RSM, D/Sergeant F. Foley; Right Flank Company, Captain A. Crabbe, Captain C. Fletcher, Lieutenant R. Petre and 124 other ranks; B Company, Major J. Elwes, Captain J. Godman, Lieutenant The Lord Hope and 124 other ranks.

Also included were some of HQ Company, including 18 signallers, two sections from the Anti-Aircraft Platoon, one detachment from the 3in Mortar Platoon, two pioneers, six cooks, two Orderly Room clerks, one ration clerk, one corporal from the Officers' Mess and one Bren Gun section of 11 men.

The loading had not been completed by the time it became dark, and owing to the strict blackout, work ceased and the job had to be finished on 12 April. The ship did sail more or less on time that afternoon.

General Mackesy commented:

During the night I got the first taste of what lay before me, personally. At 3.30 a.m. I was woken up and handed a personal, secret and confidential message from the CIGS. "I thought you had sailed yesterday, 11th. Delay should have been reported. Cable me direct of any operation orders which you have issued to your force." How anyone in the world could possibly have issued any operational orders to anyone, under the circumstances, passes my comprehension. I had of course taken the commanders into my confidence, but as I myself did not know where, in fact, I was going to end up, operation orders would have been absurd.

At the conference on board *Manchester* on 12 April, a RNR officer with some knowledge of Norway advised that some of the fjords that Mackesy hoped to use would probably still be ice-bound. Mackesy decided that he would wait and see what it was like when they got there. The senior command group then moved across to *Southampton* ready to sail. As well as Mackesy, also present were the GSO1 Colonel Dowler, the AA and QMG Colonel Whitacre-Allen and Brigadier W. Fraser, commander of the 24th Guards Brigade. Also accompanying the party were Mackesy's Naval Liaison Officer, Commander Gorton, and Captain Maund in his role as chief-of-staff to the Senior Naval Officer. Above Mackesy, Admiral The Lord Cork had been appointed as overall commander-in-chief. The two men were unknown to each other, and whilst Mackesy had received written orders to "eject the Germans from Norway", it appears that Cork had no written orders; when he did get verbal orders from the First Sea Lord, these were to "urge him not to hesitate to run risks but to strike hard to seize Narvik". It should be remembered that the Army commander had been told that "the decision whether to land or not will be taken by the senior naval officer in consultation with you".

Admiral of the Fleet the Earl of Cork and Orrery (to give him his full title) had seen active service in the Great War in command of a battle cruiser. Between the wars he was promoted to admiral and commanded the Home Fleet between 1933 and 1936. He made an unsuccessful attempt to become First Sea Lord in 1937, was made an Admiral of the Fleet (the highest rank in the Royal Navy) in 1938 and retired in June 1939, aged 66.

When war broke out in September 1939, Lord Cork offered his services but was told there was nothing for him. However, on 21 September, Winston Churchill recalled him to the Admiralty with quarters and a nucleus staff to undertake a study of a Baltic Sea offensive, to take place by March 1940. The proposed offensive was entitled Project Catherine, but the Russian-Finnish war rendered the plan obsolete .

Then at short notice, on 10 April 1940, Lord Cork was summoned to the Admiralty and given command of a hastily assembled naval force with a mission to retake from the Germans the strategic port of Narvik in Norway.

Meanwhile, at Scapa, the Army contingent, "Rupert Force", was crammed aboard HMS *Southampton* and left, escorted by the destroyers HMS *Electra* and HMS *Endeavour*. The journey across the North Sea to Norway was not a comfortable one, as. General Mackesy later wrote:

On that and the following day we had some weather; anyone who like myself suffers badly from seasickness will know how difficult it is to think at all let alone clearly, under such conditions. We discussed possibilities backwards and forwards. On the evening of the 13th April my staff and Captain Maund RN came and tried to persuade me that the only sensible thing to do was to go to Tromsö and from there get information and make a plan. During spasms of seasickness I just managed to retain enough common sense to refuse to go 150 miles to the north. I decided to go into Vaagsfjord, see if Harstad was occupied by the Germans and if so, or if no Norwegian forces were there, to try and get in touch with these in the neighbourhood of Sagsfjord. On a lovely sunny but bitterly cold morning most of us had our first view of the Norwegian fjords. Everything was snow and ice. Several feet of snow lay even down to the water's edge. The mountains showed glittering ice of glaciers and waterfalls. We agreed that the fjords could never look more beautiful than under such conditions, but never could they look less inviting from the point of view of landing and manoeuvring a military force. A few scattered houses and small villages existed at the few places where the mountains did not descend sheer to the water. My heart sank and it was difficult to crack silly jokes in a zero Fahrenheit temperature under such conditions.

There was little information coming out of Norway that could aid the British force. The Germans had taken over all means of communication with the outside world, and the Norwegian Government was almost constantly on the move and difficult to contact. The politicians, especially in London, seemed content to put their own spin on the facts as known. For example, at 1600 on 9 April, the Prime Minister, Neville Chamberlain, informed the House of Commons that it was "very possible to believe that the German landing was at Larvik not Narvik". Then two days later, on the agenda at a meeting for the Military Coordination Committee was an item about whether the Germans were in Tromsö - even though Tromsö was so far north it had little relevance to what was happening in the rest of the country and offered no real strategic value. The best estimate at the time was that the Germans had two divisions on the ground with around 200 aircraft in support.

One of the best sources of information from Norway ought to have come from the Military Attaché attached to the Embassy, but in April 1940 there was no one in the post. It was decided to invite the Military Attaché from the British Embassy in Finland to act as the Norwegian attaché. Lieutenant Colonel E. King-Salter of the Rifle Brigade reached Norwegian Army Headquarters late on the evening of 14 April. The next morning he sent several reports to London, which – probably for the first time – gave those in London some accurate information. One of these reports concentrated on Trondheim, which was a potential objective for the Allies. This report provided the intelligence that the Norwegians believed there were about 3,000 Germans holding the town itself. They were armed with light guns and automatic weapons, and were pushing out detachments to the south, occupying the areas to the east and north-east more strongly. Reinforcements were coming in, mainly by air: there were anti-aircraft batteries in the area, and one cruiser and three destroyers reported to be in the harbour. The next day, King-Salter sent further intelligence on the Trondheim position. He stated that there were 2,800 soldiers north of Steinkjer, 300 men and some artillery at Hegra, 400 troops south of Trondheim and about two battalions of troops at Åndalsnes.

On 19 April, he sent a signal summing up what the Norwegians had done:

The Norwegian troops are opposing the German advance in the four principal valleys running generally northwards from the region of Oslo … culminating eventually about 100 miles north of Oslo in easily defended defiles. These troops

57

Dear K.-S.,

I enclose you a copy of a telegram I sent to London after a visit to Trondheim.

I am afraid things are not going very well with the Norwegian forces, and I wonder whether this will ever reach you. I seem to have had very little contact with you, but I am sure you have had terrible difficulties with telephone lines being cut.

I have the following instructions for you. A representative of M.I.6 is in W/T touch with London. He is located at AALESUND, and I hope you may be able to make use of him. The following message is rather cold now, but will you deliver it if you can, and let me have an acknowledgement for it. It is addressed to the Commander in Chief of the Norwegian Forces, and runs as follows:-

1.   C.I.G.S. has received your message and thanks you for the information which you give as to your ability to cooperate with the Allied Forces, and he assures you that the Allied Forces will shortly be in a position to cooperate with you.

2.   War Office reports on the volume of W/T traffic between Germany and the Norwegian end of the Gulf of Bothnia indicate increasing German activity in this region. This would possibly indicate that the Germans are establishing refuelling bases for aircraft on the ice, and may indicate activity against LULEA. (We are asked to give any indication we can of what this means, - but how the devil we are meant to do it, they don't say).

A telegram from the Military Attaché Sweden to King-Salter part 1. (The National Archives)

are the equivalent of only a few battalions and batteries ... and consist of varied elements, many of which are completely under trained or very incompletely mobilised.

Hitherto the Germans have not concentrated in any sector and their operations appear to have been conducted by single battalions reinforced by some artillery and sometimes by light tanks.

The Norwegian detachments, too weak to resist in the open valleys, are now falling back by large bounds ... these withdrawals have given place to a number of rearguard actions in which a few prisoners have been taken. These actions have given the troops some confidence. But there are no reserves behind them and the men are without relief in the front line.

This was the background on which the Allies had to base their plans, and in London there were several important questions that needed to be answered. Where were the Allies going to land and counter-attack? Would Narvik and the iron ore trade be the focus of the landings? What about Trondheim and Bergen? What forces could be brought together

3.
I also received a message /o say that British
troops are on the way and/should be landed by the
time stated, and you wer/ to do your best to hearten
the Norwegians. I am a/raid that this message also
reaches you after Brit/sh troops have already landed,
and probably too late, - but I pass it on.

The Norwegian Legation in Stockholm is sending out

1 Field Wireless Transmitter,

and it is a station of good quality and high performance.

It will work to a Norwegian station in Stockholm. If you can

locate this, - and I can't indicate where it is going to, -

this would be a useful link between us. Next time the courier

comes through, perhaps you could indicate any sensitive points

in the German armour into which we might stick pins, as pin

factories are in the course of being set up.

Yours,

R.

(R. Sutton- Pratt

Military Attaché

Stockholm)

A telegram from the Military Attaché Sweden to King-Salter part 2. (The National Archives)

without endangering commitments on the Western Front? None were easy to answer.

Troops had been reallocated from mainly home defence duties. The 1st Irish Guards marched out of their barracks in London on the afternoon of 10 April and the 2nd South Wales Borderers from their quarters in Ulster. The Irish Guards found themselves going to Euston Station in a convoy of Green Line buses and had chalked on the sides comments like "See the Midnight Sun", "North Pole Express" and, no doubt to the horror of security personnel, "To Norway". After the train journey north, the Irish Guards found themselves in King George V dock in Glasgow and soon afterwards on the troopship *Monarch of Bermuda*. The *Monarch* had been a pre-war cruise ship before being called up for military service, and in similar luxury the 2nd South Wales Borderers found themselves on the *Reina del Pacifico*. After being loaded and unloaded several times over the previous few days, the rest of the Scots Guards found themselves on the *Batory* and the Hallamshires finally embarked on the *Chrobry*. The four ships set off on 11 April for Scapa Flow, escorted by destroyers. Following close behind were the King's Own Yorkshire Light Infantry (KOYLIs) and the Lincolnshires, who were moved from a transit camp at Dunfermline to Glasgow and put aboard the *Empress of Australia*. They still lacked much vital equipment that had been lost in the panic of getting off the Royal Navy

S E C R E T.

From:- 146th Infantry Brigade.

To :- The War Office.

Desp.
Recd.0840 17.4.40.

IMPORTANT.

G8 Cipher 25/4.

Hallam patrol action to-day Bei(γr)stad two German prisoners taken one wounded.   Our casualties nil. Germans belong 73rd Infantry Regt. identity books show Hanover.   Have been handed to French who have better interpreting facilities.

C.4.(Telegrams).   To M.O.8. (for action).

Telegram regarding the 146th Brigade regarding captured German prisoners. (The National Archives)

ships when the call had come to sail for Norway in a hurry, without the troops. These losses had not been made up, nor the equipment found, so these two units had to go as they were.

Formulated in the heady days of the rout of the German Navy at Narvik, with the expectation that Narvik would fall into Allied hands within a matter of hours, several ambitious plans were suggested.

There was Operation Henry, which following the success at Narvik on 13 April called for the landing of 300 sailors and marines at Namsos the next day; Operation Primrose, a diversionary raid by around 600 sailors and marines planned for 16 April at Åndalsnes; and Operation Maurice, the main landing of around 5,000 men on 16 April at Namsos, to move towards Trondheim that day.

Never shy of interfering, on the morning of 14 April London suggested that to implement Operation Maurice quickly, one of the two brigades currently sailing for Narvik should be diverted to Namsos. General Ironside's protests were brushed away by Churchill. After a conference call, the French agreed to divert some of their *Chasseurs*

Members of an unknown unit being issued with kit at the holding camp at Dunfermline. (The National Archives)

Men of the 24th Brigade hard at work on their way to Norway. (Imperial War Museum N8)

Alpins to Trondheim, instead of Narvik. The War Cabinet authorised the idea, including the diversion of the 146th Brigade to Namsos, but when the order reached the *Chrobry* and the *Empress of Australia* transports and their naval escort (the cruisers HMS *Birmingham*, HMS *Cairo* and HMS *Manchester* and destroyers HMS *Highlander*, HMS *Vanoc* and HMS *Whirlwind*) in the evening, they were only about 100 miles from Narvik. This meant that out of the original Rupert Force heading for Narvik, only the 24th Guards Brigade remained.

Despite all this confused planning, the voyage across the North Sea did have a few pluses for those on the ships. Sergeant J. Adams, the Signals Sergeant in the Borderers, remembers quite clearly the menu on the *Reina del Pacifico* for one of their first meals on board:

> The ship had it appears previously catered for a luxury market in South America and been requisitioned, and still had ample stores on board. On the first morning the breakfast menu was issued, which comprised about 4 pages. The wag sitting next to me asked for "everything twice please". He didn't get it – all he got was 4 or 5 eggs.

10

Rupert Force

The war diary of the 1st Scots Guards records that all ranks were issued with arctic clothing on 7 April and that a route march had been planned for the morning of 9 April, but was cancelled because of the sailing of the *Batory* for Scapa Flow. It further comments:

> A Regular Battalion of the Scots Guards had not been in Scotland for nearly 200 years. The First Battalion of the Regiment had crossed the border and embarked at King George V Dock, Glasgow, but this occurred in comparative secrecy. Had the route march, ordered for this morning, taken place, with the Drums and Pipes at the head of the Battalion, Greenock would have witnessed an occasion historic in the annuls of the Scots Guards.

While at Scapa Flow, the war diary records that, at 1100 on 11 April, orders were received for part of the unit to move to HMS *Southampton* for an amphibious landing in northern Norway.

On 13 April, while at sea, there is an entry in the war diary for the group on *Batory* which reads:

> 0930 Conference between the naval representatives and OC Troops to decide details of landing troops in Norway. There appear to be five or more plans depending upon various circumstances, but the two which seem most likely at the moment are as follows:-
>
> (a) To land unopposed at Narvik presuming that the Navy and the detachment 1 SG on board HMS *Southampton* will have driven back the enemy. This at the moment seems highly unlikely.
>
> (b) To land remainder of 1 SG at Lavangen fjord about 30 miles north of Narvik presuming again that detachment 1 SG have previously cleared away any opposition in this fjord.
>
> If the latter plan is adopted personnel would be transferred to one or more destroyers and taken 12 miles up the fjord, where they would re-transfer into the lifeboats of MS *Batory* which had been towed behind the destroyers. It is easy to see that the foregoing presents many difficulties, both naval and military.

Meanwhile, ahead of them the rest of the unit, plus the command group of General Mackesy, had reached Harstad, which is about 35 miles from Narvik.

General Mackesy recalled:

About 5 a.m. we arrived off Harstad, which proved to be quite a nice looking village; it actually has about 2,000 to 3,000 inhabitants. We were delighted to see one crane and a couple of small wooden piers. We sent a boat ashore with a naval officer and an army officer, both Norwegian interpreters, to find out what they could and bring to the ship any local officials, army or otherwise, who might be of use. To avoid disclosing the presence of troops on board the army officer was dressed up in naval uniform. He sacrificed a most becoming moustache in the cause. I have a vivid memory of our standing on the bridge of *Southampton* with our ears pricked to hear if the boat was going to be fired on or not. Owing to difficult navigation and lack of a local pilot, *Southampton* could not stand in near enough to afford the boat any protection at all, were such protection needed.

We spent an anxious hour and a half. At last the boat, accompanied by another, was seen returning. Our two officers arrived full of contradictory information, mostly based on local guesswork and rumour, together with the local chief of police, a local pilot and the local British vice-consul. Some rapid questioning followed from which it at least transpired that Narvik was strongly held, that the Germans held strongly the Gratangen Fjord and a line to the east of it, that the local Norwegian military headquarters was near Bardu, some 25 miles from the inner end of Sagsfjord. So to Sagsfjord we went. I had arranged for one boat to go into the fjord first to avoid any risk of the open boats carrying troops coming under fire. The leading boat towed a whaler carrying one section, an anti-tank rifle and an anti-aircraft Bren gun from the Scots Guards. We landed through several feet of snow at the small village of Salangsverket. The Union Jack was planted in the snow and we eyed an entirely empty village and landscape.

The first troops started landing around 1400, with no opposition, and a local man soon appeared in a car. He initially treated the new arrivals with suspicion, but the sight of the Union Jack and some basic Norwegian from the interpreters convinced him they were friendly. After what was described as "some bribery", Mackesy's GSO1 was allowed to borrow the car and set off to find some Norwegian troops. Meanwhile, the rest of the Scots Guards started to leave the *Southampton*, but it was a slow process owing to the lack of suitable landing craft and boats. Nevertheless, before night fell the two companies of the Scots Guards were established some seven miles to the east of the landing spot, at Sjoveien, and were in contact with a detachment from the Norwegian 6th Division.

Then the fog of war came into play again. Lord Cork ordered HMS *Southampton* to meet him that night in Skjelfjord with a view to landing at Narvik on the morning of 15 April, as intelligence had suggested that the Germans there were in a state of chaos following the naval action: the town was apparently ripe for an assault and could be taken with hardly a shot needing to be fired. The troops would be the 350 or so Scots Guards in the *Southampton* and around 200 sailors and marines from the ships in the Narvik area. Mackesy commented on his first real contact with Lord Cork:

This signal must have arrived about 2 p.m. and Skjelfjord must be some 250 nautical miles from our then position. I said disembarkation must continue. As my information showed Narvik to be strongly held in any case, as there had been no opportunity for reconnaissance, in fact we knew very little indeed and what little we did know made me dislike the suggestion enormously. I felt it to be my duty to refuse the offer as politely as possible.

Lord Cork had already received the following advice from the Admiralty: "We think it imperative that you and the General should be together and act together and that no attack should be made except in concert." To his credit, Cork did order HMS *Aurora*, the cruiser he was on, to the area of Harstad on the night of 14–15 April.

Harstad, to British eyes, was a fishing village of around 4,000 inhabitants but it did have a small harbour with some wooden quays and unloading facilities. It was, however, a shallow harbour and the bigger ships could not enter. On the morning of 15 April, the transports bringing the rest of the 1st Scots Guards, the 1st Irish Guards and the 2nd South Wales Borderers arrived in the area, escorted by the battleship HMS *Valiant* and nine destroyers. The remainder of the Scots Guards were moved ashore on this day, together with the Irish Guards, Brigade HQ and the 3rd Anti-Aircraft Battery, Royal Artillery. The Irish Guards war diary recording the following for 15 April:

We awoke to the most beautiful scene, the convoy steaming in formation of line ahead down the fjord towards Narvik. Admiral of the Fleet Lord Cork and Orrery led the convoy in the cruiser *Aurora*. The convoy circled round twice while the destroyers took soundings of the fjord. The scenery had all the attractions of the Swiss mountains with the added beauty of the waters of the fjord down which we sailed. The tiny fishing hamlets on either side of the waters took little notice at first of the long line of ships. Gradually, however, the villagers would gather in groups and finally they became sufficiently courageous to follow us in their well-built fishing smacks. At about noon, six depth charges were heard in rapid succession and this time the victim was successfully claimed and six prisoners were landed from one of the destroyers. At lunchtime the CO was told that a destroyer was alongside, ready to take off the first landing party of the Battalion. The Battalion disembarked in the order No. 2, 1, 3, 4, HQ. In addition to the kit, which the men wore, when embarking, they wore their arctic coats, pullovers, gloves, glasses and carried their two additional kit-bags. Those men, for whom room could not be found on the destroyer, landed in the local fishing boats.

Billets were found for the Battalion in Harstad. Battalion HQ and No. 1 Company were quartered with Brigade HQ and 1st Battalion Scots Guards in the large school about half a mile from the quay. No. 2 Company is about ½ mile from Battalion HQ with Nos 3 and 4 Companies about 4 miles away from the town.

The inhabitants of the town are friendly and the Guardsmen themselves lost no time in getting acquainted with the more attractive local inhabitants. It must be bewildering for the inhabitants to have so many soldiers thrust suddenly upon

Seemingly trying to make order out of chaos. (Imperial War Museum HU128787)

them, but they meet every problem with charming courtesy and a smile will almost requisition anything.

Force HQ are established at the Grand Hotel. Mr Borland joined Battalion HQ as official interpreter.

This somewhat leisurely and problem-free account of the landing was not confirmed by General Mackesy. He had other things on his mind on this day, as he later reported:

Flag Officer Narvik (FON) arrived in HMS *Aurora* (Admiral Lord Cork). I boarded early in the morning. I refused to carry out an unprepared and unconsidered attack on Narvik, although I was all in favour of making such preparations for such an attack later. While this was going on the troop convoy arrived, headed by HMS *Valiant*, a most impressive armada. Disembarkation should have commenced at once at Harstad, but to show his independence FON refused to accept tentative plans prepared the previous night by his own chief of staff and led the armada round and round the fjord while he argued. Imposing as the sight was, it was asking for submarine attack and it wasted five hours of precious daylight.

During the progress of this naval review, *Aurora* with two destroyers escorting, led, some miles ahead. The destroyers suddenly opened fire. Our glasses showed a German submarine just surfaced by a depth charge. It was speedily sunk. It

Waiting for the orders to go ashore. (Imperial War Museum N56)

seemed to me amazing, from a front seat in the stalls on the bridge of *Aurora*, that 39 out of a total complement of 43 were picked up by the destroyers' boats.

Eventually the first troops began disembarking to Harstad at 1.30 p.m. instead of at least 8.00 a.m. and my HQ was established at the Grand Hotel during the afternoon. My administrative staff did wonderful work in getting troops under cover somehow. As we had no anti-aircraft protection whatever, the crowding was dangerous but protection from the weather was essential.

The U-boat mentioned by Mackesy was *U49*. On the morning of 15 April, HMS *Fearless* and HMS *Brazen* were ordered to proceed ahead of the British troop convoy passing through Andfjord, and hunt a U-boat reported by a military post to be north of Andorja Island. Passage through Topsundet was made at 25 knots, and Vaagsfjord was entered at 1026, *Brazen* being then moved out to one mile on the port beam, speed being reduced first to 18 knots then to 12 knots at 1040. The course was altered to pass close to Andorja Island.

Eight minutes later, *Fearless*, then quite close to Andorja Island, gained contact ahead at 1,700 yards. When this had been reduced to 1,400 yards, the echo was confirmed as a submarine and *Fearless* increased to 20 knots to attack. A single pattern of five charges was fired. The first depth charge exploded under the bows of the U-boat and had little effect, but the second exploded close to the conning tower, with apparently fatal consequences. As one rating described it, "the boat leapt in the water". All lights were extinguished and everything was in confusion. A third depth charge exploded by the stern and the remaining two astern. The last explosion had barely subsided when the U-boat shot to the surface.

The U-boat Captain apparently lost his head, for he gave the order to blow the tanks, then changed the order to flood the tanks, but, realising this was hopeless owing to the inrush of water, once more gave the order to blow the tanks. The ballast tanks were stated to have been destroyed and the periscope was wrecked. Orders had been given to release the Marx buoy raft, but in the panic this was not done.

The first members of the crew to appear on deck made for the gun, but were discouraged by a few rounds of 4.7in from *Brazen* and *Fearless*, one shot passing through the conning tower. The Germans then took to the water with the exception of the Captain and one Petty Officer, who were seen on the bridge putting papers and confidential books into a bag. *Fearless* opened fire and they also abandoned ship. The papers were obtained, dried and sent to HMS *Aurora*. The U-boat did not appear to be much damaged on surfacing, but sank very quickly and there was a minor underwater explosion shortly after she had submerged. Survivors were picked up by whalers from *Brazen* and *Fearless* and transferred to *Aurora*, and later to *Valiant*. After some 10-15 minutes in the water, all but one of the 42-man crew – a rating - were rescued. One other rating was wounded and subsequently underwent an operation in HMS *Valiant* for the removal of a shell splinter.

At 1345, HMS *Escapade* came alongside the *Batory* and Left Flank Company, C Company and part of HQ Company of the 1st Scots Guards boarded her for transport to Harstad. Just before leaving, the CO, Lieutenant Colonel T. Trappes-Lomax, was presented by the ship with a lance flying a pennant in Brigade of Guards colours. The war diary stated this as:

> a most pleasant memento of an historic voyage. This pennant will henceforth become Battalion HQ flag. Lieutenant Colonel T. Trappes-Lomax had just time before the destroyer left to go up to the bridge and thank the Polish captain on behalf of the Battalion and said that the lance would be used as Battalion HQ sign during the war and that if it survived it would find an honourable place among the Regiment's trophy's. 1500 Battalion disembarked - Lieutenant Colonel T. Trappes-Lomax being the first to step ashore, carrying the lance direct from HMS *Escapade*, at Harstad, where they were met by 2nd Lieutenant Harvey who had been allotted accommodation in the local school. Only three pipers were available to play the Battalion up to the billets as the remainder had either been left on board *Batory* as anti-aircraft defence for the ship or had other duties to perform. All the inhabitants had turned out in force to see the British troops, who were greeted with cheers.

By the end of 15 April, the majority of the 24th Brigade was more or less ashore at Harstad and had received very little in the way of interference from the Germans. Troops were in position in a defensive perimeter around the Harstad area, but there was still conflict and confusion amongst the high command.

During the morning of 16 April, the body of 2696478 Guardsman George Johnstone B Company was brought ashore in the destroyer *Electra*. Johnstone, who became the first casualty of the war in Norway, was aged 23. He was injured while on board HMS *Southampton* in an extremely heavy sea and had died in the night from meningitis following concussion. The funeral was to take place on Thursday, 18 April. He is now buried in the Allied Plot, grave D6, in Harstad Cemetery.

The 2nd South Wales Borderers disembarked on 16 April. The advance party was brought to Harstad from the *Rio de Pacifica* by two destroyers and arrived about noon, with the remainder coming in another destroyer and arriving about 1600. They were billeted in buildings along the quayside or near the harbour. Their war diary records one thing in common with all the billets - the "stench of drying fish"! Also on this day, Harstad and the ships offshore were somewhat ineffectually bombed by the Germans, whose raids gave the 24th Brigade the honour of firing their first shots in the war at German aircraft.

The Irish Guards spent the morning settling into their new surroundings, with the officers' mess established in a house behind the school. An Orders Group was called for 1400. Just as the CO, Lieutenant Colonel W. Faulkner, was issuing orders, a loud crash was heard. Their war diary noted:

> We waited rather nervously for the next one. All the CO said was "Have we too many eggs in one basket?" but we continued, rather forcing our attention back to our maps, pencils and notebooks. The next crash, 12 minutes later at 3 p.m., forced us all without exception into an undignified but obviously practical plunge on the floor. The result of this bomb was as follows. Two craters were found on either side of a house, only 50 yards from the room in which the conference was held. The house caught fire, but none of the occupants were touched. The Carrier Platoon on the opposite side of the road had all the glass broken in their billet and one piece pierced a Guardsman's SD (Service Dress) cap without hurting him. The fire was extinguished after hard work by the Carrier platoon. All the windows of the officers' mess were broken and the clock was utterly smashed. Seven bombs were dropped in all and the only check to the Nazi pilot was some optimistic Bren gun fire by the Anti-Aircraft Platoon, which probably did more to draw the enemy fire close to Battalion HQ than anything else. One of the bombs which fell near the docks killed a military policeman and badly frightened PSM (Platoon Sergeant Major) Higgins and the Pioneer Platoon, who were unloading baggage from the Quay.

General Mackesy commented on the disembarkation:

> On Tuesday 16th April disembarkation was still proceeding slowly from ships at least ten miles away from the port of Harstad. We had no signal communication with the ships: the result was that men, nurses and stores arrived ashore in complete disorder with no advanced parties and no hope of any orderly handling of personnel and stores landed. The prodigies of overwork and improvisation

performed by my staff for days on end, during these early days, beggar description and imagination. The Navy thought of nothing but emptying ships. Neither at this time nor later did I ever meet a naval officer, however good, who could think above the high water mark with the exception of Commander Gorton RN.

On this day I had another conference with Lord Cork and once again had to refuse an immediate assault on Narvik owing to the need for reconnaissance and sorting out units, their arms, ammunition and weapons, apart from the total lack of all elementary essentials, such as landing craft, for a combined operation. As one example of my condition, my battalions were shipped with no mortar ammunition in spite of many previous representations to the War Office. At this meeting I again pressed for air photographs of Narvik to be taken by the aircraft from HMS *Furious* but until I left Narvik I never received one worth looking at.

General Mackesy had some valid points: it was all well and good for the Navy to say that the two recent actions had demoralised the Germans at Narvik, but no real intelligence was coming back as to who was there and in what numbers. With the benefit of hindsight it is easy to say that the majority of the defenders were sailors and that the non-arrival of the three expected supply ships and one of the two tankers did have an effect on German operations, but the arrival of 34 lorries carrying around 350 tons of supplies from Sweden compensated for this to some degree. Lord Cork was pressing for an immediate attack on Narvik but Mackesy stuck to his guns and refused.

Another reason for Mackesy's refusal was the weather, of which he later said:

Although nobody without personal experience of Arctic winter conditions can possibly picture the climatic difficulties we experienced in the early days, a word or two of description may not be out of place. The country was covered by snow up to 4 feet or more in depth. Even at sea-level there were several feet of snow. Blizzards, heavy snowstorms, bitter winds and very low night temperatures were normal. Indeed, until the middle of May even those magnificent mountain soldiers, the French *Chasseurs Alpins*, suffered severely from frostbite and snow blindness. Troops who were not equipped with and skilled in the use of skis or snowshoes were absolutely incapable of operating tactically at all. I had no such troops at my disposal when I first landed. Shelter from the weather was of vital importance.

It is recorded that whilst ashore on a fact-finding mission, Lord Cork attempted to walk across an area of deep snow. Almost immediately he went in up to waist and had to be helped out.

Lord Cork reported on the afternoon of 16 April that the assault on Narvik originally proposed for that day had been abandoned, but London kept up the pressure with both the Admiralty and the War Office getting involved. On 17 April, a joint signal was sent to the two commanders:

Your proposals involve damaging deadlock at Narvik and neutralisation of one of our best brigades. We cannot send you the *Chasseurs Alpins*. *Warspite* will be needed elsewhere in two or three days. Full consideration should therefore be given by you to an assault upon Narvik covered by *Warspite* and destroyers which might also operate up Rombaks Fjord. The capture of port and town would be an important success. Send us your appreciation and act at once if you consider right. Matter most urgent.

Later that day, Lord Cork wrote a memorandum to General Mackesy dated 17 April 1940, as follows:

I am sending you herewith a copy of my remarks and only wish they were supporting yours. I have, however, always held this view and there it is.

Would it now, however, be possible to attach to this a little more information as to the dates you are working to under your scheme and leave it to Whitehall to decide? The Government obviously want a quick decision; it was probably the mention of the end of April in our last message that frightened them. If you could mention say six days for capture or dispersal of enemy forces north of Rombaks Fjord and so many days for reduction of town, the Government might be glad to accept the alternative. A battleship would not be needed until you were ready and I would report to that effect.

May I say how much I sympathise with you in having this decision thrust upon you. I should like to come over tomorrow and discuss this with reference to the two messages that have just reached me and have not sent a reply.

My view is that under the overwhelming gun power a force of one battleship, two cruisers and eight destroyers could bring to bear, the troops could be landed with slight loss. If the enemy retained their morale after such an ordeal as a bombardment by heavy guns at close range, then their resistance might be successful and lead to the result the General foresees. My own belief is that their general morale would be broken and only a show of resistance made and I should gamble on that chance. Enemy defences are stronger now than they were, but my belief is that such an attack would succeed.

On 18 April there was a meeting ashore at Harstad. The minutes of this conference again show a degree of conflict between the Army and Navy:
Present:

Admiral of the Fleet Lord Cork
Major-General P Mackesy
CSO to FO Narvik
Staff Officers of GOC Rupert GSO1, AA & QMG, GSO2 & NLO
Commander 24th Guards Brigade
    1. Lord Cork referred to his attendance at a meeting of Ministers and COS Committee and indicated that the early capture of Narvik was being urged there.
    2. He explained that the naval force available would consist of:-
One battleship
Two cruisers
Eight modern destroyers

3a. General Mackesy. He reviewed the last Cabinet instruction received a week ago today and stressed the references therein to additional troops and to preliminary preparations and reconnaissance.

b. He quoted the verbal instructions given to him by Brigadier Lund on 11th April, 'We realise that it may take you some weeks to make a plan etc'. In actual fact he (General Mackesy) made a plan in 24 hours and it is now actually being carried out.

c. Troops at present in this area available for attack are inferior to the enemy in number and in equipment. *Chasseurs Alpins* have been taken away, leaving no troops trained and fit to fight in snow.

d. Defences at Narvik were taken over intact by the enemy from the Norwegians and have since been strengthened.

e. It is not a justifiable operation of war for a numerically inferior force, scarcely able to move owing to the snow, to attack an enemy who enjoys all the advantages of the defensive. When the difficulties of landing from open boats on very limited beaches are added the operation becomes sheer bloody murder.

f. Without definite orders to do so, General Mackesy will NOT carry out the proposed assault. If he receives such orders, he will do all that can be done to carry them out loyally and energetically, though he depreciates the snows of Narvik being turned into another version of the mud of Passchendaele.

4. General Mackesy's proposed plan.

Bombardment may result in demoralisation of the enemy. Suggest therefore:-

(i) Heaviest possible bombardment. But there are 5,000 Norwegians in the place; do the Admiral's instructions entitle him to carry out such a bombardment? (The Army's do not.)

[This question was not answered during the conference.]

(ii) All available troops to be kept in hand (afloat, ready to land in tactical order) out of range of MG fire.

(iii) GOC to carry out a personal reconnaissance and call the troops forward to land, if, and only if, he is satisfied that the landing is feasible.

(iv) Troops to go ashore covered by a second bombardment unless, of course, the enemy has surrendered.

5. Lord Cork agreed to the broad outlines of the General's plan. He considered the bombardment is certain to be effective, but agreed that the ships' guns cannot help once the troops get ashore.

6. The difficulties of the landings were discussed; a photograph clearly showed the limited number of beaches on which the troops could land and how the town itself is defiladed from a frontal bombardment by a hill up which the troops, if they got ashore on the western beach, would have to climb through deep snow.

7. General Mackesy stressed that the Army can land and occupy Narvik if the garrison is sufficiently demoralised, but cannot assault. Lord Cork agreed.

8. General Mackesy asked for a ship to enable him to carry out a preliminary personal reconnaissance of Narvik.

So a compromise was agreed: after a strong naval bombardment from close range, reconnaissance parties would land at Narvik. If there appeared to be weak German resistance, two of the infantry battalions would be put ashore using local fishing boats. If, however, there was strong resistance from the Germans, the bombardment would restart and a new plan would be worked out.

As General Mackesy had requested a personal reconnaissance of the Narvik area, he was taken there in the cruiser HMS *Aurora* with his ADC and the commander of the 24th Brigade, Brigadier Fraser, leaving shortly after noon. They first went to the repair facility at Skjelfjord to obtain some local intelligence. Mackesy later commented:

> As I saw a large captured German merchant ship there loaded largely with motor transport including troop carrying transport, it made me wonder a good deal as to what the German intentions at Narvik really were. The ship was to be sent to England as a prize but I suggested that we should have her contents investigated more closely, keep what was of use to us and offer the remainder to the Norwegian Army. This was done.

Whilst at Skjelfjord, *Aurora* was ordered to patrol off Narvik, as a report had been received that five German destroyers with 900 troops on board were heading for the port. It turned out to be a false rumour, and in Mackesy's eyes another day was wasted while looking for these ships. Another ship arrived to take over from them and they were at last able to carry out their close target reconnaissance. This was completed successfully, Mackesy reporting back:

> Narvik lies on a promontory, and to the west end is a steep, wooded bluff. To the north facing the Rombaks Fjord a comparatively flat foreshore runs up to low heights which defilade most of the area from the fire of ships. To the south lies the harbour, fouled by the wrecks of some sixteen ships and guarded by magnetic mines. Warships were unable to enter and no gun fire at all could be brought to bear on the ore quay area. To the east the ground rises steeply, but precipitously to the mountains.
>
> The only land exits from Narvik are on the south, a road running along the edge of Beis Fjord to the town of the same name, and on the north the mountain railway running along Rombaks Fjord. The road runs along the foot of very steep mountains. During the long days of arctic spring and summer neither the railway nor the road can be used if the high ground north and south of Rombaks and Beis Fjords respectively are in hostile occupation.
>
> To the south of Narvik lies the Ankenes peninsula within machine gun range of many parts of Narvik. To the north lies the Oijord peninsula, within 2,000 yards of some of the few possible landing places. Both the Ankenes and Oijord peninsulas are much higher and between them give perfect command of Narvik. The whole country was under some three or more, generally much more, feet of snow. Any tactical movement for British troops was quite impossible. Even if, as they might with luck, a few troops did get ashore on the north they could do

nothing more and get no covering fire of any value from ships' guns. Without proper landing craft they could not get ashore dry; the inevitable frostbite after sunset would have been devastating.

In short, my previous opinion, was, to my mind, most fully justified. Brigadier Fraser and I, after our reconnaissance, sat down independently and made notes. Our unanimous opinion was not surprising, but the similarity of phrases we used was rather remarkable. I reported to the War Office in a telegram which read as follows:

Following for CIGS from General Mackesy in confirmation of 1451 20th April.

I have now made a personal reconnaissance of Narvik, which is undoubtedly strongly held. My original opinion that the conditions essential for a successful opposed landing do not at present exist is fully confirmed. I do not rule out such a landing at a later stage, but shore artillery, shore observation and suitable landing craft will all be necessary. There are no beaches which could be used effectively under present deep snow and climatic conditions. There are two piers which might be used if destroyers can be run alongside but the prospects of successful exploitation of a landing so made are non-existent. Owing to the nature of the ground, flat trajectory of naval guns, and the impossibility of locating the concealed machine guns, I am convinced that the naval bombardment cannot be militarily effective, and that a landing from open boats in the above conditions must be ruled out absolutely. Any attempt of the sort would involve NOT the neutralisation but the destruction of the 24th (Guards) Brigade.

As regards bombardment and occupation if resistance ceases. This plan is based on Lord Cork's firm belief in the demoralising effect of naval bombardment. Those of us who have seen and experienced far heavier and better-directed bombardments than this one can be, know only too well that British and German troops are not so demoralised and that machine gun detachments always come up when the bombardment ceases. The only hope there is to bombard and to hope that the Germans will surrender as they surrendered at Duala (in the Cameroons in German West Africa) in 1914. For this reason it will be necessary to include the town in the bombardment. I am convinced that the bombardment of only such defences as are known to us would have no small chance of obtaining this effect. Narvik is reported to contain not less than 5,000 Norwegians and such a bombardment must involve them in the highest degree. I fear that the effect of such action upon my relations with the Norwegian authorities may be very grave and may prejudice all future operations in northern Norway. It is contrary to the instructions which I have received from the Cabinet and I submit that it should only be undertaken on a direct order from the Cabinet.

Nothing short of the surrender of the town, the giving of hostages and the assembly of all German troops where they can be controlled by the fire of the ships can justify the landing of troops under existing conditions. I lay the greatest stress upon this being accepted and upon no last minute action being taken to try and force my hand against my judgement. Unless I have this assurance I shall feel unable to continue with the plan.

The problem of the civilians in Narvik was answered by a restriction of the area of the bombardment. Word was also got to Tromsö Radio to urge the residents to evacuate.

The fortunes of the three battalions on the ground around Harstad should now be considered.

Most of the first unit to get ashore around Harstad, the Scots Guards, was first billeted in a school. After bombs were dropped in the town in a *Luftwaffe* raid on 16 April, the decision was taken to move the unit to the outskirts, where if possible they would be billeted in scattered houses. This move was not without difficulty, as the Guards' war diary for 17 April recalls: "Transport was practically unavailable and kit bags and cookers were either carried down by hand or pushed ½ mile in borrowed sledges." By 17 April, Battalion HQ and Left Flank Company (less one platoon) were positioned south of Harstad, with C Company, and the other Left Flank platoon, about a mile away from Battalion HQ to the north-west of the town. Right Flank Company was still some seven miles to the east of the landing spot at Sjoveien; on 18 April, 2nd Lieutenant Harvey was dispatched to Salangen in a local fishing boat with stores, maps, cigarettes, wine and spirits for Major Graham's detachment. On the same day, at Harstad, the funeral of Guardsman G. Johnstone was held at the cemetery near C Company's billets. Their war diary records:

The service was conducted by Captain Hamilton, with full military honours except that owing to the absence of blank ammunition no salute could be fired. The ceremony was made more impressive by the snow, the brilliant sunshine and the absolute quiet, broken only by the sound of the pipers and the two bugle calls.

Some of the more enterprising officers and men borrowed skis from locals to aid movement in the conditions. The CO of the unit, Lieutenant Colonel T. Trappes-Lomax, perhaps mindful of the amount of snow still falling in the area, decided to introduce skiing practice for all ranks, but this was hampered by a shortage of skis. The mayor was asked to help supply more skis. The war diary for 19 April records that as the following day was Hitler's birthday, German radio forecast a large bombing raid on Harstad as a present for him. However, the expected air raid did not materialise, possibly scuppered by heavy snow. The Scots Guards were buoyed by the news that the MT and Carrier Platoons were due to arrive at around 1900. In the event they turned up the next morning.

On 17 April, No 2 Company of the 1st Irish Guards had left in three fishing boats with the intention of landing at Skaanland, leaving one platoon at Evenes and working their way up the coast towards Lenvik. On 18 April, Major Bowen led a small party, including two interpreters, towards Bogen Bay, where it was intended that the Battalion should land the next day.

Bogen Bay is on the north side of the Ofotfjord, about 10 miles from Narvik as the crow flies, but about 30 miles by road or ferry. Skaanland was about twice as far from Narvik on the same road. On 19 April, just as the Irish Guards were leaving, enemy aircraft appeared and dropped some bombs, but with little effect. The Guards' departure was delayed until the all clear was given. They initially boarded a minesweeper, HMS *Protector*, and then transferred to HMS *Vindictive*, a repair ship which had previously acted as a light cruiser and an aircraft carrier. The unit's war diary records that "by 1900 the Battalion was comfortably settled in on board ship. The troops were loud in their praise of the naval food and were eager to take advantage of the facilities offered on board to buy tobacco and cigarettes at duty-free prices."

The war diary continues:

> The CO had a conference of Company Commanders at 1400 to give out orders for landing at Liland in Bogen Bay; HQ, 1, 3 and 4 Companies were to be billeted between Liland and Leros. No. 2 Company had one platoon at Evenes. Major Bowen and Captain Fitzgerald met the CO and his staff who landed first in the fishing fleet of Norwegian boats, which were under the orders of the FO Narvik. Billeting and unloading of baggage was completed by the early hours of the morning.
>
> It is interesting to note that all the BBC programmes we have heard so far state that British Forces are in Narvik. From news sent in by No. 2 Company, we know that the German ski patrols are active, not 10 miles from Liland.

They spent the rest of the day settling in and were unmolested by any enemy activity. Most of their problems seemed to come from their own side, as the war diary records:

> The CO received the following telegram during the day, which makes the attitude of our Allies difficult to understand; "Telegram from Norwegian Divisional HQ, stating that Norwegian volunteers at Bogen must not be used by British troops, as their task is only to defend their homes." The crying need at the moment is expert skiers, for patrolling, and by the time we have learnt to ski, the snow will have gone.

The third unit of the brigade, the 2nd South Wales Borderers, was the last to land, and after a few false starts was also moved to Skaanland on 19 April, spending the next day or so settling in, although much of the winter clothing did not arrive with the first ships. The following comment from their war diary also applied to all British units in the area: "The whole country is deep in snow and impossible to move without skis or snowshoes."

The thinking behind this dispersal of the troops seems to have been to prevent any German air raids on Harstad killing or injuring a large number of men from the brigade. They were also now relatively handily placed for the assault on Narvik.

While all of these moves were being played out, General Mackesy received information that he would not be getting any more troops, but was still expected to go for Narvik. His reply was as follows:

> Very well we will do what we can. I must point out that I have not even one field gun and I have not even one anti-aircraft gun. I have practically no mortar ammunition. My force is probably inferior to the enemy. Under the conditions, which have changed so much since Brigadier Lund brought me written and verbal instructions at Scapa, my future plans must be based on British troops

operating eastwards along the north bank of West Fjord in close co-operation with the Navy while I try to encourage the Norwegians to operate southwards from [the] Bardu area. Further details after I rejoin my headquarters. At the moment I am at sea on personal reconnaissance. No tactical movement by my troops possible for some weeks owing to snow conditions. Offensive operations without artillery must be ruled out.

General Mackesy deserves some sympathy here, as previous experience from the Great War showed time and again that an artillery barrage, supported by tanks, artillery and mortar and machine gun fire, was just about the only way to defeat an enemy in a defensive position. Mackesy and his men had been invited to attack without any realistic hope of success. The reply from the War Office can hardly have filled him with confidence: "War Office fully realises the state of your forces." Having arrived back at Harstad around midnight after a long and tiring drive from Liland, Mackesy recalls receiving a copy of a message from the First Sea Lord, Winston Churchill, to Lord Cork. The message was as follows:

First Lord to Lord Cork. We have altered emphasis of operation against Trondheim in such a way as to place *Warspite* and her escorting destroyers at your disposal. I do not understand what is intended. I thought that in this tongue of land, especially its tip occupied by Narvik port and town, fighting could certainly be dominated by fire of warships and that houses could be occupied with forces you possess. Once this is achieved we have the trophy at which all Europe is looking. We have a bridge head sic for further landings and our men sleeping under such shelter as may be left, while enemy sleep in snow. The word assault ought NOT to be a stumbling block. Obviously after harassing bombardment from sea you would feel your way with reconnaissance's and not risk full attack until all machine-gun posts were knocked out by ship's guns, as they surely can be. The fact that the enemy has spread himself out beyond Herjangsfjord and at other points is NOT important, because he has no artillery worthy of mention or comparable to match our seaborne guns.

As I see it, once you have got Narvik tip and are ensconced in houses and wrecked pill boxes, all his detachments in the country are ruined and can be reduced at leisure. I am trying to find other troops to aid in clearing outlying detachments. Pray regard this telegram as my own personal opinion to enable you after consultation with the General to let me know what you severally and jointly advise and if you do NOT agree what are the main obstacles. The movement which you are now carrying out with the General seems admirably preparatory for what we have in mind. Send also a timetable of operation and if you require more infantry we will try to find them. There seems to be no need to delay opening harassing fire. We are sending you an ammunition ship as fast as possible. Of course the less the town is knocked about the better for our own accommodation, but we must get into Narvik or its ruins as soon as possible.

Mackesy commented on Churchill's message: "I cannot find one word of sense in the whole effusion. Shades of Gallipoli: nothing learnt from that tragedy: the same mistakes: the same conceit of ignorance." Mackesy's opinion of Churchill and Lord Cork cannot have improved when at about the same time a message arrived from Lord Cork asking why he was not using his "third battalion". Matters did not improve on Sunday, 21 April, which in Mackesy's view was a black day in spite of bitter frost and blinding snowstorms. It opened with the receipt of another strong message from Churchill regarding the 24th Brigade, which ran as follows:

> To FO Narvik from Admiralty. Personal to Admiral of the Fleet Lord Cork and General Mackesy. In order to ensure concerted combined action in operations to capture Narvik, His Majesty's Government has decided absolute command should be vested in one officer. Admiral of the Fleet Lord Cork as senior will in consequence assume command forthwith of all forces committed to this task. No further troops can be made available for at least a fortnight. It is however highly desirable both for political and military reasons that there should not be any delay in capturing Narvik. Admiral of the Fleet Lord Cork will report as early as possible whether he will act now or whether delay for reinforcements will be indispensable.

Shortly after this message was received, the daily conference took place. Mackesy's plan from 18 April was agreed, with some modifications which had resulted from the *Aurora* reconnaissance. The minutes of this meeting follow:

1. Unanimously agreed that troops should be transferred from battleships into destroyers, NOT into local craft. General Mackesy attached great importance to this.

2. General explained the modern organisation of defence in depth.

3. General recounted results of his reconnaissance, which established that the western beach is quite impassable for British troops at present owing to: need for wading in deep icy water; steep hill covered in deep snow; beach enfiladed and taken in reverse by MGs on Ankenes peninsula.

4. Admiral suggested a landing on the pier on north shore. General considered this was not really possible. Admiral stressed landing was not to assault but to occupy. General agreed – but occupation must be after surrender. Admiral did not want a Gallipoli – troops are only to exploit any sign of the demoralisation caused by naval bombardment. General pointed out that exploiting means committing troops: cannot "exploit" on mere "signs" of demoralisation – must have surrender first: can then land on pier on north shore.

5. Probable effects of bombardment on MG defence in depth were discussed. Concluded that to produce demoralisation the town itself must be destroyed.

6. Action of reconnaissance party was discussed. General considered that if it went in alone, it would either be killed at once or be let in and disappear. COS added that there would be casualties in the destroyer too. Admiral urged that if

the bombardment were successful and we took no steps to ascertain its results we would have missed our opportunity. Send a destroyer in – if she is not fired on, land a reconnaissance party. If we see no signs of withdrawal, we must find out what is happening. Brigadier pointed out that the ferry pier to the north is the only place where a reconnaissance party could see anything. Agreed that reconnaissance party should comprise one platoon with some signallers. Previous reconnaissance (i.e. before D1) from ships is necessary for reconnaissance platoon commander: also for other officers of both battalions.

7. Admiral pointed out that enemy commander might surrender, but some MG posts continue fighting in ignorance of surrender. Brigadier agreed; must therefore get enemy assembled under control of ships' guns. COS said reconnaissance party should NOT land till after surrender.

8. Question of sending officers (one Navy, one Army) with flag of truce to demand capitulation was discussed. Agreed that this should not be done till after bombardment.

9. Army's lack of mortar bombs and of reserve SAA [small arms ammunition] and grenades was discussed. Navy could only help with 50,000 rounds SAA. Operation must therefore wait till store ship carrying ammunition arrives - due at Harstad p.m. 23rd April.

10. After some discussion it was agreed to postpone D1 from 23rd to 25th April. Preliminary reconnaissance to take place on 23rd. Ammunition from store ship to be put into warships. In the event of bad weather on D1, troops remain on board ships.

Things were not going well for the general, who was then firmly placed in the middle of a potentially major dispute with Cork, when later that morning two senior Navy officers, Captain Maund and Commander Hubback, came to see him. They said their orders were to plan the bombardment of Narvik and to include parts of the town known to include civilians. They were unhappy at this and were considering refusing to obey Lord Cork's order. They also stated that Brigadier Fraser supported their view and Mackesy himself later wrote that he agreed, but was in a difficult position. He persuaded them not to ruin their careers by refusing to obey an order and said he would try to find a solution. He decided to send the following secret and personal official letter to Lord Cork:

Sir,

Before the proposed action against Narvik commences, I have the honour to inform you that I feel it my duty to represent to you that I am convinced that there is not one officer or man under my command who will not feel shame for himself and his country, if the thousands of Norwegian men, women and children in Narvik are subjected to the bombardment proposed. I must ask that these views may be represented to His Majesty's Government.

I have the honour to be, Sir, your obedient servant,

P. J. Mackesy

Commander Rupert Force.

A reply came back almost immediately to say his views would be passed to London, but this was later followed by a *volte face* from Cork:

> Dear General,
> I have told Captain Maund that I wish him to revert to the original bombardment orders, as in my view to destroy even some military positions would be more effective than the damage of houses – however small these results might be – as the Germans cannot have much in the way of reserves. Your message, I take it, refers to all bombardment the town must suffer, but if it is only the form you suggested this forenoon you may not wish your protest to Government to be stopped. It won't be able to go for some little time owing to congestion so perhaps you would let me know, otherwise it will be sent.
> Yours sincerely,
> Cork and Orrery

Mackesy later commented:

> With this somewhat ambiguous letter my personal confidence in Lord Cork began to wane. I sent my GSO1 on board the flagship and gave him full powers to withdraw my protest to His Majesty's Government on an assurance from Lord Cork that no Norwegian civilians were to be deliberately bombarded. This assurance was given by the Naval Chief of Staff and one more naval mutiny was quelled, at no cost to me.

Captain Maund and Commander Hubback told General Mackesy that they were of the opinion that no one with any military knowledge would think of attacking at Narvik under the conditions that existed and with the lack of equipment the force possessed. A telegram which then arrived from the War Office compounded Mackesy's misery: "As command has passed to Lord Cork His Majesty's Government is sure that you will give him full support in any action he proposes to take." With good grace, he replied that London was fully justified in its assumption, but requested that he be allowed to deal direct with the War Office on administrative matters. This was granted a couple of days later. The daily conference on the morning of 22 April was a sombre affair. Lord Cork informed those in attendance that he was now in sole command and expressed the hope "that the Army would carry out his orders with efficiency". One attendee recalls that this was met by a stony silence.

The minutes of this meeting record the following:

> 1. Lord Cork referred to the altered situation now that he was in sole command. The primary object was now to capture Narvik as soon as possible. The First Lord is not merely the First Lord – he is also chairman of the Inter-Services Committee and a member of the War Cabinet. Messages from him are also messages from His Majesty's Government.

HMS *Warspite* pictured off Narvik in offensive mode. (The National Archives)

2. Lord Cork hears the views of the military commander and of his naval advisers; he decides and he accepts full responsibility. The orders he issues are issued in the broadest sense; he has no wish to interfere with administration. He relies on team work to achieve the common object.

3. The modification of the plan was then considered. It comprises two parts:

Part 1. A naval bombardment of military objectives only; one battalion to be in a warship ready to land if opportunity offers.

Part 2. Land operations to the north, to establish the Army in the area Bjerkvik-Oijord. For this two battalions ski troops, artillery and anti-aircraft artillery would be required.

4. As regards Part 1 - the forces to embark should be one battalion (1st Irish Guards) and one section field company.

5. The future requirements of the Army – two battalions mountain troops, one field regiment Royal Artillery, one light regiment Royal Artillery, two 3in anti-aircraft batteries and one 3.7in anti-aircraft battery.

6. Army to submit plan for future operations north of Narvik if occupation of Narvik is not carried out, remembering that from the naval point of view Harstad is unsuitable as a base as it ties up too many naval forces.

Mackesy later commented: "While all of this was going on time was being wasted. Nothing could be done because the only three battalions I had were standing by for Lord Cork's bombardment or were guarding vulnerable points and all this without the slightest hope of success." On the evening of 22 April, Lord Cork delivered instructions for the proposed bombardment of Narvik, due to take place on 24 April. The plan was to "demoralise the enemy and endeavour to destroy the enemy's defensive positions at Narvik by means of a heavy naval bombardment." The major ships to take part were the battleship HMS *Warspite*, the cruisers HMS *Aurora*, HMS *Effingham*, HMS *Enterprise* and HMS *Vindictive*, and numerous escorting destroyers. It was intended for the ships to fire one at a time at the "identified military targets." It is hard to see how this could be an effective barrage without some form of decent spotting, which appears to have been ignored. Meanwhile, the Irish Guards were to move by local fishing boats to the *Vindictive*, with the 2nd South Wales Borderers on short notice warning to move. Mackesy later commented (with the benefit of hindsight) that he felt it hard to see how such a plan would work when it was discovered that for all the weight of the 15in shells from the guns on *Warspite*, there was only one round to every 6,000 square yards or so of the target area. Most of those fired were armour-piercing shells and the craters they caused could only be worked out by discolouration of the snow.

On 23 April, a small party of Army officers- –General Mackesy and his staff and Brigadier Fraser and his key staff from the 24th Brigade – boarded HMS *Effingham* (Admiral Cork's flagship) and sailed for Narvik. Things were moving at last, although the weather was decidedly unfriendly – rough seas, bitterly cold and heavy snowstorms. On the morning of 24 April, the fleet arrived off Narvik and the bombardment began. There were two distinct views of what should happened next. Lord Cork sent a message to the Admiralty timed at 1407, which read:

> Carried out reconnaissance this morning and bombarded certain military targets. Results disappointing – most difficult to detect anything in deep snow. A ferry steamer apparently replacing one already destroyed was sunk. Weather bad – heavy snow which is our worst enemy preventing all movement. Your 0044/24, with these reinforcements it should take no time to capture town after snow melts. Thaw due any day and once it sets in snow disappears rapidly on low ground I am told. Every effort shall be made.

Meanwhile, Mackesy commented: "It shattered two things and practically two things only; such remaining confidence as may have existed amongst the military officers in the policy of relying entirely on ships' gunfire to support an opposed landing without tanks, proper landing craft and so on, and such confidence as remained in Lord Cork." It was also something of a surprise to the watching Army officers on HMS *Effingham* to see her 6in shells land in the water only about 300 yards from the ship. One commented drily that if this continued, any landing parties would have been disposed of without the Germans opening fire at all! However, there was some good news, in that despite all that had been said before, the demi-brigade of *Chasseurs Alpins* (three battalions) would be arriving at some unknown but not too distant date. Mackesy then appeared to get an agreement of a kind to his original plan: should it prove impracticable to occupy Narvik as a result of the naval bombardment (absolutely likely in his view) it would be necessary to clear the Germans from the Oijord peninsula and establish field artillery there to support a ground offensive on Narvik. Further operations would be contemplated from the Bjerkvik area towards German positions at the head of Rombaks Fjord and the occupation of the Ankenes peninsula. To achieve these objectives, the 24th Brigade would then patrol eastwards from Bogen, while the *Chasseurs Alpins* – once they had landed – would move westwards from the line Gratangen–Forbakken in conjunction with any Norwegian troops that could be cobbled together. Mackesy stressed to Brigadier Fraser the need to work together with the Navy, in particular the captain of the *Aurora*, who had been appointed SNO Ofotfjord. It now seemed that Narvik was back as the primary objective after Government eyes in London had been temporarily diverted towards Trondheim. It appeared to Mackesy that Cork wanted Narvik taken at any cost.

The plan was still to hold a line from Narvik to the ore fields of Sweden. Even if the troops did get ashore and take Narvik, the route to the ore fields was difficult and it would be a case of forcing the Germans back along the railway line, with virtually unprotected flanks. Mackesy looked at the possibility of using his troops to advance along the railway line and use the mountain troops promised by France to look after the flanks. As Mackesy commented:

> Anything seemed better than the single-file advance along the broken railway. Any idea that we would be better off in Narvik, liable to heavy air attack, had no appeal to me. By now Narvik was really a name on the map, the place itself of little use to anyone. Our real object was to defeat the German forces and get established on the Swedish frontier. All this time of course the complete absence of military air reconnaissance and of air photographs was a deadly handicap. Our maps were hopelessly out of date and inaccurate. In spite of repeated requests I could not make Lord Cork understand the importance of this matter.

On the evening of 25 April, Mackesy sent, at Lord Cork's request, the following draft comment for inclusion in a telegraph he intended to send to the First Sea Lord:

> I am satisfied that a direct assault on Narvik is impracticable and therefore intend to put the following plan into operation as soon as the arrival of the French contingent and the weather permit.
>
> 24th (Guards) Brigade (less 1st Scots Guards) with one battalion *Chasseurs Alpins* will concentrate in the area Bogen-Ballangen-Evenes. 1st Scots Guards less two companies to Harstad. French contingent less one battalion will disembark Sagsfjord. Snow continues to fall heavily and there is every indication that it will not disappear until the end of May. This limits land operations to French and such Norwegian co-operation as can be obtained. This explains the initial French disposition given above and my intention is to commence operations against the enemy about Gratangen and Herjangsfjord by a simultaneous movement of the French from north, east and west. In conjunction with the French, British troops will take the peninsula south-west of Narvik and opportunities may arise for landings in Herjangsfjord. Having defeated and cleared the enemy north of Rombaks Fjord, I intend that the French shall establish themselves across the railway about Hundalen and the frontier so as to prevent enemy reinforcements from Sweden and move westwards on Narvik if this is still necessary.

There was an additional memorandum to the Chief of Staff:

> 1. I am satisfied that a direct assault on Narvik under existing conditions is impracticable. My plan follows below. Moves already made facilitate it.
>
> 2. 24th (Guards) Brigade, less detachments for local defence of base, with, under command, one battalion *Chasseurs Alpins* and ancillary troops will operate eastwards on both shores of Ofotfjord from Bogen and Ballangen. First objectives Ankenes and Oijord peninsulas which dominate Narvik. This force will be amphibious and work in close co-operation with SNO Ofotfjord taking every opportunity of landing against weak defences, should such opportunities arise.
>
> 3. *Chasseurs Alpins*, less the battalion in paragraph 2 with ancillary troops, will operate southwards from Lund area against enemy forces north of Bjerkvik. Their task, to defeat these forces and prevent orderly withdrawal to reinforce Narvik. This force will act in close co-operation with such active help, if any, the Norwegians can give.
>
> 4. Navy will act in close co-operation with local commanders and its tasks will include:-
>
> (a) Keeping communications Narvik to north cut.
>
> (b) Constantly interrupting railway communications.
>
> 5. Later steps must depend upon circumstances but prominently in mind are:-
>
> (a) The possibility of getting *Chasseurs Alpins* across railway east of Narvik.
>
> (b) Possible landings to speed up the proposed operations.

To Mackesy's horror, his carefully worded explanation of the situation and how it could be exploited was diluted by Cork into the following message sent to London later that evening:

> Snow is several feet deep in country around Narvik and still falling; under these conditions any direct attack upon the Narvik peninsula is impossible. Present intention is to work into position to deliver such an attack immediately conditions allow.
>
> With this object troops are establishing themselves on both sides of Ofotfjord at Bogen and Ballangen. Movements already made and in progress; objectives peninsulas north and south of Narvik; troops conveyed by His Majesty's ships. Ships are now engaged stopping communication by sea with town and destroying railway.
>
> It is intended when *Chasseurs* are ready to employ them to destroy enemy detachments at Bjerkvik and to approach Narvik from the eastward.

Meanwhile, it had been decided that the command element of the 1st Irish Guards would do a close target reconnaissance of Narvik from HMS *Bedouin*. They were told at 2130 on 22 April it would take place the next day. The next morning, the CO, accompanied by seven other officers, boarded HMS *Bedouin* for the reconnaissance. The Irish Guards' war diary records:

HMS *Bedouin* off Narvik. (The National Archives)

In the morning the Commanding Officer, Major Bowen, Major Gilbert-Denham, Captain Armstrong-MacDonnell, Captain McGildowny, Captain Durham-Matthews, Captain Gordon-Watson and Lieutenant Gilliat boarded the destroyer for a reconnaissance of Narvik harbour. At first the weather was very misty and visibility very poor, but as we approached the harbour, the clouds lifted and the sun poured through, giving the watchers on the bridge, the most perfect view of their objective which they could possibly have. Captain McCoy brought us in very close to the shore and we were within easy reach of machine gun fire from the shore. The plan, explained to us the evening before by the Commanding Officer, was briefly as follows:-

The Battalion would land, after heavy naval bombardment at Vasvik pier, in the order 3, 4, 1, Advanced Battalion HQ, 2. No. 3 and 4 Companies would establish a bridge head and No. 1 Company would occupy a position astride the railway, denying all approaches east of the town. All prisoners would be collected on the beach, under an armed guard and made to lay down their arms. The whole operation depended on whether the naval bombardment with 15in guns warranted a landing, and the decision as to whether we should land rested with the naval staff.

The reconnaissance was perfect in every way, as Company Commanders had a perfect view of their areas, which is so rarely possible in the average reconnaissance. There was no sign of military activity in the town of Narvik; but all the officers on the bridge wore naval headgear to avoid a military reconnaissance being suspected. We returned to Liland at 1230.

The Scots Guards at Harstad in the latter part of April had a very quiet existence, spending most of their time either guarding key points such as the petrol dump or unloading ships. One of the more interesting comments was that from 24 April snow

General Dietl inspecting some of the men under his command. (Bob Gerritsen Collection)

seemed to fall continuously and that all ranks were ordered to wear their snow goggles when in the open to try and reduce the number of casualties from snow blindness.

For the Irish Guards it was a different matter, however. On the morning of 24 April, they embarked in local fishing boats in small groups to be ferried out to the *Vindictive*, but a strong wind was blowing and the transfer was not easy. At least one fishing boat was crushed against the *Vindictive*, but by 0830 the battalion was safely on board. But then a strange (to the Army's eyes) signal was flashed to the bridge of *Vindictive*, stating "Negative Embarkation". Their war diary commented; "What did this mean and had we embarked for nothing? We had."

Although the Navy had been shelling Narvik since the early hours of 24 April, it was decided to postpone the landing of troops. By 1230, most of the battalion was back at Liland, except No. 2 Company, which went straight back to Bogen. On the following day, Brigadier Fraser visited the battalion and arranged with the CO that No. 2 Company should move to Lenvik until the *Chasseurs Alpins* had disembarked in Bogen Bay. This was also felt to be a good gesture so that the French would not arrive straight into the front line. The Irish Guards were also told that the French were expected to arrive the following day. The CO and two of his officers, Captain Gordon-Watson and Lieutenant Young, spent that night on HMS *Aurora* prior to another reconnaissance trip to Narvik the next morning. It was reported that this was:

a thrilling reconnaissance and target practice accounted for a barracks, a telephone exchange and a chain of lorries. As the officers left the cruiser to return to Liland, three enemy aircraft at a great height dropped six bombs, which landed in the bay, at very close range to their intended targets. The Admiral, who arrived immediately afterwards in his own seaplane, was lucky to avoid this bombardment by so narrow a margin.

The South Wales Borderers did not fare much better, also suffering from the "on the bus, off the bus" syndrome.

But what was happening with the Germans under General Dietl who were bottled up in Narvik? After arriving on 9 April, they had taken a bit of a battering from the Royal Navy, and no significant reinforcements had arrived to bolster Dietl's resources. Most of their supplies had to be dropped by air. In spite of this, the Germans had attempted to push out their perimeter and there had been skirmishes with Norwegian troops, particularly in the area around Fossbakken. The main reason for focusing on Narvik was of course not just the port, but the railway line to Sweden along which the iron ore moved. General Dietl now decided he needed to secure that line. One of his first moves was an attack near Björnfell on Norwegian troops who had managed to escape the German invasion. They were quickly overwhelmed and the line was then basically under German control. The Norwegians reacted by bringing in troops from further north, coming by sea from Kirkenes, escorted by Royal Naval ships. These troops had originally been part of the Neutrality Watch. Others had been recently mobilised: all were in theory skiers and used to the snow and ice. Four battalions of troops had been brought together and were in position to launch a counter-attack towards Gratangen, west of Fossbakken. The Norwegian plan provided for a frontal attack from the north-east against the German post at Lapphaug, at the highest point on the road from Fossbakken before it descends again to fjord level at Gratangen. While the main forces were sent in there, one battalion was to advance south over the mountain from a base on an arm of the fjord further north, to cut the German line of retreat.

It was agreed that the two companies of Scots Guards should hold a rear position for the main force, but they were not to be employed offensively. They were fitted out with snowshoes and camouflage cloaks from Norwegian stores and duly moved into Fossbakken when the Norwegians went forward to the attack. Their war diary relates the following for 0730 on 23 April;

A copy of a message to Major Graham was received, stating that he might accede to the Norwegian C-in-C's request for the detachment to take up a defensive position in reserve in the Lund area, moving today. Major Graham was further authorised to take over the Norwegian defences in the Fossbakken area should this be required as a consequence of a Norwegian attack. The role of the detachment was to be partly defensive and it was clearly stated that no offensive operations were to be undertaken on whatever scale. The detachment was not to move without a Norwegian ski recce element. As a result of this news a further supply of rations, 10,000 rounds SAA, some medical supplies and pay for the detachment was despatched.

A heavy snowstorm began on 23 April and continued the next day when the attack opened. Its severity was such that a Norwegian battalion native to the country and expert on skis, not encumbered with heavy equipment, took eight hours to move less than two miles with a rise in height of about 300 feet. By 1900, the 150 Germans in their entrenched position had repulsed the attack: three feet of snow had fallen in 24 hours and there was consequently no prospect of artillery support. The other wing of their attack had achieved rapid progress, and the men made their way down to the road at Gratangen, where the battalion could get shelter for the night. A second battalion was sent forward from reserve to support this right flank, but when morning came there was still a gap between the two Norwegian battalions. The Germans, who still held Lapphaug, were able to move forward and surround the battalion at Gratangen, and opened machine gun fire upon its position in the village. A part broke through, at a cost of about 100 killed and wounded (three company commanders being among the dead) and 150 or so taken prisoner. The Norwegians had largely sacrificed one of their most efficient battalions; but the action was not without result as the Germans, to economise their forces, abandoned both Lapphaug and Gratangen within a day or two.

Meanwhile, the Allied high command was still arguing about the strategy for the campaign and what to do with the French when they arrived. The lack of action seems difficult to understand – the Army wanted to undertake small "bite and hold" operations whilst the Navy wanted to go all out for Narvik. General Mackesy was frustrated because he was not meant to contact the War Office and they complained to him that they did not know what was happening! Perhaps this comment should have been directed at the Admiralty, further down Whitehall. After a German air raid on 26 April, in which several supply dumps were hit, Lord Cork spent the rest of the day considering his options, and on 27 April he issued further instructions to Mackesy:

I have been considering over again the movements etc., which you were good enough to have explained in detail to me yesterday and make the following criticism. The primary object being as it is the capture of the port of Narvik, too much attention seems liable to be given to outlying enemy detachments – which if Narvik is once captured will fall into our hands. These detachments are isolated, snow conditions will bind them long after the Narvik peninsula is clear and they cannot move by water owing to the presence of our ships. For some considerable time they cannot interfere with our operations.

My fear is that the time may be upon us when it will be quite possible to operate directly against Narvik but we will be unable to do so because we have allowed ourselves to be involved with a secondary objective – the outlying detachments. Instead of having as strong a force as possible concentrated to achieve our object, we shall have a considerable fraction of our strength diverted elsewhere.

No doubt it will be necessary to contain these detachments but this I suggest could be done by a small force of Alpine troops, e.g. two companies or the equivalent working with the Norwegians; whatever the fighting value of the latter, they cannot be entirely negligible if supported by French troops of high quality.

The number of troops necessary to play this part is, however, an Army matter with which I do not pretend to deal – it is the principle I wish to press. If however, one whole battalion is considered necessary, this would allow two battalions of mountain troops to co-operate with the Guards Brigade for the attainment of our primary object. The conditions that will allow of our doing this may be with us within the next few days. Equally, within a very short time a great part of the German Air Force may be freed to turn their attention upon us, thus adding enormously to our difficulties. We have been warned.

If we are not able to act immediately we may find ourselves unable to do so later and judgement upon us will be that we allowed ourselves to be diverted to a secondary object when our primary object was clear before us.

I question too, whether according to the present plan full use is being made of the mobility the use of the sea confers on us. The French troops are not actually required to contain the German detachments, might well arrive fresh in their fighting area and be spared an arduous march and consequent wear and tear by being conveyed by ships.

I feel so strongly upon the general principle involved that unless I can be assured in writing that under no circumstances will such a situation be allowed to arise, I must give further consideration to what steps it is necessary for me to take in order to further the Government policy.

Mackesy replied the same day:

I can only reiterate what I have already said after personal reconnaissance, that is, a direct attack must be ruled out absolutely. I am more than ever convinced that such an attempt would be a costly and bloody failure.

The establishment of shore landings on the Oijord peninsula is, in my opinion, an absolutely essential preliminary to the capture of the town, and that is the main object of operating from Bogen and Sagsfjord. I regret I am unable to suggest any other course which is militarily sound and practicable and I am convinced this is the only course. I fully realise the implication of your last paragraph. I can only say that I, like you, must do what I consider is right.

In the meantime, in view of the imminent arrival of the French contingent, it would be extremely difficult to attempt a last-minute change in the arrangements for their disembarkation at Sagsfjord and Bogen.

I suggest therefore, that the initial locations should stand and if it is decided to use only a small French force from Sagsfjord, then the troops required elsewhere can be brought around by sea.

Things were now almost back to square one, in that troops were in the area with the French reinforcements hours away, with no real progress made as to when any actual fighting might take place. In spite of Lord Cork's comments, Mackesy stated that he received a letter from Cork just before the French arrived, saying: "We shall have to consult with the French General, but in the meantime I hope the troops will not be committed to an advance."

The French troops – the 27th Demi-Brigade of *Chasseurs Alpins* – duly arrived at Harstad and were moved ashore. In spite of their arrival, Mackesy commented that he "really felt in despair":

> After enormous difficulty I thought I had ridden off a proposal which must have had worse results than Gallipoli. I had got permission to carry on with my plan. Lord Cork had himself informed the Admiralty of it, he had himself reported that the attack on Narvik was at present impossible and now everything was at a standstill again.

Perhaps the most active unit was the 1st Irish Guards force located at Liland, with various detachments at other places, but the main "action" was conferences and defensive duties. Their war diary records for 29 April:

> The CO and Adjutant set out early for Bogen to attend a conference with the Brigadier. As the Brigadier was going on a two day reconnaissance the CO assumes command of the Brigade. No 2 Company returned from Lenvik after completing their job of protecting the landing of the *Chasseurs Alpins*. There is no doubt that No 2 Company has been the hardest worked company up to date.
>
> There is still no trace of our transport and even our local fleet has melted into thin air, to transport other battalions from one part of the bay to the other. This lack of transport is a very serious deficiency to an advancing force. The snow is gradually melting and it seems as though the aspiration of our ardent skiers may remain unattained till next winter. It is hoped that the snow may remain a while longer to enable our French Allies to frighten the enemy patrols out of their skins.

It continued for the following day: "A quiet day today, with the CO still commanding the Brigade from Bogen. The SWB's landed at Ankenes and a message reached us in the evening to say that the Brigadier had been slightly wounded while making a reconnaissance."

Back in London, it had been announced that General Sir John Dill had been appointed Vice-Chief of the Imperial General Staff and his appointment had filtered through to Norway. Dill and Mackesy had been friends for a long time, so Mackesy decided to make a "most secret and personal" appeal to him on 27 April:

> As I am not allowed to communicate direct with the War Office on the difficult problems confronting us here I have found myself compelled to make this personal appeal to you in order to ensure that someone in authority knows the facts.
>
> Narvik constitutes a defensive position of great natural strength. An assault upon it from boats covered only by ships guns would as an operation of war be comparable to attacking Messines Ridge without adequate artillery support. The result would and could only be exactly that bloody failure for which much of the world is looking.

The haversack radio is often the only link with General Dietl. (Bob Gerritsen Collection)

The military operations ahead are of great difficulty in a country and under conditions which no one at home appears to grasp at all. The problem is a purely military one. At all stages close assistance from and co-operation by the Navy is essential but in no sense is the problem one usually described by the words "Combined Operations".

I can see no smallest chance of forestalling the Germans at Gallavare. The opportunity to do that went once and for all on 14th March. No wishful thinking can bring that back. I am advised that owing to sunken wrecks Narvik harbour cannot possibly be used by ocean-going ships for a very long time indeed.

I cannot believe that the Germans will not in the end utterly demolish the Narvik railway. Its repair will be a very lengthy task indeed and there is no alternative route through the mountains. I do not know one single fact to support Lord Cork's statement to the First Lord in his 1407/24 that once the snow goes the capture of Narvik will be a matter of a few days only.

Military command is vested in Lord Cork. I am at least qualified to judge his military knowledge and I must tell you that it is exactly nil. In spite of that he has no hesitation in interfering with purely military matters and issuing directions which contain points of minor tactics. I regard this situation with the gravest apprehension.

I recommend first that a clear decision be arrived at as to what is wanted from this force and why. If it is possible it will be done but it must be possible. Second, that independent military command should revert at once to a soldier in whom His Majesty's Government not only profess but displays confidence. That Lord Cork should be immediately replaced by a suitable officer of less exalted rank such as a Commodore who is ready to co-operate with rather than dictate to the military forces. At present the situation is simple lunacy.

That the elementary need of a modern force in respect to air and anti-aircraft necessities should be supplied. As present the enemy does just as he likes in the air within restrictions of distances. I have not even managed to get photographs of Narvik worth looking at. I realise all too well the probable effect on me personally of this free expression of opinion. Were I to keep silent any longer it would be a betrayal of my responsibility to my country and the troops under my command and would leave my professional honour for ever smirched.

In conclusion I would ask whether General Gamelin knows that the fate and reputation of his *Chasseurs Alpins* will be at the personal whim of a sailor without any military experience or knowledge. If he does not know this then he will inevitably very soon learn it from his own officers.

Mackesy had been advised that should anything happen to him, Brigadier Fraser would take over. He had kept him in the loop and allowed him to see the message to General Dill. Fraser also put his feelings in writing to Mackesy on the same day:

I have read very carefully the telegram which you wished me to see. I wish to tell you that I agree with every word you have written on the military aspect of the situation here. If therefore the contingency which you suggested (removal of Mackesy in command) were to arise and I were ordered temporarily to assume command of the forces, I could do no other than to follow the plan which you have initiated.

At the same time I hope and pray with all my heart that it will not arise. Both the Brigade under my command and myself have absolute confidence in your leadership. I sympathise with you more than I can say in the position into which you have been put and if my support can be of the smallest use to you at any time, you know that it is yours without any reservations.

In the interim the French troops had arrived, under the overall command of General Béthouart, who after meeting the British Army representatives, including General Mackesy, was whisked off by Lord Cork to carry out a reconnaissance of Narvik.

General Béthouart was back on the morning of 29 April and General Mackesy gave him his orders: he was in charge of operations in the Gratangen area with the aim of clearing it, establishing himself on Oijord peninsula and studying the possibility of moving south-east from Bjerkvik. At this point one battalion of his *Chasseurs Alpins* was at Bogen and the other two at Sagsfjord. It was arranged for one of the latter units to move by sea the next day to Gratangen Fjord, the head of this fjord having just been occupied by German troops. To help the French, it was planned to land the 2nd South Wales Borderers on the Ankenes peninsula on the night of 29/30 April.

The following operational order had been issued relating to these move and the proposed assault on Narvik itself for the end of April:

Operational Order No 1
23rd April 1940
Information.
    1. Enemy.
As contained in Intelligence Summary already issued.
    2. Own Troops.
The Royal Navy is to bombard Narvik defences in an attempt to force the surrender of the German Garrison.
    (a) Should the German forces NOT surrender it is NOT intended to force an opposed landing.
    (b) Should the German forces surrender they are to be ordered to assemble in the area between Vasvik 643 6826 and Taraldsvik 644 6826, in the vicinity of the beach, so that they can be controlled by warship guns and to lay down their arms.
    1st Irish Guards are holding a bridge head covering Vasvik pier as pointed out to Company Commanders and are denying entrance to Narvik to enemy along the railway by holding a position astride the railway to the east.
    Intention.
    3. 2nd South Wales Borderers will land and occupy areas as indicated.
    4. The Battalion will transfer to HMS *Enterprise* from the small boats in the same orders as embarked from Skaanland.
    5. Orders for Disembarkation.
    (a) B Company Task - Seize and hold the high ground north of Narvik town.
    (b) HQ Company, Carrier Platoon and Mortars task - Mop up the areas as indicated. Battalion HQ and remainder of Company will follow and establish Battalion HQ.
    (c) C Company Task - Mop up north side of town south of B Company.
    (d) D Company Task - Mop up town as indicated and seize the position commanding the Quays and Harbour front so as to deny troops holding out at Fagernes 642 6822. (Entrance to Narvik to enemy.)
    (e) A Company in reserve in vicinity of Battalion HQ.
    6. Landing, in the above order, will be carried to in ships, boats covered by destroyers.
    Administration.
    7. 50 rounds per man will be carried and 25 magazines per LMG in the pouches and 12 grenades per platoon in the haversack. A supply of mortar bombs is to be sent to Narvik as soon as possible.
    8. Dress and Equipment.
The Battalion will disembark wearing fighting order with haversack on back. Leather jerkin will be worn over and white sweaters under the Battle Dress jacket.

Steel helmets and respirators will be worn but gas capes will not be worn. Kit bags, pack and Greatcoats will be left on board ship. Greatcoats will be tied in bundles so that they can be quickly unloaded and distributed. Officers' coats will be tied separately by Companies and labelled. Fur caps will be placed in pocket of Tropal coat and steel helmet will be worn. Gloves trigger/finger and white mitts will be worn.

9. Rations.

The Battalion will embark taking with them:-

(a) Unconsumed portion of the day's ration.

(b) Two days additional rations.

The Battalion will have breakfast before embarking and will land with unconsumed portion of day's and iron ration in the haversack.

10. Medical.

RAP will be established in the vicinity of Battalion HQ.

(a) An ADS will be at Liland and will have boats with them so they can move forward to Narvik at short notice if called for.

(b) MDS will be in Hospital Ship SS *Trondernes*.

(c) Evacuation from RAP will be either to ADS when established on shore or by boat to MDS in Hospital Ship.

11. Booby Traps.

Before landing all troops will be warned to be on the lookout for delay action mines and other traps. Great caution will be used when entering unoccupied buildings. Any suspected trap will be reported at once to Royal Engineers.

12. QM, Pioneer Platoon and Cooks will remain on board to unload baggage etc.

13. Battalion HQ will land and will be established as indicated to Company Commanders.

14. As soon as Battalion HQ is ashore, Companies will detail two runners to report.

15. Signal Officer will arrange W/T communication from Battalion HQ to all Companies.

16. A Company will detail four additional runners to report to Battalion HQ prior to disembarking for duty with Brigade HQ.

So by 24 April the 2nd South Wales Borderers, located at Skaanland under the command of Lieutenant Colonel P. Gottwaltz, were ready for the attack on Narvik, with all preparations completed by 0900, according to the war diary. The war diary also comments that it was snowing for the fifth day running, so preparations cannot necessarily have been easy. Then the Army practice of "hurry up and wait" came into play, with no news or orders being received. Brigadier Fraser visited the battalion on 25 April and twice on 26 April – and then the following afternoon there was some movement. A and B Companies, then in Salangen, left for Ballangen, but a proposed move by an advance party to Evenes was cancelled. Meanwhile, Commander Hopkinson, who was in charge of the puffer fleet, arrived with part of his flotilla.

A typical shot of British troops being moved around by a puffer. (Imperial War Museum N187)

The Borderers' war diary records the following for 27 April:

Advance party Scots Guards arrived, also visitation from Base HQ. Preparing for move MV *Salangen* and 17 motor puffers at our disposal. Loaded and embarked according to plan and set sail at 2130 down the fjord. On entering the tip of Ofotfjord leading to Narvik we were escorted by HMS *Zulu*. Could see Narvik burning as we turned off to Ballangen. A bit chaotic marshalling the armada but Sub Lieutenant Job i/c fleet managed it. The lack of ladders to get out of the small boats did not aid the speed of the manoeuvre. Baggage with all this arctic clothing is a big problem. The whole plan was clear by 0530.

The war diary added for the following days:

28th April 0530 CO recce on destroyer.

29th April Got W/T message about 0200 to be ready to move two companies by 1100, remainder by 1400. CO to Strand on opposite side of Ofotfjord for conference with Brigade Commander 0830 (two hour trip in puffer). Battalion prepared to move light, leaving MT and base detail personnel to look after kit left behind under Major Evans. CO returned about 1330. Battalion to move 1530 and as shown in order. Party of 10 under Lieutenant Evans put ashore at Haakvik pier near the remains of HMS *Hardy*. No opposition. So remainder of Battalion disembarked about 1900. Slow business owing to inadequate and rickety pier. Battalion was in position between Baatberget-Skole Haakvik by midnight. Roads very bad, only transport 1 car, 2 lorries and about 10 sleighs. Rained off and on during the night.

30th April. Brigadier arrived for recce of Narvik from Ankenes. Covered by 1st Scots Guards and D Company. Must have been spotted as trench mortar opened up on him. Brigadier wounded in neck eventually evacuated by sea. Covering party had difficulty in getting back. All back by 2230 intact.

Another order was given for 30 April:

Information.
    1. Enemy and own troops as given out.
Intention.
    2. 24th Guards Brigade will seize the Ankenes peninsula and the power stations at Bakkehaughen 642 6822 and Elektr Kraft station 639 6822 today.
Method.
    3. Embarkation.
    1st phase. A, B and HQ Companies will embark in puffers to *Zulu* to *Enterprise*. Lieutenant O. Evans and 10 Other Ranks, 2 Signallers and Second Lieutenant Petch will embark with B Company beginning 1515 29.04.1940.
    2nd phase. D and Mortar Platoon embark in puffers to Faulkner.
    3rd phase. C Company embark in puffers with bicycles and sleighs.
    4. Order of landing.
    1st phase. C Company will land from puffers at pier in vicinity of Skjomnes. Task – make good cross roads 635 6824 and bridge over river.
    2nd phase. D Company will land. Task – to make good Emmenes. Mortar Platoon and *Chasseurs* patrol will accompany.
    3rd phase. A Company will land. Task – make good (i) power station 642 6822 (ii) Haukan 646 6821 (iii) gain contact with enemy at Beisfjord.
    4th phase. B Company will land and pass through D Company. Task - to make good Ankenes. *Chasseurs* patrol and Mortar Platoon will accompany.
    5th phase. Battalion HQ and HQ Company will land and will proceed to Emmenes.
Administration.
    5. First store boat will be loaded up by QM with rations, cooking pots, reserve SAA, Officers Mess and Signal kit.
    6. Remaining kit will be loaded under direction of Major I. Evans on puffers and despatched to Skjomnes.
    7. RAP at Emmenes.
Intercommunication.
    8. Battalion HQ at Emmenes. Visual. Battalion HQ to Enterprise. Bicycles if possible to Companies.

The interesting thing about this set of orders is that, to this author's knowledge, it is the first time the use of sleighs by the British Army is mentioned. Whether they were commandeered from locals or made by the Pioneer Platoon is not mentioned.

By 1 May, the Germans seemed to be well aware of the Borderers' presence at Haakvik. It is recorded that in the early hours of this day a patrol of five Germans got to within 100 feet of the CO's billet before they were spotted and challenged. Shots were fired at them – apparently unsuccessfully – but the Germans fled, leaving behind their skis. Then outposts on the hills opened fire with more success on another German patrol, and when following up found an abandoned rifle, some skis and "much blood on the snow". A Company and some of the attached *Chasseurs* were also in action with the Germans south-east of the power station. One of the platoon positions of D Company was shelled by German guns in Narvik. They suffered three casualties, including the platoon commander, and pulled back as a result. The casualties were evacuated by sea. However, it was hoped that some of the French troops would arrive to reinforce the Borderers that night. Around 600 did arrive in the early hours of 2 May. Although it was May, their war diary comments that despite bright sunshine helping to melt some of the snow during the day, it froze again at night as temperatures were still falling below zero.

Captain C. Cox was a company commander in the Borderers. In an interview he related the following:

> At around 0200 on 1 May one of my patrols was visiting Ankenes village and after a short game of hide and seek with some Germans amongst the houses withdrew without any losses. A short time later a large body of German ski troops attacked us; they perhaps thought our positions were lightly held as I had withdrawn an advanced position the day before. Then at 0300, about dawn, with visibility about 100 yards due to mist, the first attack came from the right over the mountains and was carried out by ski troops firing tracer. But their fire was inaccurate luckily as their white camouflage made them difficult to see. Fortunately a Royal Navy destroyer was attracted by the noise and moved forward and asked us by signal if all patrols were in, and after an affirmative yes from me, she came in really close and opened up with everything she had. It was getting lighter and we now saw the main German attack coming in from the left flank; my left forward platoon was well equal to the situation and, supported by the Navy, we were at no time hard-pressed and they fled in some disorder to some nearby barns and woods. They left behind equipment including light mortars, machine guns and radios. Later we found about 12 dead bodies and some wounded.

Some of the French reinforcements were attached to D Company and helped to repel an attack by about 50 German ski troops, assisted by naval gunfire support. A patrol, led by 2nd Lieutenant Davies towards Ankenes, bumped into a German patrol and was only able to extract itself with some difficulty. The war diary reporting that the nights were not dark enough for effective patrolling. The troops were still vulnerable to air attack; five men were killed on this day as a result of bombing – three Borderers and two attached Royal Signals.

Although 3 May was a quiet day, the men from South Wales were cheered when some gunners arrived with two 25 pdr field guns, and the Field Ambulance supporting them finally got two ambulances. Nothing much happened over the coming days but 7 May saw the first delivery of mail from the UK and some British aircraft also appeared overhead.

The Borderers' war diary for 11 May records:

> The French are pushing on slowly towards Beisfjord. Irish Guards increased to a company in pier vicinity. Heard we have yet another Brigadier, Lieutenant Colonel Franklin Irish Guards. Lieutenant Colonel Trappes-Lomax has gone off with his Battalion under sealed orders. At the request of the French we have again taken over the power station. C Company sending out two patrols at 1130. Heard later that no further troops are to be sent to the Ankenes peninsula and that the CO, Lieutenant Colonel Gottwaltz, is OC Troops on the peninsula. We were expecting at least the Irish Guards to come here but as they are not it will mean slowing down the *Chasseurs*. No more 25 pounders and no AA guns have arrived.

Meanwhile, the French were now arriving in the area. Reaching the beach relatively unscathed, they were confident that they could clear this peninsula and the route to Narvik would be open within 24 hours. Sadly, this was not to be. Whilst progress was made, it was not as quick as they had hoped.

Lord Cork would have preferred a landing nearer Narvik in readiness for a direct attack. General Béthouart conferred with the Norwegian General Fleischer before handing over direct command of the demi-brigade to Lieutenant Colonel Valentini. The 14th Battalion was left for the moment in reserve, while the 6th was taken round by water to Gratangen for an advance up the Labergdal Pass, where on 1 May they made their first contact with the enemy. The Norwegians at this time had reorganised their expanding forces into two brigades. The 6th Brigade on the left, composed of three battalions and one mountain battery under the command of Colonel Löken, continued its fight in isolation, slowly pressing the German outposts back in the wilderness of mountains along the Swedish frontier. The 7th Brigade, composed of two battalions, one mountain battery and one motorised battery, and commanded by Colonel Faye, held the right flank and worked in close cooperation with the French, who supplied two companies and a mortar section for the main line of advance along the road from Elvenes towards Bjerkvik. The French included, however, only 70 ski troops to each battalion, which restricted their scouting; they were also short of mules and snowshoes, which slowed up the movement of supplies, and were unaccustomed to bivouacking in soft, deep snow (the depth was five feet on level ground at the top of Labergdal Pass), which cost them as many casualties from frostbite as from enemy action, air attack included. On 4 May, a battery of French colonial artillery was landed for support, and a day or two later the 14th joined the 6th Battalion in the line. But the intended manoeuvre, by which the French advance up the Labergdal was to turn the German defences along the main Bjerkvik road, was held up. By 10 May, the French ski detachment had secured the top of the 3,000 foot high mountain forming the west side of the pass, while the Norwegians were deployed ahead of them in the mountains on the east side: but along the road itself the Germans could not be dislodged from their position on the crest. It had taken 10 painful days to advance only five miles towards Narvik.

The Germans had only one battalion of infantry and the naval battalion (strength less than a little over one company, which General Dietl reallocated around the end of the month to his northern front) to cover Narvik, the railway, and Ankenes. Moreover, these troops, which had at first drawn their supplies from the *Jan Wellem*, were now dependent on what could be brought from Sweden down the railway, often under fire. But their guns in Narvik covered the direct approaches to Ankenes and machine gun posts at Beisfjord were easy to supply by seaplanes. On 1 May, a German patrol came down the mountainside at the north end of the Storvatn, and the following day a similar party of about 100 men made a more serious counter-attack along the road towards Haakvik. The guns of the *Aurora* inflicted considerable losses on the enemy, who were beaten off, but the Allies were unable to make any further progress on that side.

The 12th Battalion *Chasseurs Alpins*, serving under command of the Guards Brigade, gradually took over the operation, being better suited to it than the South Wales Borderers, who could not move at all in the snow. On 9 May, two French companies on snowshoes, supported by a skiing detachment, had succeeded in dislodging the enemy from three main heights on the ridge north of the Storvatn; they could now look down on the waters of the Beisfjord. But the approach to Ankenes by that route was clearly a task for weeks rather than days. These operations proceeded concurrently with a renewed demand for a direct assault on Narvik, where things were still not going well.

General Mackesy recalled:

> The *Chasseurs Alpins* in the snows of arctic Norway were as great a disappointment to themselves as to me. Only a small portion have skis, all are supposed to have snow shoes but many of these were packed in the bottom of some unknown store ship. Their pack mules were practically useless, the loads on their backs make them sink too deep in the snow to make any progress; the men used to the hard snow of the high Alps, could make nothing of the soft snow they now encountered. They had many cases of frostbite and snow blindness. They were very soon held up by enemy machine gun posts on the mountains and could only make slow progress. Their high hopes were soon dashed. General Béthouart, who, on the 30th April, said he had a spare battalion he did not want, but which, luckily, I had said he had better keep in the Sagsfjord area for the present, was soon using this battalion to relieve the first one. Their 75s could not elevate enough to deal with machine guns in hill tops. Some of these were cleared for them by regular Norwegian ski troops, but no real progress was being made for many weary days.

General Mackesy was signed off sick by the chief doctor for two days on 2 and 3 May, and in his words "never really recovered until I left Harstad".

On 3 May there was a further message from the First Sea Lord to Lord Cork: "Every day that Narvik remains untaken even at severe cost imperils the whole enterprise. I must regard next six or seven days as possibly decisive." For once Lord Cork took this to be the signal for strong action, and he ordered General Mackesy to get his act together by sending the following:

From Admiral of the Fleet the Earl of Cork and Orrery, Commanding HM Forces in the Narvik area.
Date 3rd May 1940.
To Major General P. J. Mackesy Rupert Force.

The following are the general lines upon which I desire to see action taken at once and I fix the date upon which preparations should be completed as Wednesday 8th May.

(1) That the movements for the object of cutting the German line of retreat be continued with energy both by the northern force and that on the southern side to secure Beisfjord.

(2) That at the same time as this progresses, a plan should be prepared for a direct attack from the sea or across Rombaks Fjord as judged best. A feint landing, capable of being pushed home if opportunity offers, also to be prepared. A reconnaissance by naval and military officers on this to take place without delay.

(3) By the time the plan is formulated and necessary craft collected and prepared, it should be evident whether the operations in (1) are likely to succeed.

(4) If not then further time should not be wasted in attempting to do this, but the impending withdrawal of the enemy forces from Narvik be compelled by (2), even if the bulk of enemy troops will be able to escape.

(5) Time is at the moment of primary importance and in order to gain time, some risk and loss involved by departure from accepted rules must be accepted.

(6) Not only may we expect considerable increase in the intensity of enemy air attack, but this particular moment when Norwegian's neutral opinion and that of potential enemies must all be affected by our withdrawal from southern Norway, a set off most necessary. Even if we occupy a heap of dangerous ruins this will be provided to the world by the capture of Narvik.

(7) Regard must be paid to this point. We cannot remain unaffected by what is happening elsewhere. All difficulties and losses will be much increased by further delay.

(8) Reports seem uniformly to show that the fighting value of German troops is not high. Under the circumstances in which they have been existing their morale must be affected.

(9) With the arrival of the Foreign Legion ample troops should be available for continuing the present movements and for an attacking force to be prepared even if it is not thought wise to move the battalion of *Chasseurs* in the north round to Ofotfjord.

Cork and Orrery Admiral of the Fleet, Commanding Combined Narvik Expeditionary Force.

Now that Cork had given a direct order to Mackesy to attack Narvik, he had no real option but to put wheels in motion for this to happen. Mackesy got his staff to work on plans aiming for an attack on or around 8/9 May. As he commented, things had improved slightly in that four armoured and six other landing craft were available. This was of course a totally inadequate number, and things worsened when one of the six unarmoured landing craft was wrecked soon after arrival. Mackesy commented:

> In spite of our new acquisitions there were great difficulties. The Narvik area is considerable. After landing, which could only take place in force on the north shore, troops had to advance some three miles. With Oijord peninsula untaken not less than two battalions should be landed in the first instance. Everyone who has studied the most difficult problem of an opposed landing with only the support of ships' guns agrees that seven armoured landing craft per battalion should be used. I could provide each battalion with two only and what this means is that a platoon would be trying to do the work of a company as covering party. My personal view has always been that an opposed landing without tanks is a very doubtful proposition.

On 4 May, the chiefs of staff of Cork and Mackesy held a briefing with the acting commander of the 24th Brigade, Lieutenant Colonel Trappes-Lomax, about the intended plan of attack and then left him to consider his options. The following day, a message arrived from Trappes-Lomax stating that he was on his way to Harstad and requested an immediate interview with General Mackesy in the presence of Lord Cork. Mackesy initially managed to sidestep this by getting Trappes-Lomax to visit his wounded brigade commander, then in the hospital at Harstad. When Mackesy and his GSO1, together with Trappes-Lomax, were in a barge going to the flagship to see Lord Cork, Trappes-Lomax asked if he could read out a statement regarding the proposed assault on Narvik. Mackesy gave him, in his words, "no encouragement, in fact I was very angry with the manner in which he had approached the problem".

At the subsequent meeting, the Scots Guards CO made a lengthy and involved statement, and demanded that his views be put before the Government in London. Mackesy later commented:

> His view, though more wordily expressed, was in fact the view which I had always maintained. It was the view of every experienced soldier. I asked Trappes-Lomax whether his grievance was against my tentative plan (which included such things as running trawlers straight on shore), in other words could he think of a better one. He replied "No", with the facilities available he could not think of a better plan, but that he regarded this, the best possible plan, as murder.

Lord Cork agreed to send this "request" to London, but the content of any reply is not known. Lieutenant Colonel Trappes-Lomax stated that if he was ordered to carry out the operation he would refuse and allow himself to be placed under arrest and tried by court-martial. He did not know what the views of his next senior in line – Lieutenant Colonel

Faulkner of the Irish Guards – were, but he felt they would be the same.

Mackesy later wrote:

> I had to speak very seriously to Trappes-Lomax, to tell him that he could not be and must not be the ringleader of a mutiny in the Guards Brigade; that he like myself was a soldier and having made a protest must obey orders to the best of his ability. After this Trappes-Lomax went off once more to see Brigadier Fraser, who expressed exactly the views I had given about Trappes-Lomax's correct attitude. I understand that Brigadier Fraser said that at all costs he would get out of hospital, resume command and carry out to the best of his ability such orders as he might be given. Trappes-Lomax returned to me and said he now realised that his duty lay in doing as ordered. To quote from notes I made that evening: "I realise all too well that everyone above me will always say that I put Lieutenant Colonel Trappes-Lomax up to this. I can only say and I say it upon my professional honour, that it is a lie." As an afterthought I added: "I cannot help feeling that it must have fallen to the lot of very few people to quell one mutiny in the higher ranks of the Royal Navy and one in the higher ranks of the Brigade of Guards and both in the space of about two weeks."

Lord Cork, in spite of being the supreme commander and appearing not to be of a strong enough character to try to impose his will, sent a message to the Admiralty on 5 May:

> For Admiralty and War Office. Reference projected direct attack on Narvik. The following unanimous representations made by senior army officers are forwarded for consideration. In view of their unanimity I feel bound to refer the matter to the judgment of His Majesty's Government which I do with great reluctance. Begins.
>
> 1. There are insufficient assault landing craft to put ashore to cover the landing of troops in unprotected craft. Only four ACLs out of the fourteen required are available.
>
> 2. Employment of local craft and trawlers is necessary to supplement motor landing craft of which there are only five. Trawlers and local craft require a steeply sloping beach and with limited information and bad charts it is uncertain whether they will ground within easy reach of the rocks.
>
> 3. This means that on the only practicable front for assault only one small beach is available for each assaulting battalion and one of these is 150 yards long. Both are bordered by high rocks and steep slopes on which men can barely clamber let alone assault.
>
> 4. Commanding Officer HMS *Aurora*, senior officer Ofotfjord patrol, supports these views.
>
> 5. During the approach landing craft will be in sight of the enemy for 1½ hours. Since it is daylight throughout the 24 hours surprise of any sort is therefore impossible.
>
> 6. Men in open boats will be subject to air attack for at least 4 hours.

7. Ships carry no smoke shells and use of funnel smoke and smoke floats is dependent on the remote chance of a suitable wind.

8. Troops will be unable to dig on account of rocks and frost and so there will be no adequate protection against air attack for the present.

9. Brigadier Fraser and all military officers experienced in war fully agree.

General Mackesy, whose attitude has been most helpful, had no previous knowledge that these representations were to be made. He has been doing his utmost to carry out my orders but I fully realised his personal view as he had always given it and as contained in his G.53 21st April.

He now adds that since that day the situation in the air has grown worse and he regards an opposed landing in the face of unopposed enemy aircraft as being absolutely unjustified. The alternative to this direct attack is to continue with development of bases while keeping Narvik blockaded and to await the result of the turning movement now proceeding, but at present making slow progress.

It is obvious that the campaign was now becoming bogged down by a lack of drive, and in London words were being exchanged amongst various committees. On 1 May, the Chairman of the Military Co-ordination Committee had called the attention of the Chiefs of Staff to the fact that these were critical days for Narvik, and the area was likely to come under attack in the coming days due to the events in the south (of which more later). He therefore urged the transfer of at least one of the carriers then stationed in the Trondheim area to cover the gap until land-based aircraft could operate. As regards anti-aircraft guns, which were also considered in a note to the Chiefs of Staff, the original allocation of just one light battery had already been supplemented by 36 more Bofors guns and a heavy battery of eight 3.7s, although it took another week or so before they were actually landed on Norwegian soil.

An estimate was made of what might be needed for anti-aircraft defence in the Narvik area, which potentially covered a naval anchorage, two airfields and other key points. The figure they came up with totalled 144 heavy and 144 light anti-aircraft guns, as against the figures of 48 and 60 actually allocated (including guns still in the United Kingdom). No further withdrawals could be made from the troops in France, who themselves had only about half as many guns as they required. To take the additional number of heavy guns from the air defence of Great Britain was judged possible: there were 900 guns there, although this was only about 40 per cent of the recognised ideal number. To take the additional number of light guns for Narvik was, however, quite impossible, as home defence possessed no more than 166 guns – of which only 36 were mobile. There were various demands for these guns to be reallocated.

The question of manpower was also being discussed, as Narvik was still attracting most of the attention from London, and Germany seemed to be either courting or threatening Sweden to secure control of the vital ore fields. Two battalions of the French Foreign Legion and the four battalions of the Free French Polish Brigade were dispatched at once to the north, as were the first five of the British Independent Companies. The second French Light Division was now stationed on the Clyde, where it was joined by the *Chasseurs Alpins*, returned from Namsos. It was intended to refit them and send them

Lieutenant-General C Auchinleck with Group Captain M Moore on board SS *Chrobry*. (Imperial War Museum HU128795)

on again to Norway. A third French Light Division remained poised at Brest awaiting transport, and on 1 May it was agreed in principle that the British 5th Infantry Division might also be brought from France as reinforcements. Meanwhile, five more Independent Companies were in course of formation, and there was even a notion of transferring Gurkhas to northern Europe. It was decided to establish a Corps headquarters for a force of about 30,000 men, and its intended commander was told in advance that he "must plan and prepare for big things".

The man chosen as commander was Lieutenant-General Claude Auchinleck. During the Great War, he had served with the Indian Army in the Middle East in Egypt, Palestine and Mesopotamia. Fighting the Turkish Army, Auchinleck was Mentioned in Despatches and received the Distinguished Service Order in 1917 for his service in Mesopotamia, promoted to Major in January 1918 and appointed brevet Lieutenant Colonel in 1919. Auchinleck took on board a number of lessons from his experiences in Mesopotamia. Firstly, that soldiers' health and well-being was critical to an army being effective; he was convinced of the need for adequate rest, hygiene, good food and medical supplies for troops. Secondly, saw the futility of inadequately prepared attacks against dug-in, well-armed defenders, which fuelled his later reluctance to initiate precipitate actions advocated by political and military superiors.

Between the wars, Auchinleck served in India. On the outbreak of war in September

1939, Auchinleck, by then a Major-General, was appointed to command the Indian 3rd Infantry Division, but in January 1940 was summoned to Britain to command IV Corps, the only time in the war that a fully British corps was led by an Indian Army officer. Then in late April he got the Norway job.

General Auchinleck was summoned on the evening of 28 April to a meeting at the War Office with General Ironside, the CIGS, and informed that he, with part of his IV Corps staff, would be required to go to Narvik in the immediate future. Auchinleck recalled:

> I returned to my Headquarters at Alresford and arranged for an Advanced Headquarters to be established in the War Office. For the next week my staff were fully employed collecting and collating information concerning northern Norway and the existing situation in that theatre. On 6th May I received my instructions from the Secretary of State for War.

Auchinleck was now commander of the North Western Expeditionary Force, or NWEF, and his orders were as follows:

Most Secret.

Instructions for Lieutenant-General C. J. E. Auchinleck.

1. The object of His Majesty's Government in northern Norway is:-

To secure and maintain a base in northern Norway from which we can:-

(a) Deny iron ore supplies to Germany via Narvik.

(b) Interfere so far as may be possible with ore supplies to Germany via Lulea.

(c) Preserve a part of Norway as a seat of Government for the Norwegian King and Government.

2. As a first stage in the achievement of this object, operations are now in progress for the capture of Narvik. The present forces assembled for this purpose are under the command of Admiral of the Fleet, Lord Cork and Orrery; the Military Commander, Major-General Mackesy, being subordinate to him. A list of the Anglo-French troops at present under Major-General Mackesy is given at Annexure 1 to this order.

3. It is the intention of His Majesty's Government that there should be no interference with the existing plans of Lord Cork and Orrery until they have either achieved success or been abandoned. At some future date, however, it will be necessary to revert to the normal system of command.

4. You are appointed GOC-in-C Designate of the Anglo-French Military Forces and the British air component in the area. His Majesty's Government will decide when the present system of unified command shall terminate. Thereafter you will be in independent command of the Anglo-French Military Forces and the British air component and will act in close co-operation with the Senior Naval Officer in the Narvik area.

5. You will proceed to the Narvik area with an officer detailed by the Chief of the Air Staff, and, in conjunction with Admiral of the Fleet, Lord Cork and

Orrery, report for the information of the Chiefs of Staffs the forces required to attain the object in paragraph 1 above and the area which you recommend should be occupied. You should take into account the necessity for making arrangements to enable any iron ore now at Narvik to be despatched to the United Kingdom and, if the situation permits, for resuming the supply of iron ore from the Swedish iron mines at Gallivare.

Your report should include recommendations as to the practicability and desirability of repairing the railway from Narvik to the Swedish frontier.

6. Scale of enemy attack up to October 1940.

Naval.

The scale of naval attack that may be expected against Narvik is:-

(a) Raids by capital ships or cruisers which although not very likely are a possibility.

(b) A heavy scale of submarine attack by both torpedo and mine.

(c) Light craft and MTB attack. Germany will probably take full advantage of such measure of control as she may be able to obtain over Norwegian waters to secure the approach of attacking light craft.

Land.

The scale of land attack that may be expected is:-

(a) Raids or attempted landings by parties carried in coastal vessels.

(b) Sabotage, especially of the railway.

(c) Parachute landings.

(d) A German advance from Sweden following invasion of that country.

Air.

The Narvik area is within reach of German bombers based on or re-fuelled in southern or central Norway. A daily weight of attack of 40 tons is possible from these bases from now onwards. To this must be added a light scale of attack from seaplanes operating from fjords. The scale and frequency of this attack would be very seriously increased if the Germans succeed in establishing air bases in Sweden, such as Boden (near Lulea) and Ostersund, or further north in Norway.

To meet this scale the Chief of Staffs estimate that two or three fighter squadrons, one bomber servicing unit and some Army co-operation aircraft are required.

7. When you have taken over command it is intended to withdraw Major-General Mackesy and the staff of the 49th Divisional HQ, less such personnel as you may wish to retain.

8. The forces operating in Norway south of the Narvik area, at present under the command of Lieutenant-General Massy, may at an early date be placed under your command. The policy as regards operations in this area is described in the attached telegram which is being despatched to Lord Cork and is at Annexure 2 (not included) to this order.

9. Should you become a casualty or otherwise be prevented from exercising command of your force, command of the Anglo-French land and air forces will pass to a British officer to be nominated by you until another British officer can

be appointed. This officer will be given the acting rank of Lieutenant-General.

10. You will act in co-operation with the Norwegian Commander-in-Chief.

11. You will maintain constant communication with the War Office.

Oliver Stanley.

The War Office.

5th May 1940.

Annexure 1:

List of Forces under command or earmarked for Major-General Mackesy 4th May 1940

Force HQ 49th Division

Royal Artillery

(a) AA Artillery

1. Now in Narvik area

3rd Light Battery 12 Bofors

2. On Passage

No 2 AA Defence HQ

193rd AA Battery (of 82nd AA Regiment) 8 3.7 inch

55th Light Regiment 36 Bofors

3. Mobilising UK

HQ 6th AA Brigade

167th Light Battery 10 Bofors

HQ 82nd AA Regiment

156th AA Battery 8 3.7 inch

256th AA Battery 8 3.7 inch

HQ 51st AA Regiment

151st AA Battery 8 3.7 inch

152nd AA Battery 8 3.7 inch

153rd AA Battery 8 3.7 inch

HQ 56th Light AA Regiment

(b) Field Artillery

Now in Narvik area

One battery 51st Field Regiment

Royal Engineers

Now in Narvik area

HQ 49th Division RE

229th Field Company

230th Field Company

Still in UK

Detachment 231st Field Park Company

Infantry
Now in Narvik area
HQ 24th Infantry Brigade
1st Scots Guards
1st Irish Guards
2nd South Wales Borderers

In Norway, this news was relayed to Mackesy by Lord Cork on 5 May as an afterthought in a letter:

> My dear General,
>   I meant to tell you, but I forgot this afternoon that Admiral Lyster (recently arrived as Rear Admiral, Narvik Base) had met General Auchinleck who is leaving for this area to take command of the troops in northern Norway.
>   You have probably heard of this, but I know curious omissions occur sometimes and in some cases do not pass it on.

Mackesy commented, "I could only, in reply, thank him for the information about Auchinleck and praise heaven that I had had the foresight to make my ADC bring a bowler hat for me."

Meanwhile, Mackesy agreed with Lord Cork that even after the arrival of some more French troops it would be impossible to launch the attack on Narvik before the night of 10/11 May.

Mackesy was officially informed of his replacement in command of land forces at Narvik on 7 May, in a telegram from General Dill advising him of Auchinleck's imminent arrival and that "his instructions, which he will show you on arrival, will make his position clear".

Mackesy commented that when Auchinleck did arrive his position was anything but clear, and he also sent a reply to General Dill: "I have strong inclinations, as I am sure you will understand, to quote to you the words of Luke 2.29 but I will not." This verse from the Bible says, "Now lettest thou thy servant depart in peace".

Despite the changes, planning still had to go ahead for the proposed attack on Narvik. Mackesy visited Béthouart and his chief of staff on 7 May and asked him to consider undertaking the following: firstly, the capture of the Oijord peninsula in order to establish a position from which artillery could be based; and secondly, to clear the Germans out of their positions south of Gratangen. As the French now had in terms of numbers about 75 per cent of the total troops in the area, Mackesy felt he should give him complete charge of these operations. Mackesy added that he would give him every assistance, and also get as much Royal Navy support as possible. Following these initial landings and operations, it was stressed that the Oijord peninsula would need to be strongly held and Béthouart should then consider operations in a south-easterly direction from the Bjerkvik area to try to get across the railway line and then attack Germans in the Hundalen-Bjornfjel area. The 24th Brigade was to remain firm and hold the north-western portion of the Ankenes peninsula, and also to move south-east with a view to taking Beisfjord

Polish troops at Brest on their way to Norway. (Author's Collection)

town. Béthouart and a reconnaissance party were sent that night by ship to look at their areas of operations, accompanied by Mackesy's GSO2 and Commander Hubback to help with planning. Béthouart requested that the two battalions of the Foreign Legion which had just arrived, and the tank company, be available for operations under his control. Mackesy also found time to visit Trappes-Lomax and advise him of pending plans.

On the following day, Mackesy stated that he had a long private talk with Lord Cork to "try and clear the air". The chief points that came out of this, according to Mackesy, were as follows:

First. To thank him for his handling of the difficult, for him, Trappes-Lomax situation.

Second. To ask him to remember our feelings and to avoid telling us we must be prepared to face losses and so on, which is tantamount to accusing the Army of cowardice. I said a plan is either a good plan or a bad plan. If it is a good plan very heavy losses may have to be incurred, but there is a chance of success. If it is a bad plan you have 100% casualties, but that will not give you victory.

Third. Whilst leaving myself in his hands, I hoped he would use his great influence to get me removed when General Auchinleck arrived. He realised the absurdity of a Corps and a Force Headquarters in the area.

It is said that Lord Cork replied that as Mackesy had been frank with him, he would be so in return. Cork said that it had for a long time been his firm intention, as soon as he got back to London, to see the Secretary of State for War and the Chief of the Imperial General Staff and to tell them that while he and Mackesy had differed over the question of the immediate direct assault on Narvik, Mackesy had every right to so differ. He ended by saying: "I consider that you have accepted what must have been a very difficult position admirably and I intend to say that I would consider it a most grave injustice if this perfectly justifiable difference of opinion were in any way to count against you."

The highlight of the day for many on 8 May was probably the arrival of the Polish Brigade, consisting of four battalions of infantry. On 23 April, Polish troops who had escaped from Poland, and were now attached to the French Army's 13th Demi-Brigade of the Foreign Legion, began boarding at Brest as part of the French contingent for Norway. To fanfares and the playing of national anthems, the Poles headed up the Channel and into the North Sea aboard three merchant ships, the *Colombie*, *Chenonceaux* and *Mexique*. The first stop was Greenock in Scotland, then on 30 April they headed for Norway. The Brigade landed in Lenvik, near Harstad – it had to be ferried ashore by Norwegian fishing boats because of a lack of harbour facilities suitable for large vessels.

11

Allied actions at Narvik

Whilst the Germans in Narvik were not particularly active, that could not be said for the rest of their forces in Norway. After successfully taking the key objectives in the early days of the invasion, they started to push out into other areas. One of the main lessons they had learned in the 1930s was the value of air power and airfields. Within weeks of getting settled in the main populated areas in the south, they felt they could concentrate on the north. The British high command believed that a German advance from the south concentrating on Mo, Bodø and Mosjöen would be of considerable danger. The British were well aware of the threat of air power, especially as they had little or no air support and not much in the way of anti-aircraft resources. The German *Luftwaffe* had been bombing them fairly regularly, although in the early days of the campaign this had been hampered by difficult weather conditions and the distances involved. The British thought that the bombers had been flying from the deep south of Norway and refuelling at Trondheim, but should the area around Mo, between Trondheim and Narvik, be secured there was a landing ground there which, it was suggested, could be improved. This would allow more bombers to attack Narvik, and more often. In London, this danger was recognised, but little was done about it apart from sending some RAF personnel ("reconnaissance parties") to Narvik to find a potential landing ground. Mackesy was particularly concerned by this, and wrote:

> I realised that it was probably a race: could the Germans occupy and use the Mo landing ground before we could install adequate aircraft to compete with them? I was afraid that unless definite measures to check them were taken without delay they probably could. When I heard that our air force said they must have a concrete runway 1,400 yards long and 50 yards wide at Skaanland before they could use bombers, the situation seemed to me to be very serious.

Some fighters had been sent to Norway but mainly to southern areas. In the meantime, British reinforcements had been allocated to the northern sector and these duly arrived, in the shape of five of the ten Independent Companies under the overall command of Colonel C. Gubbins. Ten of these companies had been formed in April 1940, with volunteers from various divisions called for. The results were:

No. 1 Independent Company, formed from 52nd Lowland Division on 20 April 1940 under the command of Major J. Ballantyne of the Cameronians; No. 2 Independent Company, formed from 53rd Welsh Division on 25 April 1940 under the command of Major H. Stockwell of the Royal Welch Fusiliers; No. 3 Independent Company, formed

A panorama of Narvik Fjord. (The National Archives)

from 54th East Anglian Division on 25 April 1940 under the command of Major A. Newman of the Essex Regiment; No. 4 Independent Company, formed from 55th West Lancashire Division on 21 April 1940 under the command of Major J. Rimmer of the Liverpool Scottish; No. 5 Independent Company, formed from 56th London Division on 21 April 1940 under the command of Major J. Pedder of the London Scottish; No. 6 Independent Company, formed from 9th Scottish Division on 25 April 1940 under the command of Major R. Tod of the Argyll and Sutherland Highlanders; No. 7 Independent Company, formed from 15th Scottish Division on 25 April 1940 under the command of Major J. Young of the Highland Light Infantry; No. 8 Independent Company, formed from 18th Eastern Division on an unknown date in April 1940 under the command of Major Rice of the Suffolk Regiment; No. 9 Independent Company, formed from 38th Welsh Division on an unknown date in April 1940 under the command of Major W. Siddons of the Royal Welch Fusiliers; No. 10 Independent Company, formed from 66th East Lancs Division on an unknown date in April 1940 under the command of Major I. Robertson of the Territorial Army General List.

Some of these officers took part in some of the early commando raids between 1940 and 1942, and in some cases beyond.

The orders given to Colonel Gubbins included the following:

Your task is to prevent the Germans occupying Bodø, Mo and Mosjöen. This you must try to do by small parties landed from the sea or dropped by parachute. Later, the Germans may be expected to advance northwards on Mosjöen from the Trondheim area via Grong. You will ensue that all possible steps are taken by demolition and harrying tactics to impede any German advance along this route. Your companies operating in this area should not attempt to offer any prolonged resistance but should endeavour to maintain themselves on the flanks of the German forces and continue harrying tactics against their lines of communications.

Lance Corporal D. Randall recalled how in April 1940, as a member of the Signal Platoon of the 1st Liverpool Scottish, he ended up in an Independent Company:

> In the middle of April a number of names were put on the Battalion notice board. These men were required to report at a certain time to the Battalion Orderly Room. My name was amongst them and I found over thirty men had been called forward from all over the unit. We were interviewed in turn. Very few declined – mostly married men – but the rest of us felt at last there would be something more practical and useful to occupy our soldierly skills.

The "volunteers" were given limited information about what they had signed up for, except that after some special training they would proceed overseas and their role would be to harass the enemy in a mountainous country. Various rumours flew around as to where they would be going: the Balkans, the Caucasus, Norway and Switzerland were all suggested. A few soldiers from each unit of a division were selected or volunteered, and within a week or so their strength was approaching the "paper establishment".

An Independent Company was to consist of 21 officers and 270 other ranks, organised into three rifle platoons. Each platoon had an HQ of one officer, one sergeant and nine other ranks, and then three sections each consisting of one subaltern, one corporal and 12 men. It was not normal for a section to be commanded by an officer – this was usually the job of a corporal. There were also normally eight men in a section. There was also a support element for each company, consisting of a LMG (light machine gun), a Royal Engineer and a Royal Signals section. Additionally, there was an ammunition section from the Royal Army Service Corps, along with medical and intelligence sections.

After undergoing training, mainly route marches and trench digging, five of the ten companies moved in early May to Glasgow, where No. 4 Independent Company at least boarded the *Ulster Prince* for the trip to Norway. Waiting for them at Glasgow were eight officers from the Indian Army, who had been sent specially to advise the group on mountain warfare. Other companies sailed to Norway on the *Orion*, *Royal Scotsman* and *Highland Queen*.

Gubbins issued the following advice to his new force:

> Your mobility depends on your requisitioning or commandeering local craft to move your detachments, watching possible enemy landing places. Keep attack from the air always in mind. Disperse and conceal, but retain power to concentrate rapidly against enemy landing parties.
>
> Keep a reserve. Get to know the country intimately. Make use of the locals but do not trust too far.
>
> Use wits and low cunning. Be always on guard.

When the companies arrived in the Bodø, Mo and Mosjøen area, Gubbins' group was placed under the orders of Lord Cork, but it was not long before Gubbins and his company commanders were asking Mackesy's staff for instructions, which the latter did their best to provide.

The policy of apparent lethargy by the Army was still rankling with Lord Cork, and during the night of 9/10 May General Mackesy received a letter from him expressing grave anxiety about so-called "delaying tactics" in the Mosjøen, Mo and Bodø area, which seemed to him to be making no progress in stopping the Germans. Lord Cork suggested sending down a battalion of Poles as the Norwegians were complaining of a lack of action, and in his eyes there was a large risk of them "throwing in their hand".

In reply, on the morning of 10 May, Mackesy wrote to Lord Cork:

> I am sorry for the delay in answering your letter, but I have waited to get in touch with Gubbins at Mosjøen again. I am now waiting for further information from Colonel Gubbins himself. I do not recommend sending the Poles (in a footnote he commented that their fighting quality on the whole was reported as being of doubtful quality. "I had not been at all impressed with the officers. They had not yet really sorted themselves out.") but I suggest sending the rest of the Scots Guards with a few field and light AA guns. I am not clear yet as to which is the best place to send them. News was later received from Gubbins that Mosjøen was being evacuated, so it was decided to send them to Mo. I am ordering troops to be at short notice to move so that there will be no delay if you decide to send them.
>
> I entirely agree with your draft to the First Sea Lord. If I had the personal responsibility for sending it I would be inclined to add something like this:-
>
> Narvik is in itself of no importance except as a well-known name on the map. I feel that all our energies should be devoted for the moment to preventing the Germans establishing themselves at or north of Mosjøen.

This message was taken by an officer to Lord Cork on his flagship, and he soon returned with a verbal message saying that Cork agreed with every word that General Mackesy had said. Orders were therefore issued to the following units to "proceed to and hold Mo at all costs":

1st Scots Guards (less company already at Bodø)
One troop 203rd Field Battery Royal Artillery
One troop 55th Light AA Battery Royal Artillery
One section 230th Field Company Royal Engineers
One company 137th Field Ambulance Royal Army Medical Corps
Signals detachment with a W/T set
Royal Army Service Corps detachment with one car and six 30 cwt lorries

Signals
Now in Narvik area
HQ 49th Divisional Signals (less C Section)

No 2 Company and K and L Sections

RAMC
Now in Narvik area
137th Field Ambulance
147th Field Ambulance
22nd General Hospital
Personnel and Ambulance Train
Base Depot Medical Stores

Stores and Transport
Now in Narvik area
Petroleum Depot
Personnel Companies

Ordnance
Now in Narvik area
Detachment Base Ordnance Depot
Detachment Base Ordnance Workshop Section
 French Troops
(a) Now in Narvik area
HQ 1st Light Division
3 Battalions *Chasseurs*
12 75mm guns
12 25mm AA and A/Tank guns

Administrative units
(b) On Passage (due to arrive 4th/5th May)
(i) 2 Battalions Foreign Legion
(ii) Polish Brigade (4 Battalions)

The order to move to Mo was accompanied by a further message outlining the objectives and future plans for the Army, albeit written by the Navy:

Annexure 1

Draft telegram to FO i/c Narvik.
To FO Narvik
From Admiralty
   Your 1645/4. Following is policy for operations south of Narvik. It is not possible to maintain large forces in face of enemy air superiority at any place well in advance of an established fighter aerodrome and even then adequate air protection would require forward landing facilities. Only place south of Narvik where it might prove possible to establish forward landing ground is Bodø.

Hence at Mo and Mosjöen only small bodies can be maintained. Role of such bodies is to carry out extensive demolitions on road leading north from Namsos which is already in a bad state and reported impassable for wheeled vehicles, and to delay advance of enemy for as long as possible and prevent landings from sea or by parachute. It is however highly desirable that Bodø should be included in the forward defences of Narvik if reconnaissance shows that a fighter forward landing ground can be developed in the area, and provided that the provision of necessary AA defences and maintenance of necessary forces does not prove too expensive a drain on our resources. In the meantime reconnaissance report from Bodø is awaited. Company Scots Guards should not repeat not be withdrawn until further orders. Intended that all military forces in northern Norway shall eventually come under command of General Officer Commanding troops Narvik at time to be decided by War Office.

At this time, the news filtered through to Norway of the German invasion of the Low Countries and the fact that a more significant campaign had started further south. If Norway was not very high on the priority order, then it was going to be competing in the coming weeks with urgent demands from the British Expeditionary Force in France.

With the arrival of the Foreign Legion units and the Polish Brigade, coupled with gradually improving weather and the arrival of some much-needed equipment (notably AA guns, a small number of landing craft and some French tanks), it seemed as though the time was right to undertake more active operations on the Narvik front. So the French were tasked with clearing the Gratangen-Bjerkvik area, while the British 24th Brigade (with one battalion of *Chasseurs* under command) were to hold firstly the northern end of the Ankenes peninsula and then advance on Beisfjord as soon as weather conditions would allow. The first move occurred at 0100 on 13 May, when the Demi-Brigade of the Foreign Legion landed at Bjerkvik. The landing was preceded by a bombardment from naval ships. A particularly troublesome machine gun post on the left-hand side of the assault beach was knocked out by this support, allowing three light tanks and about 120 men from ALCs (assault landing craft) to land safely. They secured the beach and, once established, worked their way round the head of the fjord to deal with other machine gun posts. The next assault wave came ashore using ships boats, and in the high command's eyes was entirely successful. "Without the use of tanks it might easily have ended in costly failure. It was fortunate indeed that low clouds prevented hostile air attack during the landing. Contact was made with the force operating from Gratangen and the Oijord peninsula was seized. The stage was now set for the capture of Narvik."

In spite of this encouraging start, all was still not well behind the scenes. General Mackesy commented that Lord Cork had postponed the operation twice, each time for 24 hours, Mackesy wanting the operation to go ahead on 10/11 May. On 11 May, elements of the 1st Scots Guards had also been sent to Mo and arrived safely just after a small German force had left Hemnes, another peninsula on the narrow fjord running up to Mo. During the night of 10/11 May, Mackesy came to the conclusion that the HQ of the 24th Brigade and the Irish Guards, with some support elements, should also go to the Mo area, but in theory this would need the permission of Lord Cork. Mackesy wrote:

As Lord Cork would shortly be out of touch I telegraphed my proposals direct to the War Office and repeated them to Lord Cork (then on HMS *Effingham*), expressing the hope that he agreed. The message to Lord Cork went off at 0330 on 11th May. No answer was received and *Effingham* did not reply to any signals made during her absence. I was entirely out of touch with Lord Cork until the afternoon of Monday 13th May.

From an Army point of view everything was ready for the operation to take place on the night 10th/11th May. I had a difficult task to make up my mind whether to be present in person at the French landing or not. After much thought I told General Béthouart that, strong as was my every inclination to go, I thought it might be an embarrassment to him to have a senior officer standing beside him and that I felt it my duty to stay quietly at my HQ.

With the benefit of hindsight this was a good decision, as on 10 May a message was received from the transport ship SS *Chrobry* that not only was Lieutenant-General Auchinleck arriving at 2100 the following day, but that he would be accompanied by 11 senior and 22 junior staff officers. One of Mackesy's staff officers then spent a hectic time trying to find them quarters, not helped by the arrival of the *Chrobry* at 0900 instead of 2100! Even then Auchinleck arrived unexpectedly; General Mackesy was out and two of his senior staff officers had long interviews with him to put him in the picture. Mackesy continued:

I had about a 40 minute interview with him before lunch, told him my plans and outlined the orders I had given. He did not show me his own instructions and I was left in grave doubt as to what he had really come for with a large staff. After lunch Auchinleck said he must see Lord Cork at once. Arrangements were made for him to drive to Skaanland and pick up *Effingham*'s barge there, and go down to the anchorage to see Lord Cork. He said he would be back for dinner.

Later in the evening I heard indirectly that General Auchinleck had decided to remain in *Effingham* for the French operation. After my unwilling decision not to go myself this action filled me with apprehension. There can be no doubt that it was due to the presence of this very senior officer on board that I received no reports of any sort of the operation and spent many hours of unnecessary anxiety.

In fact Lieutenant-General Auchinleck had an unpleasant duty to perform in Norway: to remove Major-General Mackesy from command. On Monday 13 May, the situation in the Mo area was changing, and it seemed not for the better. The Germans on the Hemnes peninsula were consolidating their positions and were reported to have some artillery support. Meanwhile, a group estimated at between 500 to 1,000-strong, supported by tanks and artillery, was reported to be moving northwards from Mosjöen and was believed to have reached Elsfjord. The chances of another landing at Mo did not look too good to Mackesy. He felt somewhat hamstrung without knowing what the naval position was there: "*Effingham* ignored all signals."

Then another problem cropped up. It had wisely been decided that some of the newly arrived 3.7in AA guns should accompany the 24th Brigade, but their value was of limited worth. It had been revealed by the OC of the battery that whilst he had his guns and ammunition, he was not really in a position to fire them due to lack of essential equipment. Mackesy felt enraged enough to put his feelings in writing:

> The reason for this almost incredible state of affairs is a good lesson of what must always happen if the staff machinery is not allowed to work and if snap decisions are taken by higher organisations who cannot know the essential details. The battery, complete, but without predictors, height finders and so on, had embarked. These essentials were just going to start loading when the embarkation staff received orders that the RAF party was to have absolute priority and nothing else whatever was to be loaded. So a perfectly good and badly needed 3.7 inch AA battery sailed from England unable to come into action. Apart from its effects on my operations there is irony in the thought the RAF had always refused to bring aircraft until 3.7 inch batteries were available, in action, to defend the aerodromes.

In the early afternoon of 13 May, HMS *Effingham* was reported to be due back soon at Harstad. When she arrived, Mackesy sent his GSO1 with Brigadier Fraser to discover from the naval staff what ships were in the area and the likely situation. It was intended that the GSO1 would return with the latest position, and then Mackesy and his team would sort out a definite plan. But on board things did not go as Mackesy wished, and his GSO1 reported back that Lord Cork and General Auchinleck were discussing plans themselves. Then at around 1800 that day, Auchinleck came ashore and had a meeting with Mackesy, who recalled:

> He showed me an order signed by General Dill authorising him to take command and one brief paragraph in what appeared to be a Cabinet instruction ordering him to report on a base area or something of the sort. General Auchinleck informed me that he had decided to assume command forthwith because (i) I had not accompanied General Béthouart at his landing operation, (ii) I had sent a staff officer to *Effingham* on her return instead of going myself and (iii) because the Mo operation looked difficult.
>
> General Auchinleck asked me quite frankly if I thought he was "a shit". I replied in the negative, that I presumed he was doing what he considered to be his duty, as I myself had always tried to do. He then said he was very busy at the moment but wanted to have a long talk with me next day. This remark was repeated several times in the next 48 hours. I always replied that I was entirely at his service at any time he liked to send for me, but he never did and I was never once asked for my views about anything. From now on I had no staff except my ADC and personal naval liaison officer, I had no office and the first thing the new Corps staff did was to take away the typewriter used by my ADC for secret personal work. A War Office telegram to FO Narvik referring to a message from him timed 0812 on 13th May removed me from my command and ordered me home.

Now that Mackesy was in theory out of the way, new orders were issued that night to the 24th Brigade by the newly created Headquarters North Western Expeditionary Force (NWEF); an important change was introduced, in that the Bodø-Saltdalen area was to be denied permanently to the Germans and an "advanced detachment" was to be maintained at Mo as long as possible.

Mackesy left Norway on Wednesday 15 May in company with a number of other "waifs and strays", heading for the Clyde in the *Ulster Monarch*. He arrived back in Scotland on the evening of 22 May and went straight to London, where as ordered he reported to the War Office. However, it seems nobody wanted to see him and he was told he had "better go on leave". He heard nothing more until Friday 14 June, when he received a letter from the Military Secretary advising him that there "was no other appointment vacant for which you could be considered", and that he had been reverted to unemployed pay from 23 May. This was the end of the active career of Major-General P. Mackesy.

The following report was made by Lieutenant-General Auchinleck, covering the period from 7 May, when he embarked for Norway, to 24 May:

Departure for and arrival in Norway.

I embarked with an Advanced Headquarters staff at Leith in the Polish liner *Chrobry* on the 7th May and landed, after an uneventful voyage, at Harstad on the 11th May.

Lord Cork was away in his flagship at Skaanland when I landed, but I met Major-General Mackesy and his General Staff Officer, Colonel Dowler, at once and learned the situation from them, hearing that a landing operation by the French contingent was about to take place near Bjerkvik at the head of Herjangsfjord and that Lord Cork was to direct the operation in person. I at once went to Skaanland with my Brigadier General Staff, Brigadier Gammell, and met Lord Cork.

I explained my position to Lord Cork and with his approval, remained in HMS *Effingham* with him. Neither General Mackesy nor any member of his staff was present on the flagship, though General Béthouart, commanding the French contingent, and his staff embarked just after myself and remained aboard throughout the operation.

The landing took place under a heavy bombardment from the guns of the Fleet in cold and cloudy weather in the early hours of 13th May, and in spite of the fact that there was now continuous daylight throughout the twenty-four hours and appreciable opposition from enemy machine guns on shore, was completely successful. The enemy was ejected from the area north and east of Herjangsfjord and the French landing parties not only effected a junction with their own troops advancing from the north from the direction of Gratangen but also cleared the country down to Oijord immediately across the Rombaks Fjord from Narvik.

Although I was present in the capacity of a spectator only, I am constrained to express my admiration for the way in which the whole operation was conceived and effected by all concerned. I was particularly struck by the business like efficiency of the French Foreign Legion which carried out the landing. That the landing was not interfered with by enemy aircraft was almost certainly due to the fortunate weather conditions prevailing at the time. At this period, there were no land-based aircraft available in Norway with which to counter enemy air attacks and a bombing raid might well have turned the operation from a success into a failure. I returned with Lord Cork to Harstad in HMS *Effingham*, arriving on the afternoon of the 14th May.

Assumption of Command.

Immediately HMS *Effingham* reached Harstad, Brigadier Fraser, commander of the 24th Guards Brigade, came on board with Colonel Dowler of the General Staff, to discuss plans for operations in the Mo and Bodø areas with Lord Cork. Owing to ill-health, Major-General Mackesy was not present.

With the concurrence of Lord Cork I listened to the ensuing discussion which centred round the question whether reinforcements already embarked at Skaanland should be sent to Bodø or to Mo, where an advanced detachment consisting of 1st Battalion Scots Guards and some "Independent Companies" had already been landed under heavy enemy air attack. During the course of the conference I came to the conclusion that, apparently for personal reasons, relations between Lord Cork and Major-General Mackesy were not of a nature to ensure wholehearted co-operation between the two services and I decided it was necessary for me to supersede Major-General Mackesy there and then. I informed Lord Cork of my decision and he approved of it.

I then gave verbal orders to Brigadier Fraser that he was to proceed at once with 1st Battalion Irish Guards and other troops to Bodø and not to Mo, and that he was to hold Bodø permanently and Mo for as long as he could. These orders were subsequently confirmed in writing and are attached below.

On landing from HMS *Effingham*, I at once informed Major-General Mackesy of the action I had taken and my reason for taking it. I wish to make it clear that throughout my dealings with Major-General Mackesy I found him uniformly helpful and informative. In fact, many of my subsequent actions were based on information and advice received from him.

To Brigadier W. Fraser DSO MC Officer Commanding 24th Guards Brigade

1. You will proceed forthwith with your HQ to Bodø.

2. Your object on arrival will be:-

(a) To deny the area Bodø-Saltdalen permanently to the enemy.

(b) To maintain an advance detachment at Mo as long as possible. Should it be necessary eventually to withdraw from Mo, to destroy, as possible, everything that may be of use to the enemy.

3. The following troops are placed under your command for this operation:-
24th Guards Brigade less 2nd South Wales Borderers
Independent Companies now in the area which are under the command of Colonel Gubbins

One troop 3rd Hussars

203rd Field Battery Royal Artillery

230th Field Company Royal Engineers

137th Field Ambulance Royal Army Medical Corps

24th Brigade Signal Section with detachment 49th Division Signals including one 25 watt set, one No. 9 set and two No. 11 sets

4. Of the above, 203rd Field Battery, 1 Troop 55th Light AA Regiment and HQ 137th Field Ambulance will, it is hoped, be despatched to you tomorrow by SS *Charlbury*.

5. It is intended to despatch to you the following additional troops as soon as arrangements can be made:-

2nd South Wales Borderers

Detachment 25mm guns if these can be withdrawn from the French.

6. RE stores. An allotment of wire will also be despatched by SS *Charlbury* with pickets.

7. Additional Staff:- Captain Bateman Intelligence Officer Force HQ will proceed with you tonight to assist your IO.

8. Methods of dealing with civilian population:-

It is essential that your operations should be in no way hampered or prejudiced by the presence of civilians in the area of operations. You have, therefore, full authority to take such action as you may consider necessary in this connection. In particular you should have no hesitation in taking over civilian telephones in the area, requisitioning such buildings as you may require, and evacuating the civil population from the areas in which their presence may be undesirable. Should you require assistance in this evacuation you will inform Force HQ forthwith.

Signed J. A. Gammell

BGS

NWEF

Appendix: Instructions for the preparation of a light tank troop detachment 3rd Hussars.

One light tank troop detachment of 3rd Hussars will be prepared to move overseas at 12 hours notice from 0001 05.05.1940. 3rd Hussars has already been ordered to mobilise under War Office instructions 19.04.40 and will be organised as shown in the appendices to this instruction.

Troop Detachment 3rd Hussars.

Independent Tank Troop.

A Organisation.

Troop consisting of three light tanks Mark VI B, three motor cycles and administrative transport.

B Detail.

Light tank 1 subaltern, driver mechanic and driver operator.

Light tank 2 corporal driver internal combustion, driver mechanic and driver operator.

Light tank 3 sergeant, driver mechanic and driver operator.

Motor cycles 1 and 2 (each) motor cyclist.

Relief men carried in troop transport: - one driver mechanic, one driver internal combustion and one driver operator.

Total personnel (fighting) 14 armed with 14 pistols.

30 cwt lorry 1 - one driver mechanic and one driver operator (relief drivers), fitter, driver internal combustion, proportion ammunition and petrol and various stores.

30 cwt lorry 2 - one cook, two drivers internal combustion (one as a relief driver), proportion ammunition and petrol. various stores, 1000 rounds LMG and 200 rounds A/T rifle.

Total personnel (administrative) 4. Rifles including one per B vehicle 6.

Total personnel of Troop.

Officer 1, sergeant 1, corporal 1 and troopers 17. Grand total 20.

This organisation is improvised to permit a light tank troop of three light tanks to operate independently, with, in consequence, a limited sphere of action.

Tank Maintenance.

With no LAD (Light Aid Detachment - a small group of engineers responsible for the maintenance and repair of the vehicles and equipment) or workshop organisation behind them, these troops would only be capable of carrying out running repairs. A fitter and small stock of spares is provided.

Petrol and Oil.

The petrol and oil provided would permit a radius of action of approximately 140 miles or approximately 200 miles if the tanks themselves are permitted to travel filled.

Ammunition.

One complete refill per tank is provided.

Rations.

Have been provided in bulk for seven days plus five days composite rations.

Cooking Gear.

Only Tommy cookers are allowed for - or No. 2 portable cooker if space allows.

AA and Ground Defence.

One LMG and one A/T rifle are provided with the necessary ammunition.

Medical.

A medical pannier is allowed for and each AFV has a First Aid case. There are no trained medical personnel.

Details of Loads.

30 cwt lorry 1.

14 cases petrol (112 gallons)
8 boxes (4,000 rounds) .303" SAA
18 generators smoke
20 Verey lights
1 box (360 rounds) .5" SAA
2 drums M.265
2 drums M.800
Medical pannier
50 blankets
20 groundsheets
Composite rations for 20 men for 3 days
Technical stores and spares
Spare batteries
Reserve clothing

30 cwt lorry 2.

14 cases petrol (112 gallons)
8 boxes (4,000 rounds) .303" SAA
1 box (1,000 rounds) .303" Mk VII for Bren
200 rounds .55" A/T SAA
500 rounds .38" pistol SAA
1 LMG (Bren) and spare parts
1 A/T rifle and spare parts
Rations for 7 days in bulk on special scale
Tins for water
6 rifles and 100 rounds each
5 Tommy cookers or No. 2 portable cooker
Rum ration

12

The Independent Companies and the Mo area

Bodø and Mo, where the Independent Companies and 1st Battalion Scots Guards were operating, lie south of Narvik and north of Trondheim. Bodø is 70 miles south of Mo, and in 1940 had a population of 6,000. Mo, connected by a poor quality road with Sweden, was almost chosen by the Norwegian Government for its temporary base instead of Tromsö. It is a region of mountains and fjords, and in 1940 attracted little population or traffic other than the coastal traffic through The Leads, its railway not yet functioning past Grong (the junction for Namsos). To travel north from Grong to Bodø there was the need to use several ferries to cross expanses of water, and beyond Bodø roads were non-existent until the approaches to Narvik were reached. The area was strategically important because the withdrawal of Allied forces from the Trondheim area meant that the Germans might be expected to advance northwards up the coast until, by using their air bases if not their actual troops, they could turn the besiegers of Narvik into the besieged.

The orders, part of which was referenced in the previous chapter, issued to Colonel Gubbins, commander of the Independent Companies, were as follows:

Headquarters, V Corps.
22nd April 1940.
Instructions to Lieutenant Colonel C. McV. Gubbins, MC.
    Information
    1. Force Maurice has been instructed to send a detachment of two French *Chasseurs Alpins* to Mosjöen by sea to hold it until relieved by you. This detachment should have arrived there night 1st/2nd May.
    2. A detachment from Force Rupert (one company Scots Guards) arrived Bodø area on 30th April and reported "all well".
    3. No. 1 Independent Company sailed for Mo against any attempted landings by sea or air. Copy of instructions at Appendix A.
    4. Nos 3, 4 and 5 Independent Companies together with your Headquarters will be shipped from the Clyde probably on morning 4th May 1940.
Task
    5. You will assume command of Nos 1, 3, 4 and 5 Independent Companies and any further companies that may be subsequently placed under your orders.
    6. You will send two companies to the Mosjöen area as soon as possible, after which arrangements are to be made by this Headquarters for the shipment of the

AN INDEPENDENT COMPANY - continued

(iii)   Distribution of personnel by corps

Detail	Command and administration	Intelligence section	Signal section	R.E. detachment	Support section	Medical detachment	Ammunition section	Total company headquarters	Platoon headquarters	3 sections (each)	Total, platoon	Total, independent company
Infantry												
Major	1							1				1
Captain	1							1				1
Subalterns		1			1			2	2	1	5	17
Company serjeant-major	1							1				1
Company quarter-master-serjeant	1							1				1
Serjeants	1							1	1		1	4
Rank and file	12	10	15		26	1	7	71	10	13	49	218
R.E.												
Subaltern				1				1				1
Serjeant				1				1				1
Corporals				3				3				3
Sappers				18				18				18
Royal Signals												
Subaltern			1					1				1
Serjeant			1					1				1
Rank and file			11					11				11
R.A.M.C.												
Medical officer						1		1				1
Medical orderlies						8		8				8
R.A.O.C.												
Armourer serjeant	1							1				1
Total, all ranks	18	11	28	23	27	10	7	124	13	14	55	289

Distribution by Corps. (The National Archives)

French detachment to the United Kingdom.

You will send one company to the Bodø area to relieve the company of Scots Guards whose removal is being arranged by Rupert Force.

7. Your first task is to prevent the Germans occupying Bodø, Mo and Mosjöen. This they may try to do by small parties landed from the sea or dropped by parachutes. Later the Germans may be expected to advance northwards on Mosjöen from the Trondheim area via Grong. You will ensure that all possible steps are taken by demolition and harrying tactics to impede any German advance along this route. Your companies operating in this area should not attempt to offer prolonged frontal resistance but should endeavour to maintain themselves on the flanks of the German forces and continue harrying tactics against their lines of communications.

8. Similarly, should the Germans invade Sweden and attempt to reach the Mosjöen-Mo-Bodø area across the Swedish border, you will employ harrying tactics and demolitions in order to make their advance slow and costly.

Reinforcements

9. You will report as soon as possible whether you require additional independent companies sent to join you.

SECRET

ANNEXURE 1 to War Office
Urgent Postal Telegram No.
79/Mob./3433/129(M)(Mob.1.)
dated 22nd April, 1940.

AN INDEPENDENT COMPANY.

(Consisting of a Headquarters and 3 Platoons each of 3 Sections)

(i) Summary of ranks

Detail	Command and administration	Intelligence section	(a) Signal section	(a) R.E. detachment	Support section	(a)(c) Medical detachment	Ammunition section	Total, company headquarters	Platoon headquarters	3 sections (each)	Total, each platoon	Total, independent company
Major	1							1				1
Captain	1							1				1
Subalterns		1	(b)1	1	1			4	2	1	5	(e)19
Medical officer						1		1				1
Total, officers	2	1	1	1	1	1		7	2		5	22
Company serjeant-major	1							1				1
Total, warrant officers	1							1				1
Company quarter-master-serjeant	1							1				1
Serjeant cook	(J)1							1				1
Serjeants	1		(b)1	1				3	1		1	6
Total, staff-serjeants and serjeants	3	1	1					5	1		1	8
Corporals		1	(3	3	3	4	1	15		1	3	24
Rank and file (other than corporals)	13	9	(d(23	18	23	5	6	99	10	(f)12	46	234
Total, rank and file	13	10	26	21	26	9	7	114	10	13	49	258
Total, other ranks	16	10	27	22	26	9	7	117	11	13	50	267
Total, all ranks	18	11	28	23	27	10	7	124	13	14	55	289

Summary of ranks. (The National Archives)

APPENDIX "A" TO WAR OFFICE URGENT POSTAL TELEGRAM
79/MOB./3433/119(M) (MOB.1.) DATED 20TH APRIL, 19

SECRET

Serial No. (a)	Unit. (b)	Parent Unit under whose supervision each Company will mobilize. (c)	Place of Mobilization. (d)	Assembly of Mobilization Equipment. (e)	Date by which unit is to be mobilized and ready to move. (f)	Remarks (g)
22033.	No.5 Independent Company.	1st London Rifle Bde., Beachborough Park, near Folkestone. (Tel.No. Cheriton 85122)	Weapon Training Camp, St. Mary's Bay, New Romney. (Tel.No. Dymchurch 149)	Unit.	29th April, 1940.	
22034.	No.8 Independent Company.	5/Beds. & Herts. Regt., West Tofts, Thetford, Norfolk.	Cranwich Camp, Mundford, near Brandon, Norfolk. (Tel.No. Mundford 231)	Unit.	29th April, 1940.	
22035.	No.3 Independent Company.	55 Anti-Tank Regt. R.A. Ashington, near Morpeth, Northumberland.	Methodist Hall, Cortland, Northumberland.	Unit.	1st May, 1940.	
22036.	No.4 Independent Company.	9/King's Regt. Belstead School, Aldeburgh, Suffolk. (Tel.No. Aldeburgh 365)	"A" Company Camp, 9/King's Regt., Sizewell, near Leiston, Suffolk.	Unit.	1st May, 1940.	
22037.	No.10 Independent Company.	520 Petrol Coy. R.A.S.C. (Tel.No. Catterick 301, Ext. 12)	Hooge Lines, Catterick Camp, Yorks.	Unit.	1st May, 1940.	

The raising of the Independent Companies sheet 1. (The National Archives)

AN INDEPENDENT COMPANY - continued

(ii) Distribution of rank and file by duties

Detail	Command and administration	Intelligence section	(a) Signal section	(a) R.E. detachment	Support section	(a)(c) Medical detachment	Ammunition section	Total, company headquarters	Platoon headquarters	3 sections (each)	Total, platoon	Total, independent company
					Company headquarters					3 platoons (each)		
Tradesmen												
R.Signals												
Operators wireless and line			(b)10					10				10
Instrument mechanics			(b)1					1				1
R.E.												
Carpenters and joiners				6				6				6
Fitters				3				3				3
Electricians				3				3				3
Pioneers				9				9				9
Non-tradesmen												
Batmen	1	1			1	1		4	1	1	4	16
Clerks	1							1				1
Cooks	1							1	1		1	4
Duty corporals		1			3		1	5	1		3	14
Interpreters		4						4	1		1	7
Liaison personnel	4							4				4
Medical orderlies, R.A.M.C.						(g)8		8				8
Privates		4			22		6	32	4	(f)11	37	143
Scouts									3		3	9
Regimental signallers			15					15				15
Supply duties	4							4				4
Orderly groom	1							1				1
Total, rank and file	12	10	26	21	26	9	7	111	10	13	49	258
Total, other ranks	16	10	27	22	26	9	7	117	11	13	50	267
Total, all ranks	18	11	28	23	27	10	7	124	13	14	55	289

Distribution of ranks/duties. (The National Archives)

APPENDIX "A" to War Office Urgent Postal Telegram No.79/Mob./3433/129(M)(Mob.1.) dated 22nd April, 1940.

Serial No. (a)	Unit (b)	Parent Unit under whose supervision each Company will mobilize. (c)	Place of mobilization (d)	Assembly of mobilization equipment (e)	Date by which unit is to be mobilized and ready to move. (f)	Remarks (g)
22269	No.6 Independent Company	61st A/T Regiment, Drill Hall, North Tay Street, Dundee	Buddon Camp, Carnoustie, Fife.	Unit.	4th May, 1940	
22270	No.7 Independent Company	130th Field Regiment, R.A.	Stobs Camp, near Hawick.	Unit	4th May, 1940	
22271	No.9 Independent Company	5th Battalion, K.S.L.I.	Ross-on-Wye.	Unit	4th May, 1940	
22272	No.2 Independent Company	Infantry Training Centre, Royal Irish Fusiliers, Ballykinlar.	Ballykinlar, N. Ireland.	Unit	4th May 1940.	

The raising of the Independent Companies sheet 2. (The National Archives)

AN INDEPENDENT COMPANY - continued

(iv) Table of weapons and ammunition

Detail	Number	Ammunition - rounds		
		On man or with gun	Reserve	Total
Pistols (h) .38-inch	113	24	4,100	6,812
Rifles, .303-inch	150	120	30,000	48,000
Snipers rifles	18	50	6,000	6,900
Machine carbines	18.	100	20,000	21,800
L.M.Gs.	4	750	14,000	17,000
A.T. rifles	10	40	1,600	2,000
Pistols, signal	14		450	450

(a) To be allotted to platoons as required

(b) Royal Signals

(c) R.A.M.C. personnel except batman

(d) Includes 11 R. Signals personnel of which one will be a
lance-corporal and 15 regimental personnel of which two will
be lance-corporals

(e) A proportion may be warrant officers, class III

(f) Includes 1 lance-corporal

(g) Includes 4 corporals.

(h) For -   Officers
Full N.C.Os.
Ammunition numbers
Personnel armed with machine carbines
Light machine gunners
Anti-tank riflemen
R. Signals personnel

(j) Armourer, R.A.O.C.

NOTE ON FIRST REINFORCEMENTS.
(Not included in totals on Page 1.)
Details left at base.
Orderly Room clerk (Corporal) ..... 1.

Table of weapons and ammunition. (The National Archives)

In addition, you can be reinforced at short notice by any of the following in small detachments:

(a) Light tanks.

(b) Bren Carriers.

(c) 3.7-inch howitzers or 3-inch mortars.

(d) M/c combinations.

provided you can be sure of landing them, employing them to good purpose, concealing them from air attack and maintaining them.

Administration

10. An Independent Companies Administration Group is now in process of formation and will leave for Bodø about 7th May. It will be accompanied, or followed closely, by supplies and maintenance stores for the whole force for thirty days. Thereafter Bodø will be kept stocked with thirty days' supplies and maintenance stores by periodic shipments from the United Kingdom.

Each Independent Company leaving the United Kingdom has been, or will be, accompanied by thirty days' rations (plus a proportion of mountain rations) and its G1098 equipment.

Transport

11. You will report as soon as possible what assistance you require in the way of small craft for sea transport. If considered necessary by you trawlers or other small ships can be made available.

Intercommunication

12. Signal instructions have been issued separately.

Special Reports

13. Report early on the possibility of any landing ground with 1,000 yards runway in the Bodø area.

Additional Officers

14. Eight Indian Army Officers are allotted to you for employment as you think fit. The fullest use should be made of their knowledge and experience of irregular warfare in mountainous country.

Brig., GS,

NWEF

As early as 21 April, a trawler had been sent to report on facilities at Mosjöen, a tiny port at the head of the Vefsenfjord about 90 miles north of Namsos (150 miles by road), and five days later the Commander-in-Chief, Home Fleet, mentioned it again, apparently thinking that it would be feasible to relieve pressure at Namsos if a suitable landing place could be found there or elsewhere in the same direction. But it was not until the decision had been taken to leave Namsos altogether that operations north of that town became urgently necessary. On 27 April, Major-General Carton de Wiart's headquarters passed on to the War Office information received from their Norwegian allies that the enemy intended to occupy Mosjöen. General de Wiart had been sent to command the troops operating in central Norway. Two days later, a message from General Massy (who had been appointed as commander of all troops in Norway except those at Narvik) stated that it was essential to deny Mosjöen to the enemy. His plan was that one detachment should be sent from Maurice Force direct to Mosjöen by sea, and a second detachment, with the available transport, left as a rearguard at Grong, east of Namsos, to hold up the enemy along the road north. This second detachment might, if necessary, be composed of skiers only. General de Wiart and General Audet (the French commander of all troops in Norway) were, however, equally opposed to providing the rearguard. The ski troops were not sufficiently numerous to achieve much and would be at the mercy of air attack; reconnaissance had shown the road to be impassable during the thaw for the motor transport required to supply them. In any case, the skiers were needed in their present positions to cover the evacuation. The matter remained under discussion as late as 2 May, when there was a further conference between General de Wiart and General Audet because direct instructions for a French detachment to be posted at Grong had been received by the latter from General Gamelin (the French overall commander-in-chief). But the original view that such a rearguard could not be set up because it could not withdraw by road to Mosjöen was maintained.

As to the practicability of a retirement by road on the proposed date, perhaps the views of local experts might have been sought. According to Colonel Getz (commander of the Norwegian 5th Brigade), the line of the uncompleted railway had been cleared of snow by 19 April; by 26 April, the supplies for his brigade were being brought overland from Mosjöen, and on 1 May he was advising the Norwegian Legation in London, who were purchasing stores for him, of the good connections available between Mosjöen and Grong. A Norwegian battalion based on Mosjöen had been moved south to Grong on 21 April; it moved back with no great difficulty along the same route in the first week of May. This involved travelling around 130 miles by rail and 35 miles by a shuttle service of lorries on high ground in the middle where a railway bridge awaited completion,.

The other half of the plan put to General de Wiart was carried out, though on a reduced scale. A party of 100 *Chasseurs Alpins* and a two-gun section of a British light anti-aircraft battery were sent by sea from Namsos in the only available transport, a destroyer, on the night of 30 April, arriving, unobserved from the air, late next day at Mosjöen. A week later, the French were replaced by British troops, so the defence of Mosjöen and the subsequent operations became exclusively a British-Norwegian venture. Meanwhile, the forces at Narvik under Lord Cork had received orders to safeguard the main intermediate point at Bodø and a company of Scots Guards was sent to that area, so that the delaying operations to the southward henceforth had Bodø to fall back upon as an outpost protecting operations against Narvik.

The situation was difficult, since British naval control of the inshore routes, which might have been expected to make successive advances along the coast in a southerly direction, was seen to be somewhat risky because of the threat of German air attacks in the narrow waters of the Norwegian fjords. As there was a shortage of landing grounds in the Narvik area, on 30 April the Air Ministry ordered a search for these in the area around Bodø, Mosjöen and Mo, in that order of priority. Four days later, a small party of RAF specialists came to Bodø in two flying boats chartered from Imperial Airways. The Germans spotted their arrival and an attack was launched. Within 30 minutes of the arrival of the second aircraft, both had been destroyed.

The Independent Companies (sometimes called Scissors Force in official orders) had been sent to Norway under the command of Colonel Gubbins. No. 1 Independent Company landed on 4 May at the head of the Ranfjord at Mo, 54 miles north of Mosjöen by road. No. 3 Independent Company, to be joined later by No. 2 Company, landed much farther north at Bodø, and at the same time Scissors Force headquarters was set up 11 miles east of that town at the village of Hopen, where the Scots Guards company had already established itself.

The day after No. 1 Company's arrival, some of the first actions begun at Mo were the responsibility of the 4th and 5th Companies. These were the troops that replaced the French at Mosjöen on the night of 8/9 May. No. 4 Company was positioned to protect Mosjöen from the sea and to secure the first part of the road to Mo, while No. 5 Company moved south to link up with the Norwegians. Colonel Gubbins, who had landed with them, learnt that the Norwegian battalion in the area, only 400 strong, had gone forward again. Colonel Gubbins found the Norwegians at Fellingfors, 25 miles south of Mosjöen, where a side road led to the snowbound Hattfjelldal airfield up the Vefsna valley. The defensive position had been helped by the demolition of the bridge over the river, but it was of little use as on 9 May, only four days after they had started their advance from Grong, the Norwegians were forced out by the Germans. A fall-back position for both Norwegians and Independent Company men was established, closer to Mosjöen at a point where the Björnaa river forms a lake and a long stretch of road is exposed to fire from the steep hillsides. No. 5 Independent Company had two platoons (100 strong) on one flank of the two Norwegian companies, while its third platoon defended the alternative approach along the line of the railway at the bridge over the Vefsna river. The bridge was later demolished. In the early morning of 10 May, the advance guard of the German Army appeared, cycling incautiously down the road. They were ambushed and around 50 Germans were killed. Soon after noon, German pressure along both road and rail routes drove this group back towards Mosjöen, about 10 miles away. Colonel Gubbins had hopes of taking up a new position on the outskirts of the town, but there was no natural line of defence, and both the British and the Norwegian commander concluded that a further withdrawal beyond Mosjöen would be necessary. Colonel Gubbins thereupon sent orders to No. 1 Company at Mo to safeguard the line of the Ranfjord. It was intended that the British-Norwegian withdrawal should be made as slowly as possible to delay the German advance and cause as many casualties as possible. This seemed a reasonable proposition, since the Germans had advanced a fair distance from Grong (which the British had originally thought to be impassable at that time of the year), and had extended and vulnerable lines of communication.

The Germans undertook a further operation on this day, which Norwegian historian Major General Ragnvald Roscher Nielsen, writing in 1947, described as "as audacious as the original invasion". A party of about 300 German troops had been embarked near Trondheim in the Norwegian coastal steamer *Nord-Norge*, which had a crew drawn from the German destroyers. After a 24-hour delay caused by a submarine alarm, the *Nord-Norge* left Trondheim fjord under the escort of two aircraft, and set its course north towards the Narvik area. The movement was observed by the Norwegian coastal watch in the early morning, and reported to British Naval HQ at Harstad. The first report was received at 1015, but it was not until 1155 that orders were sent to the only ships available - the anti-aircraft cruiser HMS *Calcutta*, which was with a convoy 50 miles west of Skomvaer Lighthouse, and the destroyer HMS *Zulu* at Skjelfjord. *Calcutta*, had she proceeded at once, alone, might have intercepted the enemy; but more than two hours elapsed before a second signal gave Mo as the possible destination, and in any case *Zulu* could not meet the cruiser earlier than 1700, off the Myken Lighthouse. The two ships were then about 40 miles north of the Ranfjord, which they entered behind the *Nord-Norge*.

By 1900, the *Nord-Norge* had completed its voyage, as its objective was Hemnesberget, 15 miles west of Mo on the seaward edge of the Hemnes peninsula. From here, the route between Mosjöen and Mo could be effectively cut. The arrival of the steamer was preceded by that of two *Dornier* seaplanes, which put ashore about 40 men with mortars and machine guns west of the town, and then dropped bombs on it. A platoon from No. 1 Independent Company put up some resistance, but they were outnumbered and outgunned and so could not realistically hold the town. They were forced to withdraw as best they could, by boat to Mo or to the neck of the peninsula at Finneid, where they were joined that night by the rest of No. 1 Company and by about 120 Norwegian troops with four heavy machine guns. Meanwhile, the two British ships arrived about 90 minutes behind the Germans and sunk the *Nord-Norge*, but not before two mountain guns had been landed as well as all its cargo of troops. In spite of this loss, the Germans kept this force supplied over the next few days by using seaplanes.

Meanwhile, Colonel Gubbins had already withdrawn No. 5 Company through No. 4 Company to a position north of Mosjöen, but more Germans now blocked any further moves in that direction . Mosjöen and the surrounding area therefore had to be abandoned, leaving the Germans free to improvise a forward air base in this area if they could. No. 4 Company was embarked in a small Norwegian steamer the same evening in the area around Mosjöen, with No. 5 Independent Company leaving the next morning at a point further down the fjord. The light AA section, which had originally accompanied the French to Mosjöen, was also embarked but had to spike its guns. They were landed at Sandnessjöen, on the north side of the large island at the mouth of the Vefsenfjord, where two destroyers made contact with them in the early morning of 12 May, and were brought into Bodø, some on destroyers and the rest on a local steamer. By 0400 on 11 May, Mosjöen was in German hands.

The reserve Norwegian detachments which had assembled at Mosjöen were then despatched to Mo by sea, but the battalion which was working with the Independent Companies went back overland from Mosjöen to Elsfjord, halfway to Mo. Here the road was split by a ferry route terminating at Hemnesberget, but it was not possible to land there. They had to leave the ferry at a point further down, on the road north from Korgen, which would bring them past the neck of the Hemnes peninsula to Mo. However, they had to leave most of their heavy equipment behind, with a consequential decline in their offensive and defensive capability.

But even before this disaster at Hemnesberget, Colonel Gubbins' initial report from Mosjöen had aroused serious concerns at Harstad, where General Ruge's liaison officer also had instructions to give a daily reminder about the importance of stemming the German advance from the south. Lord Cork's proposal that the southern front be reinforced, made on 9 May, was welcomed by General Mackesy, who that evening put the Scots and Irish Guards at short notice to move to Mo. Brigadier Fraser, who had now returned to duty after being wounded, was given command of all British troops in the area, and three companies of Scots Guards, with four 25 pdrs and four light anti-aircraft guns, landed at Mo in the early morning of 12 May. The ships conveying them fired on the wharf at Hemnesberget on their way. Although they included an anti-aircraft cruiser and a sloop, the weight of air attack, both at Mo itself and in the approaches through some 40 miles of narrow waters, was such that an agreed report was sent back, saying that other than anti-aircraft cruisers, large ships ought not to enter the fjord. Two further attempts were made to harass the enemy on the Hemnes peninsula by naval bombardment, but it was not deemed possible to meet the Army's request for ships to be kept in the area to hamper any German advance across or alongside the water.

The Norwegians had made an attack from Finneid against Hemnesberget on 11 May. They penetrated about halfway along the road between the two places but were then driven back by German gunfire. The recapture of Hemnesberget was considered again next day when the Scots Guards arrived, but Lieutenant Colonel Trappes-Lomax decided to await further reinforcements, establishing in the meantime a defensive position at

Stien, on the road which skirts the fjord between Finneid and Mo. The other possibility, that the Germans might cross from Hemnesberget to the north side of the Ranfjord to attack Mo from the west, was covered by the Norwegian reserve troops evacuated earlier from Mosjöen. Next day, the Germans had pushed so far across the peninsula that their mortars and heavy machine guns commanded the road to Finneid, along which the Norwegians who had made the detour from Elsfjord would have to pass. A counter-attack was launched which enabled the Norwegians to pass through, but on 14 May the Germans pressed forward again, and that evening, after some serious fighting, No. 1 Independent Company and the Norwegians abandoned Finneid and retired through the position at Stien.

By this time Brigadier Fraser, who received instructions from General Mackesy's successor, General Auchinleck, to maintain an advanced detachment at Mo as long as possible, was on his way down to view the situation. Having conferred with Lieutenant Colonel Trappes-Lomax and the newly appointed Norwegian area commander, Lieutenant Colonel R. Nielsen, he formed the view that the position in the Mo area was untenable. In the first place, the Navy could not maintain an adequate flow of reinforcements and supplies because of the air threat. There was no good alternative route of communication overland, since the road north from Mo to Bodø was a mountain road climbing well above the snow line. This could be dominated by the *Luftwaffe*, which was already operating in the skies above Bodø. Moreover, Lieutenant Colonel Trappes-Lomax said that he required another battalion if he was to hold Mo against serious attack. The Germans, however, were increasing their strength daily. Hemnesberget was being reinforced and supplied by seaplane. A German battalion was already using horse-drawn transport to make the difficult mountain crossing (which the thaw might soon render temporarily impassable) to Korgen from a point near Elsfjord, where the ferry and other boats had been withdrawn to delay them. Other German columns were reported north of Mosjöen. They had not yet been identified as troops of the 2nd Mountain Division under General Feuerstein, which the Führer had diverted from the attack in Western Europe and shipped to Trondheim as an additional division, with a special mission to penetrate at top speed towards Narvik. This meant that in the area the Germans now had five mountain infantry battalions and at least three troops of mountain artillery.

For the Allies the importance of holding on for as long as possible was evident both to Lord Cork and to General Auchinleck, while at the same time the Norwegian Commander-in-Chief, General Ruge, and the Divisional General Fleischer were renewing their representations that a further withdrawal would be disastrous. Attention was (at last) being focused on air power, or – for the Allies – the lack of it. Suitable airfields were becoming a priority and thoughts turned to a partly developed airfield site at Rösvik, 10 miles north-east of Mo. This was in German-held territory, though they did not appear to use this site (or Hattfjelldal) much. But there was still confusion as to how to achieve the aim of taking Narvik: demonstrated when, on 15 May, Brigadier Fraser reported that in his opinion to continue to hold Mo was "militarily unsound". Lord Cork, meanwhile, was informing the Admiralty of his feeling that the Allies must hold on and fight at Mo, since otherwise the whole Narvik situation would become precarious. There was also the unvoiced consideration of British prestige at stake. As Mr Churchill had commented in one of the several meetings about the position at Mosjöen, many miles further south, only 11 days earlier: "It would be a disgrace if the Germans made themselves masters of the whole of this stretch of the Norwegian coast with practically no opposition from us and in the course of the next few weeks or even days."

The position at Mo, already difficult, was made worse by two disasters occurring in quick succession at sea, beginning with the sinking of the Polish liner *Chrobry*, which was attacked by German dive bombers as she left the seaward extremity of the Lofoten Islands to steer across the Vestfjord.

On the morning of 13 May, the Polish Carpathian Brigade took over responsibility for the Ankenes peninsula, and so from all round the fjord the scattered units of the 24th Guards Brigade converged on Skaanland. The orders were for the battalions to sail at four-hour intervals: the Scots Guards first in two destroyers, then the Irish Guards in the *Chrobry*, and finally the South Wales Borderers in HMS *Effingham*. Three old river boats and one flat-bottomed barge put in to Liland to transport the Irish Guards and three times the normal reserve of ammunition. The barge was dangerously overloaded. The steamers were so top-heavy that men and kitbags had to be packed as ballast into the water-logged holds. All three steamers and the barge left Liland together and arrived alongside the *Chrobry* at 1700. Part of Brigade HQ, a battery of field gunners and some Fleet Air Arm officers were already on board, but no preparation had been made to load the Battalion. It was 0300 before the last man and box of ammunition were loaded.

"It is a hard thing to say", Captain M. Gordon-Watson of the Scots Guards wrote later, "but it is possible that this delay contributed to the loss of much valuable life when the ship was again bombed and hit". It certainly gave the Germans the intelligence that a troop ship was in the area and troops seemed to be on the move.

At 1830 hours the *Chrobry* steamed slowly down the fjord, followed by a German observation plane. When she reached the open sea, the *Chrobry* was sailing alone through the peaceful evening sunshine. The German aeroplane had disappeared; the naval escort, the destroyer *Wolverine* and the sloop *Stork*, were out of sight over the horizon. As the evening grew chilly, the Battalion went below to eat and sleep. The *Chrobry* was a new Polish motor ship, comfortable and well-provisioned. "This is the way to go to war," said one officer. "It's all very well," said Lieutenant Colonel Faulkner, "but it only needs one bomb. It would go through this ship like a hot knife through butter. I do not know whether our landing will be opposed or not, but I think it will be pretty sticky, particularly if the German aircraft spot us. We will land about four o'clock, so I will advise you all go to bed early and get some sleep while you can."

One of the survivors from the *Chrobry*, Captain D. West of the Cheshire Regiment, who was Staff Captain of the 24th Brigade, commented:

About 0015 on 15th May, three German *Heinkel* aeroplanes approached; one flew very low over the ship and secured direct hits or hits amidships. There was one violent explosion which brought everyone from their beds. The luxury state rooms containing most of the senior officers collapsed like a pack of cards, lights went out, the whole of the top decks amidships were immediately ablaze and very soon the main staircase seems to have disappeared. Some officers managed to extricate themselves and rescue others from beneath the wreckage of the cabins, but further rescue was out of the question owing to the dense black smoke which made both re-entry and visibility impossible.

Troops came up quickly to the promenade and boat deck assembly stations and the Polish crew helped to lower the first flight of boats, principally the ones aft owing to fire amidships, but one boat on the starboard side fell empty and was waterlogged. Some military personnel were able to get into these boats, but the moment they were ready for lowering, the Polish crew made a wild rush and got into them, leaving the military personnel almost without aid to lower any more boats.

I am told this may not have happened in other areas but it certainly did in mine at No. 3 assembly station.

Efforts were made to lower the second flight of boats with the aid of one Polish Officer or Petty Officer, but power was cut off and the electric winches were unworkable; the Herculean efforts of Guardsmen on hand winches proved of no avail. At this point, I think, Lieutenant Payne of the Fleet Air Arm gave me valuable advice not to attempt further to lower these boats. Some rafts were thrown overboard and the men, admirably controlled by the junior officers of the Irish Guards, were prevented from jumping into the water, as the ship did not seem to be in imminent risk of sinking, unless of course she exploded. The escorting vessels HMS *Wolverine* and HMS *Stork* were approaching fast from astern, whilst at the same time keeping the *Heinkels*, which were still attacking, at bay.

Stork stopped astern, firing her AA guns and taking up occupants of such boats as had been launched whilst *Wolverine* came alongside starboard abaft the bridge. Several seriously wounded men had by now been brought up and were lying on the deck; everything that could be done was being done to make them comfortable. We now removed a section of rails from the promenade deck aft and attached and lowered all available ropes, hawsers and baggage slings over the side of the ship to enable men to climb down to the destroyer's deck many feet below, at the same time calling a large party of men up to the boat deck to make use of the boats' falls for the same purpose.

The problem of the seriously wounded still remained and Lieutenant Payne devised a means of lowering them by attaching ropes round both men and stretchers. Several were lowered in this way until the destroyer's commander announced he would have to cast off. The only remaining living seriously wounded man, I think it was Major Potter, the ship's staff officer, was therefore carried up along to where the destroyer's bridge was level with the deck and the stretcher passed across to it. A hasty search of the decks revealed no more men, so after throwing down all spare clothing and blankets that could be found, we boarded the destroyer's bridge, and when the ship's captain and the Commodore had come down from the *Chrobry*'s bridge and done likewise we cast off. *Wolverine* launched her whaler to pick up any further survivors who might appear.

Throughout the whole of the abandon ship operations the conduct of both officers and men was admirable, despite the fact that at one time after the ship's crew had gone and the second flight of boats could not be launched, and the situation seemed pretty serious.

Aboard *Wolverine* everything humanly possible was done to make survivors comfortable and succour the wounded, the crew even stripping their own clothes to clothe those who had been in the water and all the while maintaining their anti-aircraft and anti-submarine defence.

The Commodore on the *Chrobry* was Rear Admiral Burke, he later wrote to the Admiralty:

The calm courage shown by the troops can hardly – if ever – have been surpassed and is best illustrated by the following: Embarked 2 a.m.; under frequent bombing attack all day cooped up at anchor – 300 or more were collected on the forecastle – whole midship part of the ship a raging furnace – enemy planes overhead – 50 tons of ammunition in the hold – rescuing destroyer alongside. Not a man moved until I gave the order, which was not until I judged that men from the rest of the ship had got off. When they did move, they did so at a deliberate walk, some even refusing to part with their rifles. It was naturally not possible to single out anyone particularly, but I did notice the very admirable conduct of the Roman Catholic Chaplain.

One of the Fleet Air Arm officers, Lieutenant Compston, said:

I turned in about 2230hrs and went to sleep almost immediately. The next thing I remember was the crack of machine guns and the roar of aircraft engines overhead. Familiarity truly breeds contempt, and my cabin companion and I decided it was no good getting up and hoped the enemy would miss us as he had done for the past few days. Unfortunately this was not the case, and no sooner had we turned over to go to sleep again than there was the most deafening roar I have ever heard or want to hear. The ship had been struck abaft by large calibre bombs – one at least incendiary. My cabin collapsed immediately, and the lights went out. I left the cabin and ran through the adjoining dining saloon – the floor of which was covered with glass and debris – cutting my feet rather badly, and on reaching the port side of the ship saw that she was already ablaze.

Lieutenant J. Gilliat, who shared a cabin with Lieutenant C. Scott, both of the Irish Guards, recalled:

He had the bottom bunk, because I am more agile than he. At about 2330 I was awakened by a bang, not a big one, as I thought it might be stores being moved. As my feet touched the floor, the lamp burst and glass flew around the room. I grabbed my watch and life-belt, put my feet into boots (unlaced) and went out into the passage, followed by Scott in similar undress. I must have looked like a slightly obscene pantomime dame. The passage was dark and thick with acrid smoke, it gripped one's throat. I thought we were done for.

"It was the unluckiest thing in the world that the bombs all landed near by the senior officers' cabins," wrote Captain Gordon-Watson. "I'm afraid the first one must have killed Jack Mathews and Freddie Lewin and the second or third the CO, John Bowen, Tommy Pain and Brian O'Neill." Guardsman Draper, the sentry at the head of the stairs, was killed at his post. Of the servants and orderlies sleeping in the corridor outside the cabins, Guardsman O'Connell had his arm broken and Armer was pinned to the ground, badly burnt. Guardsman Armer, the CO's orderly, extricated himself from the wreckage and struggled through the smoke to his cabin. There was no trace of Lieutenant Colonel Faulkner. Guardsman Allen dragged Major Gilbert-Denham out of his cabin and carried him up to a lifeboat. Captain D. Fitzgerald was having a shower when the first bomb exploded. He and his servant, Guardsman O'Shea, were trapped in the bathroom and had to get out into the sea through a porthole. Lieutenant F. Lewin, who shared his cabin, was killed in his sleep.

The fire spread rapidly, for the explosion had wrecked the sprinkler system. PSM Morrow and Guardsman Sullivan, the Battalion Fire Orderly, struggled to get the hoses working, but there was no water in the hydrants. "Theirs was a very creditable performance," said Lieutenant I. Powell-Edwards, "since this task appeared almost hopeless from the start." The crackle of .303 ammunition and the red and green flares of exploding Verey lights mingled with the steady firing of the AA barrage. The *Heinkels* circled overhead at a respectable height, "waiting to machine gun the boats", thought Lieutenant J. Gilliat gloomily. So, too, thought Lieutenant Compston, "but to our surprise they were gentlemanly enough not to machine gun us in the water as we expected. Their main interest seemed to be to take photographs."

After the first explosion, the Battalion was ordered up on deck. The fire divided the ship into two halves, with the result that the most of the men had to go forward and most of the officers aft. The companies filed up from their mess decks, in full kit, carrying their rifles and Bren guns. "Get on parade – face that way"- at the sound of RSM Stack's familiar voice the companies formed up en mass, Drill Sergeant Hoey in front, Drill Sergeant Peilow in rear. The sentries already on deck acted as markers. Only one man jumped overboard; he broke his neck on his lifebelt.

The lifeboats forward could not be lowered, for the power was cut off, the electric winches were unworkable and the hand winches proved temperamental. There was nothing to do but wait until the escorting destroyer came alongside. Father Cavanagh began to recite the Rosary. On a burning ship in the Arctic Circle, men said the prayers that they had learnt in the quiet churches and farmhouses of Ireland. Rescue parties searched the burning wreckage and brought the wounded up on deck. Sergeant Johnson, the Medical Sergeant, cleared an area on the promenade deck for an RAP (Regimental Aid Post) and there collected and tended the casualties. His first two casualties were the doctor, Captain O'Neill, and Captain McGildowny, both of whom were unconscious. Only four men were now reported missing - Guardsmen O'Donnell, Widdison, Killian and Tweed. Guardsman Callaghan – "Mushy" of No. 3 Company – knew that they must be trapped by fire down below in the hold. He threw a rope over the ship's side and swung from porthole to porthole until he discovered them, then hauled them out one by one up on to the deck.

The winches aft were still working, so the Polish crew lowered the first flight of lifeboats. These were already full with mixed loads of soldiers, sailors and wounded. Lieutenant Compston, with his boatload:

> We cast off and drifted away from the *Chrobry* to see the escorting destroyer, HMS *Wolverine*, approaching fast to come along the starboard side. We headed for the other ship – the sloop *Stork*. At this moment I must praise the courage and devotion to duty of the men of your Regiment who, in spite of finding themselves in an element which is certainly not their own, showed the greatest calm – many of them carrying their kitbags and rifles to the lifeboats and waiting patiently to embark – without the slightest sign of panic. We had great difficulty in parting them from their weapons.

No mere naval disaster could shake the effect of the Guards Depot training, reinforced by a sergeant shouting at them: "Take care of those rifles, they are government property." Lieutenant Compston continued:

> In the lifeboat they were magnificent, and once they had been told to obey orders of one officer, they never faltered. I shall always be grateful to one Guardsman who gave me his battle dress tunic to put over my cold and wet silk pyjamas which was all I stood up in. Another Guardsman gave me his scarf and they all did their best to keep the most scantily clad of us from freezing in the incredible cold. We had rather difficulty in getting the Polish crew to row and do as they were told – possibly this was because I was a British officer and they had their own ideas —but on the whole they were calm. Eventually in the crowded lifeboat we managed to get Guardsmen to man the oars. They did as we asked them and after about thirty minutes in the water we managed to row alongside the sloop *Stork*. They still behaved with the greatest reserve, obeying every calmly given order of the NCOs. As the boat was crowded there was a great possibility that if they disembarked too quickly she might have overturned.

The crew lowered the second flight of boats aft while they could, and then slid down the rope after them. Some men, led by the Quartermaster, who ruptured himself, followed them and swam to the half-empty boats.

Lieutenant B. Eugster also started to go down a rope, very slowly in the orthodox PT style, hand over hand. A solid block of six Polish sailors slid down on top of him and swept him into the sea. He was wearing bright pyjamas when he went into the water; he came up stark naked. Lieutenant H. Young could not swim; Lieutenant P. Fitzgerald did not like the look of the water; Lieutenant C. Scott questioned the Polish Captain and learnt that it would take the ship 24 hours to burn herself out and sink, though she might blow up at any time. The three of them decided to stay on board and stop anyone else from sliding down into the water. If the ship blew up, everyone would go into the water anyway; if it did not, they might as well keep warm and dry.

By the time the escort came up there were some 20 heads bobbing about in the sea, for the fire amidships was spreading and forcing isolated men overboard. The *Stork* launched her whaler to pick them up. She herself stood off astern, engaging the bombers with her guns and taking on board the lifeboats. HMS *Wolverine* came alongside starboard.

Commander R. Craske on *Wolverine* commented:

> We closed on their burning and sinking ship. I never before realised what the discipline of the Guards was. We got a gangway shipped forward and the men were ordered to file off on to us. There was no confusion, no hurry, and no sign of haste or flurry. I knew that there might be only a matter of minutes in which to get them off. I had four ropes fixed so as to hurry up the transfer. They continued to file steadily off in one line. I cursed and swore at them, but they had orders to file, and they filed. I saw someone who seemed to me to be a young officer and in no measured terms I told him to get them off by all four ropes. In a second they conformed to this order by one of their own officers, still steadily and without fuss or confusion. Their conduct in the most trying circumstances, in the absence of senior officers, on a burning and sinking ship, open at any moment to a new attack, was as fine as, or finer than, the conduct in the old days of the soldiers on the *Birkenhead*. (In 1852 HM Troopship *Birkenhead* was transporting troops to South Africa when she ran into difficulties and the order came to abandon ship. There were not enough lifeboats and so the soldiers on board stood fast and allowed the women and children to go first. This incident led to the 'women and children first' call on abandoning ship and gained the soldiers much credit for their chivalrous action.) It may interest you to know that 694 were got on board in 16 minutes.

Two years later, Admiral Craske wrote to the Regimental Lieutenant Colonel:

> You will not know me. My son, Commander R. Craske, RN, was in command of HMS *Wolverine* in May, 1940. He lost his life in HMS *Barham* in November, 1941, and amongst the papers he had treasured is your letter to him referring to the rescue of the Battalion from the *Chrobry*. He never mentioned the affair till the following December, when he was awarded the DSC, and then told us very little, except that any rescue would have been impossible but for the superb discipline of the men of the Battalion.

The letter mentioned was a message from the CO of the 1st Irish Guards, dated 16 May 1940, which read:

> I wish to convey to you the deepest gratitude and admiration of all ranks for the bravery and skill displayed by officers and crews of HMS *Wolverine* and *Stork*. It was entirely due to your gallant action that so many lives were saved.

"The sailors were wonderful," wrote an officer, "and made coffee and cocoa and gave us clothes. We had a seven hour journey back to Harstad and were bombed all the way. Not a good ending."

The destroyer *Wolverine* arrived at Harstad first and discharged its load of survivors on the quay. "What a funny feeling it is to have nothing except what you stand up in." The Guardsmen came ashore wrapped in blankets and naval greatcoats over pyjamas and dungarees. Stretcher bearers carried the wounded off first, and laid them in a tin shed. From there, the worst cases, Major Gilbert-Denham, Guardsman Corbett and Guardsman Sliney, were taken straight to the Base Hospital. Drill Sergeant Peilow jumped ashore and doubled away to look for a square. He found one and put out company markers, while RSM Stack ordered the men straight on parade. They fell in – "a proper Battalion parade" – and waited for the other boat to arrive. The Scots Guards RQMS, still at Harstad with their Base Details, with real charity, sent down containers of tea and mounds of "wads" (military slang for buns). The Officers and the Company Sergeant Majors waited on the quay for the *Stork* to come in. Everybody was desperately hoping that Lieutenant Colonel Faulkner would be on board. As the *Stork* came in, they saw Captain Gordon-Watson in pyjamas standing on the bridge, and shouted enquiries. "Where's Colonel Faulks?" "No sign." "Jack?" "Never seen."

The Company Sergeant Majors collected their men off the sloop and called the roll on the square. The Battalion was then marched out of the town to the village of Ervik. The attack on the *Chrobry* could have been a whole lot worse; the fatal casualties only amounted to 12. These were as follows: Major C. Bowen, 44, 15 May 1940 (Narvik New Cemetery, grave XI K 3); Guardsman J. Corbett, 26, 16 May 1940 (Harstad Cemetery, grave Allied plot D4); Guardsman E. Draper, 29, 15 May 1940 (NKG Brookwood Memorial to the Missing, Panel 8 Column 3); Captain J. Durham-Matthews, 36, 15 May 1940 (NKG Brookwood Memorial to the Missing, Panel 8 Column 2); Guardsman J. Elliot, 24: 14 May 1940 (Harstad Cemetery, grave Allied plot F4); Lieutenant Colonel W. Faulkner, 42, 14 May 1940 (Narvik New Cemetery, grave XI K 5); Major T. Hacket-Pain, 40, 14 May 1940 (NKG Brookwood Memorial to the Missing, Panel 8 Column 2); Lieutenant F. Lewin, 25, 15 May 1940 (NKG Brookwood Memorial to the Missing, Panel 8 Column 2); Guardsman D. McLoughlin, 20, 15 May 1940 (NKG Brookwood Memorial to the Missing, Panel 8 Column 3); Captain B. O'Neill (age not given), 14 May 1940, (NKG Brookwood Memorial to the Missing, Panel 8 Column 2); Guardsman W. Rigby, 20, 15 May 1940 (Harstad Cemetery, grave Allied plot E5); and Guardsman E. Sliney, 38, 15 May 1940 (Harstad Cemetery, grave Allied plot D5).

Another result of the sinking of the *Chrobry* – which was scuttled by aircraft from the carrier HMS *Ark Royal* on 16 May - was that when news of its loss was received by HMS *Somali* at Mo, she went to render what assistance she could. On the way *Somali* was bombed and suffered such damage that she had to return to Scapa Flow; Brigadier Fraser, who was on board, having to transfer across to HMS *Curlew* to continue to Harstad. However, it was clear to General Auchinleck that Fraser did not appear to be too well. He managed to get a medical board convened, which decided that he was unfit and he was ordered home.

On the evening of 17 May, the second naval incident occurred when the cruiser

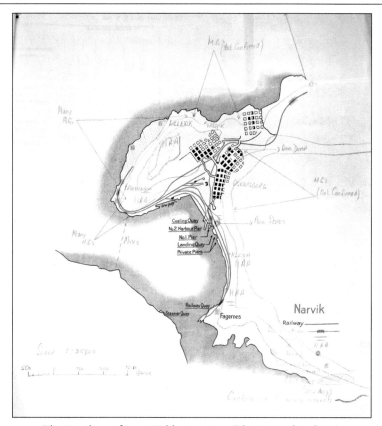

The Narvik area from a Welsh viewpoint. (The National Archives)

HMS *Effingham*, carrying 24th Brigade Headquarters and the South Wales Borderers to the same destination, ran aground whilst steaming at 23 knots. Its log book records:

> Ran aground at 23 knots on Faksen Shoal in Vestfjord, near Bliksvoer, when taking short cut. Position 67° 17' N 13° 58' E. Troops transferred to the cruiser HMS *Coventry* by the destroyer HMS *Echo* but equipment including Bren Gun carriers were lost.

The other escort ships were the cruiser HMS *Cairo* and the destroyer HMS *Matabele*. This is from the 2nd South Wales Borderers war diary about this time:

> 15th May. Mild air activity. Warning order to move at 1030. No mention of a relief. Discussions with French re re-organising position. Eventually got a message saying Poles were relieving us. CO protested re timings as it would mean embarking in plain view of enemy aircraft as relief could not possibly be completed before late in the morning.
>
> 16th May. Puffers with Poles appeared about 0200. All baggage stacked at the

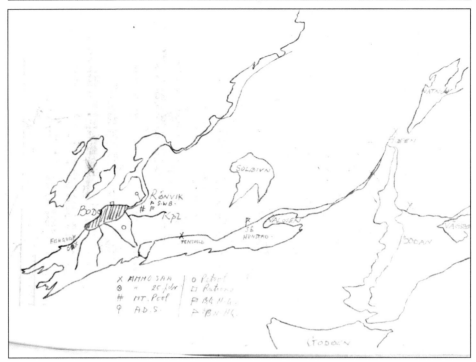

Another view of the Narvik area from the 2nd South Wales Borderers. (The National Archives)

pier. Started embarking 0430. Managed to complete the handing over of the positions on the heights to the very weary Poles by 1100. Final embarkation effected about noon. Discovered (no orders received) we were to board *Effingham* at 2000 at Harstad. Very pleasant journey, a perfect day, took about 6 hours. A good many enemy aircraft about but there were ships about which offered more tempting targets. Almost continuous raids in Harstad itself. The first companies taking refuge outside the town before re-embarking. Brigade HQ and 147th Field Ambulance are with us. Carriers and MT personnel on board. An alarming quantity of stores which were still in process of loading when we sailed at 0400. The tide will only permit ships to be alongside for 3 hours at Bodø, where we presume we are going.

17th May. Harstad 0400. Air attack during the night. An uneventful trip until about 2000 when we hit a rock doing about 23 knots. Ship started to settle forward and the order to Abandon Ship was given. *Echo* came alongside and took all troops and a very limited amount of equipment off. Luckily it was very calm and we had no visitors from the air. Everything went off very smoothly. From *Echo* we were transferred to HMS *Coventry* while the destroyer went back for the crew, which they took off. Only saw one man in the water – Private Kimberly, who was pulled out none the worse. *Effingham* said to be drifting towards shore.

18th May. Harstad 0700. Landed at Harstad – no one seemed to have done very much about us. CO went ashore and tried to arrange for breakfast, which

Copy of telegram.

From F.O. to Mr Vereker.

No. 86 February 29th.

Following for M.A. from DMI :

Much warmer weather in Finland is reported by press. Please report (if?) there are signs of early thaw and xx what effect of such will be.

Halifax.

Replied — no signs at present.

A typical request from London. (The National Archives)

we eventually got at the Irish Guards billets, where they were very helpful. After many orders and counter-orders we got into billets at Borgenes about 19 kms from Harstad, with D Company at Ervik about 16 kms away.

A personal account involving this incident comes from one of the Borderers company commanders, Captain C. Cox:

There was a frightful crash and I personally thought we had been torpedoed, much later I was to realise a torpedo was a very much different matter. The ship remained upright but had struck an "uncharted rock" and her bottom was torn out. The Captain ordered all watertight doors to be closed and so we were unable to get any kit together – then came the order "abandon ship" and a destroyer came alongside and took us off. I was told later that *Effingham* was the first cruiser lost in the war.

Sergeant Adams recalled that a rumour went round that the pilot was a Quisling and had deliberately run them aground!

An idea of the background to the Scots Guards' arrival at Mo and some of the difficulties faced there can be gauged from the regiment's war diary:

10th May 1940.

1000. Major Graham witnessed a rehearsal by Right Flank of their proposed landing at Narvik. This landing entailed a climb of 150 yards up a steep slope through snow which was in places over four feet deep. The rehearsal was not so well carried out as that of B Company yesterday, but it is only fair to say that the conditions for Right Flank were more difficult than those of B Company.

1400. Cipher message received, ordering the Battalion to be prepared to move immediately and to remain at 2 hours notice until further orders. No information was given to show whether this was a local move or a withdrawal from Norway.

1600. Lieutenant Colonel T. B. Trappes-Lomax arrived back from Bogen, having handed over command of 24th Guards Brigade to Lieutenant Colonel W. D. Faulkner 1st Irish Guards.

1800. A telephone message from Force HQ at Harstad ordering Battalion to be ready to embark at Skaanland at 2300 tonight.

15 lorries were put at the disposal of the Battalion for moving baggage and the trek to Skaanland began. Personnel of Left Flank left their billets at 2030 and Right Flank at 2130 to march to the quay, arriving at 2300 and 2330 respectively. The road about two miles east of Skaanland was in an extremely bad condition and it was fully expected that the loaded vehicles would be unable to get through the mud. All, however, crossed this bad patch safely.

2400. Embarkation was carried out as follows:-

(a) Two platoons of Right Flank in HMS *Hesperus*

(b) B Company in SS *Margot*

(c) Battalion HQ, HQ Company and Left Flank in HMS *Enterprise*

(d) One platoon of Right Flank in HMS *Fleetwood*

None of the above vessels could come alongside the quay and all personnel and baggage had to be conveyed to them on local puffer boats.

11th May 1940.

0300. Embarkation was complete. Role of 1st Scots Guards. The Battalion less C Company, about whom there has been no news for several days, was to proceed to Mo, a port some 300 miles south of Skaanland and 60 miles south of Bodø. The chief importance of this port lies in the fact that from it runs the only road at present in the hands of the Allies which leads to Sweden. The Battalion is ordered to hold Mo at all costs. The Operational Order for the move to Mo was received in a cipher message which had been wrongly coded, but a printed copy in 'clear' reached Battalion HQ before embarkation took place, together with a few maps. The remainder of the maps were put on board SS *Margot* at Harstad.

Lieutenant Colonel T. B. Trappes-Lomax, who received further instructions over the telegraph, after having been told that the only other Allied troops at Mo were an irregular force of approximately 200 officers and men under a Colonel Gubbins beside some Norwegians, requested firstly that C Company should rejoin the Battalion at Mo, and secondly that 1st Irish Guards should be despatched from Bogen as quickly as possible to reinforce the garrison at Mo.

Lieutenant Colonel T B Trappes-Lomax formed a plan prior to his recce, whereby 1st Scots Guards was to take up a defensive position some 8 miles south-west of Mo, with its right flank on the sea and its left flank on the side of a glacier. The remainder of the day was spent at sea. There was a strong wind which produced quite a lot of seasickness. The officers and the men in the *Hesperus* and *Enterprise* were looked after with true Naval hospitality, but the same could not be said for those on board SS *Margot*.

12th May 1940.

0400. *Enterprise* shelled the town of Hemnes and set alight to a house which was believed to contain German troops and then continued up the fjord towards Mo.

0500. Anchored off Mo. It was essential to disembark men and baggage as quickly as possible owing to the extreme likelihood of enemy aircraft attack.

0745. All baggage and personnel had landed. The bulk of the baggage was left on the pier to be loaded on transport later.

Lieutenant Colonel T. B. Trappes-Lomax had left the *Enterprise* early in order to carry out a recce and had decided after his recce to hold a position in the Stien area 317 6615 with two companies (Right and Left Flank) forward and B Company in reserve just in advance of Battalion HQ at Skjaaneset 1½ miles to the north.

One company of Colonel Gubbins' force is holding a position at the eastern edge of the peninsula across to Hemnes.

1030. All companies were by now out of the town marching towards their positions, with the exception of the baggage party on the quay, when six German bombers were seen approaching from the south-west. Having circled the quay once they dropped three bombs, one of which narrowly missed the SS *Margot*. The warships fired very rapidly at the bombers, who quickly withdrew without causing any damage. They launched a second attack about 15 minutes later; this time they changed their tactics and commenced to dive bomb. The warships got under way and they commenced fire, zig-zagging about the fjord whilst doing so, and two of the aircraft were seen to falter and afterwards came to earth, apparently out of action, hits having been scored.

13th May 1940.

Consolidated Dalsklubben position. B Company sent to Langeset for defence of quay at Mo against enemy landings. Second Lieutenant Rose with one section went to Finneid to assist Independent Company.

14th May 1940.

1000. Lieutenant Colonel T. B. Trappes-Lomax made recce Yttern position and B Company in billets at Mo for defence of quay. Withdrawal from Finneid fixed for 15th/16th May.

1730. Enemy from Hemnes attacked Finneid and No. 3 Independent Company were ordered to withdraw, covered by RA.

1900. Destroyer arrived and bombarded Hemnes. Battalion signallers attempted to get in touch in order to divert destroyer to Finneid Fjord. Independent Company withdrew without casualties and came under command of 1st Scots Guards as reserve company. Second Lieutenant Rose acted as rear party for their withdrawal and was of great assistance.

15th May 1940.

1100. Much aerial activity. Enemy aircraft brought down by Bofors. Gunner escaped by parachute. Pilot badly injured, but both taken prisoner with valuable information. Brigadier Fraser arrived night 14th/15th and after short stay was bombed on the way out and returned to England. Lieutenant Colonel T. B. Trappes-Lomax, now in command of the British Forces at Mo, held a conference at Grubben in the evening; position anything but satisfactory.

The position would shortly deteriorate. Trappes-Lomax was undoubtedly not the only person who felt the position was "anything but satisfactory". Back in London they were still getting the impression that not a lot was happening in northern Norway, but it is probably fair to say that events in Belgium and France were of far more significance and swamped any attention that might have been given to Scandinavia. Now that he had established his command, Lieutenant-General Auchinleck felt able, on 16 May, to send his demands for extra resources to London, as follows:

Provided the situation generally remained unchanged and that no serious threat of aggression developed from Russia through Finland or from Germany through Sweden, it should be possible to maintain the integrity of northern Norway with the forces outlined below, and, as well, develop a limited offensive so as to deny the air base at Mosjöen to the enemy.

Forces Required.

(a) Sea.

Four cruisers

Six destroyers

Four escort vessels

Twelve anti-submarine trawlers

Two submarines

Auxiliary vessels as at present

(b) Land

One Divisional Cavalry Regiment

One Squadron Armoured Cars

One Mounted Infantry Unit (Lovat Scouts)

Five Batteries Field Artillery

Two Batteries Medium Howitzers

Thirteen Batteries (104 guns) Heavy Anti-Aircraft Artillery

Eight Batteries (96 guns) Light Anti-Aircraft Artillery

Five Companies Engineers

Seventeen Infantry Battalions

One Machine Gun Battalion

(c) Air

Two Squadrons Hurricane fighters

One bomber Squadron
One Army Co-operation Squadron

Auchinleck added in this message that his first objective, namely denying the movement of iron ore through Narvik,

> … seemed already to have been achieved by the destruction of the facilities at the port, partly by the Germans and partly by naval bombardment; secondly, that the interference of ore to Germany through Lulea did not seem to be a practical proposition unless the active and full co-operation of the Swedish armed forces could be assured; and that therefore the third object, namely the maintenance of the integrity of northern Norway, seemed to be the only one of the three that required immediate consideration.

The answer from London arrived the next day from the Chiefs of Staff: "Owing to events in France and Belgium, your force will be limited to 12 French and 3 British Battalions, ten Independent Companies, disproportionate artillery, engineers and services, 48 heavy and 60 light anti-aircraft guns, one Hurricane Squadron, one Gladiator Squadron and possibly, one Army Co-operation Squadron."

Meanwhile, further south around Mo, the Scots Guards were coming under increasing German pressure. On 16 May, B Company occupied a position to the left of Yttern with Norwegian troops on its right. The Battalion HQ was moved to a new position in a quarry, and from advance positions it was reported back that six seaplanes landed at Finneid. They were thought to have brought more troops into the area. Trappes-Lomax, feeling his unit was rather exposed in the face of a German attack, therefore ordered the Blasklubben bridge to be blown up, which it duly was. According to the war diary, a *Junkers* flying boat was shot down on the far side of the fjord and a patrol from the Guards was sent to capture the crew who had been seen to struggle ashore. However, the Norwegians beat them to it and took four prisoners.

The rest of that day and the next, up to about 1400, was fairly quiet. Then a German bicycle patrol was seen coming from the direction of Finneid, but was stopped in its tracks by artillery fire from the few 25 pdrs supporting the Guards. At 1830 there was an attack in greater strength. The war diary records:

> All went well to begin with and many casualties inflicted as the Germans attempted to cross the broken bridge with planks. Estimated at over 100 dead. Enemy field gun, mortars and machine guns established on high ground across the river and it was very noticeable, that their fire was chiefly directed at nodal points such as the old Battalion HQ, Company HQ and signal exchange. Forward movement became most difficult owing to machine gun fire along the road and forward slopes of the position.
>   Night 17th/18th.
>   Enemy attack developed frontally and along the valley to our left front. Parachutists were reported in Lundenget valley where C Echelon were located.

Major Graham reported the serious situation to HQ and B Company were moved up to hold a covering position in front of Lundenget at about 2359. About 0200 18th May, enemy had enveloped the left of Left Flank and fierce fighting took place at close quarters in the woods. The Tommy gun and their light equipment gave the Germans a marked advantage and Left Flank, though fighting magnificently, especially 16 Platoon encouraged by Lieutenant Ramsey, who had been wounded, suffered considerable casualties. Lord Garnock was also wounded and Left Flank, now completely surrounded from their left and the rear, were forced to withdraw. All forward communication had been cut in the early stages in spite of the efforts of Captain Sanderson, aided particularly by Guardsman Howard to maintain them. A line still worked, however, to Force HQ and Major Graham was ordered to withdraw.

The Germans had built up a force of about 1,750 men in this area, giving them local superiority in numbers To counter these troops, the Guards had positioned two companies at Stien itself, where the small river Dalselva empties into the fjord, and their third company and the Independent Company placed farther back on the road towards Mo. The four 25 pdrs were also sited in the rear. The Germans suffered a good many casualties at the bridge itself, but then made a thrust down the river valley, which they had approached over the snowbound mountains from a point south of Finneid, collecting skis from farms as they went. Because of a lack of satisfactory equipment, the Guards had not been able either to get to, or put positions on the heights, in spite of local warnings, and three small Norwegian ski detachments, which were supposed to watch the flank, were of little effect. The Germans also dropped paratroops on the mountainside nearer Mo, and these developed a subsidiary flank attack at Lundenget. Along the Dalselva valley the fight continued through the short twilit night, with the Germans making full use of their mobility and firepower as they pressed along the north side of the valley towards the road, until at about 0200 the Scots Guards were forced to fall back through the reserve position near Lundenget, where their third company still guarded the road to Mo.

Brigadier Gubbins had arrived on the scene during the night, having been appointed with an acting rank to command the troops in the Bodø-Mo area in place of Brigadier Fraser. After a telephone conversation with Lieutenant-General Auchinleck, Gubbins gave orders for the retirement to continue to the north of Mo. The information was conveyed to the Norwegians by Lieutenant Colonel Trappes-Lomax, who said that he had been outflanked by superior German forces and had lost two companies.

The Scots Guards war diary has the following illuminating comment for 0230 on 18 May:

Orders were issued for a withdrawal towards Mo, Left Flank and Right Flank coming first, covered by Independent Company, who were in turn covered by Battalion HQ. This was successfully carried out with few casualties and the Battalion passed through B Company position at about 0430. All kit etc., had to be left behind as there was no transport in which to remove it. There is little doubt that enemy troops had been collecting in the valleys leading to the position for some days before the attack, which was admirably timed and took place from all directions, simultaneously. These troops were probably landed by parachute but although the continual arrival of seaplanes had been reported daily, no action either of an offensive or recce nature had been possible, owing to the complete absence of any air support whatsoever.

About 0600 orders were received to delay enemy advance on Mo and after recce with company commanders Major Graham ordered a position to be held on the ridge north of Lundenget; at the same time a message was sent to B Company to come into Battalion reserve behind this line. This message failed to reach Major Elwes and no further contact was maintained with his company as the enemy had penetrated between his position and the rest of the Battalion. C Echelon had been evacuated from Lundenget, but as only a few broken-down lorries were available everything but rations and SAA had to be abandoned.

Whilst the British were not in headlong retreat, the Germans had certainly caused chaos. The men cannot be blamed for this; with the absence of proper winter warfare equipment, little artillery support and no air cover, it was an all but impossible situation. A fighting withdrawal was what was intended, and it was only due to the discipline of the Guards that this was to some extent achieved. The Guards war diary continues:

18th May 0900. Lieutenant Colonel Trappes-Lomax visited Battalion HQ in a wood outside Mo and ordered a further withdrawal north of the town. The enemy had reached Landnget area about 1200 and there was considerable machine gun and mortar fire. In spite of this the withdrawal was carried out successfully, with the exception of B Company with whom no contact had been made. PSM Washington covered the withdrawal of the forward companies from a post established on the road. By his splendid example and gallant stand, he enabled these companies to withdraw towards Mo while the Independent Company made their way into the town down the side of a precipitous mountain. Elements of Battalion HQ again acted as rear party through Mo and at 1500 hours the two bridges over the River Rana were blown by Major Graham's order. The enemy entered Mo between 1500 and 1530. One incident is worthy of note, when two Germans swam, presumably with a machine gun, in an endeavour to land in the rear of PSM Washington's post; both were shot. The Battalion had suffered approximately 70 casualties and in addition the whole of B Company was missing.

1500 to 2000. A long weary march of 10 miles brought the Battalion to Sandstraein after passing through a covering position held at Rosvold by C Company, who had hurriedly been brought up in MT, from Bodø, 130 miles to the north. A total distance of 15 miles was covered during the day, throughout which a succession of rear guard actions had been fought.

The British strategy for the area was in tatters and it was now a case of damage limitation. The Scots Guards group spent the night in Sandstraein and left on the next day, 19 May, marching from about 0930 until 1600. They rested until about midnight and then carried on to Storvold, a total distance of about 20 miles, and arrived there in the early hours.

However, there was good news in that Major Elwes had succeeded in extracting B Company from the clutches of the Germans, after hard fighting and marching over the mountains, mainly knee-deep in snow. They turned up south of the River Rana in the vicinity of Sjseon. Meanwhile, the rest of the Battalion had crossed the Rana, but this was a tortuous affair as there were only three boats available and each could only carry three men. B Company rejoined their comrades on 19 May, and had only suffered four casualties during their engagement.

On 20 May, Lieutenant Colonel Trappes-Lomax and Major Graham attended a conference with Brigadier Gubbins at Krokstranden. At this they learned that orders had come from Harstad that they were now to conduct a fighting withdrawal towards Bodø, about 100 miles to the north. This, it appears, was greeted with dismay, as when looking at the route on a map, it was a single road with no possibility of an alternative way, no cover and an easy target for any German aircraft once the withdrawal had started. Trappes-Lomax took back command from Graham and, after a quick recce with the company commanders, three positions were chosen to set up ambushes, to slow down the German advance. Battalion HQ was set up at Krokstranden and the companies were in position by around midnight. The first contact was not long in coming when a German bicycle patrol bumped into the C Company position. With the exception of German air activity, 21 May appears to have been a fairly quiet day. The war diary records: "No sign of British fighters whose help has been promised daily." An attack came in from the Germans at around 2100, at "Position A", an area held by Right Flank and C Company; after some skirmishing, they withdrew to "Position C on the edge of the snow belt".

The Official History of the Norway Campaign gives a description of the area that the Scots Guards group were fighting in and the general situation as follows:

The first part of the long route to be traversed follows the valley of the Rana in a generally north easterly direction for fifty-five miles. It then descends again by a second valley system in a more northerly direction to where the Saltdal debouches into the fjords leading out to Bodø. The distance from the watershed to Rognan on the Saltdalsfjord is about forty-five miles, making about a hundred miles in all. Population is very thin even in the lowest reaches of the respective valleys; the barrenness of the mountain plateau between may be imagined from the fact that it lies within the Arctic Circle and includes a belt of perpetual snow. The German advance was not, at first, pressed hard: the demolition of the bridges imposed a serious obstacle, and the speed with which Mo had come into their hands had probably something of the effect of a windfall. Thus the British force (less the Independent Company, which was carried straight through to Rognan) was able to spend the second day after its withdrawal from Mo resting about thirty-two miles from the town in a position covered by the freshly arrived company at Messingsletten bridge. At this juncture Lieutenant Colonel Trappes-Lomax received orders from General Auchinleck, saying: "You have now reached good position for defence. Essential to stand and fight … I rely on Scots Guards to stop the enemy". The Colonel maintained, however, that it would be throwing away the only battalion available for immediate defence if a major stand were attempted before his men were safely across the vulnerable area of the snow belt, beginning about twenty miles up the valley. After reference to General Headquarters by telephone, Brigadier Gubbins issued modified instructions for "hitting hard" and withdrawing only if there was "serious danger to the safety" of the force.

By midnight three defence lines had been manned, where the wide and rather featureless floor of the upland valley seemed most suitable. The enemy did not attack in earnest until the evening of the next day (21st May), when they outflanked our first line and followed up as far as the main position at Krokstrand, where the road crosses the river and a demolished bridge was defensible from good cover on the far side. But this likewise was held only for a few hours, until the Germans were able to enfilade it from higher ground on their side of the river, while it was also being machine gunned from the air. It took the enemy (whose force included two bridging columns) one day to build a new bridge here in the wilds, and the British troops were not seriously pressed in their withdrawal to their third position, from which they moved in small parties that evening across the plateau, where the road for twenty-three miles ran between steep walls of snow. Three Bren gun carriers which had been salvaged from HMS *Effingham* successfully screened the embussing. Thus the attempt to stop the enemy in what General Auchinleck called "the narrow defile north of Mo" had been abandoned. As in so many other instances, German air supremacy played a large part – not so much in the actual assault on our positions, but in providing unhampered reconnaissance of our movements and in restricting within the narrowest limits the use of our lines of communication back to Bodø.

In the early hours of 22 May, Position B was attacked by the Germans, who managed, using their skis and bicycles, to move round the Guards' Left Flank Company on the far side of the river. At 0430, both Left Flank and B Companies withdrew, Left Flank to an intermediate position about a mile back, with B Company another two miles further back. There was no further contact with the enemy in these new positions and both companies withdrew further. The first to move was Left Flank at 1300, with B Company at 1700. They were moved in commandeered buses to Viskiskoia. Second Lieutenant Anderson, using two of the dried-out carriers and helped by some Independent Company men, gained recognition in the war diary:

> … played an important role as rear party to the Battalion MT column from the edge of the snow belt to Viskiskoia and from there during the long march to Pothus. This officer's courage and ability undoubtedly helped to secure the safe withdrawal of the Battalion by engaging cyclist patrols. He was continuously in action for about 70 hours and his conduct is worthy of the highest praise.

The journey back to Viskiskoia was also remarkable because no German aircraft appeared, unlike previous days. Had they done so, it is highly likely a large number of casualties would have been sustained.

The war diary for 22 May continues:

> The journey was accomplished without incident although during the previous two days every car crossing the snow belt had been chased and machine gunned from the air. Major Graham met companies on their arrival and showed them their areas and the Battalion was in position by midnight, with No. 2 Independent Company under command on the right flank. The high ground on the right of the position constituted a severe menace, but after a consultation with the officers of the Indian Army, it was agreed that it was not applicable for the Independent Company to hold and maintain themselves across the river on a succession of false crests. The men were utterly exhausted and a certain demoralisation had set in, in consequence of fatigue, loss of kit, a succession of rear guard actions and continuous menace from the air, which invariably disclosed every position to the enemy and enabled him without interference to harass the Battalion and base his plans on certain knowledge.

New positions were taken up at Viskiskoia, where the road crosses to the east bank of the river as it descends towards the Saltdal. Most of the Guards were deployed to cover the demolished bridge, while No. 3 Independent Company, which had marched up from Rognan, supported by a few Norwegian ski troops, was posted on the far side, high up and well in front, to deter the enemy from a flank advance.

On 23 May, a somewhat disturbing development for the Scots Guards occurred. Lieutenant Colonel Trappes-Lomax received a telephone call at Storjord from Brigadier Gubbins. When he returned early in the afternoon, it was with the news that he had to hand over command. The war diary records:

> … informed Major Graham that he was to command the Battalion while he (Lieutenant Colonel Trappes-Lomax) was to report to Harstad on the grounds that he had failed to carry out his orders. This crushing blow took place in the middle of an enemy attack and it is hardly to be wondered at that the morale of both officers and men was still further shaken by the loss of a CO for whose personality and ability everyone had the highest respect and in whom everyone had the greatest confidence.

This German attack was supported by low-flying attacks from a single aircraft and by mortar fire. Two of the Bofors guns were out of action and the Scots Guards had only one 3in mortar left (which did some damage); the field guns could give only very limited support. By 1600, the Independent Company had been driven back, so the position of the Scots Guards was once again in danger of being outflanked. At around 1800, therefore, Brigadier Gubbins gave the order for another retirement to Major Graham. (Gubbins had, as you have read, been given local temporary rank of Brigadier, so future references to him will be in his new rank unless quoting direct from a war diary: for example, the Scots Guards still called him Colonel Gubbins.) The Scots Guards war diary records this as follows:

On realising the situation Colonel Gubbins told Major Graham at 1800 that he could withdraw to a position at Storjord. The withdrawal began at 2000 and in spite of enfilade, sniper and machine gun fire, was successfully completed by 2359, at which time the Battalion had occupied the Storjord position and the bridge had been destroyed. During this action the work of Lieutenant Petre and Lieutenant Burgess RAMC is worthy of special note: casualties were evacuated in the very inadequate transport by a succession of journeys along a road subjected to enemy fire.

The situation did not improve much on the following day, with German aircraft still ruling the skies and machine gunning targets as they saw them. The new CO of the Scots Guards had a lucky escape when his car was riddled with bullets while he was sleeping inside. Fortunately he was not hit, but it would have been a rude awakening! Whilst plans to withdraw further were being drawn up, the Brigade Major of the 24th Brigade imparted the news that any withdrawals would have to be delayed for as long as possible in order that the 1st Irish Guards could be brought into position at Pothus. Major Elwes was sent back to reconnoitre two positions in the rear, and around 1830 the order to withdraw was given, just as the Germans appeared. The Germans did not really press home their attack, so the old positions were successfully abandoned by about 1900 and the new ones occupied without interference, except from the air. The foot-weary Scots Guards trudged back to the small village of Pothus, where at about 0100 on 25 May they passed through the positions of the Irish Guards. After some confusion, the Scots Guards were moved to Hopen and the surrounding area by buses. Here, some welcome rest was obtained.

General Auchinleck, looking at the bigger strategic picture, was becoming concerned at the apparent growing strength of the Germans and the inability of his forces to hold any ground. It must be pointed out that the Allies were severely outnumbered and the threat from the air was proving far more deadly than the senior commanders had estimated. Intelligence suggested that the Germans now had about 4,000 men with tanks and artillery in the Mo-Mosjöen area. Auchinleck's policy was to strengthen the defence of Bodø with whatever ground forces he could get together, but there were really very few options. It was intended to land a further battalion of *Chasseurs Alpins*, and bring over three of the five remaining Independent Companies from England. Help was also sought from the Fleet Air Arm, while the landing ground at Bodø was being hurriedly prepared for aircraft to be transferred from Bardufoss. It was decided to put into the line the elements of the 1st Irish Guards, 2nd South Wales Borderers and four of the Independent Companies. The new position at Pothus was, therefore, manned in more strength, though Brigadier Gubbins, hampered by lack of transport, kept about half his men strung out along the lines of communication to Bodø in anticipation of a turning movement from the sea or air.

The village of Pothus is about 10 miles from the mouth of the Saltdal, and stands on both banks of the river, which widens out there. There were two bridges: a substantial girder bridge which carried the main road from the east to the west bank, and a smaller structure crossing a tributary that flows into the Saltdal from the east a few hundred yards further downstream. A platoon of around 50 men of No. 2 Independent Company

A list of weapons that potentially were going to be sent to help the Norwegians. (The National Archives)

reached the area first, with the 1st Irish Guards and No. 3 Independent Company following. They had occupied their positions by midnight on 24 May, just in time to welcome the Scots Guards.

Meanwhile, after their mishaps aboard ship in mid-May, the Irish Guards had, as their war diary puts it, been "refitting" at Harstad, with Captain Gordon-Watson taking over command. But their respite was short-lived; on 20 May they were ordered to Bodø, with HQ and No. 4 Company going by puffer boats and the rest in the comparative luxury of destroyers. The Battalion arrived at Bodø. Their war diary curtly reported: "Arrived at Bodø. No staff work. No orders. One puffer nearly sinks." However, someone must have known something as within a few hours they were bundled back in boats and sent to Hopen. Captain McGildowny, who had been released from hospital after the *Chrobry* incident, caught up with the Battalion and took over command, with Captain Gordon-Watson reverting to his Adjutant's role. By 22 May, most of the Battalion was at Godones, with No. 4 Company on the Stromnes peninsula. The Germans were very active in the air, so these moves would not have gone unnoticed. On 23 May, after several conferences, the Irish Guards were ordered to Rognan to relieve the Scots Guards, this move being accomplished by a combination of puffers, steamer, mail-boat and ferry.

The Irish Guards' war diary entry for 24 May reads:

The general position in the Saltdalen valley, when the Battalion arrived to cover the withdrawal of the Scots Guards and their embarkation at Rognan, was as follows:- Ten days before, the Scots Guards took up a defensive position at Mo and were to be joined as soon as possible by the 1st Battalion Irish Guards and the 2nd Battalion South Wales Borderers. Both Battalions were held up, once by the disaster to the Irish Guards on the *Chrobry* and once by the grounding of the *Effingham* with the South Wales Borderers on board. The other reinforcements available were the Independent Companies.

These Independent Companies were raised purely to harass enemy lines of communication and were never meant to act as defensive troops. They were ordered to do so and through no fault of their own, proved quite inadequate to the task. When supporting our flanks throughout the forthcoming operations, it was very difficult to contact them and more than often impossible to know if they were even there. They lived up to their names as Independent Companies and retired and advanced at will. Colonel Gubbins (although not a Guardsman) controlled Stockforce, as it was now called, from Rognan, and his commander in the field was Lieutenant Colonel Stockwell, Royal Welch Fusiliers.

The Scots Guards had been withdrawing, helped only on the flanks by isolated platoons of the Independent Companies, with no support, no lines of communication and in the face of completely unopposed air superiority. To make matters more difficult, Lieutenant Colonel Trappes-Lomax was relieved of his command in the middle of this difficult operation of withdrawal.

By 25 May, as their war diary puts it:

> The Irish Guards were ordered to take up and hold a defensive position along the line of Pothus bridge. The main feature of the Saltdalen valley was a road running through wooded country from the river at Pothus bridge to the town of Rognan. The high ground south west of the bridge was deemed vital to the defence.
>
> No. 1 Company was to hold the high ground on the far side of the river. No. 4 Company was to hold the wooded area on the right flank, overlooking the bridge. No. 3 Company was to cover the left flank on the eastern side of the road. No. 2 Company was held in reserve. Units of the Independent Companies were on both flanks, on the high ground, which dominated the valley. The defence was to be thickened up by a battery of 25 pounders, a section of Norwegian machine guns under Captain Ellingar and 2 Norwegian mortars.
>
> Communication, which was of vital importance to the holding of the position, broke down completely, the river proved unfordable and the W/T set, sent to No.1 Company, was sent to a different place to the operators who, when they did arrive, had not the remotest idea how to use the set. Completely overshadowing these factors was the unopposed air superiority. On Friday at 1545, the Germans machine gunned from the air. That evening the last rations were sent out to No. 1 Company by truck. Apart from the air gunning the front was quiet, until after the 1st Battalion Scots Guards had passed through.

In the early hours of the next day, the Pothus bridge was blown, it appears much to the surprise of the Irish Guards and according to them, "contrary to all orders and due to a misunderstanding between a junior RE NCO and a Scots Guards officer". It appears that this Scots Guards officer was with the rearguard, and was under the impression that the bridge should be blown as he was the last man across, with only the Germans behind him. The consequence of this was that No. 1 Company of the Irish Guards was stranded on the other side of the river. They tried to regain contact, but the war diary records:

> Ferry service across river to No. 1 Company tested; a few hours later, deemed impractical. No. 1 Company was now cut off, because: 1. The W/T set did not work. 2. The bridge was blown too soon. 3. The ferry was impossible and the signal cable (which it was planned to take over the bridge before it was blown up) could not reach No. 1 Company.

The Norwegians had sent forward two mortars and some patrol troops in addition to their machine gun company already posted with the rearguard. Their mortar detachment was placed on the high ground to the west of the British positions to the rear of the road bridge, while the main road was further covered by the single troop of artillery which had survived the withdrawal from Mo. The HQ of Stockforce was close to the reserve position, hidden in a wood to the west of the road.

Enemy cyclists made contact with the outlying positions along the main road on the east side of the Saltdal around 0800 on 25 May. By 1100, the support section had been driven back to the main defensive position protecting the girder bridge, where the Guards in slit trenches held the ridge firmly with support from the 25 pdrs and the Norwegian mortars on the other bank. In the early afternoon, while five *Heinkel* aircraft were machine gunning to create a diversion on the far side, the Germans tried to storm the ridge. They were driven back, but then proceeded gradually to outflank the position and eventually forced its defenders to withdraw. The last platoon to move back found that the bridge on the flooded side river had been blown up and had to cross under fire by a rope improvised from rifle slings. The men from the ridge then made their way along a track down the Saltdal to a hanging footbridge about a mile below the reserve position on the other side. Meanwhile, No. 4 Company Irish Guards, posted immediately behind the main road bridge, came under heavy fire, but with the help of Norwegian troops prevented any enemy advance across the river on to the west bank and inflicted considerable casualties.

Lieutenant Colonel Stockwell was burnt out of his HQ, after it had been set alight, presumably by tracer bullets, in one of the air attacks, but about 1800, when he heard of the difficulties on the east bank, he sent in his few precious reserves: No. 2 Company of the Irish Guards and No. 3 Independent Company.

They were sent across the river to hold positions on and near a high shelf protected by cliffs at the northern angle of the river junction. These were occupied by around 0400 on the 26th and made the situation on the left flank reasonably secure. However, during the night, the Germans had built a pontoon bridge over the river a little way upstream, so it was possible to outflank the defenders. The advance positions on the hillside were forced to withdraw towards the Guards positions, preventing access to the wrecked girder bridge. The last remaining uncommitted troops, a small number of men from No. 2 Independent Company, were sent up on to the hill in the forlorn hope of halting the

German advance from there and preventing the whole force being surrounded. By the late morning, the Germans were pressing hard nearly everywhere, and shortly afterwards Brigadier Gubbins at Rognan gave orders for a withdrawal. The situation was somewhat confused , with things not helped by how the orders for the withdrawal were handled. The Irish Guards war diary states: "No. 2 Company received their order to withdraw, five hours after dispatch of order. Message had been given personally by Force Commander to Norwegian interpreter, Captain Hartman, to deliver as he knew the way. Message pocketed by Sergeant of Independent Company, hence the delay."

No. 4 Company of the Irish Guards had better luck, positioned as they were across the wrecked girder bridge. They seized their chance to sneak away when a Gladiator fighter appeared out of the blue and machine gunned their opponents. This is one of the first instances when the RAF was able to give some air support to the hard-pressed soldiers, and was probably as much of a shock to the Germans. The withdrawal down the road to the mouth of the valley at Rognan then proceeded according to plan, except for a party from Battalion Headquarters, who had been kept back to load the reserve ammunition on the last of the motor transport. They were ambushed from a roadside farm as they marched back, but managed to extricate themselves from this situation. By 2359, the remnants of the Irish Guards left Rognan by local puffer boats from Finneid, and arrived at Finneid in the early hours of 27 May. Meanwhile, No. 2 Company Irish Guards, unable to cross the river into Rognan, extricated themselves by means of a forced march of 20 arduous miles across steep and pathless mountains, arriving ultimately at Langset, where the road resumed at the other end of the ferry journey. On the following day they made contact with the rest of the unit.

The Irish Guards, now reunited with No. 2 Company, spent most of the day widely dispersed around the Finneid area. Lieutenant Colonel Stockwell and Captain McGildowny conducted a recce of the area, decided it could not be held, and orders were issued for a withdrawal to a line near Aaseng, which they reached at about 0300 on 28 May.

Meanwhile, after their adventures on HMS *Effingham*, the South Wales Borderers had been licking their wounds at Harstad and trying to sort themselves out when, on 23 May, orders were received for a move. Their war diary records:

> More air activity over Harstad. 2 of the 16 Gladiators were up, one pilot had to abandon his plane owing to oxygen trouble and was nearly shot by the QM who saw him descending by parachute. Orders for move tomorrow received. A Company are to be left behind. Still short of equipment.
>
> 24th May. In the evening starting at 2000 D and HQ embarked in puffers for Bodø.
>
> 25th May. Arrived Bodø 1800 after a pleasant, uneventful journey. All troops were kept below decks and the few aircraft seen were not interested in the convoy, which was well strung out. Rejoined B and C Companies who had been having a somewhat harassing time with low-flying air raids and local false alarms. Moved into billets.
>
> 26th May. Reorganised the defence of Bodø. Much coast line and a lake to be

watched. Too many civilians about, no control, no transport. Three Gladiators arrived. Seen by enemy. Greatly assisted Irish Guards in withdrawal. One credited with five victims. One Gladiator crashed.

27th Biggish air raid – fighters and bombers. The last of our air force for the present. Received a plain message in early hours warning us to move as Independent Companies and Irish Guards were withdrawing. Very serious air raid at about 1830 lasted for two hours, concentrated on pier and W/T station. Many hundreds of bombs dropped, many planes involved. Most of the town on fire including hospital, which must have been done deliberately. D and HQ busy saving personnel, remainder in positions. Very few casualties, the platoon on the quay having the only two suffered by the Regiment. Move of Battalion forward cancelled.

29th May. Orders to withdraw Bodø Force received, to be done in three nights, 29th, 30th and 31st. We are sending 50 tonight. Party got away without interference of any sort on destroyers.

30th May. Battalion moved across to take up final position on left of peninsula. Two carriers taken over from the Irish Guards. No air activity, very low cloud and drizzle. Further embarkation completed without incident.

31st May. Probably the longest day most of us have experienced waiting. The leading company of the Scots Guards withdrew from their forward position about midnight. All bridges were destroyed and only a few cyclists were seen all day. The two carriers were most useful. The weather was cloudless at first but about 1800 it began to cloud over. We were due to embark at night. Considerable air activity. Many planes over, some very low indeed. Six bombs dropped in the northern area of the harbour, target unknown. Withdrawal went according to plan, A, B, D and HQ getting aboard HMS *Arrow* in 12 minutes. C Company and Carrier platoon went on another destroyer at 0045.

The embarkation was carried out without incident by three destroyers. No enemy planes appeared at all. Very fortunate, particularly as they had been harassing the destroyers on their way down to fetch us.

The war diary of the Scots Guards says of the withdrawal:

31st May. 0001. A considerable amount of fighting took place at Hopen. Enemy mortar and machine gun fire was considerable and artillery inflicted a number of casualties on Germans east of the bridge. In the early hours of the morning, the left flank of B Company was threatened and about 0200 Captain Godman decided to withdraw covered by one South Wales Borderers carrier.

0400. B Company reached position in Battalion reserve. No contact during the day, which turned out to be the longest on record.

1900. Six enemy aeroplanes made recce of Battalion area and bombs were dropped in the vicinity of Bodø, after which the aircraft luckily withdrew. The final withdrawal commenced at 1915 in the following order: Left Flank, C, with Right Flank at 2015, covered by B Company who finally abandoned at 2120 in order to hold a last position covering Bodø in conjunction with one company South Wales Borderers, although Right Flank sighted an enemy cyclist patrol just before withdrawing. There was no interference and the Battalion successfully embarked on two destroyers - HMS *Echo* and HMS *Delight* - between 2359 and 0030. As usual the Navy offered us every hospitality.

During the period from 17th-31st May the Battalion suffered 97 casualties (2 officers and 95 other ranks) and marched about 130 miles.

These are Lieutenant-General Auchinleck's comments about the events at Bodø:

Prior to the receipt of instructions from HM Government to evacuate northern Norway, it had been my intention to use every means to reinforce the troops in the Bodø area. I had already in mind a plan to send down a battalion of *Chasseurs Alpins*, in order to have troops specially trained in mountain warfare to oppose the advance of the German infantry which was being carried out with great skill and vigour. Once the decision to evacuate Norway had been made however, it was obvious that the evacuation of the troops from Bodø must be carried out as promptly as possible, as I had already received reports from Brigadier Gubbins that, without further reinforcements, he was doubtful whether he could hold on for more than a few days. On receipt of the instructions for evacuation from the Chiefs of Staff, I therefore immediately despatched Colonel Dowler, my GSO1, to Bodø in a destroyer, which was conveying the last company of the South Wales Borderers to join the rest of its battalion, to concert plans with Brigadier Gubbins for the withdrawal of his Force.

In view of the heavy and repeated air attacks which were being made upon the town, docks and aerodrome at Bodø, it was decided in consultation with Lord Cork, that evacuation by destroyers provided the best chance of evacuating personnel without serious loss. This decision meant abandoning the few wheeled vehicles and guns with the force, but in view of my instructions that the first consideration was to save personnel, and also in view of the fact that no suitable ship for embarking wheeled vehicles and stores was immediately available, no other course was practicable. Arrangements were therefore made to send two destroyers to embark 500 men each at 2300 29th May and three destroyers on each of the two succeeding nights, 30th and 31st May, to embark two further parties of 1,500 men each. Early on 26th May when the orders to prepare for the evacuation reached Brigadier Gubbins, the main positions held by his Force was some 40 miles from Bodø, in the neighbourhood of Fauske. Orders were issued by Brigadier Gubbins for two Independent Companies and administrative details to concentrate at Bodø at once and for the withdrawal from the position north of Fauske to start next day.

The general plan was that the 1st Battalion Irish Guards and three Independent Companies, which were all under the command of Lieutenant Colonel Stockwell, should withdraw from the position north of Fauske and pass through the Scots Guards, who were to be placed in position on a neck of land between the sea and a lake near Hopen. Having passed through the Scots Guards, the Irish Guards and the Independent Companies were to move straight to Bodø and embark. The third battalion of the 24th Guards Brigade, namely the 2nd Battalion, The South Wales Borderers, was to be placed in position across the Bodø peninsula further to the west astride Lake Soloi. The withdrawal of the Irish Guards and the Independent Companies was carried out without interference from the enemy's land forces, though the rear party passed through the Hopen position less than an hour before the enemy's advanced troops, consisting of cyclists and machine guns, made contact with the Scots Guards. The enemy were at once engaged and the bridge at Hopen was destroyed. This checked the pursuit and the Germans made no movement during the next day. During the withdrawal on the last night the enemy again followed up with cyclists and machine guns, but no serious pressure developed and no delay occurred. One company from the Scots Guards and one company from the South Wales Borderers with four 25 pounder guns were placed in position some four kilometres east of the town and formed the final rear guards. These companies withdrew to the quay without difficulty by previously reconnoitred routes.

A small incident in Bodø was recalled by Captain C. Cox of the South Wales Borderers, whilst waiting for the impending evacuation:

We moved to Bodø by puffer and my company relieved a company from the Scots Guards. A large flight of German aircraft came over and offloaded incendiaries which caused a lot of buildings to catch fire. I think the whole civilian population had left except one, who was the owner of the house I had chosen as my HQ. On arrival I had put my steel helmet on top of a male bust on a table and I was so tired I went to sleep on a sofa, then the owner returned and expressed his displeasure at my battle bowler being on his father's bust and my dirty boots on his sofa. We expressed surprise at his surprise as the whole town was in flames and the Germans were advancing. In any case we placated him and within a few days we left anyway.

A final few words on these events from Auchinleck:

During the three days covering the period of the re-embarkation several bombing attacks were carried out by the enemy on Bodø and its vicinity, but during none of the three periods when the actual embarkation of troops was in progress was there any interference from enemy aircraft in spite of the fact that there was continual daylight. This was probably due to unfavourable flying conditions during the first two days. On the last day however, the weather cleared. The times chosen for the evacuation were around midnight when enemy air activity was normally at its lowest. Fortunately the quay at Bodø had not suffered from enemy air attacks and this enabled destroyers to go alongside without difficulty. The embarkations were carried through with great rapidity, 500 men of one battalion embarking with their kit in less than ten minutes. The swiftness and efficiency with which the evacuation was carried out reflects great credit on Brigadier Gubbins and his staff. The destroyers of the Royal Navy were very well handled and carried out the programme laid down to the minute. Four 25 pounder guns, four Bofors guns and three Bren carriers which had been saved from HMS *Effingham* had to be abandoned, together with such material as could not be moved by the men, but some wireless sets and all the arms and equipment, including Bren guns and anti-tank rifles, which could be carried by the men, were brought away. The first echelon to be embarked were transferred at sea from the destroyers to HMS *Vindictive* and conveyed direct to the United Kingdom. Owing to the fact that transports for the second and third echelons had not arrived in time to admit of their direct transhipment, the troops comprised in these were landed at Borkenes to the east of Harstad and re-embarked later as part of the general evacuation programme.

The plan that the Bodø-Saltdalen area was to be denied permanently to the Germans and an advanced detachment was to be maintained at Mo as long as possible, thought up only a few days before, was now completely in tatters.

By mid-May, Lieutenant-General Auchinleck, mindful of the threat posed by the *Luftwaffe*, was doing his best to gain some more anti-aircraft assets for his troops. He commented:

> Throughout this period the installation of such anti-aircraft artillery as had been made available for the force, namely 48 heavy and 58 light anti-aircraft guns, was pushed forward with skill and energy by Brigadier Rossiter, commanding the anti-aircraft defences. Except at Harstad itself the disembarkation of these guns had to be carried out by transferring them into MLCs (motor landing craft) and then to ferry them ashore. The extremely mountainous nature of the country increased the difficulty of finding suitable positions for the guns and the indented character of the coast complicated the maintenance of isolated detachments. In spite of these obstacles the establishment of the anti-aircraft artillery was effected with commendable speed and efficiency and materially added to the security of the Force and its bases.
>
> The allotment of the limited guns available was made on the principle that it was only possible to give a minimum degree of protection to really vital areas and that smaller and less important areas must go without.
>
> On 20th May I decided that the best disposition of these guns would be:

Situation	Heavy Guns	Light Guns
Bardufoss	8 (16)	12 (24)
Harstad and Skaanland	24 (48)	18 (36)
Bodø	8 (16)	16 (24)
Tromsö	8 (24)	16 (24)
Total	48 (104)	58 (96)

The figures in brackets show the number of guns considered necessary to give really adequate protection to each area. In addition, there were demands for anti-aircraft artillery to protect French troops in the forward areas round Narvik, at Lødingen at the mouth of Tjelsundet fjord to protect the coast and naval anti-submarine defences there, to cover the RDF stations to be installed in the Lofoten Islands and elsewhere, and also for the protection of a third landing ground under preparation at Elvenes, near Salangen.

The actual number of guns in Norway and their locations at the end of May were as follows:

Location	Heavy Guns	Light Guns
Bardufoss	12	12
Sorreisa	-	2
Elvenes	-	4
Tromsö	4	4
Harstad	12	5
Skaanland	15	10
Ballangen	-	4 (protecting French forward troops)
Ankenes	-	4 (protecting French forward troops)
Bjerkvik	-	2 (2 lost at Mo)
Loaded for Bodø	4	4
With the Navy	-	1 (in a Q ship)
Total	47	52

As well as trying to address the anti-aircraft artillery position, Lieutenant-General Auchinleck was also fully aware of the need to sort out air support for his men. He summed up the position as follows:

On 13th May the Germans had a powerful air force in southern Norway and several excellent air bases from which to operate it. We, on the other hand, had not a single aerodrome or landing ground fit for use. The enemy thus had complete mastery in the air, except on the somewhat rare occasions when the Fleet Air Arm were able to intervene with carrier-borne aircraft. The vigour and daring of the Fleet Air Arm when they were able to engage the enemy earned the admiration of the whole force, but even their strenuous efforts could not compensate for the absence of land-based aircraft owing to the unavoidable relative weakness of performance of carrier-borne aircraft.

Shortly before Group Captain Moore RAF, who had been selected to command the Air Component, and I arrived in the theatre of operations, an energetic and inspiring start in the selection and preparation of possible landing grounds had been made by Wing Commander Atcherley, who carried out his difficult task with great energy and perseverance.

Group Captain Moore pushed on the work with the utmost determination and was ably assisted by Brigadier Pyne, my Chief Engineer. The work of preparation was hampered by much of the country being still under deep snow, making it impossible to determine whether expanses of a reasonable size and flatness would prove suitable for landing grounds in respect of their surfaces. The mountainous nature of the country forced upon us the selection and development of the most unlikely sites, of which Skaanland was an example. Few laymen would have thought that this site could possibly be made into a landing ground for Hurricane fighter aircraft.

The need for some support in the air for both the sea and land forces was urgent, particularly for HM Ships which were suffering heavily from the daily and almost continuous attacks made on them in the narrow waters round Narvik by the thoroughly efficient enemy bomber aircraft. Nevertheless, Group Captain Moore rightly, in my opinion, resisted all pressure to induce him to call for the aircraft to be sent before he was quite satisfied that the landing grounds could be said to be reasonably ready to receive them.

The existing landing ground at Bardufoss, 50 miles north of Narvik, was selected to be the main air base and work to make it fit for fighters was pressed on with the utmost energy and in the face of considerable difficulties, not the least of which was the conditioning of the road to it from Sorreisa at which place all stores, vehicles and equipment had to be disembarked from the ships in landing craft.

The preparation of the new landing ground at Skaanland also presented great difficulties and even the laying of a specially prepared mat brought out from the UK failed to overcome the softness of the surface caused by the peaty nature of the soil. Another possible site was found at Elvenes near Salangen, north east of Harstad, and was put in hand as an alternative landing ground, while work was also commenced at Elvegaard, near Bjerkvik, as soon as the enemy had been ejected from this area by the successful French landing on 12th May. The possibility of operating aircraft from Laxelvn on Forsanger Fjord, east of Hammerfest was also considered as there is an excellent landing ground there capable of taking two squadrons and relatively free of snow, but it was too far from the scene of active operations.

Eventually the first squadron of Gladiator fighters flew off the carriers on 21st May and was safely established at Bardufoss, with a few casualties caused by physical difficulties. Just before their arrival, anti-aircraft artillery, heavy and light, had been installed at Bardufoss after much labour and energy had been expended in their disembarkation and subsequent transport by road from the sea. The importance of giving this one and only aerodrome the maximum degree of protection against air attack was so great that its defence was given priority over all other needs. Twelve heavy and sixteen light anti-aircraft guns were installed there.

It was not until 26th May that it was possible to receive the second squadron, consisting of Hurricane fighters, at Skaanland. Even then, this landing ground proved unequal to the weight of these aircraft and they too had to be operated from Bardufoss, which remained the sole landing ground in regular use.

At the cost of a great amount of skill and energy on the part of Wing Commander Maxton, an advanced landing ground was got ready at Bodø and used with great effect by our aircraft in support of the troops in that area until it was so heavily bombed by enemy aircraft as to be unusable without extensive repair.

Once established, the RAF soon proved their superiority over the enemy bombers and fighters and I have no doubt that the comparative immunity from air attack enjoyed by the forces during the later phases of the campaign was due to the severe losses inflicted by our aircraft on those of the enemy. The effect on the morale of the force as a whole of their vigorous and successful operations was most marked.

Now that some fighter aircraft had arrived in the area, HQ NWEF felt able on 20 May to issue Operational Order No. 3, titled "The Employment of Fighter Aircraft". This read:

1. General Task.
The main areas it is desired to protect from hostile air attack are those containing:-
    (a) The naval anchorage at Skaanland and the approach thereto.
    (b) The military base at Harstad.
    (c) Allied sea or land forces in contact with the enemy.
    (d) RAF occupied aerodromes.
    2. The primary aim of your fighter aircraft should be to destroy enemy aircraft approaching these areas.
    3. I shall require you on occasion to co-operate closely with the land forces operating against the enemy. For this employment of fighters you will receive special instructions on each occasion.
    4. Particular tasks.
I appreciate that until you have established a forward landing ground at Bodø you will be unable to operate fighters effectively over the Bodø-Mo area. I understand that the Hurricanes' range, however, will enable them, when established at Skaanland, to operate for very brief periods over the neighbourhood of Bodø.
    5. If opportunity affords, therefore, you should endeavour to effect a brief, occasional patrol over the Bodø area, even if only to serve as a valuable moral support to the troops engaged in that area.
    6. When Bodø landing ground is ready for use patrols over the forward troops near Mo should be effected as often as the general air situation elsewhere in the Allied-occupied area permits.
    7. Subject to the provisions in paras 3, 5 and 6 your fighter effort for the time being should be directed to the destruction of enemy aircraft attempting to approach:-
    (a) The general area Trondenes-Lodingen-Narvik.
    (b) Our occupied aerodromes not situated within the area at (a).
Brigadier General Staff
NWEF

In the days prior to the German invasion of Norway, some photographic reconnaissance missions had been flown over the northern German ports and a build-up of ships noticed, but it was considered that as ships had "patrolled" north before it might not be too much to worry about. Blenheims sent out on 8 April to find the ships failed, and – probably due to bad weather – were also unable to find anything of real intelligence value. In fact, of course, a German armada was on the way to Denmark and Norway, and all ships arrived at their destinations relatively unscathed.

The RAF was goaded into action and on 10 April a number of Blenheims were sent to the Bergen and Stavanger areas with orders to attack any enemy aircraft seen. Bad weather hampered the mission, though one Blenheim made it to the Stavanger area and saw a fair few German aircraft on the ground. The pilot's report stated 18 ME110s, 20 *Heinkel* bombers and about 20 seaplanes were in the area. The airfield was attacked with incendiary bombs and machine guns, and one *Heinkel* and a petrol dump were claimed as destroyed. On the following evening, as darkness was falling, six Wellingtons and two Blenheims again visited Stavanger airfield and some parked bombers believed to be *Junkers* 88s were hit. One of the Wellingtons failed to return.

The problem for the Allies was that the two main German air bases were at Stavanger and Oslo. These and all other potential airfield targets were some distance from British airfields. For example, Stavanger was around 350 miles from the closest RAF base in northern Scotland, and about 500 miles from airfields in England. Oslo was about 500 and 600 miles respectively from the same places, and Trondheim 600 and 800 miles. It was obvious that any air support for ground troops in Norway would be a major undertaking, made difficult by the lack of suitable airfields. In the interim, however, Bomber Command was still trying its best to disrupt the Germans, mainly in the Stavanger area. It sent bombers over twice on 14 April. The first raid, by three Wellingtons, was around dawn, with four Wellingtons going in at dusk. Some damage was caused by these raids, but one Wellington failed to return. There were other small-scale raids on 15 and 16 April using a variety of aircraft, but the results were very sketchy as not all aircraft found their targets.

Then on the night of 16 April, a Whitley was sent to bomb Oslo, the aircraft taking off around 1900. The pilot later reported:

The first sight of Norway was at 2212 when a snow-covered hill was sighted in brief moonlight in a gap below the aircraft. Course was then altered to cut the south east coast of Norway in order to secure a landfall. At 2245 height was reduced to 3,000 feet through cloud and the sea was observed with the aid of the aircraft's landing light through a gap. Course was then set to port till the coastline was picked up at 2,000 feet and was identified by the line of white breakers. At 2255 at 3,000 feet in and out of cloud the aircraft proceeded up the entrance of Oslo fjord. At 2320 at 1,500 feet the port of Drammen was identified. Great activity was observed alongside the docks on the southern bank of Drammen fjord immediately east of where the railway crosses the fjord. At least ten cargo vessels of all sizes were observed alongside. At least ten more ships were moored in the centre of the fjord leading to Drammen. Riding lights were displayed on all these ships. One vessel was seen under way east of the railway bridge with navigation lights on. The docks were brightly lit by overhead floodlights and great activity prevailed.

All the marine navigation lights appeared to be lit in the fjords, but no marine lights were observed on the open coast or outside the fjords. At 2325 course was set for Oslo at 3,000 feet. Fornebu aerodrome and its immediate vicinity were obscured by a snow storm and cloud. Several attempts were made to penetrate this area down to a height of 500 feet. Severe ice was encountered at each attempt. At 2335 one small ship with navigation lights on was observed heading east off Oslo. From east of Oslo Öieren fjord was observed with the northern extremity obscured in snowstorm. At 2355 course was set for base. Aircraft landed at base 0436.

It is worth adding here that at no time was any mention made of actually dropping any ordnance and the flight was a mammoth duration of nearly 10 hours. In these early days of the war, bombs were a scarce commodity for the British, and pilots were under instructions to bring their loads back if they were unable to identify their target. This pilot stated that he did not drop his bombs on Fornebu due to the snowstorm. It is also worth adding that only a few months before, a flight of nearly 10 hours would probably have been so unusual as to be mentioned in the newspapers.

Over the next few days, more Blenheims and Wellingtons were sent out, mainly to the Stavanger area, and some bombs were dropped, but again a number of aircraft failed to return and the lack of cloud cover (the RAF was mainly launching daylight raids) caused a number of sorties to be abandoned. It was now clear that unless there was the cover of darkness or cloud, the RAF was potentially facing large losses. But the reverse was also true: good weather was just what the Germans needed to provide ample air support, not only for their ground troops in their advances steadily northward from the Oslo area but also for attacks on the Allied bases that were being established.

Flights by Sunderland flying boats bringing vital supplies across from the UK were one of the more useful RAF support activities. As Norway was a neutral country, large stockpiles of explosives for demolition work were not readily available. What was in stock was being quickly used in blowing up bridges to slow the German advance. An urgent appeal went out for explosives, and over a ton of explosives was crammed into the fuselage of a Sunderland flying boat. It was able to land successfully on one of the fjords in central Norway and its vital cargo was sent off to the front to assist in trying to slow the German advance. Around this time – towards the end of April – with landings by Allied troops taking place at a number of locations, the need for airfields with fighter aircraft was paramount. On 21 April, a small party (six officers and 60 other ranks) from the RAF, together with essential stores, was despatched from the UK on a warship to try and sort out an airfield. Meanwhile, 263 Squadron, then equipped with Gloster Gladiators, was put on standby to go to Norway.

The Gloster Gladiator, which entered service with the RAF in 1937, was the last British biplane fighter and the first fighter with an enclosed cockpit. It had a top speed of 257mph yet, even as it was introduced, the design was eclipsed by new-generation monoplane fighters, such as the RAF's Hurricane and Spitfire and the *Luftwaffe*'s ME109.

However, in 1940 Norway was not seen as a vital theatre and so the rather old-fashioned Gladiator was chosen for service, rather than the more up-to-date Hurricanes or Spitfires . To move them to Norway, 18 Gladiators of 263 Squadron were flown first to Scapa Flow, where Fleet Air Arm pilots landed them on the aircraft carrier HMS *Glorious*, sailing for Norway on 22 April. The advance party arrived at the small port of Åndalsnes and soon moved inland, the vital aviation fuel being stored in the first instance in a railway tunnel about five miles outside the port.

A few days earlier, on 17 April, Squadron Leader W. Straight was sent out to Norway to find the most suitable landing ground to the south of Trondheim. This would not be an easy task in one of the most mountainous areas in Norway. The choice lay between two iced-over lakes - Lake Lesjaskog, which was south-east of Åndalsnes, and Lake Vangsmjösa, which lies high up in Valdres on another route from south-east to north-west parallel to the Gudbrandsdal-Romsdal route, and about 60 miles south-west of Kvam. Straight's preference was for Lake Vangsmjösa because it was free of snow, could take two squadrons of any type of aircraft and was connected by road to the inner reaches of the Sognefjord, where stores and equipment could be landed independently of the existing lines of communication. Lake Vangsmjösa was already being used as an emergency base by a few Norwegian aircraft. The Air Staff decided otherwise, partly no doubt because they feared that the Norwegian forces in Valdres might not be able to prevent the Germans from overrunning the lake position, but chiefly because it was too far away from the area of Allied operations. It was also decided that only a single squadron should be sent, although the 18 aircraft on its paper strength could not possibly provide a constant patrol of six aircraft. Opinion inside the Air Ministry was that this was the minimum number to maintain a reasonable level of cover.

Lake Lesjaskog is a long, narrow lake, surrounded by woods. High and desolate mountains skirt the southern shore but there is easy access on the north from the road and railway connecting nearby Dombas and Åndalsnes. The servicing flight arrived there in two parties on 23 and 24 April, having had great difficulty in sorting their stores (which were neither listed nor labelled) and getting essential items sent forward by the only two lorries which were found in Åndalsnes.

A runway of about 800 by 75 yards had been prepared by local labour, which had swept snow from a track between the main road and the lake's edge. Only a single inadequate route had been swept from the edge to the runway, half a mile long and a foot deep in snow, and stores had to be transported over it on three horse-drawn sledges, which were only intermittently available. Lesjaskog village was two miles away, so even provision of forage for the horses was difficult.

By 1700 on 24 April, the servicing flight had laid out fuel and ammunition along the runway in small dumps and collected all available tins, jugs and other containers for refuelling. It had immediately been perceived that the essential task of refuelling and starting aircraft would be difficult: just two refuelling troughs had been sent, and the starter trolley could not be used because the batteries were uncharged and no acid had been sent with them. Among the ground staff there was only one trained armourer to maintain 72 Browning guns for the squadron. Two guns from a naval battery of Oerlikons, which was landed at the same time as the RAF stores, had arrived for anti-aircraft defence, along with a platoon of Royal Marines to guard the petrol supply.

This was the situation when the aircraft of 263 Squadron, commanded by Squadron Leader J. Donaldson, took off in a snowstorm from *Glorious* 180 miles from the coast, with only four maps among 18 pilots, none of whom had previously seen action. The only advantages Gladiators had were their comparative ruggedness and short take-off and landing distances. Escorted by two Skuas of the Fleet Air Arm, they descended on the lake at around 1800 without serious mishap, although the heaped-up snow at either side of the runway had melted during the day so that its ice surface was half covered by trickling water. Meanwhile, the Germans had been flying high above the lake and were probably aware that it was being turned into an airfield. The Gladiators were immediately refuelled and one section placed at instant readiness, but the *Luftwaffe* did not return that evening.

The situation on the ground was still disorganised, with fuel and ammunition having to be left in the open, whilst jugs and tins were collected, hopefully to speed up the refuelling of scattered aircraft. Peace-time regulations were still much to the fore, as the trolley starter batteries were sent uncharged (a normal precaution for shipping) and, worse still, the acid that was needed to charge them was difficult to locate in the mass of stores; efforts to commandeer batteries from local sources were not very successful.

One section (of three Gladiators) had been placed at readiness and the pilots sat in their cockpits ready to go. There was no system of early warning and, once airborne, no way for the pilots to communicate with the ground. Around 2130, as it was falling dark, two aircraft were spotted. The pilots were told to take off, but one of the Gladiators' engines refused to start, so only two were airborne. The aircraft were intercepted and seen to have Norwegian markings, so no fire was exchanged. The Gladiators returned to the airfield and in the growing darkness had a difficult landing. One pilot used his brakes too much and burst one of his tyres. Within about an hour, all the aircraft had been refuelled and dispersed around the area. Four remained close to the runway but spaced about 100 yards apart, with the others placed as close to the tree line as the many snow drifts allowed.

During the night, it was agreed that a standing patrol over the airfield would start at dawn (around 0300) and continue until dusk, with each patrol lasting about two hours. Two other sections would be at stand-by, with pilots waiting in the cockpits, and one section to be at 15 minutes' notice.

The night was bitterly cold. When daylight came, carburettors and aircraft controls were frozen stiff, and in the absence of batteries the engines were difficult to start. The first aircraft did not manage to take off until about 0445, but they were able to intercept and shoot down a *Heinkel* 118. At 0700, two aircraft were sent to patrol the battle area, but the ground crews were still struggling to get more engines started when the first of a large number of German bombers attacked. The attacks continued at regular intervals throughout the day. The first attack appears to have been timed to coincide with the opening of a ground attack at Kvam, and the Germans disrupted any air support that the Gladiators had planned to give. During the raid, two Gladiators waiting to be refuelled were hit and set on fire, and another was also struck whilst the pilot was trying to start his engine. During a later attack, around 0900, it was possible to get the engine started on one of the Gladiators and this aircraft took off, preventing attacks on the area for about an hour. As the temperature rose, another six Gladiators could be got airborne. Some of these patrolled around the lake whilst others headed to the front line to try and prevent German airborne artillery observers spotting for their guns. Several aerial combats took place, but while damage was claimed on a number of German aircraft it is doubtful any were actually destroyed. A number of the German aircraft intercepted were *Junkers* 88s, with a top speed greater than that of the Gladiators! When carrying bombs it had a top speed of about 300mph, and about another 20mph when not, giving it a speed advantage of about 60mph.

Around noon, a HE111 was shot down over the lake, and the crew who escaped were taken prisoner. But this was an isolated success, as eight of the 18 Gladiators had been put out of action by around 1230 as a result of the air raids. Four of these had been destroyed without even taking off. The lack of suitable facilities such as bowsers on the ground was making refuelling a long and painful process. It took about 90 minutes to refuel and rearm each one, and the aircraft were vulnerable during this time: four were destroyed whilst in this cycle.

At around 1300, more German bombers appeared. More Gladiators and RAF personnel were damaged and injured in a further attack. Some aircraft were airborne and over the next few hours managed to beat off a few attacks, causing damage to the Germans, but it was really a hopeless cause. The idea of an ice runway had not really been thought through. The Gladiators were themselves outclassed, and when airborne the squadron commander's aircraft suffered severe damage from a *Heinkel* bomber. It made a successful landing at an emergency landing ground on a small plateau at Setnesmoen, near Åndalsnes, which had been partly cleared for use. Norwegian Army troops guarding the airfield there opened fire on Squadron Leader Donaldson as he landed, but fortunately their aim was not too good! He felt that Lake Lesjaskog was now a dead duck and wanted his remaining aircraft moved here. There was – of course – no communication with Lake Lesjaskog, so a despatch rider had to be sent with the news. This obviously also involved transporting the ground crew, petrol, ammunition and other stores. An additional instruction was that any aircraft not immediately serviceable were to be destroyed. At Lake Lesjaskog, 11 of the 18 aircraft were already destroyed, with a further two damaged ones soon to join that number. So when the orders arrived, just four aircraft were left to fly to their new home. It was a good decision, as by the end of the day Lake Lesjaskog had been raided so many times by the Germans that the runway was totally unusable. Whatever transport could be got together was used to move the remaining pilots, some of the ground crew and whatever stores could be crammed aboard, to the new landing ground at Setnesmoen.

Meanwhile, the Army was calling for heavy bomber attacks to be made on German positions south-west of Åndalsnes, but there were no bombers in the area and nor was the region in range of bombers based in the UK. Another suggestion that was put forward, but this time from London, was that a squadron of Blenheims could fly to Åndalsnes and bolster resources there. A curt message came back from RAF HQ in Åndalsnes that unless they came accompanied by fuel, oil, ammunition, spares and ground crews with their necessary tools and equipment, it would be pointless to send them. The five remaining Gladiators at the new landing ground were then given the mission for 26 April included to try to locate other suitable areas that could be used as landing sites. They were also to attack the German positions with machine guns, as requested the previous day by the Army, and finally reconnoitre Sundalen, at the head of Sundals Fjord, north-east of Åndalsnes, where it was reported that the Germans had made a

The 'last' Gladiator of 263 Squadron pictured near Åndalsnes. (Imperial War Museum HU2872)

landing. That day's mission did not go well. Of the two Gladiators sent to Sundalen, one returned with oil-pressure problems and seized-up engine parts, which made it unserviceable. The engine of the other aircraft sent there broke down over Sundalen and the pilot was forced to bail out. He landed in the village itself and found himself in the arms of the Norwegian Army! There were no Germans in the area and he was eventually returned to Åndalsnes. This left three aircraft from the original 18. Two of them were on a combat air patrol over Setnesmoen at around 10,000 feet when a number of German bombers were seen approaching Åndalsnes at around 25,000 feet. As was usual with the Norwegian campaign, the Gladiators had a limited supply of oxygen and were unable to reach these heights, so the *Luftwaffe* was able to bomb virtually unhindered. The docks area was particularly badly hit and an ammunition dump exploded. By the evening, a number of fires were burning fiercely. By the end of this second day, flight operations had to be stopped owing to a combination of losses and mechanical failure. The fact that the petrol had run out was almost immaterial, as on inspection the last surviving Gladiator was found to have serious airframe problems and would probably have been a death trap had it got in the air. It was not even possible to cannibalise other aircraft to get this survivor airworthy. In these two days, 49 sorties had been flown and claims for attacks against 37 enemy aircraft made. How many were shot down is unclear, but the wreckage of at least six German aircraft was visited by squadron personnel in positions where pilots claimed to have shot down their opponents. The Norwegian adventure for 263 Squadron was over. On the night of 28 April, they embarked on a cargo ship and were back in the UK on 1 May.

Aircraft based in the UK had been doing their best to support the Army and Navy operations in Norway. On 25 April, six Blenheims were sent on a sortie to the Hardanger area. They attacked a range of opportunity targets, including German flying boats, the harbour at Granvins and German shipping at Ulvik. One of the Blenheims failed to return. On the night of 26/27 April, six Whitley bombers were sent to the Oslo area and claimed to have successfully attacked oil tanks and a refinery there.

Then on 27 April, the CO of 46 Squadron – Squadron Leader K. Cross – arrived in Norway in a Sunderland flying boat. His squadron of Hurricanes was stationed at RAF Digby in Lincolnshire, and although he had been warned that they might go to France this was cancelled. Squadron Leader Cross was sent to visit Setnesmoen landing ground and see if it was suitable for use by Hurricanes. Squadron Leader Cross reported on his return to the UK that it was possible to fly Hurricanes from Setnesmoen, but the Allies' evacuation of the area curtailed this plan. However, 46 Squadron's involvement with Norway was not finished.

Further north, the initial centre of attention was the port of Narvik, well outside the range of RAF aircraft based in the UK. The Fleet Air Arm, however, was able to provide support using carrier aircraft. But until it was possible to either capture or manufacture an airfield in northern Norway, the RAF was effectively powerless to take any part in the fighting. Allied troops had landed in northern Norway fairly quickly after the German invasion on 14 April, but the deep snow had made it almost impossible for the troops to venture far. The Germans, with the benefit of less distance to fly, started aerial resupply operations towards the end of April, flying in from Trondheim, a round trip of around 800 miles. But the Allies were unable to operate effectively against this vital lifeline. It had been intended to hold Narvik indefinitely, so an RAF HQ element to go with the NWEF was formed on 22 April under the command of Group Captain M. Moore. The intention was to send three fighter squadrons, a bomber squadron and an Army co-operation flight, backed by the normal support facilities including a balloon squadron, engineers, stores and supply units, with medical and photographic support. As well as the command element, it was also planned to send a base area team, but for various reasons most of the units did not leave until 8 May. Meanwhile, the selection and initial preparation of suitable landing strips was undertaken by an advance party, which flew to Harstad in a Sunderland flying boat, arriving there on 29 April. On the next day, Wing Commander Atcherley, accompanied by a Royal Engineers officer, visited a senior Norwegian officer to ask for permission to use and extend a Norwegian airfield at Bardufoss, north-west of Narvik. Another potential landing site was identified at Banak, at the head of the Porsangerfjord, which might be suitable for bombers. It had the advantage that it was not snow-bound, but it lay 200 miles north-east of Narvik. The distance might not prove an insuperable obstacle to the operations of the aircraft concerned, but it involved a heavy drain on naval resources, which would have had to be stretched to protect seaborne communications round the North Cape. Banak was never actually used, though Lord Cork and General Auchinleck urged persistently that without the help of at least one bomber squadron it would be difficult to stop the German offensive. It was planned for one of the fighter squadrons to be based at Bardufoss, 50 miles north-east of Narvik, a small Norwegian military airfield equipped with two short runways. The nearest point on the fjord for landing supplies was the little wooden jetty at Sorreisa, more than 17 miles away via a narrow lane requiring immediate reconstruction. The other fighter squadron was to be based on Skaanland, south of Harstad, where a stretch of level ground was found which had been partially drained.

As well as the potential problem of using the small lane to move supplies to the landing ground at Bardufoss, the reconnaissance party found Bardufoss under four-and-a-half feet of snow and Skaanland under two feet, though at sea-level; beneath this was a layer of ice and under the ice a further penetration of frost deep into the soil. Snow clearance, blasting of ice, drainage of the site and surface rolling had all to be taken in hand, while the spring thaw hindered as much as it helped because the melting heaps of snow flooded back on to the cleared area. Other obstacles were raised to begin with by the Norwegian General Fleischer, who demanded a written promise from the RAF that there would be no sudden withdrawal as from Åndalsnes, and resisted the introduction of British or French troops at Bardufoss to clear the snow as he felt they should be fighting at the front. A Norwegian staff officer accompanied the British delegation back to Harstad to see Lord Cork, and over a glass of wine on board his flagship an agreement was reached.

Work began at Bardufoss the following day. The airfield had two runways, one measuring 650 yards and the other 760 yards. Both were at this time buried under five feet of snow, with under this about a foot of ice. The second runway was never prepared for operations, as the first one was almost parallel to the Bardufoss road and only about 100 yards from it, so easier to use from a logistical point of view. The British and French troops never materialised, and in their place the Norwegians sent one of their territorial battalions to help with snow clearing. This was eventually supported – and later totally replaced – by civilians from all over Norway "conscripted" by the National Labour Organisation. The locally raised labour was paid 1½ kroner an hour (at today's exchange rate this is approximately 15p) and there were never less than about 750 men working. There were two shifts, each of 10 hours, the work aided by the very long hours of daylight. The cleared snow was loaded into carts, wheelbarrows and lorries, and moved as far from the runway as possible, so that when it melted it would not flood the site. Efforts were aided by the use of a bulldozer and a 200-strong mule train – no doubt another first for the RAF. Bardufoss was eventually equipped with one runway, having a usable length of rather more than 800 yards, and up to 20 camouflaged blast-proof shelters for aircraft in the surrounding woodland. It was given the nickname of the Clock Golf Course because of a number of taxiways that centred on the runway. A rudimentary operations room was constructed underground, and an extensive system of air raid shelters was gradually developed. It was hoped that this, together with the safe dispersal of aircraft, would prevent a similar disaster as that which had befallen the Gladiators at Lesjaskog.

At Skaanland, however, in spite of a similar expenditure of effort, the airfield never became fit for use and reverted to farmland. As for Bodø, the site there was crossed by two large ditches and a network of power and telephone lines: 176,000 grass tufts also had to be cut from surrounding fields to cover a section which had been ploughed. There was, though, no snow and plenty of labour in the neighbouring town. The Norwegians had the field prepared in 10 days in spite of air raids, which were probably precipitated by a broadcast appeal from the Chief of Police for 500 men to report on the site. The lack of suitable communication in the area meant that the civilian radio network had to be used, with the inherent problem of the Germans eavesdropping.

Bodø landing strip came into service on 26 May. But Bardufoss was the main landing ground. Anti-aircraft defence was being taken seriously; eight heavy and twelve light anti-aircraft guns had been positioned around the area. Forward anti-aircraft observer posts in the form of two lines were also set up, which was about as good as it got in terms of early warning of air raids as it was found impossible to establish radar stations in northern Norway. One such line was in the south, from Bodø east to Fauske; the other covered the western approach through the Lofoten Islands. Unfortunately it was found that the wireless sets supplied were far too weak to send messages across the high mountains. It was still more unfortunate that these initial preparations were made in ignorance of the fact that the Norwegians had their own system of air raid precautions, operated chiefly by women volunteers, which stretched down into enemy-held territory along the coast to a point south of Mosjöen. However, by the time the first squadron arrived at Bardufoss, the two observer screens between them were reporting enemy movements to the RAF HQ at Harstad, with a delay of between two and ten minutes. Thus the air base got general warnings, but they depended upon the eyes and ears of the watchers and that the messages were transmitted in a timely manner by the local telephone network. For local ground defence, a company of *Chasseurs Alpins* was located at the airfield to guard against attack by paratroopers.

There had been a lull in German air activity the day of the Bjerkvik landing, but in the days after it was renewed more fiercely and many ships were attacked and damaged. In spite of the best efforts of the Fleet Air Arm, which operated fighters from HMS *Ark Royal* until 21 May, more than a dozen ships were bombed within a fortnight. The most important were the battleship *Resolution*, which was sent home for safety on 18 May after a bomb had pierced three decks, the transport *Chrobry* and the anti-aircraft cruiser HMS *Curlew*, lost with many of her crew on 26 May after a large number of attacks whilst trying to protect the construction of the Skaanland landing ground. HMS *Curlew* was attacked by a number of JU88s and hit by several bombs whilst on passage off Skutenes, Lavangfjord, near Narvik. She sank in Lavangfjord, position 67°32' N 16°37' E. The loss of this valuable ship, one of the few with an aircraft warning radar outfit, deprived the force of invaluable air cover at a critical stage of the Norwegian campaign.

A possible site for the landing ground in the Bodø area had been inspected on 14 May. It was found to have a potential runway length of 900 yards but the ground was very boggy and some of it had been ploughed up. Two wide ditches helped to carry water away from the area, but there were also a number of local hazards, with power pylons and cable and telephone lines crossing the area. It was hoped it might be possible to get some Gladiators here to support the British troops in the area to try and stop the Germans moving northward. Around 100 locals were hired to assist with the project, working in two shifts at the rate of one kroner per hour. One of their first jobs was to improve the drainage by using concrete pipes in the ditches. Again there was a shortage of transport. In the early days there were only 25 horse-drawn carts. The Norwegians drafted in some more labour – about another 100 men - so a three-shift working pattern was introduced. Work progressed at a good rate, underground cables were laid to replace the overhead ones and admin buildings and shelters were taking shape. But on 21 May, at around 1600, a *Heinkel* bomber attacked the area and according to reports dropped six bombs, which caused some damage and killed three soldiers. On the following day, work started on laying a thick wire "mat" over the runway and on 25 May, the landing ground at Bodø was declared ready, with a runway 700 yards long and 50 yards wide. Ground crew and admin staff arrived from Harstad and set up refuelling points. It was decided to base three Gladiators, again from 263 Squadron, at Bodø. The pilots had returned to the UK at the end of April, been allocated new aircraft and arrived back in Norway, being initially based at Bardufoss. The three Gladiators arrived at this new landing ground around noon on 26 May, but it was then discovered that the surface would not take the weight of the aircraft, and all three became bogged down. A rethink was called for. After some trial runs, an area was discovered about 300 yards long by 50 yards wide which could bear the weight. This was just about long enough for a Gladiator to take off. The aircraft were in the interim dug out and in a few hours local workmen laid a wooden runway, about 700 feet long and 100 feet wide, to lengthen the strip. Later, one aircraft was on a combat air patrol over the airfield when two HE111s appeared. Of the two aircraft on the ground, one crashed on take-off. The senior airborne pilot ordered the other to land after his patrol around the airfield but to take off again, whilst he went to the Salt valley as planned to try and stop German aircraft attacking the Allied troops there. This Gladiator had some success. It came across two JU52 transport planes, shooting at least one of them down, and also damaged a HE111. The pilot returned to Bodø airfield and had his aircraft refuelled and rearmed before taking off within an hour or so. The less experienced pilot, who had been "borrowed" from the Fleet Air Arm, was temporarily grounded owing to the dangerous state of the runway. Whilst he was airborne, wooden planks were laid over some of the boggier areas and when he landed he declared that conditions were much improved. After talks with the Army, it was requested that the two remaining Gladiators patrol the Mo evacuation area between 2300 that night and 1000 the following day. Because there were only two aircraft, it was only possible to have one aircraft over Mo at a time - but there were three pilots. The Navy pilot took off first and was joined briefly by the other aircraft in the early hours of the 27th. No enemy aircraft were seen and the third pilot (in the Navy pilot's aircraft) took over at around 0200. The senior RAF pilot, on his arrival back at Bodø, decided to cancel the standing patrol, because of the risk of damaging the two remaining aircraft during the frequent take-offs and landings. The Wing Commander in charge of the base told the Army that they should call for assistance if the transports were attacked by enemy aircraft. Both aircraft were safely on the ground by 0430 when the second aircraft landed. Around 0800, around 12 *Stuka* dive-bombers, escorted by a number of ME110s, attacked the airfield, Bodø and the port facilities. One of the Gladiators refused to start, but the other got airborne safely and it was left to the Fleet Air Arm pilot to fly off alone to meet this threat. He duly attacked the German formation and appeared to scare them off. However, they regrouped and attacked him, and he was wounded in the neck and shoulder. He returned to Bodø, but as there were still some German aircraft in the area he decided to fly to Bardufoss. Here he landed safely, but his aircraft was a write-off as it had been badly damaged. Back on the landing ground at Bodø, one of the remaining pilots noticed that the bombing was haphazard and so decided to try his engine again. With the help of one of the ground crew, he got it started and took off. The unnamed pilot later recalled:

I circled round the aerodrome and attacked a JU87 at the bottom of its dive from a quarter above to astern. It appeared badly hit and turned over and dived low over the sea and seemed to be making off slowly. Later the hospital authorities confirmed having seen two *Messerschmitts* circling over a spot on the south side of the fjord where the *Junkers* was seen to sink out of sight. My next recollection is of another *87* which was rearing up in front of me, unaffected by my fire. There was a sharp crack and I lost consciousness for a moment and recovered to find two bullet holes in the windscreen and blood pouring into my right eye. Soon after I felt my aircraft hit by bursts of bullets and went into a right-hand turn. The aileron controls locked and I spiralled down feeling bursts of fire from behind. At about 200 feet the control column came free, but although the aircraft righted itself, there was no further lateral control. A burst from the engine took me over some rocks and then I crashed. A Norwegian assisted me in getting to Bodø hospital, where I got treatment for my injuries.

This pilot was awarded a Distinguished Flying Cross for his actions in Norway.

The cumulative effect of the three pilots' actions was to keep the skies over Bodø relatively free of German aircraft, enabling the evacuation to be carried out in an orderly manner. But all three Gladiators were now out of action and later that day a large number of German bombers – some reports saying as many as 100 – bombed the airfield and the town of Bodø. Damage was caused to the runway by around 20 bombs, and it was estimated that repairs would take several days. The Germans continued their steady advance and the area was evacuated by the end of May, as previously described.

Lieutenant-General Auchinleck was inevitably concerned about the lack of air support. The first fighter squadron to arrive in the area was 263 Squadron, which came in on board the aircraft carrier HMS *Furious*. Now that the landing ground at Bardufoss had been prepared, they took off on 21 May in sections, each led by a Swordfish from 818 Squadron of the Fleet Air Arm. They were about 100 miles off shore when they left the *Furious*, but on crossing the coast they ran into bad weather. One Swordfish and two Gladiators crashed into a mountain, Høystakktind, between Sifjord and Osterfjord. The Swordfish crew survived the crash and was rescued. One of the Gladiator pilots, Pilot Officer W. Richards from the RAFVR, was killed and is buried in the Allied plot at Harstad Cemetery (grave E4). He was aged 24. The other pilot, Pilot Officer S. Mills, was injured in the crash but survived and was shipped back to England. The decision was taken for the surviving Gladiators to return to the carrier, and in spite of the fact that none of the pilots had done a deck landing before, all got down safely. With better weather the next day, the remaining 16 Gladiators took off, arriving at Bardufoss around 0900. They flew combat air patrols around the Narvik area, but on their first full day ashore contacts with the Germans were scarce. The next day they faired slightly better but found that their lack of speed against most of the German aircraft was a severe handicap. Pilot Officer A. Craig-Adams failed to return to Bardufoss, and when a search was carried out his crashed Gladiator was seen from the air close to a *Heinkel* bomber on a mountainside east of Salangen. Eyewitnesses reported hearing machine gun fire high up in the clouds and seeing an aircraft dive steeply into the hills, on fire and trailing smoke. It was later assumed that Craig-Adams had collided with the *Heinkel* in or above the clouds, and he was credited with a kill. His body was later recovered by the *Chasseurs Alpins*, and he now lies in Narvik New Cemetery (grave XI K6).

The few RAF aircraft did their best to provide as much support as possible, but they had to be spread between the landing strip, Harstad, Skaanland and Narvik. Each aircraft was flying at least two patrols a day, and their time airborne was helped by the closeness to the patrol areas, meaning that not much fuel had to be expended. On 23 May, there were a number of incidents with German aircraft. Again it was a difficult time for the Gladiator pilots, as the German bombers could often use their superior speed to draw away without the Gladiators getting in range. However, one pilot did manage to shoot down a *Dornier 17* south of Harstad after a number of attacks, but soon afterwards his oil pump failed and he was forced to bail out. The aircraft crashed and was destroyed.

An idea of how much of an advantage the German bombers had can be gathered from when a Gladiator chased a *Heinkel* bomber for about 15 miles without being able to overtake it, and ended up firing at an extreme range without apparent effect. But the Germans were scoring some successes on the Gladiator force. Within days, four aircraft had been destroyed or damaged beyond economic repair, and another was badly damaged. This reduced the force to 13 aircraft and 15 pilots. The long hours of daylight meant that the number of hours being flown by both men and machines was much higher than normal, with a consequent increase in stress and strain. They all found it difficult to sleep at night, and ground crews were putting in long hours in basic conditions trying to keep as many aircraft as possible serviceable. What was really needed was some reinforcements.

These finally arrived towards the end of May in the shape of 46 Squadron, equipped with Hurricanes under the command of Squadron Leader K. Cross. He had been warned in April 1940 that his unit was earmarked to go to Norway. The first plan was for them to go to central southern Norway, but this fell through. Then on 9 May orders were received to embark the squadron in the aircraft carrier HMS *Glorious*. The squadron flew to Glasgow and the Hurricanes were trucked to the quayside. During the next two days the Hurricanes were hoisted aboard the carrier. On 12 May, *Glorious* sailed, only to be recalled. No airfields in northern Norway were yet ready to receive the fighters. No 46 Squadron's ground crews and advance party embarked on the troop carrier *Batory* in Glasgow on 13 May, and on the following day *Glorious* sailed again. On 21 May, *Glorious* reached a fly-off position off the Lofoten Islands, but the airfield at Skaanland was not ready. *Glorious* returned to Scapa Flow, arriving on 23 May. She took on fuel and supplies and sailed again in the afternoon of 24 May. The landing ground at Skaanland was finally declared ready in the early hours of 26 May. Orders were issued that if the ground conditions were unsuitable for Hurricanes, they were to divert to Bardufoss. In the interim, a Gladiator had landed at Skaanland to test the runway, and whilst it landed safely, when moving over the wire net the wheels sank in about four inches. The surface did not spring back when the load was removed. It was clear the Skaanland landing ground would need continual care and maintenance if prolonged flying operations were to be carried out. Nevertheless, the Hurricanes managed to take off successfully from *Glorious*; the first time a Hurricane had been launched from a carrier. Matters were slightly helped by the stokers on board cranking up the engines, so that 30 knots was achieved – pretty good for a ship built in the Great War. Squadron Leader Cross was the first man away and led his 18 machines to Skaanland, where they proceeded to land. Ten aircraft landed successfully, but two pitched up so badly that their noses touched the ground. Cross ordered the remaining eight aircraft to Bardufoss. On the following day another Hurricane ended up nose-first in the ground. It was decided that enough was enough, and the remaining seven Hurricanes were despatched to Bardufoss. The three stricken Hurricanes were partially dismantled and shipped back to the UK. The ground crews, other personnel and stores were also "cross decked" to Bardufoss.

Excluding the Fleet Air Arm aircraft, there were now 27 aircraft actually on Norwegian soil, ready to face around 1,000 German aircraft. The Norwegian campaign was set to come to a head in the coming days in the skies above Narvik.

For the Allied landings at Narvik on 27 and 28 May, Lieutenant-General Auchinleck, the commander of the NWEF, requested that a maximum effort be put in place by the RAF so that there was continuous fighter cover over the area from 0800 until 2000 each day. The senior RAF officer, Group Captain Moore, responded that they would do their best but it was likely that there would only be three aircraft at a time, owing to the shortage of numbers. There were 15 Hurricanes airworthy out of the original 18, and of the 18 Gladiators of 263 Squadron, six had been written off, two had been damaged and were in the repair cycle after suffering machine gun attacks, one had a broken wing and three more were slightly damaged.

One air combat of note was on the morning of 27 May, when Sergeant George Milligan of 263 Squadron, flying in a Gladiator, took off at around 0900 on patrol, attacking two HE111s at 6,000 feet between Bardufoss and Narvik. He was in turn attacked by a third bomber, so turned his attention to this and made four passes at it. Pouring smoke, it dived into a valley in low cloud. As with many other aircraft which were not seen to crash during combat, the Norwegians confirmed later it had come down.

On 28 May, the Hurricanes made their first real impact in the campaign, flying 53 sorties from Bardufoss over Harstad, Skaanland, Sorreisa and Salangen. Their first success was not long in coming. At approximately 1100, Flying Officer Lydall shot down a JU88 which was attacking a Royal Navy destroyer in Narvik Fjord. Later, between them, Flight Lieutenant Jameson, Flying Officer Knight and Pilot Officer Johnson destroyed two four-engined flying-boats parked on the Rombakssfjord.

However, three HE111s bombed Bardufoss from low level in the morning of 29 May, causing damage and two fatalities suffered. Sergeant Milligan from 263 Squadron was scrambled, and after a prolonged chase was able to catch up with one of the bombers at around 15,000 feet. Milligan closed to 250 yards and fired long bursts at the bomber. Several pieces flew off the bomber, but before he could see any further results his engine began to malfunction – possibly having ingested debris from the *Heinkel* – and he had to break away. The German pilot had to crash land his damaged aircraft near Ankenes, where the whole crew was captured and shipped back to the UK. Sergeant Milligan was able to nurse his damaged Gladiator back to Bardufoss, but it meant another aircraft temporarily out of action and more work for the ground crews.

Other Gladiators undertook ground attack roles. One of these unnamed pilots reported later:

While on offensive patrol I carried out seven ground-strafing attacks on German road convoys and troops. All attacks were made out of the sun from approximately 3,000 feet. A convoy of six lorries spaced 3-2-1 with approximately 200 yards between each group was successfully strafed. Troops were strafed leaving the lorries for the shrubs and numerous casualties were observed. Also troops transferring from a lorry to a fishing smack were successfully strafed and the fishing smack was the subject of a well-directed burst. A black sedan was attacked and put out of action and a house adjacent to the point where the troops were transferring was severely strafed. Throughout the engagement the aircraft was subjected to return fire from the southern side of Beisfjord, but no damage was caused. Subsequent reconnaissance over the same area showed that two lorries and one sedan car had been abandoned, evidently owing to previous action.

Nine Hurricanes from 46 Squadron were up on patrol on the same day when they met a group of 26 *Luftwaffe* bombers approaching Vestfjord. The Hurricane pilots attacked three *HE111* of KG 100 and KG 26, north of Lødingen. At least two of the *Heinkels* were shot down, but the escort of a number of ME110s fought back and shot down three Hurricanes, with two of the pilots being killed.

Pilot Officer N. Banks shot down a ME110 in this combat but was himself brought down. He crashed into the Skjæringstad River at Strand in Lødingen and died. He now lies at Narvik New Cemetery (grave XI L4). It is believed that previously in the action this ME110 had shot down the Hurricane of Flying Officer J. Lydall, who crashed at Tjeldøya and was also killed. He is also in Narvik New Cemetery (grave XI K9). The crew of the ME110 survived the crash-landing and were taken prisoner. It is also believed that a HE111 was forced down by Flying Officer Lydall, making a forced landing at Dverberg on Andøya.

The third Hurricane shot down was flown by Pilot Officer J. Drummond. His aircraft was hit by machine gun fire and set on fire, so he was forced to bail out. He landed in the Ofotfjord, and was picked up from the water by HMS *Firedrake*.

There was bad weather over the coming days which prevented much flying. An additional factor was that there were now only six serviceable Gladiators and so far six Hurricanes had been lost, an attrition rate of 33 per cent in just a few days.

However, the decision had now been made to evacuate Norway. The NWEF was evacuated from the Narvik area between 2 and 8 June. This withdrawal went remarkably unhindered by the *Luftwaffe*. Perhaps a combination of the bad weather and the fact that the RAF was flying standing air patrols (albeit in small numbers) over the region stopped the Germans being too nosey, or maybe they did not believe that an evacuation was in place. The problem for the RAF was how to thin out the aircraft and personnel without jeopardising the air cover over the evacuation ports and maintaining a resemblance of security. The story was "leaked" that the remnants of 46 and 263 Squadrons were to be transferred to Skaanland, now in a serviceable condition, to make way for two Blenheim bomber squadrons that would take their place at Bardufoss. On the night of 7 June, 10 Hurricanes took off from Bardufoss. They were escorted to HMS *Glorious* by a Swordfish and the plan was for them to land on the carrier. This was expected to

Pilot Officer J Drummond. (The Drummond family)

be a risky venture, as it had not been tried before and the Hurricanes lacked the normal arrestor gear that aircraft required to land on a carrier. This consisted of a hook at the rear of the aircraft, which could be dropped on landing on the deck. Hopefully it would catch wires stretched across the deck, slowing the aircraft before it shot off the end of the deck and the pilot got wet feet. It would appear the Hurricane pilots had discussed this difficult landing process and one of them suggested that a 15lb bag of sand in the tail might help to cut down the braking distance. It seems this idea worked well and all the aircraft landed safely. They were followed by the remaining Gladiators, again escorted by a Swordfish. The slower landing speed of the Gladiators meant that they did not need the sand. As the last Gladiator left, the ground crew and others started work on wrecking the landing ground. Craters were blown in the runway and anything that had to be left behind was made unserviceable. By 0400, they were on their way to Narvik to be evacuated by sea.

What follows are two accounts from members of 46 Squadron who served in Norway. Sergeant Stanley Andrew, who had reached the age of 21 just a month before deployment there, recalled:

In May 1940, we were selected to form part of the Expeditionary Force in Norway. Modern fighters were urgently needed to augment the handful of Gladiators operating in that area. Because of the urgency of the situation it was decided that the air component would be embarked onboard an aircraft carrier and launched off the Norwegian coast. This was the first time when modern land-based fighters were to take off from a Royal Navy carrier. On 14th May, the Hurricanes of No. 46 left the Clyde on board HMS *Glorious* for an airfield near Harstad, but had to return with the carrier to Scapa Flow when the landing ground was found to be unusable.

The second attempt took place on May 26th. The Hurricanes were to be launched from the flight deck of HMS *Glorious* 40 miles off the Norwegian coast and 100 miles north of Skaanland. On receipt of a signal saying that Skaanland was ready to receive the squadron, the first six Hurricanes were ranged on deck. Owing to the flying-off deck having a ramp at the forward end, there was some doubt whether the aircraft would be airborne by the time they reached the top, as, according to the figures produced by the Air Ministry, 272 feet was required for take off, provided a 30 knot wind was obtained. Unfortunately a flat calm prevailed at the time but thanks to the Captain and the Commander Engineer, almost 30 knots was obtained over the deck. The first take off was carried out by the Squadron Commander and proved quite successful, the Hurricane taking off easily just before the top of the ramp. All 18 aircraft were flown off successfully.

The first flight landed at Skaanland at 2130, still clearly visible due to the midnight sun which permitted round-the-clock flying at this time of the year. On attempting to land, one accident occurred owing to the soft surface of the aerodrome. On the arrival of the second flight another Hurricane was damaged for the same reason and the decision was then made to send the remaining aircraft to Bardufoss, 60 miles north. Orders were given to this effect to aircraft by R/T from aircraft on the ground. These aircraft arrived safely at Bardufoss.

Operations commenced on the following day. At 0720, a patrol consisting of Squadron Leader Cross, Flying Officer Frost and Pilot Officer Bunker took off to intercept three HE111s approaching the aerodrome. The enemy formation was sighted but as they were going away from the landing ground they were not engaged, orders having been received that aircraft were not to be attacked unless Skaanland itself was attacked. One aircraft - again - crashed on landing from this patrol and permission was asked for 46 Squadron to evacuate the airfield until such time as the aerodrome surface should prove suitable. This permission was received and by 1800 all fifteen serviceable aircraft had arrived at Bardufoss.

From Bardufoss, the first combat patrols over Narvik were put up the same evening by a section of three aircraft led by the Squadron Commander. Patrols were maintained until 0415 of 28th May when fog covered the aerodrome and the eighth returning patrol was fortunate in having half the runway clear to land.

At 18,000 feet, pilots had a clear fine view of the attack by naval vessels and land forces. At one time as many as seven large fires were seen in Narvik town and ten at Ankenes on the side of Veissfjord. A column of smoke reached a height of 7,000 feet.

In the morning, patrols were resumed by the same pilots, who had no sleep for two nights. This time the *Luftwaffe* showed up in numbers. At approximately 1100 hours Flying Officer Lydall shot down a JU88 over Ofotfjord. Later, Flight Lieutenant Jameson, Flying Officer Knight and Pilot Officer Johnson destroyed two four-engined flying boats on the surface of Rombakssfjord.

Patrols and combats continued until the morning hours of the 29th. At 0040, Flight Lieutenant Jameson shot down a JU88. Pilot Officer Drummond went missing during this patrol. Later a message arrived from HMS *Firedrake* saying that Pilot Officer Drummond had descended by parachute and had been picked up by them. *Firedrake* confirmed the destruction of a JU88 by Flight Lieutenant Jameson and also that Drummond had shot down a HE111 which crashed in the nearby fjord. Drummond's aircraft had been set ablaze by the defensive fire from the German bomber.

No respite was given throughout the afternoon, when Pilot Officer Banks shot down a four-engined *Junkers* which was bombing Tromsö. In the evening, 26 enemy aircraft approached Vestfjord from the south and split up into formations of five aircraft. Nine Hurricanes were on patrol at the time and in subsequent encounters with superior forces Flying Officer Lydall and Pilot Officer Banks were shot down and killed. Flight Sergeant Shackley shot down one JU88 and two more enemy aircraft were destroyed, probably by a joint effort of Flying Officer Lydall and Pilot Officer Banks.

On 30th May, weather closed down, bringing a much-needed opportunity for the pilots to rest. The next day, Bodø was evacuated by British Forces, 46 maintaining patrols over the area. The rear party of the squadron, which had left Britain onboard a merchant ship on 28th May, finally arrived at Harstad. Unfortunately, orders for total evacuation were already given and they were sent back by sea to Scapa Flow.

June started with two days of very bad weather, which started improving in the afternoon on the 2nd. Pilot Officer Drummond and Sergeant Taylor on patrol over Narvik saw two JU87 *Stukas* attacking a destroyer by dive bombing. They attacked, and the JU87s separated and made off, twisting and turning. The Hurricane pilots waited for their chance and shot them down south east of Narvik. To the astonishment of Pilot Officer Drummond, the rear gunner of the JU87 continued firing from the rear gun after his aircraft had crashed.

Flying Officer Frost and Sergeant Tyrer chased another JU87 and severely damaged it before it dived into the clouds. Frost's windscreen was hit by a bullet which splintered it, but did not penetrate.

Flight Sergeant Shackley and Pilot Officer Bunker engaged five twin-engined *Messerschmitt* ME110s without result. The 110s on sighting our aircraft formed line astern and then went into a defensive circle. Each time the British aircraft joined in, two more would get on their tails. After a time the 110s went off south, easily out-distancing the British pilots. All that Flight Sergeant Shackley could to was to try a long distance shot, with no results.

On 3rd June, weather turned out bad. The next day, seven patrols were carried out over Skaanland, Harstad and Narvik, but it became clear that evacuation was imminent. Squadron Leader Cross was given orders by the RAF to send off the ground crew for evacuation by sea and either destroy the remaining 10 Hurricanes, or fly north and be possibly evacuated, with no further statement as to how and where such evacuation could take place. That night, fifty men including Pilot Officer Westcott and 3 Warrant Officers left for an unknown destination, carrying only marching order kit; Flight Lieutenant Peock left on 5th June with a further 29 men. Only the essential crew to maintain air operations remained at the site.

Chances to evacuate the remaining aircraft were slim, but Squadron Leader Cross was determined to explore all remaining possibilities in that direction. He decided that rather than flying their aircraft north into the unknown, it was better to try and get them back to a Royal Navy carrier. On 5th June, he went by Supermarine Walrus to HMS *Ark Royal* and HMS *Glorious* to make arrangements in secret for the flying on of 46 Squadron. Both carriers were within range of the fighters, but *Ark Royal's* lifts weren't large enough to take the Hurricanes down to the hangar deck without removing their wings. This left HMS *Glorious* as the available option and it was agreed that such an operation should be attempted, even though the Hurricanes lacked arrestor hooks and the type wasn't previously tested for deck landings. Cross returned the same day with this encouraging news.

On 6th June, patrols were carried out over Narvik, Skaanland, Lødingen and Harstad. Two aircraft provided an escort for 5 Walruses bombing in the neighbourhood of Norfold, without contact with the enemy. On the following day, Squadron Leader Cross and Pilot Officer Lefevre engaged four HE111s over Bardufoss with unknown results. Flying Officer Knight and Pilot Officer Drummond engaged 3 HE111s over Narvik, once again with results unknown.

Pilots were warned that they would have to evacuate Norway that night, and volunteers were asked to fly on to HMS *Glorious*. 100% volunteered, even though it was clear that landing a high-performance Hurricane without the aid of an arrestor hook on a carrier was coupled with enormous risk. One of the flight commanders, Flight Lieutenant Jameson, came up with the idea of tying a sandbag to the Hurricane tails to give extra weight and reduce the landing run. A quick test was carried out and proved a success. The Fleet Air Arm would help by guiding in the first three aircraft led by Flight Lieutenant Jameson and the ship's engineer would co-operate in giving instructions on speed and direction needed to get them down. In the end, Cross selected six of the most senior pilots to fly with him to *Glorious* in the second wave.

At 1800 Flight Lieutenant Jameson, Flying Officer Knight, and Sergeant Taylor took off for HMS *Glorious*, and landed successfully. Before receiving them, *Glorious* took most of her own aircraft below to clear the deck. Unfortunately, her own air component would remain immobilised during the fateful following day, despite the fact that the Hurricanes could be stowed away in the hangar and so their presence did not prevent air operations.

Report of the success was sent by radio back to the unit ashore, which by the time was busy with its final combat patrols. Flying Officer Mee and Pilot Officer Drummond had engaged four HE111s over Narvik, each pilot claiming to have shot down one enemy aircraft. Pilot Officer Drummond attacked and damaged the other two. On 8th June, the remaining seven Hurricanes left for *Glorious*, piloted by Squadron Leader Cross, Flight Lieutenant Stewart, Flying Officers Cowles, Frost, and Mee, Pilot Officer Bunker and Flight Sergeant Shackley. They all made successful deck landings. The remainder of the officers and men embarked on the SS *Arandora Star*.

A shot down RAF airman at Fornebu airfield. (Imperial War Museum HU290440)

The second 46 Squadron account is from the family of Pilot Officer John Drummond:

46 Squadron assembled at Bardufoss in the far north of the country and began operations on 27th May.

John saw action shortly after his arrival when, on 29th May, he took off from Bardufoss in Hurricane L1794. He sighted four enemy aircraft at 12,000 feet south of Narvik and moved into attack the nearest, a HE111. Although John hit the starboard engine he had been hit by return fire causing his cockpit to fill with smoke. He turned to go back to Bardufoss but his engine failed. He had no choice but to bail out. He landed in the near freezing waters of Ofotfjord and was picked up by HMS *Firedrake*, an F-Class destroyer later to take part in The Battle of the Atlantic. John Drummond had scored his first solo kill, a HE111 of *2/Kampfgeschwader 26*.

Four days later, in the early afternoon of 2nd June, John took off in Hurricane W2543, with Sergeant Taylor, for a routine patrol over Narvik. An hour or so into the sortie he spotted two *Junkers* JU87s attacking a destroyer in Ofotfjord. He went after the first, firing around five six second bursts. Smoke coming from the starboard mainplane confirmed he had scored a hit. John watched as it force landed, bursting into flames.

The 7th June was certainly John's busiest day during his time in Norway. It was also the day he cheated death by an inch, and earned his Distinguished Flying Cross. He was in the air at 0400 hours patrolling the Narvik area when he spotted three HE111s flying in formation. He attacked the first plane but

The RAF were able to cause some damage at Fornebu as this picture shows. (The National Archives)

it disappeared into a cloud, so he attacked the other two, hitting the starboard *Heinkel*. The other one attacked his Hurricane, causing him to seek cover in a cloud. On emerging from his cover John saw the damaged *Heinkel* heading towards the border with neutral Sweden, and so John returned to Bardufoss, claiming this as a victory.

After some rest John was in the air again at 1715, patrolling Narvik with Flying Officer Mee. They sighted four HE111s at around 10,000 feet. Mee attacked the port enemy aircraft and John the starboard. John hit his target, causing it to turn for cloud cover. John left it there and went after another of the HE111s. Spotting two, he attacked one, hitting the rear gun, but was hit himself by the other one. A shell pierced his windscreen, clipping his goggles and helmet before ricocheting out of the cockpit hood, making a large hole in the process. John returned fire again but lost the enemy planes in cloud. He claimed one victory and two damaged. On landing, John learnt that Operation Alphabet had been activated and the squadron had been ordered to evacuate Norway immediately. They had to fly their Hurricanes back to HMS *Glorious*. Perhaps because of the day he had had – two sorties in fourteen hours – John was not chosen for this task. Instead he went with ground crew of 46 Squadron on the SS *Arandora Star*. John Drummond disembarked at Gourock on 13th June and returned to RAF Digby (their home base) the next day.

John Drummond's overall record in Norway was four enemy aircraft shot down and two damaged, for which he was awarded the Distinguished Flying Cross. The citation in the *London Gazette* of 26 July 1940 read:

The King has been graciously pleased to approve the under mentioned awards, in recognition of gallantry displayed in flying operations against the enemy:-

Awarded the Distinguished Flying Cross. Pilot Officer John Fraser Drummond (40810).

During operations in Norway, this officer shot down two enemy aircraft and seriously damaged a further three. On one occasion, as pilot of one of two Hurricanes which attacked four *Heinkel* 111s, he damaged one of the enemy aircraft and then engaged two of the others. Despite heavy return fire, Pilot Officer Drummond pressed home his attack, silenced the rear guns of both aircraft and compelled the *Heinkels* to break off the engagement.

According to official records, the total number of enemy aircraft claimed to have been destroyed by 263 Squadron is 26, while the Hurricanes of 46 Squadron claimed a further 11. To this number for the air war we can add another 23 claimed by the anti-aircraft batteries.

Appendix A

German order of battle for the Denmark and Norwegian campaigns

On 1 March 1940, the German 21st Army Corps was renamed Group XXI and placed in charge of the invasion of Norway. The group was allotted two Mountain and five Infantry divisions for this task. It was led by the commanding officer of the XXI Corps, General der Infantrie Nikolaus von Falkenhorst. His Chief of Staff was Colonel Erich Buschenhagen.

Corps Troops:
German 730th Heavy Artillery Battalion
2nd Mountain Division:
136th & 137th Mountain Light Infantry Regiments; 111th Mountain Artillery Regiment
3rd Mountain Division:
138th & 139th Mountain Light Infantry Regiments; 112th Mountain Artillery Regiment
69th Infantry Division:
159th, 193rd & 236th Infantry Regiments; 169th Artillery Regiment
163rd Infantry Division:
307th, 310th & 324th Infantry Regiments; 234th Artillery Regiment
181st Infantry Division:
334th, 349th & 359th Infantry Regiments; 222nd Artillery Regiment
196th Infantry Division:
340th, 345th & 362nd Infantry Regiments; 233rd Artillery Regiment
214th Infantry Division:
355th, 367th & 388th Infantry Regiments; 214th Artillery Regiment
170th Infantry Division:
391st, 399th & 401st Infantry Regiment; 240th Artillery Regiment
198th Infantry Division:
305th, 308th & 326th Infantry Regiments; 235th Artillery Regiment
11th Motorised Rifle Brigade:
110th & 111th Motorised Infantry Regiments

Appendix B

Instructions for Protective Action by the Air Component during Re-embarkation.

Operation Instruction No. 3
To OC Air Component
Provision of Aerial Protection for Re-embarkation.
1. The NWEF is to be embarked over a period of five days, commencing 2200 hours on 2nd June.
2. The general method of embarkation will be:
(a) Transfer of troops from shore by puffers or quays to destroyers in four main areas: Harstad, Skaanland, Ofotfjord, Sorreisa and Salangsverket.
(b) Transport from destroyers to transports, lying off some 60 miles to the westward.
The responsibility of the Air Component will be to provide protection for the embarkation of troops in the first three areas given above until the last possible moment.
3. Embarkation will not be a continuous process, but will be carried out in varying periods during each 24 hours, as shown in schedule attached.
4. You should therefore arrange to provide sorties to achieve a maximum degree of protection during these periods in each embarkation area allotted to the Air Component.
5. Information regarding the action of the Fleet Air Arm.
Flag Officer Narvik is arranging for the fighters of the Fleet Air Arm to:
(a) Provide protection for the embarkation from Sorreisa and Salangsverket as shown in schedule attached and particularly to provide cover for the final evacuation of Bardufoss on June 7th.
(b) Provide protection for the transfer of troops from destroyers to transports at the selected rendezvous.
(c) If resources permit after providing for (a) and (b) above, to provide fighter patrols at the mouth of Ofotfjord.
6. Flag Officer Narvik is also arranging for Swordfish from the carriers:
(a) To carry out reconnaissance to discover movement of the enemy up the coast along the tracks leading north from Sorfolda to the Tysfjord.
(b) To bomb enemy headquarters at Hundalen daily.
(c) To be prepared to carry out further bombing tasks in the Hundalen area if required.
(d) To provide two Swordfish at Bardufoss at a time to be fixed later to guide the Gladiators of 263 Squadron to the carriers where they will finally be flown on.

7. The time at which the final evacuation of the RAF and other personnel from Sorreisa will be carried out, will be fixed on 5th June in accordance with the situation on that date.
Alphabet Patrols
To be provided by RAF Bardufoss.
Object: To prevent hostile air attack on embarkation assembly points and embarkation itself. Patrols are not to leave patrol area, however tempting an opportunity presents itself at a distance.

Date	Number of aircraft on patrol	Patrol Area	Time over Patrol Area
3rd June	3	7	2130-2330
	3	8	2200-2330
3rd/4th June	2	5ˣ	2300-0200
4th June	3	8	0745-0915
	3	5ˣ	2100-2300
	3	8	2130-2300
	3	7	2130-2330
4th/5th June	3	5ˣ	2359-0200
5th/6th June	3	5ˣ	2100-0200
6th June	3	8	0715-0845
	2	5ˣ	2100-2359
	2	7	2130-2330
	3	8	2130-2300
7th June	3	5ˣ	0100-0300
	3	8	0715-0845
	3	7	2130-2330*
	3	8	2130-2300*
	3	5ˣ	2200-2350

x Hurricanes land Skaanland after last patrol on 7th June. Gladiators land Bardufoss and fly to carrier, 0300 8th June.
* FAA Skuas or Gladiators may be operating near Area 5 at intervals. All embarkations in Area 2 will be patrolled by FAA. Last embarkation in Area 7 (0130 8th June) will be patrolled by FAA.

Bibliography

The National Archives

War Diaries:

WO168/53 1st Battalion The King's Own Yorkshire Light Infantry
WO168/54 1st Battalion The York and Lancaster Regiment
WO168/55 1st Battalion The Green Howards
WO168/56 1st Battalion Scots Guards
WO168/57 1st Battalion Irish Guards
WO168/58 2nd Battalion The South Wales Borderers
WO168/59 4th Battalion The Royal Lincolnshire Regiment
WO168/60 The Hallamshire Battalion, The York and Lancaster Regiment
WO168/61 4th Battalion The King's Own Yorkshire Light Infantry
WO168/62 8th Battalion The Sherwood Foresters
WO168/63 5th Battalion The Royal Leicestershire Regiment
WO168/86 229th Field Company Royal Engineers

Other Reports at the National Archives:

CAB106/1168 Report from Major-General Mackesy
DEFE2/675 Report from Lieutenant-General Auchinleck
WO222/1480 Medical Services Norway report
ADM1/11658 Loss of HMS Glorious
ADM199/280 Interception and Boarding of German Auxiliary *Altmark*
CAB106/1161 Report by Lieutenant Colonel King-Salter
WO106/1904 Major-General Paget's report on Sickle Force
WO106/1938 Maurice Force Historical Statements
WO106/1889 Independent Companies in Norway
WO106/1905 Reports on Sickle Force

Imperial War Museum
Interviews at the Sound Archive Imperial War Museum:

Robert Brackenborough
Charles Cheshire
Charles Cox
Donald Creighton-Williams
Vernon Day
Albert Harris
Basil Keeble
Alistair Mackenzie
Ronald Mills
Frank North
Richard Partridge

Printed sources

T. Derry, *The Campaign in Norway*, HMSO, London 1952.

G. Haarr, *The German invasion of Norway: April 1940*, Seaforth, Barnsley 2009.

W. Hingston, *Never Give Up, a History of the KOYLI* volume 5, Lund-Humphries, London 1950

J. Kynoch, *Norway 1940: The Forgotten Fiasco*, Crowood Press, Marlborough 2002

F. Kersaudy, *Norway 1940*, Arrow Books, London 1990.

N. Macmillan, *The Royal Air Force in the World War. Volume 1, 1939-1940*, Harrap, London 1942.

W. Synge, *Story of the Green Howards 1939-1945*, Green Howards, Richmond 1952.

Internet sources

The HMS Cossack Association
Hansard
Uboat.net
WW2 talk

Index

Index of People

Adams, Sergeant J. 198, 279
Atcherley, Wing Commander 298, 307
Atkins, Petty Officer 34–35
Auchinleck, Lieutenant-General C. J. E. 240–241, 244, 246, 253–255, 269, 276, 282–284, 286–287, 289, 295–298, 307, 311, 313

Banks, Pilot Officer N. 314, 317
Berger, Captain 122, 156
Béthouart, General 228, 234–235, 244–245, 253–255
Bey, Captain 122, 128, 131–132, 140, 142, 147–148, 155
Bonte, Commodore 116–118, 122, 132
Bowen, Major 211–212, 221, 273, 276
Bracken, Lieutenant H. H. 162, 164, 171
Brandis, *Oberleutenant* von 60, 63–64
Brathen, Johan 71–72
Bräuer, Kurt 68, 73, 76, 78–79, 82, 84, 87
Bruun, Captain Niels 65–66
Bunker, Pilot Officer 316–318
Burgess, Lieutenant W. 191, 289
Buzzard, Commander A.W. 105–106, 109, 111

Capito, *Hauptmann* G. 60–63
Carton de Wiart, Major-General A. 265–266
Chamberlain, Neville 15–18, 20, 23–24, 36, 193
Churchill, Sir Winston 23, 30, 33, 36, 112, 157, 192, 196, 213–214, 269
Compston, Lieutenant 272–274
Cork and Orrery, Admiral of the Fleet the Earl of 192, 200–202, 206–208, 210, 213–220, 224–228, 234–238, 241–242, 244–246, 250, 252–256, 266, 268–269, 295, 307–308
Cox, Captain C. 233, 279, 296
Craig-Adams, Pilot Officer A. 311–312
Craven, Paymaster Sub-Lieutenant 34–35
Cross, Squadron Leader K. 307, 312-313, 316–318

Dau, Captain Heinrich 28–30, 37
Dietl, General 52, 133, 155–156, 222–223, 227, 235

Dill, General Sir John 226, 228, 244, 254
Donaldson, Squadron-Leader J. 303, 305
Dormer, Sir Cecil 77, 79–82
Dowler, Colonel 192, 255–256, 295
Draper, Guardsman E. 273, 276
Drummond, Pilot Officer John 314–321
Durham-Matthews, Captain J. 221, 276
Durnford, Captain J. 157–160, 169

Edwards, Flying Officer G. 157–158
Elwes, Major J. 191, 285–286, 289
Engelbrecht, General 73, 76
Erdmenger, Captain 118, 140
Evans, Admiral Sir Edward 88, 187
Evans, Major I. 231-232
Evans, Lieutenant O. 231-232

Falkenhorst, *General der Infantrie* Nikolaus von 40–42, 70, 74, 76, 323
Faulkner, Lieutenant Colonel W. D. 232, 238, 270, 273, 276, 280
Fitzgerald, Captain D. 212, 273
Fleischer, General 234, 269, 308
Fleming, Lieutenant-Commander A. 157–158, 161, 164, 169
Forbes, Admiral Sir Charles 49, 88, 100, 104–105, 110–112, 114, 116–117, 134, 136–138, 142, 144, 152, 155
Forbes, Lieutenant-Commander J. 177-178
Fraser, Brigadier W. 192, 209–210, 215, 218–219, 222, 228, 230, 238–239, 254, 256, 268–269, 276, 282, 284
Friedrichs, Captain 119, 151
Frost, Flying Officer 316–318
Führer see Hitler, Adolf

Gamelin, General 228, 265
Gammell, Brigadier 255, 257
George, Sergeant Ogwyn 71-72
Gilbert-Denham, Major 221, 273, 276
Gilliat, Lieutenant J. 221, 272–273
Godman, Captain J. 191, 294
Gordon-Watson, Captain M. 221–222, 273,

270, 276, 290

Gorton, Commander 192, 206

Gottwaltz, Lieutenant Colonel P. 230, 234

Graham, Major H. 191, 211, 223, 280, 284–286, 288–289

Gregg, Petty Officer 92, 98

Gubbins, Lieutenant Colonel C. McV. 247–250, 256, 260, 266–268, 280–281, 284, 286–289, 291, 293, 295, 297

Hàche, President Doctor Emil 17-18

Hague, John 129–130

Häkon VII, King 11, 22, 68, 76, 84-87

Halifax, Lord 15, 23, 36–37, 86

Hambro, Carl Joachim 36, 82

Hansen, Lieutenant H. 62-63

Hansen, *Oberleutenant* W. 69–71

Harvey, 2nd Lieutenant 204, 211

Hatledal 80, 84–85

Heppel, Lieutenant G. 116, 118, 124, 126

Heye, Captain Helmuth 90–91

Hitler, Adolf 13–18, 20–22, 37, 40, 42–43, 50, 74–76, 87, 155–156, 211, 269

Holtorf, Captain 117, 119–120

Horton, Vice Admiral Max 173–174, 179–180

Hubback, Commander 215–216, 245

Hutchinson, Lieutenant-Commander C. 174–176

Ironside, General Sir Edmund 23, 25, 190, 196, 241

Jameson, Flight Lieutenant 313, 316–318

Johnson, Pilot Officer 313, 316

Johnstone, Guardsman George 205, 211

King-Salter, Lieutenant Colonel E. 193–195

Knight, Flying Officer 313, 316, 318

Koht, Professor Halvdan 36, 68, 77, 79, 82, 84

Kummetz, Admiral 67–68

Laake, General K. 50, 77, 80, 84–85

Layton, Admiral 100, 104–105, 111–112

Lent, *Leutenant* Helmut 69, 71

Lewin, Lieutenant F. 273, 276

Ljungberg, Defence Minister 80, 84–85

Lund, Brigadier 188–190, 208, 212, 220, 223

Lütjens, Admiral 101–103, 113–114

Lydall, Flying Officer J. 313–314, 316–317

Mackesy, Major-General P. J. 25–26, 187–192, 199–200, 202–203, 205–210, 212–220, 224–226, 228, 235–239, 241–247, 250, 252–256, 268–269

MacWhirter, Lieutenant (A) W. R. J. 163-164, 172

Massy, Lieutenant-General 242, 265

Maund, Captain 191-192, 215–216

McGildowny, Captain 221, 273, 290, 293

Mee, Flying Officer 318, 320

Merritt , Able Seaman 92, 98

Metscher, *Oberleutenant* Wilhelm 68–69

Micklethwait, Commander 145, 149, 151–152

Moore, Group Captain M. 240, 298–299, 307, 313

Mussolini, Benito 15–16

Netzbandt, Captain 101-102

Nickelmann, Oberst 70, 72

Nygaardsvold, Prime Minister 72, 76–77, 84–85

O'Neill, Captain Brian 273, 276

Olav, Crown Prince 68, 85

Peilow, Drill Sergeant 273, 276

Petre, Lieutenant R. 191, 289

Quisling, Vidkun 74–76, 82, 84, 87, 279

Raeder, Grand Admiral 40, 74

Rainer, Acting Petty Officer Telegraphist Bob 98, 109, 111

Ramsay, Lieutenant 91-92

Redgrave, Petty Officer V. 163, 170

Ribbentrop, Ambassador Extraordinary, Joachim von 14, 18

Rice, Petty Officer F. 146–147, 151–152

Rieve, Captain 66, 174, 176

Roope, Lieutenant-Commander Gerard Broadmead 89–92, 94–95

Rose, Second Lieutenant H. 191, 281–282

Ruge, General Otto 85–86, 268–269

Ruhfus, Captain 54, 58–59

Schmundt, Admiral 53–55

Schrader, Admiral von 54–55

Schuschnigg, Kurt von 15–16

Scott, Lieutenant C. 272, 274

Scott, Petty Officer Walter 92, 98

Shackley, Flight Sergeant 317-318

Sherbrooke, Commander 150, 153

Spiller, *Hauptmann* E. 70, 75, 82

Stack, RSM 273, 276

Stalin, Josef 18, 21

Stanning, Paymaster Lieutenant G. 116–117, 123–124

Stansberg, Lieutenant 55, 62

Stockwell, Lieutenant Colonel 247, 291–293, 295

Tangvald, Lieutenant 64–65

Thiele, Captain 67, 177-178

Trappes-Lomax, Lieutenant Colonel T. B. 204, 211, 234, 237–238, 245, 268–269, 280–286, 288, 291

Vian, Captain Philip 29–31, 33–34, 38, 105, 111

Scandinavia 23–25, 28, 37, 40, 43, 187, 282
Scapa Flow 49, 61, 88–89, 93, 112, 155, 157, 159–161, 164, 170, 190–192, 195, 199, 212, 276, 303, 312, 315, 317
Scotland 29, 31, 41, 48, 56, 66, 71, 130, 138–139, 157–159, 162, 164, 170–171, 191, 199, 246, 255, 301
Setnesmoen 305–307
Shetland Islands 28, 40, 112–113
Sjoveien 200, 211
Skaanland 211–212, 229–230, 247, 253, 255–256, 270, 280, 297–300, 308–309, 312–314, 316–318, 324–325
Skagen 173, 177–179, 182
Skagerrak 29–30, 42, 44, 49, 62, 68–69, 88, 99–100, 138, 173–174, 182–183
Skjelfjord 133, 142–143, 145, 152, 154, 200–201, 209, 267
Skjomnes 120, 232
Skomvaer lighthouse 100–101, 115, 155, 267
Skudeneshavn 157, 179
Sola 61–66, 81, 138–140, 156–159
Sorreisa 298–299, 307, 313, 324–325
Soviet Union 15, 18, 23–24
Stade 60-61
Stavanger 25, 30, 39, 41, 44–45, 47, 50, 61, 63, 65, 82, 88, 100, 138–139, 156, 158, 162–164, 170, 173–174, 179, 185, 301–302
Stien 269, 281, 284
Storjord 288–289
Strand 231, 314
Sudetenland 16–17
Sundalen 305–306
Sweden 12, 23, 25–26, 38–39, 41, 43, 85–86, 130–131, 156, 183, 185, 188, 190, 194–195, 206, 219, 223, 235, 239, 242, 260–261, 280, 282, 320
Switzerland 13, 249

Tärstad 142, 147
Tranøy 115–116, 120, 133, 135, 140, 145
Tromsö 155, 192–193, 211, 260, 297–298, 317
Trondheim 22, 25, 39–44, 46, 48, 53, 81, 89–90, 92, 100, 104, 112–114, 134, 136–142, 185, 187, 190, 193–194, 196, 198, 213, 219, 239, 247–248, 260–261, 267, 269, 301, 303, 307

Vaagsfjord 193, 203
Vasvik 221, 229
Vefsenfjord 265, 268
Vefsna 266-267
Vestfjord 49, 93, 100, 104, 113, 115–116, 131, 134, 142–143, 155, 161, 270, 277, 314, 317
Viskiskoia 287–288

Wesermünde 46–47
West Fjord 92, 134, 213
Whitehall 92, 207, 224
Wilhelmshaven 27–28, 55, 99, 114, 140

Yttern 281, 283

Index of Military Formations & Units – British Army
3rd Anti-Aircraft Battery 201, 243
3rd Hussars 256–257
24th (Guards) Brigade 25, 41, 185, 188, 192, 197-198, 204-205, 207, 209, 214, 218-219, 225, 232, 235, 237-238, 244, 252-253, 255-257, 270, 277, 280, 289, 296
49th (West Riding) Division 25, 188, 190, 242-243, 250, 257
55th Light AA Battery 243, 250, 257
137th Field Ambulance 250-151, 257
146th Brigade 41, 185, 196, 198
147th Field Ambulance 251, 278
148th Brigade 41, 185, 190
203rd Field Battery 250, 257
230th Field Company 243, 250, 257

Avonmouth Force 25–26, 187, 191

British Expeditionary Force 21-23, 188, 191, 252

Force Maurice/Maurice Force 260, 265
Force Rupert *see* Rupert Force

Hallamshire battalion 88, 185-186, 190, 195

Independent Companies 191, 239–240, 247-249, 256, 260-264, 266, 268, 281, 283-289, 291, 293-296
  Independent Company, No. 1 247, 260, 266-267, 269
  Independent Company, No. 2 247, 266, 288-289, 292
  Independent Company, No. 3 247, 260, 266, 281, 288-290, 292
  Independent Company, No. 4 248-249, 260, 266, 268,
  Independent Company, No. 5 248, 260, 266-268
Irish Guards 195, 201, 205, 211, 218, 220, 222, 234, 238, 252, 268, 270–272, 279–280, 289–294, 296
  Irish Guards, 1st Battalion 25, 185, 195, 201, 211, 217, 220, 226, 229, 244, 256, 275, 280, 289–291, 295

King's Own Yorkshire Light Infantry (KOYLI), 4th 88, 185, 195

Leicestershire Regiment, 5th 88, 185
Lincolnshire Regiment, 4th 88, 185, 195
Liverpool Scottish 248–249

North Western Expeditionary Force 241, 255, 257, 265, 300, 307, 313–314, 324

Royal Army Medical Corps 250, 251, 257, 289
Royal Army Service Corps 249–250
Royal Artillery 201, 217, 243, 250, 257, 281
Royal Engineers 230, 243, 250, 257, 292, 307
Royal Signals 233, 249
Royal Welch Fusiliers 247–248, 291
Rupert Force 192, 198–199, 215, 236, 260- 261

Scots Guards 190-191, 195, 200, 211, 221, 223, 231, 237, 252, 260-261, 266, 268, 270, 276, 279, 283-286, 288-291, 294-296
    Scots Guards, 1st Battalion 25, 88, 185, 199, 201, 204, 219, 232, 244, 250, 252, 256, 260, 280-282, 291, 326
    Scots Guards, 5th Battalion 25, 185
Sherwood Foresters, 8th viii, 88, 185
South Wales Borderers, 2nd Battalion 25, 185, 195, 198, 201, 205, 212, 218, 223, 229–231, 233-235, 244, 256–257, 270, 277–279, 289, 291, 293-296
Stockforce 291–292

York and Lancaster Regiment 88, 185

Index of Military Formations & Units – British Royal Navy
Royal Navy 11–14, 17, 29, 31–32, 40–41, 51, 56, 61, 88, 92, 109, 111, 119, 123, 130–131, 133, 140–141, 144, 147, 156, 159, 173, 177, 179–180, 184, 192, 195, 223, 229, 233, 238, 244, 297, 313, 315, 318
1st Cruiser Squadron 100, 109, 138, 169
2nd Cruiser Squadron 100, 106, 109, 112, 133, 142
18th Cruiser Squadron 100, 104–105, 107–110, 112, 191
1st Destroyer Flotilla 89, 112, 133, 142, 156
2nd Destroyer Flotilla 114–115, 133
3rd Destroyer Flotilla 105, 138
4th Destroyer Flotilla 106–107, 109, 111-112, 121
6th Destroyer Flotilla 105, 109-110, 112
12th Destroyer Flotilla 113, 142

Fleet Air Arm 56, 59, 136, 141, 160, 270–272, 289, 298, 303–304, 307, 309–311, 313, 318, 324-325
800 Squadron 56-57, 59-60
801 Squadron 59-60, 105, 160

803 Squadron 56–57, 59-60, 160
816 Squadron 105, 136, 141
818 Squadron 105, 136, 141, 311

Force B 154–155

Home Fleet 34, 49, 61, 88–89, 100, 104–107, 109, 111–113, 141, 158, 166–169, 191–192, 265
Royal Marines 59, 161, 303
Whitworth force/group 100–101, 104, 114, 142, 145, 154–155

Naval vessels:
HMS *Afridi* 105, 110–111
HMS *Arethusa* 29–31, 49
HMS *Ark Royal* 60, 276, 309, 318
HMS *Aurora* 29, 88, 106–112, 187, 201–204, 209, 214, 218–219, 222, 235, 238
HMS *Bedouin* 104, 115–116, 135, 143–144, 147, 149–152, 154, 220–221
HMS *Berwick* 49, 88, 111-112
HMS *Birmingham* 105, 198
HMS *Brazen* 203-204
HMS *Cairo* 198, 277
HMS *Codrington* 111–112
HMS *Cossack* 29–31, 33–35, 38, 144, 148, 150, 153–155
HMS *Coventry* 277–278
HMS *Curlew* 276, 309
HMS *Devonshire* 41, 49, 88, 111–112
HMS *Echo* 277-278, 295
HMS *Effingham* 218, 253–256, 270, 277–279, 287, 291, 293, 297
HMS *Electra* 111, 192, 205
HMS *Enterprise* 218, 229, 232, 280–281
HMS *Escapade* 111, 204
HMS *Esk* 41, 101, 115, 155
HMS *Eskimo* 104, 115–116, 134, 142–145, 147, 149, 151–152, 154
HMS *Fearless* 203–204
HMS *Firedrake* 314, 316–317, 319
HMS *Forester* viii, 71, 144, 148–149, 151–155
HMS *Foxhound* 144, 146, 150, 153–154
HMS *Furious* 105, 111–113, 136–137, 141–142, 144–145, 148, 155, 206, 311
HMS *Galatea* 49, 111
HMS *Glasgow* 49, 88, 105, 109, 112
HMS *Glorious* 60, 303, 312, 314–315, 318, 320
HMS *Glowworm* 88–97, 113
HMS *Greyhound* 89, 101, 115, 133–134
HMS *Gurkha* 105–112
HMS *Hardy* 101, 104, 114–116, 118–121, 123–125, 127–131, 154–155, 231

HMS *Havock* 52, 101, 114, 118–120, 123, 128, 131–132, 134
HMS *Hereward* 156, 161-162
HMS *Hero* 89, 129, 144, 151–153
HMS *Hesperus* 280–281
HMS *Hostile* 104, 114, 117, 119–121, 128, 131, 133, 137, 154
HMS *Hotspur* 101, 114, 117, 119-120, 129, 131, 133, 142
HMS *Hunter* 101, 114, 118–120, 128–131
HMS *Icarus* 41, 52, 101, 115, 142, 144, 151–153, 155
HMS *Intrepid* 29, 32–33
HMS *Ivanhoe* 29, 101, 115, 154–155
HMS *Janus* 156, 161-162, 166
HMS *Juno* 156, 161-162
HMS *Jupiter* 111, 144
HMS *Kimberley* 104, 115–116, 143–144, 148, 150, 152, 154–155, 159
HMS *Kipling* 156, 158–159, 161–162, 166, 168
HMS *Manchester* 49, 105, 109, 112, 191–192, 198
HMS *Mashona* 105-106, 109-110
HMS *Matabele* 105, 110, 277
HMS *Mohawk* 105, 107, 110
HMS *Penelope* 49, 104, 115–116, 131, 133–134, 140–144
HMS *Punjabi* 104, 115–116, 141, 144, 147, 149–150, 152–153
HMS *Renown* 41, 88–89, 92–93, 97, 100–104, 115–116, 121, 131, 142, 144, 155, 159, 166–168
HMS *Repulse* 49, 100–101, 104, 113, 115, 142, 159, 166–168
HMS *Rodney* 49, 100, 110–112, 142, 144, 155
HMS *Seal* 157, 162-164
HMS *Sealion* 173, 181
HMS *Sheffield* 49, 105, 109, 112
HMS *Sikh* 29, 105, 107, 110
HMS *Snapper* 181–182
HMS *Somali* 105, 110, 276
HMS *Southampton* 49, 98, 105, 109, 112, 191–192, 199–200, 205
HMS *Spearfish* 177-178
HMS *Sterlet* 182, 184
HMS *Stork* 270–271, 274–276
HMS *Suffolk* 53, 156–172
HMS *Sunfish* 173–174, 180–181
HMS *Swordfish* 173, 182
HMS *Tarpon* 180–181, 184
HMS *Tetrarch* 182–183
HMS *Thistle* 174, 178–179, 184
HMS *Trident* 100, 173, 180
HMS *Triton* 76, 173, 180
HMS *Truant* 174–176, 183

HMS *Unity* 173, 184
HMS *Unity* 173, 184
HMS *Valiant* 49, 92, 100, 111–112, 201–202, 204
HMS *Vindictive* 211, 218, 222, 297
HMS *Warspite* 112–113, 129, 141–142, 144–148, 150–155, 206, 213, 217–218
HMS *Wolverine* 270–272, 274–276
HMS *York* 49, 88, 111-113
HMS *Zulu* 231-232, 267

Non-Royal Navy ships:
Empress of Australia 195, 198
MS *Batory* 88, 187, 190, 195, 199, 204, 312
Reina del Pacifico 195, 198
SS *Arandora Star* 318, 320
SS *Chrobry* 88, 187, 190, 195, 198, 240, 253, 255, 270–272, 274–276, 290–291, 309
SS *Margot* 280–281

Index of Military Formations & Units – British Royal Air Force
Royal Air Force (RAF) 21, 23, 25, 30–31, 48, 54–57, 71, 88, 105, 138–140, 157, 159, 161, 169, 174, 187, 247, 254, 266, 293, 298, 300–303, 305, 307–314, 317, 319–320, 325

9 Squadron 9, 54, 139
46 Squadron 307, 312, 314–321
107 Squadron 139, 159
115 Squadron 54, 139
233 Squadron 57, 157, 159
254 Squadron 138–139, 158
263 Squadron 302–303, 306, 310–311, 313-314, 321, 324

Bomber Command 48, 56, 138–139, 301
Coastal Command 48, 138–139, 157–158, 161, 164, 169, 172

Index of Military Formations & Units – Allied (miscellaneous)
6th Infantry Division (Norwegian) 22, 200

Chasseurs Alpins 25–26, 188, 190, 196, 198, 206, 208, 218–220, 222, 226, 228, 232-236, 239, 251-252, 260, 266, 289, 295, 309, 312

French Army 21, 187, 246
French Foreign Legion 26, 190, 236, 239, 245–246, 251–252, 256
French Navy 14, 111

Haerens Overkommando (HOK) 80, 84–85
HOK see Haerens Overkommando

Indian Army 240–241, 249, 265, 288

Norwegian Army 42, 50–51, 77, 80, 193, 209, 305–306

Polish Army 19–20
Polish Brigade 26, 239, 246, 251–252, 270

Royal Norwegian Air Force 22, 62, 69
Royal Norwegian Navy 22, 30, 51, 65–66

SDD2 63, 77

Index of Military Formations & Units – German
2nd Mountain Division 43, 269, 323
3rd Mountain Division 43, 52, 323
11th Motorised Rifle Brigade 45, 323
69th Infantry Division 43, 46–48, 53, 55, 323
138th Mountain Light Infantry Regiment see
    Gebirgsjäger-Regiment 138
139th Mountain Light Infantry Regiment see
    Gebirgsjäger-Regiment 139
163rd Infantry Division 43, 48, 69, 73, 323
170th Infantry Division 43, 45, 323
181st Infantry Division 43, 323
193rd Infantry Regiment 47, 62, 65–66, 70, 323
196th Infantry Division 43, 76, 323
198th Infantry Division 43, 323
214th Infantry Division 43, 323
307th Infantry Regiment 48, 323
310th Infantry Regiment 47–48, 323
324th Infantry Regiment 48, 69–70, 323
340th Infantry Regiment 180, 323
345th Infantry Regiment 180, 323

Fallschirmjägers 9, 43, 61, 64-65, 68-70, 75-76, 82, 87
    Fallschirmjäger Regiment 1 47–48, 60, 68

Gebirgsjäger-Regiment 138 46, 48, 323
Gebirgsjäger-Regiment 139 46, 51, 156, 323
German Army 14, 20, 60, 156, 267
German Navy 13, 17, 27, 40–41, 43, 48, 66, 74, 93, 113, 117, 133, 140, 152, 156, 180, 196
    Kriegsmarine see German Navy
Group West 54, 113, 140
Group XXI 42, 48, 323

Infantry Regiment 159 46–47, 70, 323

Kampfgeschwader 26 158, 159, 314, 319
Kampfgeschwader 30 158-159
Kampfgeschwader 4 66, 158-160

Luftwaffe 15, 29, 43, 45, 57, 64, 66, 85, 112, 137, 156, 158–159, 211, 247, 269, 297, 302, 304, 306, 314, 316

OKW 21, 40, 42

Supreme Command of the Armed Forces see *OKW*

Wehrmacht 13, 16, 156

X Fliegerkorps 45, 69

Naval vessels:
Admiral Graf Spee 27, 32
Admiral Von Hipper 53, 90-92, 94, 96–98, 113–114, 136
Albatros 66, 68, 177
Alster 52, 142
Altmark viii, 27–40, 74
Antares 76, 180
Arnim see *Bernd von Arnim*
August Leonhardt 66, 181
Bärenfels 52, 54, 59–60
Bernd von Arnim 51–53, 89–90, 122, 124, 128–129, 131–132, 140, 142, 147–148, 150–152
Blücher 67–68, 73
Bremse 53, 55–56, 59–60
Brummer 181–182
Carl Peters 55-56, 59
Emden 73–74, 76
Falke 179, 181
Friendenau 76, 180
Giese 53, 122, 132, 140, 142, 147, 149–150
Gneisenau 43, 46, 89, 101–104, 114, 140
Greif 66, 174, 176, 179
Hans Lüdemann 50, 52, 89, 119–122, 124, 132, 140, 142, 150-152
Hans Rolshoven 55, 57
Heidkamp 51–52, 118, 122, 132, 140, 156
Jaguar 179, 181
Jan Wellem 44, 52, 119, 121, 131–132, 155, 235
Karlsruhe 174, 176, 179
Kattegat 44, 52
Koellner 51, 53, 122, 132, 140, 142, 146–147
Köln 54–55
Königsberg 53–59
Kreta 66, 100
Künne 51-52, 119, 132, 140, 142, 146–147, 149, 156
Leopard 54–55
Luchs 174, 176, 179
Lützow 67–68, 73, 76, 177–179, 184
Möwe 177, 179
Rauenfels 52, 131–132
Rio de Janeiro 49, 54, 99-100, 173
Roda 65–66
Scharnhorst 43, 46, 89, 101–104, 113–114, 140
Schmitt 50, 52, 117, 119, 132, 140
Seeadler 174, 176, 179
Skagerrak 53, 140, 161

Thiele 51, 53, 122–123, 128–129, 131–132, 140, 142, 147, 150–152
Tübingen 62, 66
U25 135, 147–148, 153–154
U48 141, 145
U51 116, 147
U64 134, 147
von Roeder 50, 117, 119–120, 132, 140, 142, 150
Wigbert 76, 180
Wolf 54–55
Zenker 51, 53, 121, 132, 140, 142, 147–148, 150–152

Index of General & Miscellaneous Terms
Air Ministry 136, 266, 303, 316
Altmark Incident 27, 29, 31, 33, 35, 37, 39–40, 74

BBC 17, 38, 212
British Embassy, Oslo 30, 79, 193
British Government 15-16, 23, 25–26, 36, 39, 81-82, 137, 187, 207, 214-216, 219, 225, 228, 237, 241, 295

Cabinet (British) 21, 31, 80, 174, 181, 208, 210, 216, 254
Cabinet (Norwegian) 77, 79, 84
Case Yellow 42–43
Commonwealth War Graves Commission 59, 154
Czechoslovakian Government 16-17

Distinguished Flying Cross 311, 319–321
Distinguished Service Order 92, 240

Fall Gelb see Case Yellow
Finnish War 186, 192
First Lord of the Admiralty 23, 30, 33, 157, 213, 216, 227
First Sea Lord 30, 184, 192, 213, 219, 235, 250
Flag Officer Narvik 202, 207, 212, 214, 251, 254, 324
FO Narvik see Flag Officer Narvik

German Embassy (Oslo) 30, 70, 79
German Government 20-21
Great War 11–14, 16, 19, 21, 27, 40, 51, 157, 180, 192, 213, 240, 313

HM Government see British Government

House of Commons 36, 193

League of Nations 11, 13–15, 23–24
London Gazette, The 92, 320

Merchant Navy 129, 131
Military Coordination Committee 193, 239

Nazi party 13, 15, 21
Norwegian Government 11, 22, 36, 39, 42, 50, 66, 68, 74–77, 79–82, 84-87, 193, 241, 260
Norwegian Leads, The 13, 23, 28, 30, 39, 55, 77, 260
NSDAP see *Nazi* party

Operation Duck 156, 158, 161, 164–165, 169–171
Operation *Weserübung* 37, 40-41, 61, 113
Operation Wilfred 38–39, 41, 173
Operation/Plan R4 39, 41, 185

Phoney War 9, 22, 111, 173
Polish Government 18-19

Ships:
 Æger 65–66
 Eidsvold 51, 117
 Emile Bertin 49, 111
 Kjell 33–34
 Nord-Norge 267–268
 Norge 51, 117
 Orzel 54, 99, 173–174, 180
 Pol III 66–67
 Trygg 29-30, 33
Spanish Civil War 15, 27, 88, 93, 130
Storting, The 36, 82
Supreme War Council 24, 187, 190
Swedish Government 25, 39

"Trojan horse" ships 41, 44, 52–53, 65, 117

Versailles, Treaty of 13-15, 27
Vice Admiral Commanding, Orkneys and Shetlands 161, 166-168
Victoria Cross 91–92, 124

War Cabinet see Cabinet (British)
War Office 25, 188, 190, 206, 210, 213, 216, 224, 226, 238, 241, 243, 252–255, 257, 265
W-Day 43–45, 47–48, 66
Western Front 23, 138, 187, 190, 195